THE STORY OF
MANAGING PROJECTS

THE STORY OF MANAGING PROJECTS

An Interdisciplinary Approach

Edited by

ELIAS G. CARAYANNIS

YOUNG HOON KWAK

FRANK T. ANBARI

PRAEGER

Westport, Connecticut
London

Library of Congress Cataloging-in-Publication Data

The story of managing projects : an interdisciplinary approach / edited by
Elias G. Carayannis, Young Hoon Kwak, and Frank T. Anbari.
p. cm.
Includes bibliographical references and index.
ISBN 1-56720-506-2 (alk. paper)
1. Project management. 2. Organizational learning. 3. Industrial management.
I. Carayannis, Elias G. II. Kwak, Young-Hoon. III. Anbari, Frank T.

HD69.P75.S755 2005
658.4'04–dc22   2004018111

British Library Cataloguing in Publication Data is available.

Library of Congress Catalog Card Number: 2004018111
ISBN: 1-56720-506-2

First published in 2005

Praeger Publishers, 88 Post Road West, Westport, CT 06881
An imprint of Greenwood Publishing Group, Inc.
www.praeger.com

Printed in the United States of America

The paper used in this book complies with the
Permanent Paper Standard issued by the National
Information Standards Organization (Z39.48-1984).

10   9   8   7   6   5   4   3   2

CONTENTS

TABLES AND FIGURES

Tables

Figures

PREFACE

I n *The Story of Managing Projects,* we have compiled a number of chapters that deal with the process as well as the content, context, and impact of project management from a number of disciplines and industries. This manuscript is meant to serve as a platform for project management practitioners to team up with project management academics in order to provide cross-disciplinary threads of insights, lessons learned, and best practices from a variety of professions and settings as well as regions of the world where project management is enacted and shaped in the process.

Thematically, the book has a "multilegged T" (MLT) structure with the introductory chapters providing an overview/overlay of key project management concepts and subsequent chapters delving into specific project management context and practice areas (such as project management in health care, project management in construction, project management in S/W, project management in telecom, etc.). The concluding chapter synthesizes and integrates insights and lessons learned across thematic areas and functional contexts for best practices in project management. It also provides the foundation for identifying and forming interrelated communities of practice and interest with regards to project management across different practices (law, engineering, medicine, movie-making, research, etc.), and a roadmap for future research based on the foundation this book provides.

The book audience encompasses professional project management practitioners, academic researchers, and graduate students as well as professionals from other specialties with an interest in understanding how best to benefit from and practice project management in their domain of expertise (such as doctors, lawyers, accountants, movie producers, book authors, etc.).

The chapters in this book provide both a horizontal coverage in breadth of key current and emerging issues in the discipline of project management (such as the chapters by Kerzner and Hartman as well as those focusing on Stakeholder Mapping, Knowledge Flows, and the use of Multimedia and Digital Storytelling) as well as a vertical coverage with more focus on a specific area of project management practice (construction, telecommunications, software, health care, transportation, etc.).

We believe that the reader will benefit from the juxtaposition and critical synthesis of the insights and findings in those chapters to provide a more solid foundation for developing better project management theories as well as tools, methodologies, and practices.

——— 1 ———

Brief History of Project Management

YOUNG HOON KWAK

P roject management has been practiced for thousands of years, ever since the Egyptian era. It has been only since about half a century ago, however, that organizations started applying systematic project management tools and techniques to complex projects. In the 1950s, the U.S. Navy employed modern project management methodologies in their Polaris project. During the 1960s and 1970s, the Department of Defense, NASA, and large engineering and construction companies utilized project management principles and tools to manage large-budget, schedule-driven projects. In the 1980s, manufacturing and software development sectors started to adopt and implement sophisticated project management practices. By the 1990s, the project management theories, tools, and techniques were widely received by different industries and organizations.

FOUR PERIODS OF PROJECT MANAGEMENT

Snyder and Kline (1987) noted that the modern project management era started in 1958 with the development of CPM/PERT. Morris (1987) argues that the origin of project management comes from the chemical industry just prior to World War II. He further notes that project management is clearly defined as a separate discipline in the Atlas missile program, especially in the Polaris project. Some literatures pointed the origin of project management to Henri Fayol's (1916) five functions of a manager: (1) to plan, (2) to organize, (3) to coordinate,

TABLE 1-1. Four periods of project management

Periods	Theme	Sub context
Prior to 1958	Craft system to Human Relations Administration	▪ Project management ▪ Actual projects
1958 – 1979	Application of Management Science	
1980 – 1994	Production center: Human Resources	
1995 to Present	Creating a new environment	

(4) to control, and (5) to direct or command. Kerzner (1998) observes that project management is an "outgrowth of systems management."

Four periods have been identified to capture the history of modern project management: (1) prior to 1958, (2) 1958–1979, (3) 1980–1994, and (4) 1995 to present. Table 1.1 summarizes these periods. Following is a brief history of each period and representative actual projects.

PRIOR TO 1958: CRAFT SYSTEM TO HUMAN RELATIONS ADMINISTRATION

Project Management

The origin of the modern project management concept started between 1900s and 1950s. During this time, technology advancement shortened the project schedule. Automobiles allowed effective resource allocation and mobility. The telecommunication system increased the speed of communication. The job specification was widely used and Henry Gantt invented the Gantt chart. The job specification later became the basis of developing the Work Breakdown Structure (WBS).

Actual Representative Projects

T. D. Juhah's Project Plan for Building Pacific Railroad
In T. D. Judah's (1857) "A Practical Plan for Building the Pacific Railroad," engineers and clerks at the project office prepared a formal report when survey information arrived from the field managers. Once the data was updated and analyzed, the project office forwarded orders to resident engineers, and field managers initiated the project. The project office also dealt with relationships with investors as well as conducting the field survey, cost estimation, feasibility study, and other necessary tasks. The project office simply functioned as an administrative office.

Hoover Dam (1931–1936)
In 1928, Congress passed the Boulder Canyon Act, assigning $175 million to the Hoover Dam. The "Big Six," Utah Construction, Pacific Bridge, H. J. Kaiser,

W. A. MacDonald and Kahn, Morrison-Knudsen, and J. H. Shea, formed a consortium to work as a general contractor. It was crucial for the companies to have a detailed project planning, controlling, and coordinating strategy because the project involved six independent companies. The construction site was located in the middle of the desert with no infrastructures. Boulder City was created to accommodate their workers to stay near the construction site.

The project required both physical and human resources. Approximately 5,200 workers were employed, and large amount of construction resources including concrete, structural steel components, steel pipe, and so on were required (Bureau of Reclamation 1985). The project was completed under budget and ahead of schedule (Moore 1999). The Hoover Dam is one of the highest gravity dams in the United States and generates more than four billion kilowatt-hours of electricity a year.

Manhattan Project (1942–1945)
The Manhattan Project was the pioneer research and development (R&D) project that designed and built the atomic bomb. The initial project was proposed in 1939 to defend against possible threats from Germany. In 1941, the Office of Scientific Research and Development (ORSD) was established to coordinate government-sponsored projects, and the Manhattan Project was initiated in 1942. The OSRD coordinated universities and resources for the research and development of the atomic bomb. The project was tested successfully in July 1945, a month before the bomb was dropped on Hiroshima, Japan. The project involved 125,000 laborers and cost nearly $2 billion.

APPLICATION OF MANAGEMENT SCIENCE, 1958–1979

Project Management

There were significant technology advancements between 1958 and 1979. In 1959, Xerox introduced the first automatic plain-paper copier. In the 1960s, many industries were influenced by the development of silicon chips and minicomputers. In 1969, Bell Laboratories developed the programming language UNIX, and the computer industry started to develop rapidly. NASA's successful Apollo project earmarked a historic event of humankind. In 1971, Intel introduced 4004, a 4-bit microprocessor, which was the foundation of the evolution of Intel's 80386, 80486, and Pentium processors in the 1990s. While many dedicated scientists developed ARPANET, Ray Tomlinson in 1972 introduced the first e-mail software. In 1975, Bill Gates and Paul Allen founded Microsoft. Several project management software companies were founded during the 1970s including Artemis (1977), Scitor Corporation (1979), and Oracle (1977).

Between 1950 and 1979, several core project management tools, including CPM/PERT and Material Requirement Planning (MRP), were introduced. CPM/PERT was calculated in large computer systems, and specialized programmers operated the CPM/PERT mainly for the government-sector projects. The common organizations used the project office as "brokers of information," with a small number of skilled schedulers and estimators (Vandersluis 1998).

Actual Representative Projects

Polaris Project (1956–1961)
The Polaris Project refined the project management concepts as known today (Sapolsky 1972). The $11 billion project was undertaken by the U.S. government to deliver nuclear missiles, fleet ballistic missiles, by submarines. The U.S. Navy initiated the project in late 1956 and successfully launched its first Polaris missile in 1961. The navy created a new unit called Special Project Office (SPO) to avoid giving the Polaris Project to Bureau of Ordinance and Bureau of Aeronautics (Sapolsky 1972).

Apollo Project
In 1958, the National Aeronautics and Space Administration (NASA) was created. Between 1969 and 1972, NASA successfully led six missions to explore the moon. In 1960, NASA set up the Apollo Program office to maintain and schedule Apollo missions using PERT, procure and contract with suppliers such as GE, develop a management system to measure the performance, and establish a focal point of the Apollo Program.

ARPANET

> The Internet is as much a collection of communities as a collection of technologies, and its success is largely attributable to both satisfying basic community needs as well as utilizing the community in an effective way to push the infrastructure forward. This community spirit has a long history beginning with the early ARPANET. The early ARPANET researchers worked as a close-knit community to accomplish the initial demonstrations of packet switching technology described earlier. Likewise, the Packet Satellite, Packet Radio, and several other DARPA computer science research programs were multi-contractor collaborative activities that heavily used whatever available mechanisms there were to coordinate their efforts, starting with electronic mail and adding file sharing, remote access, and eventually World Wide Web capabilities. Each of these programs formed a working group, starting with the ARPANET Network Working Group. Because of the unique role that ARPANET played as an infrastructure supporting the various research programs, as the Internet started to evolve, the Network Working Group evolved into Internet Working Group.
>
> —Leiner et al. 2000

The Internet project began its journey in 1962. It started with series of memos discussing the concept of a "Galactic Network," by J. C. R. Licklider of MIT (Leiner et al. 2000). The U.S. Department of Defense initially funded the project, and the Advanced Research Projects Agency (ARPA) coordinated it. The ARPA's objective was to schedule and coordinate the activities of the heterogeneous set of contractors (Hughes 1998). The ARPA started to develop its ARPANET, the origin of the Internet.

The ARPA project was a R&D project initially developed by the ARPA and then managed by several organizations. In the 1970s, a federal networking council was formed to support international organizations and coordinate federal agencies such as NASA, the Department of Energy and others (Leiner et al 2000). Different from single organization-driven projects, many researchers and organization drove the development of the initial ARPANET. Currently, the Internet is coordinated by several organizations including the Internet Engineering Task Force (IETF), the Internet Engineering Steering Group (IESG), the Internet Architecture Board (IAB), and the Internet Society (ISOC).

PRODUCTION CENTER: HUMAN RESOURCES, 1980–1994

Project Management

During the 1980s and early 1990s, the revolution of IT/IS sector shifted people from using a mainframe computer to a multitasking personal computer that had high efficiency in managing and controlling complex project schedules. In the mid-1980s, the Internet served researchers and developers, and local area networks and Ethernet technology started to dominate network technology (Leiner et al. 2000).

During the 1950s through 1970s, most computer engineers were responsible for operating the project management systems because the mainframe systems were not easy to use. During the late 1970s and early 1980s, project management software for the personal computer became widely available by a number of companies, which made project management techniques more easily accessible.

Actual Project Cases

Three projects were selected to portray the era of 1980s and early 1990s: the English-France Channel Project (1989–1991), the Space Shuttle Challenger Project (1983–1986), and the XV Calgary Olympic Winter Games (1988). These projects illustrated the applications of high technology and the project management tools and practices.

The English Channel Project was an international project that involved two government agencies (British and French government), several financial institutions, engineering construction companies, and other various organizations. The project goal, cost, schedule, and other factors needed to be adjusted to conduct the project. The language, use of standard metrics, and other communication differences needed to be coordinated.

CREATING A NEW ENVIRONMENT, 1995–THE PRESENT

We are on the verge of a revolution that is just as profound as the change in the economy that came with the industrial revolution. Soon electronic networks will allow people to transcend the barriers of time and distance and take advantage of global markets and business opportunities not even imaginable today, opening up a new world of economic possibility and progress.

—Albert Gore Jr. 1997

Project Management

The Internet started to change virtually every business practices in the mid-1990s (Turban et al. 2000). It provided a fast, interactive, and customized new medium that allowed people to browse, purchase, and track products and services online instantly. As a result, the Internet permits organizations to be more productive, more efficient, and more customer oriented. Between 1995 and 2000, the project management community adopted Internet technology to become more efficient in controlling and managing various aspects of projects. While the information technology revolutionized the traditional business practices, various industries started to adopt and to apply project management practices.

Actual Project Cases

Year 2000 (Y2K) Project
The Year 2000 (Y2K) problem, known as the millennium bug, referred to the anticipated belief that computers would not function correctly on January 1, 2000, at 12 A.M. It was a man-made problem that started back in the 1950s. President Bill Clinton issued Executive Order 13073, "Year 2000 Conversion," in February 1998, which required all federal agencies to fix the Y2K problem in their systems (Executive Order 1998). Several government agencies and state governments initiated the year 2000 awareness program back in 1996. The order established a centralized focal point for monitoring all Y2K activities within the U.S. government.

The Y2K Project integrated several aspects of PM. First, the Y2K Project had a specific objective (to fix Y2K problems) and sharp deadline (January 1, 2000, at 12 A.M.). Second, the project was globally and independently conducted since virtually every organization using computers were at stake. Each organization focused on correcting Y2K problems within their particular organization, but the problem was interrelated due to the dependency of various computer systems via computer network. Third, there were various methodologies and tools to remedy the problem. Fourth, from initiation to completion, detailed progressive reports were widely available. The Y2K Project became the most documented project in project management history, because millions of organizations in the world conducted virtually similar projects.

The Y2K problem prompted many organizations to adopt project management practices, tools, and techniques to conduct their own Y2K project. Many organizations set up the project office to control and comply with their stakeholders regarding Y2K issue. Furthermore, use of the Internet was common practice for Y2K projects, which led to set up a virtual project office. The goal of the Y2K project office was to deliver uninterrupted turn-of-the-century monitoring of Y2K project efforts, to provide coordination, to develop a risk management plan, and to communicate Y2K compliance efforts with various stakeholders. The Y2K office was a focal point for all the project works, and its functions were so highly visible that it boosted the awareness and importance of the project office. In addition, it increased the awareness and importance of risk management practices to numerous organizations.

Iridium Project

Motorola's $5 billion Iridium Project aimed to provide global communication service virtually anywhere at anytime (Barboza 2000). In November 1998, the Iridium network was established and started to provide global network services. In March 2000, Iridium filed for bankruptcy terminating its services. Once viewed as a technological breakthrough, the project ended quickly and mysteriously. The program office was established with full-time project control managers, software engineers and analysts were also relocated. In addition, the project control managers utilized sophisticated project management software, Primavera Project Planner, to handle complex and interrelated project scheduling management. (Fabris 1996).

SUMMARY AND CONCLUSIONS

Historians and dedicated scholars contributed to project management history over the years. Most of the documents were written in narrative format that covered only a few aspects of project management. A set of standards will make it easy for the project management community to build its history and take advantage of lessons learned from the past. Literature reviews suggest that technology and advanced management tools strengthened the functions of the project office. More organizations are adopting and applying project management practices, tools, and techniques to their various operations. Therefore, a permanent project-supporting entity that provides comprehensive project management knowledge is needed. Advanced Internet and computer technology is assisting organizations to support the needs of project management. Eventually, the project office will function as a heart of the project management community. Table 1.2 summarizes the brief history of project management.

TABLE 1-2.   A brief history of project management

	Technology	Management Science	Project Management & Technology	Major Projects	Project Office
– 1958	- Telegraph - Telephone - First computer - Automobile - Airplane - First database	- Adam Smith - Frederick W. Taylor - Henry Fayor - Henry Gantt - A McGregor's XY theory	- Parametric Cost Estimating - PERT/CPM - Gantt Chart - Monte Carlo simulation - Systematic application	- Intercontinental railroads - Hoover Dam - Polaris - Manhattan project - Panama Canal	- Focal point - "proximity" - Traditional project office functions - Navy Special Project Office (SPO)
1959 – 1979	- IBM 7090 - Xerox copier - UNIX - Microsoft founded	- ISO - Total Quality Management - Globalization - Quality management	- PMI - Inventory control - Material requirement planning	- Apollo 11 - ARPANET	- Project supporting office
1980 – 1994	- Personal computer - Wireless in-building network - First Internet browser (MOSAIC)	- Manufacturing resource planning - Risk management	- Matrix organization - PM software for PC	- Boeing 777 - Space shuttle Challenger - The English-France Channel project	- Project headquarter - War Room
1995 – Current	- Internet	- Critical chain - Enterprise Resource Planning	- PMBOK (PMI)	- Iridium - Y2K project	- Virtual project office - Web-base project office

BIBLIOGRAPHY

Barboza, David. 2000. Iridium, Bankrupt, Is Planning a Fiery Ending for Its 88 Satellites. *New York Times* (April 11).

Bureau of Reclamation. 1985. *Hoover Dam*. U.S. Department of the Interior, U.S. Government Printing Office, Washington, D.C.

Department of Defense. Y2K History. Retrived from: http://www.defenselink.mil/specials/y2k/y2k_hist.htm, January 2001.

Executive Order. 1998. Executive Order 13127. Vol. 64. No. 116. Retrieved from: http://www.archives.gov/federal_register/executive_orders/1999.html#13127, October 2004.

Fabris, Peter. 1966. Ground Control. *CIO Magazine* (April 1).

Gore, Al. 1997. *A Framework for Global Electronic Commerce*. Retrieved from: http://www.technology.gov/digeconomy/framewrk.htm, October 2004.Hauben, Michael. History of ARPANET: Behind the Net—The untold history of the ARPANET. Retrieved from: http://www.dei.isep.ipp.pt/docs/arpa.html, October 2004.

Hughes, Thomas P. 1998. *Rescuing Prometheus*. New York: Pantheon Books.

Judah, T. D. 1857. A Practical Plan for Building the Pacific Railroad. San Francisco, January 1.

Kerzner, Harold. 1998. *Project Management: A System Approach to Planning, Scheduling, and Controlling*. 6th ed. New York: John Wiley & Sons, Inc.

Leiner, B. M., V. G. Cerf, D. D. Clark, R. E. Kahn, L. Kleinrock, D. C. Lynch, J. Postel, L. G. Roberts, and S. Wolff. 2000. A Brief History of the Internet. Retrieved from: http://www.isoc.org/internet-history/brief.html, October 2004.

Moore, David. 1999. The Hoover Dam: A World Renowned Concrete Monument. Retrieved from: http://www.romanconcrete.com/HooverDam.htm, October 2004.

Morris, P.W.G., and G. H. Hough. 1987. *The Anatomy of Major Projects: A Study of the Reality of Project Management*. Chichester: John Wiley & Sons.

NASA. Center Responsibilities in the Apollo Program. NASA Apollo Program Directive No. 33, November 8, 1967. Concept to Apollo. Retrieved from: http://www.hq.nasa.gov/office/pao/History/SP-4009/v1p1.htm, October 2004.

Sapolsky, Harvey M. 1972. *The Polaris System Development*. Cambridge, Mass.: Harvard University Press.

Snyder, James R., and Kline, Smith. 1987. Modern Project Management: How Did We Get Here—Where Do We Go? *Project Management Journal* (March).

Turban, E., J. Lee, D. King, and H Chung. 2000. *Electronic Commerce: A Managerial Perspective*. Englewood Cliffs, NJ: Prentice Hall.

Vandersluis, Chris. 1998. Now is a good time for a project office comeback—project management techniques—Industry Trend or Event. *Computing Canada*. 24: April 27, 1998. Retrieved from http://www.findarticles.com/p/articles/mi_m0CGC/is_n16_v24/ai_20541445 on October 26, 2004.

2

Background to Project Management

HAROLD KERZNER

Arguments exist among project management project management educators as to when it actually began. The most common belief is that project management dates back to the construction of the great pyramids. Other beliefs focus on the construction of the Hoover Dam. In any case, the construction industry was probably first to embody project management principles. But the real growth of project management can probably be attributed to the aerospace and defense industries following World War II.

THE LATE 1940s

Following World War II, the United States entered into a "cold" war with its adversaries. In a "hot" war, you win by outshooting your enemy. To win a cold war, you must outspend your enemy by developing a vast arsenal of mass destruction weaponry.

By the end of the 1940s, it became apparent to the Department of Defense (DoD) that traditional forms of management would not suffice for cold war projects. Traditional management advocated the use of over-the-fence management where each function area would perform its own activities in support of the project and then throw the ball over the fence to the next person in line. Work was performed entirely sequentially. In time of crisis, the last person holding the ball bore the brunt of the pain and the ultimate blame.

With over-the-fence management, customers were often clueless as to the exact status of the project. Without project management in place, customers had to rely heavily on the sales force for status reporting. The sales force were gods, standing between the customer and the workers, and filtering all information. If the project were successful, the sales force would be first in line to receive credit. If the project were a failure, blame would be placed on the project manager. The sales force would receive large year-end bonuses even if the project failed. Blame was certainly never placed on the sales force.

As projects began to grow in size, weaknesses in the over-the-fence management approach became apparent. The customer could not get ready access to technical data, and the information that had been received was filtered several times. Schedule compression was difficult at best because all work was performed linearly. The majority of the project management work was given to line managers, who favored the best interest of the line over the best interest of the project. There was nobody truly dedicated to the best interest of the project. Real project management simply did not exist. The government was becoming increasingly concerned that large military projects would suffer under current contractor management practices.

THE 1950s

During the 1950s, the government decided that the cold war could not be based entirely on the B52 Bomber Program as the only deterrent weapon system. The race was on to build a multitude of advanced technology weapon systems, specifically missile weapon systems. The challenge facing the government was how to get private industry to grow rapidly in regard to both facilities and staffing. Private industry had limited financial resources and was certainly unable to maintain the growth that the DoD might need. The solution was the award of cost-plus-percentage-of-cost (CPPC) contracts. These contracts were basically bottomless pits of money, encouraging contractors to spend as much as they wished and then being paid a profit for whatever they could spend. Some companies doubled and even tripled in size overnight. New facilities were constructed at the government's expense. The aerospace and defense industries grew thanks to government-provided facilities and equipment.

Today, this type of contract is illegal in the government, but in the 1950s it did cause the aerospace and defense industry to grow rapidly. Because the government now had a vested interest in these companies, contracts were spread over all companies. The government wanted all of the aerospace companies to survive. Contracts were sometimes awarded to the second or third most qualified supplier just for the sake of keeping them in business. Cost was not an issue for aerospace and defense projects. The government then funded two programs that were larger than anything the government had up to that time: the Minuteman Intercontinental Ballistic Missile Program and the Polaris Submarine Program.

These programs involved thousands and thousands of contractors. With programs of this magnitude, there were several concerns that worried the government, first and foremost being project management. The government wanted industry to assign a full-time, dedicated project manager who would be on board for the life of the project. Furthermore, the government wanted direct access to this individual for response to technical inquiries. This mandated that the contractor's project managers be engineers, preferably with advanced degrees. The single most important criteria to become a project manager was a command of technology. The government wanted one person to be assigned who would possess (or have immediate access to) all of the technical knowledge on the project. Project managers were paid to manage people and provide daily technical direction; today, project managers focus on managing deliverables rather than people with the technical direction being provided by the line managers.

Initially, industry provided resistance to such a move. Since most organizations at that time were considered sales or marketing driven, this could lead to a change in strategic direction and have a serious affect on the Christmas bonuses paid out to the sales force. The sales and marketing forces did not support project management for fear that all customer contact would now go through the project manager. The power and authority of the sales force would therefore be diminished.

Senior management also resisted the implementation of project management. The government wanted a project manager assigned who had a "command" of technology, not merely an understanding. There were two serious concerns facing senior management. First, because of the command-of-technology requirement, it was possible that the person assigned as the project manager would come from the technical ranks and therefore not be on the management career path ladder. The second concern, and the more serious one, was that project management would most likely work better the nearer it was to where the work actually took place. This meant that senior management would have to decentralize authority and decision making.

Senior management was not ready to surrender decision-making responsibility. Instead, they changed their official titles to read: John Doe, Vice President for Engineering and Project Manager for the XB3 Project. This certainly did not fool the DoD personnel. The problem of obtaining timely and accurate answers to technical questions still existed. Also, DoD personnel had limited access to senior management at the contractor's organization.

To resolve the problem, the DoD decided to invoke the golden rule that states, "Those who have the gold, rule!" Senior management at the contractor's company finally succumbed to the pressure and made project management a career path ladder. However, there still had to be an umbilical cord connecting the project to the senior levels of management. Senior management still had to be informed of project status and problems that would require senior management's involvement. This problem was resolved by creating the position of the project sponsor. Initially, all sponsors for the critical projects came from the senior levels of management.

This approach of using project sponsors pleased both corporate senior management and DoD. From the DoD's perspective, project sponsorship, especially if at the executive levels, could be used to: get immediate resolution to conflicts between DoD personnel and the contractor's project manager, verify that the project management was spending the government's money wisely, and resolve conflicts within the contractor's organization quickly. Another benefit of executive sponsorship was rank. Some military officers believed that the project managers were below them in rank, even though the project manager was earning two to three times the salary of the military officer. Since rank was important to military personnel, the role of the executive sponsor also included stroking those military officers who refused to communicate directly with the contractors' project managers.

CAREER PATHS

As project management began to grow, industry contemplated whether or not project management should have its own career path ladder. At first, there was tremendous resistance to creating a separate career path ladder for project management. The reasons for this included: line managers were fearful that they would no longer be allowed to communicate directly to the customers, something often done under over-the-fence management; line managers would be treated as second-class citizens compared to the project managers; the project managers would have more influence over workers than the line managers; salaries on the project management ladder would be greater than on the technical ladders; technically oriented personnel would migrate to the project management ladder thinking the "grass is greener," thus diluting the line organization's technical strength. Line managers, who previously had control over various parts of the project, now appeared to have very little control. They argued strongly that project management belonged on the technical ladder, which meant that the project managers would still report to the technical line managers.

Executives began to recognize the importance of project management and its potential to generate more profits than using over-the-fence management. Reluctantly, project managers were given the responsibility for profit and loss. How can a company rationalize that the project manager has the responsibility to generate hundreds of millions of dollars in profits for the stockholders and not be regarded as a professional manager? Also, how could the company rationalize to the customer that someone who was just an engineer and not regarded as a professional manager was managing their money? The solution was clear. Project management had to become a career path. The companies now had three career path ladders: a technical ladder, a management ladder, and a project management ladder.

Making project management a career path at the contractor level certainly pleased the DoD. During competitive bidding situations, the DoD began requiring that contractors show the resumes of the project manager and project sponsor in their proposals. In some cases, companies identified two or three project managers and project sponsors, allowing the government to make the selection on contract award.

For military officers, a project management assignment was viewed as a mixed can of worms. Senior military officers who were managing programs rather than projects, had the authority to make decisions and were responsible for the implementation of the weapon systems promoted. Program management became an opportunity to get to the rank of general or admiral. But for the lower ranking military officers, project management was viewed as a nonpromotion slot because lower level project managers were seen as monitors or expeditors rather than managers, simply tracking progress and reporting upstairs to senior military officers. Lower ranking officers had very little authority to make project decisions.

Frustration set in among junior military officers who believed that project management would be their future. Promotions that did occur were often based on the size and nature of the project, the branch of service, and the magnitude of the cost overruns. This frustration became more severe when the junior military officers had to interface with industrial project managers who were on a promotable project management career path ladder.

Civilian personnel working for the DoD did not fare much better. The government did not know how to prepare job descriptions that would differentiate between different grade levels of project managers. Using the dollar value of the project would not work because you could be managing a $10 million project today but your next project might be only $500,000. Does that imply that the workers would agree to a reduction in pay? Eventually project management was integrated into the acquisition management career path for government employees.

THE 1960s AND 1970s

Without any firm guarantees that project management would enhance their career path opportunities for advancement, government employees began drifting away from project management. Those military officers who believed that project management would enhance their careers soon discovered the downside risks:

- If a project were terminated while you were managing it, your military career would most likely be over.
- If a project were terminated while you were managing it, the career of your boss, who fills out your performance review, might also be over.
- If there were significant overruns or schedule slippages, the results could be equally as bad.

- If the project were completed but at less than acceptable quality or performance, the project manager holding the ball at that time may be nonpromotable.

Military project management then took on a new meaning:

- When managing a project, do everything possible to make sure your project remains alive until you are either promoted and/or transferred off of the project.
- Delay approval of all necessary scope changes until your replacement arrives. Then the cost overruns become someone else's responsibility.
- If possible, avoid becoming the project manager right before project implementation, otherwise you will be the one explaining to Congress the reasons for the cost overruns and inability to meet specifications.

While government personnel were becoming frustrated with project management as a career path, project management at the aerospace and defense contractors was flourishing. Pushing through highly profitable scope changes became a way of life. The scope changes and add-ons were becoming so profitable that both the prime contractors and subcontractors were underbidding the initial contracts by as much as 40 percent and planning on making up the additional profits and revenue on scope changes and follow-on contracts.

At first, military personnel were hesitant to approve the scope changes for fear that the projects (and their careers) would be terminated. But soon the project managers began to realize that scope changes that increased the likelihood the weapon system would be funded, as long as the requests were made after significant investment was incurred in the project. Now it was cheaper for Congress to fund the scope changes rather than cancel the project. Contracts began pushing through both necessary and unnecessary scope changes to increase profitability. Military officers began to believe that approved scope changes would extend the life of their projects.

On large projects, cost overruns could be as much as 300 to 400 percent over the initial budget. Many government contractors had built up large empires on the belief that this level of government funding would continue indefinitely. As the government began cutting back on funding, the contractors' senior management was pressuring their project managers to generate more and more scope changes, even if unnecessary, to solve the company's cash flow problems. The alternative would be to downsize the organization. The scope changes were now being used for cash flow rather than profits.

By the mid-1980s, nine of the top ten DoD contractors and forty-five of the top one hundred were under investigation for allegations of wrongdoing.[1] These allegations included cost mischarges, bid rigging, defective pricing, product substitution, kickbacks, bribery, false claims, and falsification of performance records. The allegations involved billions of dollars. Industries other than aerospace and defense now believed that project management might have been part of the problem. There were common misbeliefs that project management:

applied only to aerospace, defense, and heavy construction; was restricted to engineering companies only; was the root cause of major cost overruns; was a fad, soon to disappear; would elongate project schedules; would reduce quality; and would generate excessive scope changes.

RECESSIONS AND THE 1980s

Although recessions are often viewed as being bad, the results of recessions can be good, as was the case for project management. By the mid-1980s, the U.S. economy was beginning to recover from a lengthy and painful recession. Managers who were resistant to change were now looking for better ways of managing, convinced that the hierarchical management structures would not suffice for future competitiveness. Project management was now being revisited. Managers became convinced that the principles of project management could be applied to a multitude of industries.

There were several factors that offered encouragement for the use of project management processes. First, industry finally realized that the cost overruns in the aerospace and defense fields were not due to project management, but more so to the length of the projects. For projects that were less than two or three years in length, technology was assumed to be known over the life of the project. But for projects that ran ten to fifteen years, as in aerospace and defense, numerous scope changes occurred due to technological advances. Now the cost overruns were being attributed to the inability to forecast technology rather than to project management.

The second important factor was that government had developed excellent templates for risk management and other project management processes. In addition, the government was dealing with thousands of contractors and needed consistency in the way that financial data was being prepared and reported back to the DoD. The result was the earned value performance measurement, which is the standard today for all of project management.

Perhaps the biggest factor was the establishment of the Project Management Certification Exam administered by the Project Management Institute (PMI). By passing the exam and meeting other criteria, participants became project management professionals (PMP). Industry looked very favorably on PMPs, and customers were requiring that the contractor's project manager be a PMP. This provided the customer with some degree of assurance that the assigned project manager had at least an understanding of the core knowledge necessary to lead the project and that the chance of project success would be greatly enhanced.

THE 1990s

Growth in project management during the 1990s can be attributed to the auto industry. The recessions of 1978–1983 and 1989–1993 had a devastating affect on the auto industry. To remain competitive and recover lost market share, the

U.S. auto industry had to improve automobile quality and compress new product development time from six years to three years.

Under pressure from Detroit, automotive suppliers accepted project management as a way of life. This affected the steel, rubber, textile, computer, electronics, and automotive components industries. Detroit was requiring the tier one suppliers to get their project managers certified as PMPs. The tentacles from Detroit spread to a multitude of industries. Many of today's best practices in project management came out of the auto industry and its suppliers; twenty years ago, the best practices came from aerospace, defense, and construction.

THE PROJECT OFFICE

By the mid-1990s, the successful use of project management permeated virtually every division within a company. Management began to believe that for sustained project management growth to occur there must be strategic planning for project management. One major roadblock identified as part of the strategic planning process was the fact that the project managers reported to various managers through the organization and lessons-learned information was not shared. To solve this problem, management looked toward the project office concept as the focal point for controlling all intellectual property on project management.

The project office concept was not new. For almost forty years, the project office (or program office) existed within the defense contractors as a group of project management personnel assigned to a specific project, usually a large project, in support of government contracts. Aerospace and defense contractors created multiple project offices for grouping U.S. Army, Navy, and Air Force customers. Some companies created project offices exclusively to serve either large projects or small projects.

The initial concept behind the project office approach was to get closer to the customer by establishing an organization dedicated to that specific customer. The majority of the so-called projects were actually programs that were very large in dollar value and multiyear in duration. It was not uncommon for people to spend ten or fifteen years working on just one project.

Although the members of the project office had unique primary roles and responsibilities, they essentially worked together as a project management team. Each person in the project office was required to have both primary and secondary responsibilities. The secondary responsibilities were to function as a backup for other project office personnel who might be reassigned to other projects, leave the company, or were out sick.

Headcount in the project office was not important because the customer paid the bills. Technology and schedules were significantly more important than cost. Customers preferred to have more people than necessary assigned to the project offices. The cost of having someone assigned full time to the project was considered an insignificant overmanagement cost compared to the risks of undermanagement, where individuals were assigned part time but may have been needed full time. The only people who were trained in project management, and truly understood it, were the project office personnel. Project offices were reviewed as profit centers, whereas the functional hierarchy was treated as a cost center.

During the 1980s, military and government agencies became cost-conscious. Project offices were pared down as personnel, other than in the project office, underwent training in project management. Line managers were asked to better understand project management and share accountability with project managers for project success.

The 1990s began with a recession, which took a heavy toll on the white-collar ranks. Management's desire for efficiency and effectiveness led them to take a hard look at nontraditional management techniques such as project management. Project management began to expand to nonproject-driven industries. The benefits of project management, once seen as applicable only to the aerospace, defense, and heavy construction industries, were recognized now as being applicable to other industries. Typical benefits were:[2]

- accomplishing more work in less time with fewer resources and without any sacrifice in quality
- an increase in profitability
- better control of scope changes
- more efficient and effective operations
- better customer relations
- better risk identification and problem solving
- applicability to a multitude of projects, irrespective of size
- an increase in quality
- a reduction in power struggles
- an improvement in the sharing of information
- better company decision making
- an increase in business and competitiveness
- the ability to provide complete solutions rather than just products

As the benefits of project management became apparent, management understood that there was a significant, favorable impact on the corporate bottom line. This led management to three important conclusions: Project management must be integrated and compatible with the corporate reward systems for sustained project management growth. Corporate recognition of project management as a profession must occur to maximize performance. There must be a control point for project management intellectual property.

Consideration was being given to create a project office for control of all critical activities related to project management. This included such topics as strategic planning or project management, project management benchmarking, project management mentorship, continuous improvement, problem-solving hotlines, maintaining lesson-learned files, methods and standards, and training and education.

Each of these activities brought with it advantages and disadvantages. The majority of the disadvantages were attributed to the increased levels of resistance to the new responsibilities given to the project office. Today, the project office has become commonplace in a multitude of companies. As project management continues to grow, so should the responsibilities of the project office.

NOTES

1. See "Problems in the Development and Manufacture of Defense Systems." *Harvard Business School Case Study*, 9-390-055, © 1989 by the President and Fellows of Harvard College.

2. Adapted from Harold Kerzner, *Project Management: A Systems Approach to Planning, Scheduling and Controlling*, 7th ed. New York: John Wiley & Sons, 2001, p. 64.

3

Redefining the Foundations
for Project Management

FRANCIS HARTMAN

A s project management evolves and, hopefully, becomes a distinct and recognized professional discipline, we will see emergence of a solid foundation
of proven theory and practice. We are not there today, as the profession is yet
young. This chapter takes a look at the fiction behind the facts in project management. Understanding what is real and what is not in the theory and practice
of managing projects can help us understand why even the most careful use of
project management tools and processes can still lead to failure. The chapter is
deliberately provocative. The intent is partly to stimulate thought and partly to
challenge what we do as project management practitioners. It is through such a
challenge (critical thinking), as well as through the search for better solutions
(productive thinking), that we improve on what we do.

UNDERSTANDING WHERE WE ARE

Where is the boundary between project and operation management? What is a
project today? More to the point what is not one? As the ideas behind project
management get more attention and both people and practice challenge the new
traditions of the emerging profession, we find several interesting things happening. First, we see that blind or mechanical use of project management tools
can lead to poorer performance and can even lead to misinformation and bad
decision making. Next we look at the real and empirically validated theories and
find most do not pass the test of adequate and objective research, let alone

rigorous study. Much of what we have in project management theory and practice is founded on experience of professionals and on traditions and legends. What does this mean?

What Is Project Management?

Traditionally, we have defined projects as work with a defined beginning and end. Projects have a specific defined outcome that needs to be achieved, typically with limited resources and in a predetermined time frame. But does not just about everything we do fall into this definition in one way or another? Most enterprises now look at operations in a new way. It is not good enough to do things the way we did last year; we need better products, higher productivity, lower cost, or some other target needs to be met in order to maintain competitive advantage. Are these not the factors that turn operations into a form of project? Yet many managers resist "projectizing" their work. Is this because by doing so, clear accountability for the target results becomes one of the outcomes? Observation would suggest a growing interest in using the project model to increase the probability of success in achieving results—not just on the more traditional project types, but increasingly for softer projects and operations-related targets for performance or process improvements.

Redefining project management in this way makes it harder to understand what good project management really is. This is exemplified in the growing number of special interest groups (SIGs) that are being formed to address the specific needs of specialist project types. We can see that project management is evolving to encompass a growing inventory of project types. But it does not stop there.

Is CPM Fundamentally Flawed?

If the meaning and scope of project management is growing and changing, what else is (or should be) changing? One of the cornerstones of project management theory is the process for building a Critical Path Method (CPM) Schedule. Theory states that the critical path is the longest path through connected activities in a schedule. Based on this premise, we have in the past defined those activities on the critical path as being the critical ones. Traditionally, we have promoted the idea that it is these critical activities that should get our management attention over the others. Yet even when we do this, we end up with problems and they are rarely to do directly with the activities on the critical path. All too often we have a problem with an almost-critical activity that goes awry.

Should we rather be looking at some other criticality than just the likely time to complete a task? How about which resources are most critical? Or should we be focusing on the most volatile activities. Try it for yourself. Consider three concurrent activities: A, B, and C. All have the same likely duration of ten days. Activity A is on the critical path. Which one would you manage? Add the fact that activity B needs a key person to do the work, and that person is only available on certain days that have to be booked many months in advance. Now which one is more important? Activity C is very volatile. Under perfect conditions, you would not even need to do it. But if things went wrong, it could delay the project by six months. Now which activity will you focus on?

What do we learn? A classical CPM schedule does not give you all of the information you need to make the decisions we routinely make based on what we see. This does not mean that the scheduling technique is fundamentally flawed. Rather, that it can easily mislead a project manager who relies on theory and limited information alone. The trick is to know how to collect the right information for the decision at hand, and not to be overwhelmed by the data that might be available as opposed to what you really need to know to make the right decision.

Why Do The "Bits" of Project Management Not Fit?

We have just seen how important it is to have all of the relevant information available to us for decision-making purposes. Yet, if we look at how we structure the parts of project management (consider Project Management Institute's [PMI] Guide to the Project Management Body of Knowledge [PMBOK], as just one well-known example), we see that there is a propensity to separate and categorize the knowledge areas. Both the knowledge areas and their impact on decisions and behaviors are closely interlinked. Yet they have their roots in traditional roles of estimators, schedulers, purchasing specialists, human resources specialists, auditors, contract administrators, risk management specialists, accounting departments, and so on. Each of these disparate specialized professions has a different and unique perspective on the issues involved in management of a project. That is good and bad. The good part is that the perspectives, while different, are relevant and important. The bad part is that the connections between the parts are essentially lost because they have been isolated and developed independently. What is needed is a more cohesive review of these important elements of a project, so that we regain the linkages between, for example, cost, team morale, and how risks are managed on a project.

While we can see the disconnect manifest itself in many ways, one of the most common is the need for complex maps to link responsibility to cost codes to the work breakdown structure and to other bits of information on a project. In other words, we have a body of knowledge that is disconnected and leads to problems in management of the projects we are trying to deliver. This is so insidious that we see it as a "normal" part of project management and not as a problem in itself. The root cause of this problem lies in the history of how we have added knowledge to the profession by drawing on other operations-based management specializations. Projects are not about operations. They are about step change. And step change requires a deliverables-based approach.

Is This Just the Tip of the Iceberg?

If we look at our existing body of knowledge as being based on what may well be the wrong foundation, how big is the problem of how project management information and knowledge is structured? Is this a Titanic iceberg? And if so, are we looking at something we have not yet fully understood in terms of what we are trying to do?

Although no effective study has been done to compare projects delivered using current project management knowledge versus those projects that did not use any or much of the project management body of knowledge, it would not surprise me to find that any such study would reveal little or no difference. There are studies that explore the relationship between the use of planning techniques (based on PMI's PMBOK), but all appear flawed in that the research methodology will inevitably lead to the conclusions that are drawn.

The suggestion that the results of a well-executed study might show little or no discernible difference between project management-informed delivery and random delivery is based on the following sad observations.

- People who do not recognize their role as that of a project manager deliver many projects.
- Three independent private studies of the correlations between delivering projects on time and within budget and repeat business suggest that there is no relationship between use of project management techniques and metrics and the perceived success of the project.
- If we look at projects, regardless of the use of "best practices" in project management, there seems to be a consistent failure rate (or success rate if we are optimists) across any particular industry.

For a growing number of organizations, there seems to be little difference in the delivery of projects and the performance of project managers with training (e.g., a certificate or other designation in project management) compared to those without the training. There may be a correlation between the experience of a project manager and their rate of success, though the reason for this is not known. It may be that the experienced project manager has learned from that experience. It may be natural selection at work (experience means we are dealing with a survivor, or bad project managers never get any more experience). Good project managers who have earned that label based on the commendations of their clients seem to have just one thing in common: they can make connections and through that ability can make better judgments and thus better decisions.

So maybe we have a huge iceberg, and we do not even know its composition, let alone the extent under the waterline. Research in project management is still quite young. Much of the work being done is based on building on, or validating the existing claimed theories. We look at industry practices. We develop improvements to existing tools, and we try to understand why theories work. Is this the right approach, or are we building on the wrong set of assumptions?

UNDERSTANDING WHAT WE NEED TO DO

What Are Real Results and Research Really Telling Us?

This is an unfair question because it asks about "real results." The assumption in any quality research is that the results are arrived at objectively. Part of that objectivity includes use of assumptions. A significant portion of the work done to build the theoretical framework we currently rely on is arguably flawed. Consider the following.

- When looking at sample sizes, ask if samples of two or three are truly representative of the project management world.
- If a sample is drawn from members of a particular professional or technical association, is the result likely to be biased?
- If the questions in a survey are presented in a way that the respondent is likely to come up with the "right" (or expected) answer, have we distorted the findings?
- If we have a good and random sample, but the results are interpreted based on a set of incorrect assumptions, do we simply reinforce these assumptions?

In literature reviews conducted as part of the University of Calgary projects, a significant number of the empirical studies have shown one or more of the above cautionary indicators. And many of the papers published in project management journals, magazines, trade magazines, and other related publications are based on experience and stories rather than on rigorous and objective empirical data. As a consequence, many of the texts include information based on these stories and observations where we are not dealing with the mathematical theory behind, for example, CPM scheduling or earned value calculations. This begs a frequently asked question in the Calgary research program: "What is really real, and what could be telling us something else?"

Ultimately, we can see the picture of the profession as one of slowly shifting awareness of what is "real" as opposed to merely opinion. This is scary, as we are all reluctant to discard what we have held to be true and profound in the past. So what do we keep and what do we discard? Is there any litmus paper out there that can help us rebuild the foundations of theory and practice for the profession? To answer these questions we need to test some basic assumptions.

Can We Recognize What Works and What Is Just "Comfortable"?

One of the assumptions we were able to test in a cursory way, and by observation in a few organizations, was the impact of formal training in project management. Here are three cases.

The first company is a financial services organization based in the United States. They trained all of their project managers at the time, and required them to complete a master's certificate program that basically covered PMI's PMBOK, but has its own testing and certification program. The success rate of their projects did not improve measurably. This led to a requirement that project managers should qualify as Project Management Professionals. As this really added little to the knowledge base of the managers who had already completed the master's certificate program, and did nothing about their management style. The result was that there was no measurable improvement in project delivery. Predictable. The third round of training was to use an online provider of training. The basic premise on which project management training is founded seems to be similar in most instances, and again the predictable result occurred—no measurable performance change. The fourth step was to pilot a new approach that yielded significantly better results. Unfortunately this did not seem to be sustainable, as the process of embedding the new approach in company procedures was done largely by traditionally trained project mangers who eliminated all of the "wrong stuff," reducing the new approach to what was used before.

In the second case, a large government agency with no particular approach to management of projects adopted a new paradigm and associated methodology. The adoption was part of a grassroots movement and was applied in carefully selected project situations at the outset. The rampant success of the projects that used this new approach led to growing demand for training and support in this new delivery method. Because there was no tradition around project management (despite annual project spending of about $450 million!), the adoption of the new framework and the basis on which the approach was based, was relatively easy. An internal champion and a small core team that were certified trainers in the approach formed the core that supported this initiative.

The third case is still evolving at the time of this writing. This is a large oil and gas exploration and extraction business. It is embarking on a multibillion dollar expansion and has started to build an internal infrastructure to manage and deliver the projects in this program. The staff who are being recruited are seasoned project professionals. This means that they have experience in doing things the way that this industry (and some related industries) has traditionally done business in delivering these projects. The executive of the sponsor company has decided to try a new approach to management of projects that is based on modified theory. The team on one significant project has accepted the implementation of this new approach. However, the communication challenges are huge. One of the key issues is that the well-understood and comfortable traditional approach is so well understood that any new idea is measured or referenced against this standard. By doing this, the comparison leads to confusion and misunderstanding. For example, traditional projects plan in great detail at the outset. Because we know that, once you are guessing what will happen more than six weeks ahead, such detailed plans tend to be incorrect in the detail—though not in the outline—the new approach does not plan in detail beyond a six-week time horizon. Within the six weeks, greater care is taken to make sure the plan is right. The translation by traditional project management practitioners is that there will be a much larger effort in planning with questionable advantage or benefit. Yet the reality is that more people plan their own work, coordinate more effectively, and have fewer problems in that they do not have to keep explaining why the original plan keeps being out of touch with what is really happening on the project!

What can we learn from this? The more comfortable we are with the way we do things (regardless of whether the approach is good or indifferent), the more likely we will tend to stick to comfortable ideas. Only those of us who do not know any better will try—and succeed—in delivering projects more effectively.

Can We Effect Change in Project Management?

It would seem that making a change in how we do business will require either a determination to do better (apparently rare) or a desperate need to survive (probably less rare). Making a change will depend on many factors. Some of the barriers for change are:

- I know how we manage projects today, it is safe and predictable—so there is no need to change.
- All new ideas need to be proven and time-tested before they can be used for the first time (a death-defying piece of logic, commonly encountered!).
- We have taken years to get what we have in place, train our staff, and develop our systems and procedures. We do not give up on such a significant investment easily.
- We tried something different before and it did not work.
- Who else is using it? If we do not believe that these companies are as good as we are we see no reason to do what they are doing.

There are many more barriers, and most will be familiar to anyone who has worked in the change management field. Change in how we manage projects will likely be both slow and frustrating for those trying to improve on current practices.

If We Must Change, What *Do* We Change?

The primary reason for change in an area such as how projects are managed is usually an imperative such as survival or a need to remain competitive. Under those circumstances, we typically see people already working under considerable stress. And under stress, we need as little new material to work with as possible. So, in many ways, the driver for change is also one of the biggest barriers. What do we change under these circumstances? Typically, we change as little as possible! Perhaps the most important change lies in the way a project is planned. A good plan is also a stress reliever. This is so because a good plan will identify most of the things that can go wrong and will provide a solution or a way of eliminating the risk. The downside to a good plan is that it may demonstrate that the project is not achievable within the parameters set by the sponsor. Another view is that this will help to cancel the project—or modify the parameters so the project can succeed—before the wrong "go" decision is made.

Some of the emerging and reemerging tools that are being used to help with better planning include a set that are slowly being adopted to build living charters for projects. These living charters—a new idea in itself—are also the project plan. The charter, just as a plan would, changes and adapts over the course of the project to reflect reality. By the end of the project the charter is a record of what happened. Because the format does not change, it is useful as a document of what was learned during the course of the project.

Some of the main elements of a charter/plan include the following components:

- Milestone schedule and supporting schedules: Replacing the traditional CPM schedule, there is a suite of schedules from the main milestone schedule that spans the entire project to increasingly detailed ones that span ever shorter durations, but in increasing detail.
- Deliverables-based work breakdown structure: This is a familiar tool that is based on deliverable components that support the key results for the project.
- A priority triangle: This sets the priorities for the project or for phases of the project so that the right approach to tactical management and decision making is obtained for the team and its leadership.
- Alignment tests: There are a number of ways of checking that the stakeholders are aligned on key issues. The results of these tests (usually in the form of answers to specific questions) are documented once consensus has been achieved.
- A rigorous risk assessment and mitigation process: The key outcomes of this exercise are a good understanding of the risks in the execution of the project, together with an appropriate mitigation plan for the more critical risks. In addition, a risk communication plan is produced and implemented.
- A communication plan at both the strategic and tactical levels.
- Simple comprehensive and timely reporting on progress and detailed planning on a regular basis throughout the life of a project.

These and other tools have diminished the role of the more traditional tools such as scheduling and estimating in favor of a broader range of hard and soft tools that focus on the expectations of the stakeholders and their needs. Balance between people, business, and technical issues is the result. The newer approach theoretically develops a more complete plan, at the right level of detail, while retaining an appropriate degree of flexibility to accommodate the realities of future changes to project circumstances and stakeholder expectations.

Are Any of These Ideas Being Tested?

So, where do these ideas all come from? What has driven the work that led to a change in thinking? A series of projects investigating a number of identified critical issues was undertaken at the University of Calgary over a five-year period. These resulted in a prototype modified approach to project planning and subsequent management. The prototype was developed through field trials. The concept of a combined charter and plan for projects with the ingredients outlined previously, among others emerged. The results of the trials indicated not only that the projects were more successful, but also that their management was simplified.

One of the important things that were learned was that we needed to see an evolution from a best-practices search (based on what is being done today) to development of a focus on the importance of balance and connections (common elements in successful projects). We could not do this without touching on the importance of the role of people and how they are managed in a project context (temporary organizations) and the key role of trust. This led to the work on trust over the next four years. This has, in itself, led to a prototype model to map the genome of a successful project using "Enterprise DNA" or EDNA. Following is a brief explanation of the EDNA model.

UNDERSTANDING THE FUTURE AND LEARNING FROM THE PAST

Just understanding today's project management and trying to work out the theory behind it has relatively little value. The reason for this is that by the time we understand what we do today, the world will have changed again, and the results of our work will be outdated. The research program that led to EDNA was based on trying to understand the world of tomorrow and find out what the basic drivers are for how projects will need to be managed. EDNA grew out of the trust research, as the team found more and more parallels to the three basic types of trust that form the basis of the research.

The DNA of Enterprises (EDNA)

EDNA is one way of modeling the culture of an enterprise. To build the DNA model of an enterprise, we use five steps. The first two steps use a six-by-six matrix of elements that reflect the relative relationship of six general characteristics of enterprises. The matrix works in a similar way to the Myers-Briggs approach to understanding personality types with its four-by-four matrix. The relative priorities of the resulting thirty-six characteristics are then set out in a list. This is done twice: the first time reflects the management perspective of priorities; the second one is based on real decisions and analysis of these, particularly those decisions made under pressure or in difficult and stressful situations. The result is a double helix of thirty-six elements of a business that have been prioritized based on beliefs and then again based on practice. It is not expected that the two sets of priorities will coincide.

What Use Is EDNA?

EDNA tells us how we perceive ourselves as well as the difference between this and how others see us as derived from actual behaviors. When we compare the EDNA of two enterprises that might work together on a project, we can identify differences in priorities between them. It is these differences—and the corresponding similarities—that will influence the behaviors of the two organizations toward each other. If we can build an understanding of this, we can also explore other basic ideas regarding the complexities and drivers of enterprises. This analysis will, we hope, help us to better understand other factors as well.

Sample uses of EDNA include: understanding where communication problems will occur through a better understanding of others' perspectives, selecting the team for better effectiveness by understanding and managing expectations more effectively, contracting strategies to align EDNA of each enterprise in order to reduce conflict and achieve better working relationships, building more effective charters that reflect the needs and aspirations of the stakeholders more effectively, and managing change (a key outcome of virtually every project) so that resistance to such change is minimized and the outcomes are balanced more effectively.

SO, WHAT COMES NEXT?

This chapter started with a look at some of the things that we have taken for granted in the world of project management. From that we looked at some current research that is largely exploratory. The research is uncovering some interesting ideas, including issues around sustainability of projects and project organizations. We are at an interesting time for the profession of project management. As we start to dig under the foundation of what we do, we start to unearth a range of opportunities to explore the factors and issues we need to understand if we want to manage the projects of tomorrow.

EDNA and the related trust research is just one of the areas being investigated by researchers from around the world. All of this work, as well as the knowledge of practitioners, will help reshape project management for the future. We can expect the future versions of project management to be quite different, as the shapes of the foundations of theory evolve, gain strength, and change shape.

BIBLIOGRAPHY

Canfield, J. M., V. Hansen, and L. Hewitt. 2000. *The Power of Focus*. Deerfield Beach, Fl.: Health Communications Inc.

Hartman, F. T. 2000. *Don't Park Your Brain Outside*. Newtown Square, Pa.: Project Management Institute.

Hartman, F. T., and G. Jergeas. 1997. Simplifying Project Success Metrics. *Cost Engineering AACEI* 39(11): 33–37.

Koehn, Daryl. 1996. Should We Trust in Trust? *American Business Law Journal*. 34(2): 183–203.

McKnight, D. H., L. L. Cummings, and N. L. Chervany. 1998. Initial Trust Formation in New Organizational Relationships. *Academy of Management Review* 23(3): 473–90.

Neal, R. A. 1995. Project Definition: The Soft-Systems Approach. *International Journal of Project Management* 13(1): 5–9.

Shaw, Robert B. 1995. *Trust in the Balance*. San Francisco: Jossey-Bass.

Ward, S. C., and C. B. Chapman. 1995. Risk Management Perspective on the Project Lifecycle. *International Journal of Project Management* 13(3) 145–49.

———— 4 ————

Stakeholder Mapping and the Execution of Successful Projects

Embedding and Institutionalizing Learning as a Key Project Management Competence

ELIAS G. CARAYANNIS
FRANK T. ANBARI
ROBERT JAMES VOETSCH

This chapter examines the customer management aspects involved in a knowledge-based service-focused project. We will consider the following factors that influence customer management: customer mapping interfaces in knowledge-based service projects; the manner in which knowledge is created, managed, and diffused in any project; customer expectations issues in knowledge-based service-focused projects versus quality of the product and process; the role and necessary insights for project management in this process, with specific reference to the role and need of postmortem evaluation roles in internal knowledge-based service-focused projects; requirements gathering methods for internal projects such as software development projects; and embedding and institutionalizing learning processes in knowledge-based service-focused internal project management? When, how, and why? In summation, the overall objective is to consider how the embedding and institutionalizing of learning processes can improve the mapping of all project customer needs and expectations. A secondary consideration is how these processes can add to the historical information produced by the project during postmortem reviews. Finally, this chapter will considers how project management tools and techniques can be empowered with knowledge management methodologies and skill sets to better enable projects to deliver performances that fall within the primary triple constraint: on time, within budget, and according to customer expectations.

The primary question that needs to be asked when considering any knowledge-based service-focused project is the nature or categories that exist for such projects. The secondary issue in this question is the role that customer expectations plays in determining whether a completed project is considered to be of high or low quality.

In any research and development work, there are two categories of projects: "upstream" projects and "downstream" projects. Each of these categories possesses different types of product or process development. Therefore, the nature of the customer and his expectations is also different according to whether or not the project is an upstream or downstream project.

Another key question is the content and purpose of a postmortem project review and the place of this review in the project life cycle presented in the Project Management Body of Knowledge. To answer this question, it is necessary to discuss the nature of a postmortem review and where it fits into the project life cycle. Such a discussion must consider the value of these reviews and how they can assist and organization to improve on the manner in which its projects are conceived, planned, implemented, reported on, and evaluated.

Central to this consideration are these key questions:

- How might postmortem reviews differ between a construction project, on the one hand, and a knowledge-based service-focused project on the other?
- What information is needed in order to know definitively what the requirements are for an internal—in this case software development—project?
- What types of knowledge exist in an organization and how can these be accessed and used to further goals and mission of the organization?
- What roles do project management and knowledge management play within an organization?
- What roles do organizational culture, organizational structure, communication protocols, and communication technology use play in facilitating or impeding an institutionalized learning process within a knowledge-based service-focused internal project?

LITERATURE REVIEW

To assist in answering the above questions, we reviewed a number of literature sources that address some of the key issues motivating this chapter. For instance, The Dimensions of Customer Requirements (Ireland 1991) identified two categories of customers: Apparent Customers—these customers are easy to identify. They are the sponsor, buyer, workers, and end users of the project; and, Invisible Customers—those customers not readily apparent to a project. They are persons or communities who are not interested in the project's goals but who want to shape the project—for example, pressure groups and government officials.

Ireland (1991) also offers the "9-ilities," a list of characteristics that describe the quality of a product. These are: Producibility, Usability, Reliability (Mean

Time Between Failures; MTBF), Maintainability (Mean Time to Repair; MTTR), Availability (MTTR + MTBF), Operability, Flexibility, Social Acceptability, and Affordability. Finally, Ireland states that customer requirements consist of two categories of specifications: Functional Specifications, which are the functions that the product will display over its useful lifespan, and, Detailed Specifications, which concern the size, functions, and assembly of the product to the level of detail required by the customer.

Cabanis (1997) who argues, "the idea of having requirements be customer defined is silly. . . . The reason he argues is that doing so amounts to pass[ing] off . . . responsibility to [a] mysterious group of people called customers, who don't always know what they want." Since the external, customer-focused approach is fraught with the peril of customers not knowing what they want, and since some customers are internal to an organization, the immediate suggestion is that an internal organizational process may be the source of knowledge on clarifying project specifications.

The literature review has indicated that organizations can become learning entities when they review, document, and archive the lessons learned from completed or terminated project. This review process has been variously described as either a post-project review or a postmortem review.

Busby (1999) argues that post-project reviews are necessary since people do not always automatically learn from their professional experiences. He describes two types of post-project review structures: chronological reviews in which the lessons learned are compiled for each phase of the project life cycle, and categorical reviews in which all lessons learned are compiled by all project team members on the basis of whether they were positive and negative experiences. A formal learning exercise is needed in order to extract from project team members as much knowledge as possible on what occurred in a project. This lesson-learned knowledge is essential to disseminate project management experiences and lessons learned within an organization in order to avoid repeating the same mistakes again and again. Busby cautions that post-project reviews can be time consuming, embarrassing to project managers and project team members, potentially damaging to social and professional relationships, and rejected by people who think that professional experience by itself is sufficient to acquire lessons learned from a project.

Collier, DeMarco, and Fearey (1996) argue for a postmortem project review process that is formal and required by a senior management commitment. They see the goal of a postmortem review to be a means to improve future project management methods and practices.

Both Busby (1999) and Collier et al. (1996) identify proactive problem-solving tools. These tools include documented procedures and guidelines, established communication channels, positive/blame-free analysis, balanced costs and benefits of postmortem reviews, and published results. The result of this process is the establishment of an organic link between postmortems and future projects—in this phase all postmortem output is documented and sorted according to the category of the lessons learned by project team function and the affected project management process or knowledge area. Senior management must see the results at regular organization reviews. Each lesson learned should be assigned to a staff member who is then responsible to investigate the lesson further and then implement a solution.

A number of literature sources focused on the need to embed knowledge management within an organization. Githens (1999) argues that good requirements management is the key to ensuring project success. He believes that projects fail at the beginning of the project life cycle and not at the end. This is the result of *scope creep* that does not increase the time or cost parameters of the project to accommodate increases in the scope of the project.

The author also contends that there are four processes of project requirements management: problem understanding—this process models the customer's problem and the desired future state; requirements elicitation—this process consists of gaining customer and developer knowledge relevant to the problem; requirements specification—the purpose of this process is to produce a formal notation of the requirements; and requirements validation—the purpose of this process is to make certain that the requirements are consistent with the customer's intentions and that they are unambiguous, complete, stable, traceable, and not too complex.

Olonoff (2000) compares knowledge management and project management and then offers a way to marry the two "umbrella disciplines" into a "project knowledge orientation." He discusses knowledge management as "knowledge orientation" or "organizational learning" and describes organizations that master knowledge creation as "learning organizations." Finally, Olonoff argues that knowledge management differs from project management in the following respects: knowledge management assumes that the world is uncertain and full of unforeseen change; it views unforeseen contingency as bringing the greatest new opportunities; the business value of knowledge management is the creation, sharing, use, and re-use of knowledge, and knowledge management-oriented organizations share knowledge across organizational boundaries.

Olonoff (2000) views project management as focused on a conventional model of operation in which planning and allocating are done for known resources and variables. In addition, he views project management as being focused on lessons learned as knowledge sharing, when in fact these learned lessons can be too little too late in the project life cycle to affect positively the project outcome; and, project teams tend to be cut off from their larger organizations, thus impeding knowledge and information sharing.

Olonoff goes on to describe "project knowledge orientation" as consisting of the following attributes: porous boundaries between organizational units, project managers being responsible for knowledge issues (e.g., knowledge creation), using convenient methods of cross-unit communication (e.g., intranets and groupware programs such as Lotus Notes), and establishing "communities of practice" within organizations to share ideas, experiences, and newfound knowledge.

STAKEHOLDER/CUSTOMER MAPPING

In order to embed a learning process within an organization, a thorough map of stakeholders and customers is needed. This map would not only identify all project stakeholders and customers but also indicate what the interests and expectations of each were for the project. An example of such a map can be seen in figure 4.1. This map presents our view of how the various actors intersect with one another to influence the direction and output of the project team. Each actor is a customer—internal or external—of the project. Depending on the type of project being implemented, some of these customers may not be present in the project map.

For example, the project customer in an upstream project might be a functional department; it would not necessarily be a commercial customer. Also, in an organization that has instituted an enterprise project management approach, the functional departments might be replaced by the Project Management Center of Excellence, the project support office, or the office of the chief project officer, depending on the type of organizational architecture was in place in the organization implementing the project.

The project stakeholder/customer map (figure 4.1) displays the goals, interests, and expectations that each actor brings to the project. If all of these sometimes opposing expectations are to be met in a downstream project, they should

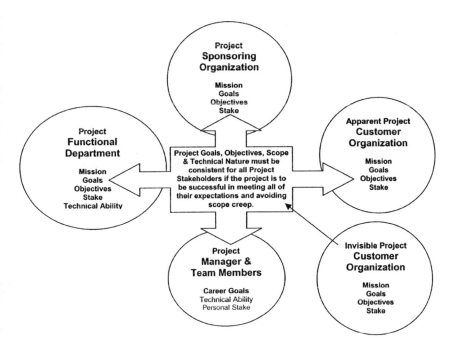

FIGURE 4-1. Project stakeholder/customer map.

be reflected in the goals and objectives of the project document and scope statement. In our opinion, the ultimate success of a downstream project in both producing a quality project or process and in meeting the expectations of the customers is entirely dependent on how well prepared the project stakeholder/ customer map is and how this is reflected in the project document.

In figure 4.1, the role of the invisible customers is present as an outside force. These customers are on occasion the single most important customers of a project. For example, government regulators, judicial authorities, nongovern- mental interest groups, the media, and the general public can force a project to be altered radically or even discontinued. Thus, the project manager can only identify what external project customers may exist and—based on any historical information available within the company or in the public record—determine to what extent they may influence his project. The primary project concern remains satisfying the expectations of the commercial customer by involving him the planning process through the Quality Function Deployment (QFD) process, thereby increasing the likelihood that the product or process produced would meet the "9-ilities" of quality identified previously.

THE POST-PROJECT REVIEW

The literature sources cited suggest a bridging phase between project closeout and project initiation: The postmortem project review or the post-project review. In our opinion, the authors of the cited articles are absolutely correct in arguing that the postmortem review process is an essential exercise to be conducted for all projects—and programs too for that matter. The lessons learned from this exercise provide a consolidated body of data and information that can serve as the baseline historical information for future projects. This database will enable future project managers and their team members to make more accurate esti- mates on cost, schedule, and technical specifications.

Organizations that routinely schedule and hold post-project reviews can use the advise of the authors to improve the conduct and benefits of this exercise. Those organizations that hold such reviews sporadically, or not at all, can use the above articles to learn valuable tips on how to organize and conduct post-project reviews. Most of all, the cited literature indicate the crucial importance of in- volving both senior management and other project managers in the post-project review process. When these organization members are involved in the process, the lessons learned from the reviewed project can be disseminated immediately and used by other members of the organization.

Impact of the Post-Project Review

In view of the benchmark literature sources, we believe that it is essential for knowledge-based service-focused projects to be approached in a project- oriented as opposed to program-oriented manner. There are a number of reasons for this. First, the primary triple constraint of delivering projects on time, on budget, and according to specifications requires that these knowledge-based service projects be implemented by a team of personnel deployed for the single purpose of implementing the project. Second, the triple constraint of delivering projects, that of quality, meet customer expectations, and succeed in managing and mitigating all risks (technical, schedule, cost, quality, etc.), is best met by a single-purpose project team. The Luther Gulick project type organizational structure argues that risks can be contained and that time and resources for a project can be predicted accurately. I believe that project postmortem reviews provide organizations an opportunity to generate the historical information that will allow time and resources to be accurately predicted and for any and all project risks contained.

In our experience, the majority of knowledge-based service projects (e.g., software programs, communication networks) are customized products/processes for a specific customer. Thus, an "off-the-shelf" product/process most likely will not succeed in meeting the customers' expectations. After all, if there was an off-the-shelf product available in stores, customers would probably have already purchased it. Thus, a project approach that is unique to the special needs of the customer is the best approach.

The work of Funtowicz and Ravetz indicates that the increasingly ambiguous project operating environment requires a systematic approach to learning lessons from completed or terminated projects. The postnormal scientific paradigm compels organizations to provide their project managers with as much information as possible at the conceptual stage of a project on how to develop project objectives, structure project management decision making, and access other information sources as no one has all the requisite expertise.

The "virtuous circle" model of organizational postmortem reviews can lead to the institutionalizing and embedding of organizational learning and knowledge sharing processes. These processes bridge the gap between project teams and the larger sponsoring organization.

INFORMATION-GATHERING PROCESS PROTOCOL

In discussing how to go about gathering information on the requirements for a software project, the following five-step process is recommended.

Step 1

First, we seek out information in the company on the results of any previous or ongoing projects of a similar technical nature for the same customer and in the same department of the company. The purpose of this search is to obtain baseline information on the range of possible parameters of these projects with respect to: scope, cost, time frame, human resource requirements, contract types, communication methods, project organization, identified risks, and quality parameters. To briefly recapitulate, we access the project archives to obtain any relevant information from other projects that would enable us to complete our benchmark requirements data for our project.

Step 2

Second, we obtain information on the technical requirements and specification for the software product from the customer via either the state of work in the Request for Proposal (RFP) or the project document—in the event that one has already been developed. At this stage, we consider the needs, expressed expectations, and any possible hidden agenda of the commercial customer for this software project. The use of the QFD would be very helpful in reaching an agreement with the customer(s) on what the final software product will be. If this planning stage regarding the quality and customer end-use requirements is done well, the risk of producing a software product that will not meet the secondary triple constraints of quality and customer expectation will be greatly reduced.

The creation of a project stakeholder/customer map would facilitate our understanding of the various customers—apparent and invisible, internal and external—who have a stake in the project. We would need to confirm that these potentially disparate interests were reflected in the project scope statement of the project document. Once the scope of the project had been confirmed and compared with the project customer's interests we would develop a scope management plan.

We would ensure that the scope management plan included a clear and well-known scope change control plan that was agreed to by the customer. Such a clearly defined scope change control process would assist the project in avoiding any scope creep risks that might arise during project implementation. We would make clear in communication with the customer that any changes in project scope would have to be reflected in corresponding changes in the project schedule, budget, and quality specifications. Without this customer agreement to change the parameters of the primary triple constraint, it might become impossible to deliver the project within budget, on time, and according to project specifications.

Step 3

The next step of our requirement gathering process concerns the identification of the specific human resource needs of the project. Once again, access to an organization database on project historical information would greatly facilitate this assessment. The human resource requirements consist of the technical skill sets and number of staff required as well as the costs associated with them. In addition, it is important to know the names of specific individuals who could either assist or hurt the project team in being successful in the project. With this information, a team would have a better chance of successfully producing the software product. Finally, any team development and conflict management issues related to software products must also be obtained.

As mentioned previously, historical information from the company project database is an essential element in the successful finalization of human resource requirements for this software project. However, if this historical information was lacking in a formal sense, company staff and project managers with experience implementing similar projects could be located to assist in determining what the probable human resource needs were for those projects. To the extent possible—and necessary—the project sponsor and the project customer could be approached to determine what their views on the human resource—or at least skill set—requirements for the project.

Step 4

The organizational structure for the team is also important to obtain. If there were no historical information available, we would consult the RFP or project document to determine if there was a requirement for a projectized structure. Finally, and ultimately, the organizational culture of our employer as well as the history of software project implementation would determine what type of project team organization we would have—functional, matrix (strong or weak), or some form of projectized structure.

It would be necessary to ensure that the terms of reference for the project manager would be consistent with the needs of the project. In this respect, we would need to have the necessary authority of all project resources—money, staffing, and equipment—needed to implement the project. Finally, the communication and reporting periodicity and protocol would also need to be determined to avoid any future conflict or communication breakdowns between the project team and its sponsor(s) and customer(s).

Finally, we would ensure that the project charter reflected our needs as the project manager with respect to our authority over project resources, scope change control, customer communication, and periodic reporting. We would ensure that this project charter had the endorsement of senior management and was disseminated to all project team members, internal customers, and external customers. In this way, we would always have an official and unambiguous point of reference with respect to our authority—or lack thereof—over project resources and decision making.

Step 5

The risk management plan for the project would be an essential requirement as this would determine the threats to the successful completion of the project. Related to this would be not only the specific risk events of each deliverable and task of the project plan, but also the probability of their occurring, their quantitative impact on the project, who could best manage this risk, and what type of contract arrangement (legal regime) would enhance the ability of the project team to successfully manage and mitigate the identified risks.

For example, if there were risks to the completion of specific project tasks or deliverables that only the customer could control, these would have to be identified clearly as such and communicated to both the customer and the project sponsor. In this way, the project team—and the project manager—could not and would not be held accountable for cost overruns, schedule slippage, or product quality that was not under their control.

With the above steps completed, we would then work with customer and all project team members and any subcontractors to devise and design a comprehensive project plan—work breakdown structure—that would incorporate the assumptions on what the requirements were for the project in terms of: scope, cost, schedule, quality, legal provisions, human resource requirement, communication patterns and protocol, and finally risk management and mitigation.

TYPES OF LEARNING PROCESSES, ORGANIZATIONAL CULTURE, AND KNOWLEDGE MANAGEMENT ISSUES

The two main categories of learning that can be embedded and institutionalized in any organization are formalized training and orientation programs for organization members, and informal education and knowledge sharing between the members of an organization. In both instances, the organization benefits from the knowledge and learning that its membership experiences and generates.

In the case of the formalized training and orientation programs, an organization can easily embed and institutionalize this learning mode through policy statements, human resource procedures, and technical skill development programs. Participation in these formalized training programs can be arranged, scheduled, and streamlined to ensure the participation of those deserving such training opportunities.

The informal learning and knowledge sharing experienced by members of the organization, and thereby the larger organization itself, is the organizational learning that has been given the name knowledge management. This term means different things in different settings. However, this term can mean the ability of an organization to provide its membership with the knowledge they need when they need it, and to the extent that they need it at any time.

Methods to Facilitate Knowledge Creation

Given the ways in which knowledge can be created, Nonaka (1995) argues that there are two basic methods that facilitate knowledge creation within an organization. These methods are the development of mutual trust to facilitate the sharing of tacit knowledge and the externalized conceptualization of tacit knowledge through a continuous dialogue between organizational members.

Methods of Knowledge Transfer

Nonaka (1995) also states that there are three directions that knowledge transfers (information flows) can take within an organization: top-down—in this method, top management plays the key role in transferring explicit knowledge through computers or documents; middle-up-down—in this method, middle managers, and self-organizing teams transfer both tacit and explicit knowledge in many different ways; and, bottom-up—in this method, individual members of the organization act like entrepreneurs in using tacit knowledge.

To summarize: There are two types of knowledge in an organization, tacit and explicit. These two types of knowledge are created in one of four ways and are transferred to the members of the organization in one of three basic directions. The facilitating factors in this process are the extent of mutual trust in the organization and the degree to which staff communicate continuously with one another.

THE ROLE OF ORGANIZATIONAL CULTURE

The next step in determining how learning processes can be embedded and institutionalized in an organization is to consider the role that technology use can play in this process. In our opinion, the key factors that determine the role technology can play in organizational learning are the history and personal culture of technology use in the organization. In this vein, the research work of Orlikowski (1993) is instructive. She argues that organizational culture and personal culture are the key determinants in the manner and degree to which knowledge transfer take place.

If an organization has a culture of staff members hoarding information, this will not change with the introduction of a groupware communication system such as Lotus Notes. On the other hand, if the culture of the organization is one of information sharing, then the knowledge management software will be used in a cooperative and sharing manner. The key point is that culture of the organization drives the use of knowledge management technology and not the other way around. Furthermore, the extent to which staff members personally use technology also factors into this dynamic. For example, if staff members were acculturated to the typewriter before the computer, they will tend to use computers like they did typewriters—for written communication only. Similarly, if staff members were acculturated into communicating with colleagues on a need-to-know basis, they will tend to use intranets in the same way. Thus, the boundaries of personal technology use and communication patterns determine how well used technology is in organizational learning.

THE ROLE OF INFORMATION TECHNOLOGY
IN KNOWLEDGE MANAGEMENT

In her research study, Orlikowski (1993) studied a large international consulting firm and how it used a groupware implementation of Lotus Notes to improve internal organizational knowledge management and transfer. Her basic findings were these: information technology use is not necessarily knowledge management, technology is merely a tool for knowledge management, and technology amplifies the existing work culture and does not necessarily transform it.

The types of technology that can be used to facilitate organizational learning and knowledge transfer (management) are many. Figure 4.2 displays a knowledge management structure for specific technologies whose use can be institutionalized and embedded in an organization.

A graphical representation of this knowledge management technology model is shown in figure 4.3. The key point conveyed by this model is that workers (knowledge workers in this model) can use knowledge management technologies in three ways: to communicate structured information, to communicate unstructured information, and to connect with other workers in daily communication.

The specific technologies in this knowledge management technology model that influence the selection, deployment, and application of knowledge management tools are as follows:

- Connectivity—these technologies affect the organization's communication infrastructure and interfaces, workflow software, Internet Web portals, e-mail, and Internet, intranets and extranets.
- Structured Information—these technologies affect the organization's search engines, data cataloging and indexing, data mining and warehousing, and metadata management.
- Unstructured Information—these technologies affect an organization's Web-enabled tools and document management.

Structured		*Unstructured*
Connectivity	*Information*	*Information*
Universal Interface	Business Intelligence	Document Management
Collaborative Space	Data Mining	Voice/Video
Internet/Intranets/Extranets	Data Warehousing	Media Rich Format
Portals	DSS	Push/Pull technology

FIGURE 4-2.   Knowledge management technology.

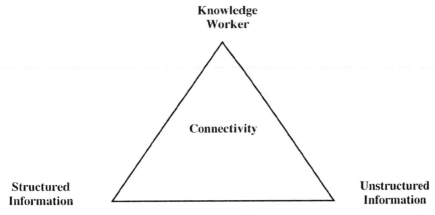

FIGURE 4-3.   Knowledge management technology graphical representation.

Thus, to summarize this section, the choice of technology in organizational learning and knowledge management is influenced greatly by personal and organizational histories and cultures in technology use. There are many types of technology that can be used to embed and institutionalize organizational learning. However, the selection of a specific technology type should be a reflection of the culture of the organization and not the characteristics of the technology by itself.

CONCLUSION

The use of technology to facilitate organizational learning must take into account the degree to which project management is a part of organizational culture. The work of Olonoff (2000) in the development of the Problem Knowledge Couplers (PKC) software is a step toward integrating knowledge management and project management to create project knowledge management. This approach calls for project managers to consider knowledge creation and transfer within their project team and from their project team to the rest of the sponsoring organization as part and parcel of their daily activities. We agree with Olonoff that knowledge management and project management are compatible and not competitive managerial approaches. For the purposes of organizational learning, the post-project review exercise discussed earlier could be easily integrated with knowledge management practices. In fact, an organizational culture of knowledge management and learning could facilitate the dissemination of project lessons learned throughout the organization.

To conclude, there are a number of key factors that lead to the successful management of customers in a knowledge-based service-oriented project. First, the successful management of customer expectation and the delivery of a quality project is a function of the following factors: project deliverables and goals that are compatible with the expectations and needs of all stakeholders and customers, a project stakeholder/customer map that completely and accurately depicts the actual project situation, a good project scope statement incorporating the interests of all stakeholders and customers, and the recognition that projects can have different categories of stakeholders depending on whether they are an upstream or downstream project.

A good project stakeholder/customer map enables the project manager to integrate these sometimes competing interests in a manner that allows him to monitor the success of his project in meeting their needs and expectations. To this end, the QFD and subsequent monitoring and regular communication with the project stakeholders and customers is essential. Table 4.1 presents a summary of our ideas on the level of involvement needed by project actor(s)

TABLE 4-1. Upstream/Downstream Project Involvement and Actors

Project Actor	Upstream Project Involvement	Downstream Project Involvement	Combination Project Involvement
Sponsor	Involvement useful	Not needed but useful	Not needed but useful
Project Manager	Involvement essential	Involvement essential	Involvement essential
Project Team Members	Involvement essential	Involvement essential	Involvement essential
External Customer	Not needed	Involvement essential	Involvement essential
Internal Customers	Involvement essential	Involvement essential	Involvement essential
Invisible Customers	Not needed	Useful	Useful

during each phase of the project life cycle. This table presents our personal ideas based on our professional experience.

The information above provides the historical information database from which future project teams can begin to put together a comprehensive project plan that addresses all nine knowledge areas of the PMBOK. Most of all, this database of project histories and lessons learned could provide project managers with information they need on specific staff skill set needs, specific staff members to recruit or to avoid, and the profile of the customer and the operating environment. All of these can impact the final success or failure of the project.

Table 4.2 presents a summary of our ideas on the type of information source(s) available to the project team during each phase of the project life cycle. This information depends on the type of project learning (lessons learned/ historical information) cycle the organization is in. This table presents our personal ideas based on our professional experience.The purpose of table 4.2 is only to display the types of information that a project team can access in each of the above organizational project learning cycles. The final postmortem project review phase indicates the extent to which this phase is a part of the project life cycle of the different organizational types.

Finally, in our opinion, post-project reviews enable organizations to create a virtuous circle in which each project implemented—regardless of whether or not it was a success—adds to the repository and the depository of information and lessons learned on such projects, their sponsors, customers (both apparent and invisible), and the project manager and project team members. The result of this

TABLE 4-2. Project Life Cycle Stages Critical Information

Project Phase	Vicious Cycle	Functional Cycle	Virtuous Cycle
Initiation	Team member knowledge	Team members, other organization staff, previous project archives.	Team members, other organization staff, previous project postmortem reviews
Planning	Team member knowledge	Ibid.	Ibid.
Executing	Team member knowledge	Ibid.	Ibid.
Controlling	Team member knowledge	Ibid.	Ibid.
Closeout	Team member knowledge	Ibid.	Ibid.
Postmortem Project Review	These are rarely if ever done. If conducted, they are very superficial.	These are usually conducted. However, results may not be well disseminated throughout the organization.	These are always conducted. Information is detailed and well disseminated throughout the organization.

process is an ever-climbing spiral of project management and project implementation improvement to the benefit of the organization.

The gathering of requirements includes two separate activities: determining the technical and quality requirements of the customer with respect to the deliverable(s) of the project and determining the requirement of the project to produce these deliverables with respect to time, cost, quality, and resources needs. In our opinion, the best way to go about determining the technical and quality requirements of the customer—that is, customer expectations—is for the project team to use the QFD. Once implementation begins, the project team can use the seven key quality management tools to ensure that project results comply with customer requirements and technical specifications.

The other requirements for the project can best be obtained from the project archives and historical information database of the organization. The key reason for having clear requirements for the project with respect to its various dimensions is to avoid scope creep once project implementation begins. If the requirements are determined in a team effort by the project team and the project customer(s), and if the project institutes a clear and mandatory scope change control process, the likelihood of scope creep greatly diminishes. Scope creep is the one project risk event that can prevent project delivery within the primary and secondary triple constraints.

Finally, all of the various requirements of the customer and their impact(s) on the project parameters must be reflected in the project document, scope statement, and contract elements.

Table 4.3 presents a summary of our ideas on how the project team can address and satisfy project requirements and specifications . Also included in the table is our assessment of the risk level to final project success for each phase of

TABLE 4-3   Project Requirements and Specifications

Project Life Cycle Phase	Requirements Satisfaction	Specifications Satisfaction	Risk Level to Overall Project
Initiation	Historical information & Customer RFP & Statement of Work	Historical Information & Customer RFP & Statement of Work	Low
Planning	QFD Stakeholder map	QFD Stakeholder map	Low
Executing	Quality Management Tools	Quality Management Tools	High
Controlling	Ibid. Joiner -Step™ method	Ibid. Joiner -Step™ method	High
Closeout	Project document and legal contract	Project document and legal contract	High
Postmortem Project Review	Involvement of key project actors	Involvement of key project actors	Low

the project life cycle phase. These are our personal ideas based on our professional experience.

The point of departure (Initiation Phase) for all project requirements gathering is the official statement of work in the request for proposal. Equally important, in our opinion, is any historical information available from the organization database on projects, specific project customers, and project-related knowledge creation in general. We view the overall risks to the project during this phase of requirements gathering as low as little has been invested in the project and no plans finalized.

During the Planning phase, the QFD is crucial to determine precise customer requirements or expectations for each project deliverable or outcome. Related to this is the project stakeholder/customer map. The purpose of this map is to identify all customers and their interests in the project in order to make sure that the same are reflected in the project scope statement and work plan. As with the Initiation phase, we view the overall risks to the project during the Planning phase of requirements gathering as low as little has been invested in the project, actual project implementation still not under way and thus, all finalized plans subject to correction without serious impact on project delivery.

During the Executing and Controlling phases of the project, requirements and specifications are best realized through use of the seven key project management tools a well as the Joiner–step method. We view the overall risks to the project during these two phases of requirements gathering as being extremely high. Since funds are being used, tasks implemented, and the field of operation is in a fluid and dynamic state, any mistakes in requirements gathering can cause significant schedule slippage, cost overruns, and customer concern with the overall progress of the project.

During the Close-out phase, use of the project document and legal contract are the best ways to determine if the requirements and specifications have been satisfied and the project deliverable acceptable to the customer. As with the Executing and Controlling phases of the project, this is a very high-risk phase. In fact, it is the most risky phase in the project life cycle as customer rejection can mean a serious loss of money, professional prestige, and ultimately project failure. However, if the requirements gathering of the earlier phases of the projects were done properly, then the project deliverable(s) should meet the expectations of the customer.

Finally, the requirements of the project postmortem review phase can be best met with the involvement of the key actors in the project as well other project stakeholders and internal customers—for example, senior management and other project managers in the organization. We view the risk level here as low to nonexistent as the project has been completed. The real risk is that valuable lessons will not be documented for future organizational reference and/or disseminated to other personnel in the organization.

The embedding and institutionalizing of learning processes (knowledge management) in organizations is possible and desirable. Integrating knowledge management and project management is both desirable and possible. In our opinion, the foundations of institutionalized organizational learning are: the culture of the organization with respect to organizational learning both by the organization as a holistic entity and by its constituent functional parts—departments—and ultimately by its individual membership; the formal policies of the organization with respect to formal training for staff, communication protocols, decision-making processes, and general procedures regarding information access and usage; the personal attitudes of senior management to technical training and information and skills transferal among and between the staff members of the organization; the collective attitude and opinion of the rank and file of the organization toward the organization and the value the organization places on the unique abilities, knowledge (tacit), and ideas of its individual staff members regardless of seniority, tenure, skill set, or pay level; the type and extent to which information technology is used in the process of organizational learning; and the extent to which technology procurement decisions must take into account the cultural aspects of the organization. If done successfully, the embedding and institutionalizing of learning processes in an organization can have many positive impacts on learning in an organization. Through the creation of a virtuous circle, the lessons learned from previous projects serve as the historical information and baseline data needed by new projects when devising and setting the estimates of the project plans.

In order for an organization to successfully embed and institutionalize informal knowledge creation and transfer (learning) methods, the overall culture of the organization must be one that encourages and enables such learning. This cultural paradigm of organizational learning must be initiated at the top level if it is to have any credibility with the rank-and-file membership. If the organization is a start-up one, then this open learning process can be easily embedded and institutionalized within its rank-and-file membership. However, if another type of learning process has been embedded and institutionalized—or, for that matter, none at all—then the process of organizational change will be a long-term affair born of persistence, patience, and ultimately staff attrition.

BIBLIOGRAPHY

Busby, J. S. 1999. An Assessment of Post-Project Reviews. *Project Management Journal* 30(3): 23–29.

Cabanis, Jeanette. 1997. "I'm the Guru Who Was Wrong." An interview with Philip Crosby. *PM Net* 11(6): 20.

Charette, Robert N. 1996. Large-Scale Project Management is Risk Management. *IEEE Software Journal*, July, 110–17.

Collier, Bonnie, Tom DeMarco, and Peter Fearey. 1996. A Defined Process for Project Postmortem Review. *IEEE Software Journal*, July, 65–71.

Dewhirst, H. Dudley. 1998. Project Teams: What Have We Learned? *PM Net* 12(4): 33–36.

Duncan, William R. 1999. Requirements versus Specification and Other Comparisons. *PM Net* 13(7): 21.

Funtowicz, S. O., and J. R. Ravetz. 1990. *Uncertainty and quality in science for policy.* Dordrecht: Kluwer Academic Publishers.

Githens, Gregory D. 2000. Capturing Project Requirements and Knowledge. *PM Net* 14(2): 249–59.

Ireland, Lewis R. 1991. Quality Management for Projects and Programs. Upper Darby, Pa.: Project Management Institute.

Nonaka, Ikujiro. 1994. A Dynamic Theory of Organizational Knowledge Creation. *Organization Science* 5(1): 14–36.

Olonoff, Neil. 2000. Knowledge Management and Project Management. *PM Net* 14(2): 61–64.

Orlikowski, Wanda J. 1993. Learning from Notes: Organizational Issues in GroupWare Implementation. *The Information Society* 9(3): 237–50.

5

From Abstract User Requirements to Tangible Business Solutions

An Iterative Approach

ABDUL SAMAD KAZI
IAN WILSON

The construction industry has for long been under the modus operandi of the virtual enterprise. This reality has only been recognized recently, however, in the wake of a need of information and communications technologies to support noncolocated teams in project-based industries striving to deliver one-of-a-kind products. While the recognition of the need of new methods of working, tools to enable this work, and business change requirements exist, a systemic approach outlining different steps of the development and furthermore migration strategy has been for long lacking.

This chapter presents an iterative approach that was used to translate abstract user requirements from different organizations involved in interenterprise communications under the modus operandi of virtual enterprises into tangible business solutions through an iterative process. In summary, the approach entailed the encapsulation of user requirements based first on their current modes of operation within the organization (intraorganizational practices) and then their modes of operations in an interenterprise setting (interorganizational practices). While the requirements initially were abstract, they were structured using some well-identified templates. The next step entailed the synthesis and generalization of the requirements and modi operandi of different participant organizations (organization types that would typically interact in a one-of-a-kind product delivery project). Participant organizations were asked then to ensure that there exists a clear mapping of their practices into the now generalized and structured requirements. Once this was confirmed, individual use cases were identified for each possible process. An analysis continued that used a systemic methodology to analyse, translate, and present the user requirements in a meaningful manner to the system designers and developers. Both information modellers and system designers consumed this process and presented the user requirements in a form and language that the system developers understood. The developers then developed a solution (details of which are out of the scope of this presentation) that was assumed to be compatible with the requirements of the end users. This was then "field-trialled" by the participant organizations to check and ensure if compliance with their needs is achieved. It furthermore provided an opportunity to come up with some initial business process change recommendations. The approach was repeated several times leading to revisions and modifications from the user requirements down to the final business process change recommendations. In the end, a tangible business solution was achieved that enables organizations to interoperate and share information.

INTRODUCTION

Project-oriented modes of operation under the modus operandi of virtual enterprise have been a long-established practice in the construction industry. One-of-a-kind products, such as buildings, encompass the involvement of multiple organizations during the product life cycle. At the same time, most of the currently available commercial Information and Communication Technology (ICT) tools are geared toward internal use with organizations and their associated supply chains. There is, therefore, a need for ICT support for dynamic and at times geographically and organizationally dispersed project teams. A good starting point to understand the complexities of construction is to observe the collaboration between different organizations' converging competencies to deliver the product, a constructed facility.

In our example, there are two distinct set-ups: a virtual enterprise and the traditional supply chain. At the same time, while information flows seem to stem from the architect, contractual flows are around the client. Despite small variations in configurations of the above, it has been reported that rarely, if at all, information and contract flows are in coherence (Kazi, Hannus, and Laitinen 2001).

Hannus and Kazi (2000) reported some typical characteristics of construction when operating in a set-up similar to the example:

- temporary relationships,
- some participants are not known in advance,
- complementary competence is provided by distinct companies,
- absence of a dominant actor,
- disparity between contractual relationships and information flows, and
- participation of some actors in other distributed engineering settings concurrently.

The construction industry revolves around a project-based working environment, the actual workings of which differ between companies and indeed consortia as the industry epitomises the virtual enterprise (VE). In their research of virtual teams, Lipnack and Stamps (1997) proposed a Virtual Team Model, encapsulating the elements they believe capture the essence of virtual teams: people, purpose, and links. In this model, the *people* populate groups and teams at every level; in terms of teams, the task to be completed is the *purpose*, and the *links* are the channels, interactions, and relationships within the virtual team. As the greatest difference between working teams in situ, and virtual teams lies in the nature and variety of their links (Lipnack and Stamps 1997), it is these that the digitally enabled VE must provide in a way that is accessible and acceptable to the people involved in order to achieve their purpose.

THE OSMOS PROJECT

We now present some elements of the OSMOS project that was harnessed to enhance the capabilities of construction enterprises, including Small or Medium-sized Enterprises (SMEs), to act and collaborate effectively on projects by setting up and promoting value-added Internet-based flexible services that support team work in the dynamic networks of the European construction industry. Its main objectives include: specification of Internet-based services for collaboration between dissimilar construction applications and semantic cross-referencing between the information they manipulate; specification of Internet-based services allowing the coordination of interactions between individuals and teams in a construction VE; specification of a model-based environment where the release of, and access to, any shared information (including documents) produced by actors participating in projects is secure, tracked, and managed transparently; provision of low entry-level tools (cheap and user-friendly) to small enterprises to act and participate in construction virtual enterprises; set-up two OSMOS Internet-based team work service providers for the purpose of the project, and ensure their take-up as commercial offers after the completion of the project. An iterative and incremental approach was employed to address the objectives of the project. The work was carried out across three iterations spanning a twenty-seven-month period.

INTRAORGANIZATIONAL PRACTICES

In terms of the initial requirements for the OSMOS project, the first element of the methodology involved an elaboration of the core business processes of each of the end-user organizations. In order to make the resultant information easily accessible for analysis purposes, the IDEF0 (NIST 1993) methodology was used to build business process models. The information input to the process models was based on current working methods in the construction industry. As there are limitations of IDEF0 diagramming alone for process description, an OSMOS standardized format was created to provide capture of further information related to each process/functional activity. This format allowed the end-users to present their current processes as IDEF0 diagrams and to include additional information as required. This information included a description of the activity being modelled and the operational context in which it is applied. Additionally, the actors involved in the activity, any existing preconditions and/or post-conditions, exceptions, and other remarks pertinent to the activity could also be provided. The resultant models (The OSMOS Consortium 2001a, appendixes) provided a comprehensive view of the intracompany business activities and the methods of information handling between actors. This formed the first step toward the specification of the OSMOS generic solution.

INTERORGANIZATIONAL PRACTICES

The next element in the methodology was an analysis focused on the current management of teams and other actors in the context of a VE. This analysis provided a comprehensive view of the intercompany interactions of the actors commonly involved in a construction project. The results of the analysis indicated the many variables to be taken into account during the life of a VE. It became clear that a VE in the construction industry is contemporaneous with the life cycle of any specific building project. Depending on the actors involved, therefore, a single VE may exist for the complete life cycle of a building, while others may exist only during the design phase or facilities management (FM) phase. Each of these purposes would require different infrastructures, available services, information management practices, and indeed teams to be managed. The analyses showed that a generic VE solution, therefore, had to take into account at least the following variables:

- required infrastructure for the project,
- a methodology to agree on procedures and protocols,
- contractual agreement,
- available services according to the contract,
- setting up of a VE administrator account,
- structure of information and information entities,
- training of personnel (e.g., project administrator, personnel using services provided by third parties, etc.),
- management of changes—including actors, classes, access rights, information, infrastructure and configuration data, rapid change in technology, the building itself, and so on,
- data security, and
- transfer of accumulated data.

The IDEF0 models produced (The OSMOS Consortium, 2001b) highlighted the interactions and processes that were common to all of the end-user companies, and also those that were specific to each. The analysis also identified three potential "roles" within the VE as perceived in the OSMOS model. The three roles are:

OSMOS Service Provider (Role A): The companies adopting this role are primarily concerned with hosting the OSMOS core infrastructure through provision of and access to both OSMOS core services and third-party services (TPS). Role A, through the OSMOS core, has the capability to host multiple VE projects and to make available different services (both core and TPS) to different projects.

OSMOS Third-Party Service Providers (Role B): These companies plug in their services and register associated methods through a Role A provider and make them available for use in a VE. Typically, these services would be geared to serving a particular purpose for the VE to which they are being made available. Examples of these services include HVAC, facilities management, document management, and CAD services.

OSMOS Clients (Role C): These companies use and take part in VEs that are supported and enabled through the OSMOS platform. While one company would configure and administer the VE, others would make use of the core and TPS services made available to the project.

GENERALIZATION OF THE REQUIREMENTS

The next step entailed the synthesis and generalization of the requirements and modus operandi of the different participant organizations (organization types that would typically interact in a one-of-a-kind product delivery project). This work resulted in the specification of a Generic Virtual Enterprise Process Model (GVEPM) developed by abstracting from the processes in the preceding analyses.

At the highest level, the model represents all the actions required to manage and use the OSMOS platform to run a complete VE project from initial client requirements to the end of the contract. (See The OSMOS Consortium 2001b for the complete IDEF0 model.) The management and use of the OSMOS platform was found to decompose to two key activities. First, provide and maintain VE Services incorporates the processes required to provide and maintain all services currently available to companies that wish to run a VE. This activity is equivalent to the OSMOS Role A, and must provide and register the availability of TPSs, maintain them once provided, and remove or replace them as changes in technology and/or requirements dictate. Second, provide and maintain VE project is the totality of processes required to run any individual project—which is the purpose of the specific VE. A project management committee would be formed and a contractual agreement made between the actors (including the OSMOS Role A company) involved in the prospective VE, and these then control the processes required to set up and configure the particular VE project environment and operate the project from inception to completion. The activities required to operate a VE project, once configured, are shown in figure 5.1.

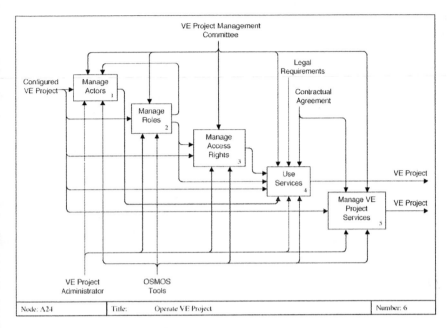

FIGURE 5-1. Operate a VE Project.

The concept of actors and their roles and access rights was very carefully considered in order to keep the OSMOS solution as generic as possible. Any one project (and therefore VE) comprises a set of actors at the organization/company level, a unique set of individuals, required services, information objects, and varying degrees of access to services and information depending on legal, contractual, and intellectual property rights (IPR) considerations.

One or more individuals within one or more companies/organizations will hold a specific project role. It is through the project role that access rights will be given to an individual within the project. A project role in one VE, however, may not necessarily have the same profile in another VE, even where the actors for the two VEs may be exactly the same (due to the fact that the agreements, protocols, and procedures will differ). The result is that through the OSMOS approach, access rights are assigned to specific defined roles, which themselves are assigned to actors at the company/organization level within the VE. The company/organization then delegates the available role to the individual(s) as required.

The GVEPM revealed the high-level generic processes that are required to enable the VE, and the participant organizations were asked to ensure that there existed a clear mapping of their practices into the now "generalized" and "structured" requirements. By generalizing the processes involved in the VE, it is hoped that the model will also be usable within industrial contexts other than building and construction, thus ensuring that the approach taken in terms of requirements capture need not be repeated each time a VE is formalized in differing contexts.

OSMOS TOOLS

Leading on from the IDEF0s, and following a translation process to Unified Modeling Language (UML), some tools were developed to heed the requirements provided by the end-users. A brief mention of the developed tools is worthwhile before we elaborate on the findings of the field trials that were conducted on the basis of these tools.

Overall, the OSMOS project has yielded a collection of solid models enforced and executed through an Application Program Interface (API). On top of this, several tools were developed to enable users to invoke API methods and get back responses (available both as Java objects and XML strings). The main tools are:

Role A Server Tool: This tool (implemented using Java Swing classes) provides functionality to a server administrator to manage the server. Main functionalities include the registration and management of different core and third-party services, API invocation logging, and so on.

VE Server Administration Tool: This tool (presented using Java Server Pages) is a Web-based environment for facilitating the configuration and maintenance of the OSMOS platform in term of projects, organizations, employees, and so forth. It is to be noted that this tool is a simple interface to relevant API calls for initializing a VE project.

VE Project Administration Tool: This tool is basically a subset of the VE Server Administration tool and is developed in particular to configure and manage a particular VE project. Once a project has been set up, control is passed over to a VE Project Administrator who then uses this tool to configure and manage it.

Web-based Information Browser: This tool acts as a low-level entry environment to the OSMOS workspace. In simple terms, the objective of this tool is to present and expose to VE participants, based on their roles and associated access rights, the different objects and their associated service methods to which the VE participants have access.

TESTING AND VALIDATION

The principal means of testing and evaluating the OSMOS approach is being provided through field trials simulating work in a construction VE. Criteria have been determined for technical, social, and economical evaluation of the OSMOS system together with legal, contractual, and organizational aspects. Throughout the project, the consortium has recognized that the integration of human, organizational, and technical elements is a prerequisite for a successful specification of the strategy required to identify and implement the potential changes resulting from the proposed OSMOS approach. The research has therefore included analysis of factors often neglected in similar industry/business and ICT research efforts. An information technology and construction questionnaire was completed by employees working at the operational/tactical level in the end-user organizations, and provided initial company profiles. Further to the questionnaires, semistructured interviews were also carried out with more senior people at the tactical/strategic level. Results from this research provided initial validation of the OSMOS approach and the requirements of the resultant system being developed, plus valuable information that, coupled with the results from the final field trials, will ultimately enable the formulation of business recommendations.

Field trials were designed and performed, enacting scenarios including real-life processes that the participant organizations carry out in their core business operations, to check and ensure that compliance with their needs is achieved. Overall, the field trials aim to address three high-level concerns: to ensure that the proposed system works (i.e., to evaluate its usability), to ascertain that it meets and achieves its intended business goals, and to ensure its acceptance by the intended users. The field trials carried out to date have been based on separate work scenarios within two of the end-user companies in France and Finland, and have allowed evaluation of the OSMOS tools developed for administration at the VE Server level and at the VE Project level. In the French field, trial the OSMOS tools were manipulated to simulate the set-up and management of a construction VE. The individuals taking part, including information technology and construction professionals, represented the roles of VE Server administrator, TPS provider, VE Project administrator, and VE Project participants. In the Finnish field trial, the testing scenario involved using the OMSOS VE administration tools to set up a new VE and the use of a proprietary Web-enabled FM software application (representing a specific purpose for which a particular VE may be formalized). Representations of a building owner, a maintenance company, and a facility consultant were created as organization actors, to which employees were registered and given project roles with access to specific services.

In terms of usability, four aspects were taken into account: *System functionality, Efficiency, User-friendliness,* and *Technical aspects.* Analysis of the results from the field trials showed generally satisfactory results overall according to the usability criteria. Some issues were noted regarding the intuitiveness of the user interface, and there were navigability issues, but these are minor points as the tools tested were reference implementations only. It is interesting to note, however, that cultural differences were apparent between the results from the two countries involved.

The results validated the GVEPM in terms of the processes involved in administering the VE at both the server and project levels. The trials also validated the OSMOS Roles (A, B, and C). The roles were accepted as a strong and logical underlying concept within the OSMOS consortium, and it is an excellent result that the users who took part in the field trials—who were not previously associated with the project—found agreement in these concepts.

The approach taken in OSMOS will inevitably lead to some business process reengineering, and as the processes around which the system is based are generic, there may be some need for training within companies wishing to enable their construction VE through OSMOS. It was possible to make some preliminary business recommendations specific to the companies involved in the project from analysis of the interim field trials results, combined with the research into human and organizational issues. The adoption of the OSMOS system shows potential to improve communications and information sharing. The conceptual basis for the process involved in setting up and maintaining the construction VE through the OSMOS platform was proved to be accepted, with the information management capabilities of the OSMOS solution built in to the tools so far developed, meeting the requirements specified by the end-user organizations, both in terms of the human and organizational issues raised through the questionnaire and interview research efforts and also the limitations and inconsistencies expressed with current methods employed.

SYNTHESIS OF RESULTS AND CONCLUSIONS

The shift toward the VE is related with a fundamental change in organizing and managing daily operations. The VE is more complex as it connects multiple organizations and teams coming from diverse locations in a dynamic environment. Virtual teams bring people together across disciplines, departments, functions, and geographical locations. Information technology provides the platform, but ultimately it is the people who make the projects work. The importance of the human element and the way that people cooperate with each other should not be taken for granted, particularly in a virtual context. In terms of the business aspect of the VE, recommendations can be made following the recognition of problems existing in terms of information sharing, organizational culture, and teamworking, acceptance of change, and training requirements. These problems are summarized below, together with an exploration of possible solutions.

Information sharing: All end-users face difficulties with information sharing because of technical and business reasons. Due to a perceived lack of trust and clarification of objectives, the concept of sharing information through knowledge databases is still treated with disagreement. As a result, technology has to play a very important role enabling communications and information sharing, supporting and improving business process, and integrating services. Moreover, the role of culture is very important. There is a need for building an organization, which will support information sharing and knowledge dissemination and will allow learning to take place. Explaining the strategic vision, encouraging participation and involvement, and managing performance and linking it with the right rewards are three important steps toward enhancing information sharing.

Organizational culture and teamworking: Characteristics of the participatory type of culture such as flat structure, open communication channels, participation and involvement in decision making enhance sharing of information and facilitate virtual teams. The analysis of results indicated that teams in the construction industry face many problems including the lack of availability and time planning. Bureaucratic cultures cannot facilitate these cross-functional teams, and as a result, they can hinder the change process. An important finding from the OSMOS research is related to motivation as part of the culture. High motivation levels and job satisfaction are critical success factors in any organizational environment and even more important in a virtual environment. Introducing interesting work and a choice of varied tasks within the same project are two important suggestions, which have been tested in two of the participating end-user organizations, and have shown good results.

Acceptance of change: It is very interesting to note here that there were positive attitudes toward changes. Although some of the end-users face continuous changes, some of which were not successful, the results indicated a positive climate toward that direction. This finding may be explained by the fact that there is dissatisfaction with the existing system, which underlines the need for change. However, there is a need for planned change in order to manage virtual environments, which are characterized by continuous changes. It is important to note here that age was found to be a crucial factor in all of the end-user organizations. As expected, younger employees are able to use technology more effectively, and they are more open to new ways of working than the older employees. The difference between age groups in the frequency and capability of the use of technology causes tension in all the participating companies. Understanding people's fears and concerns, encouraging involvement and participating, and explaining the objectives of the change are the main targets in order to cope with potential resistance to change.

Training: The results indicated that training is important particularly in project management and software packages. On-the-job training is suggested as a feasible solution although (certainly within the construction sector) there is the problem of hectic schedules and lack of availability. Another suggestion is to build and implement a training plan, which will take into consideration skills required for setting up virtual teams. The tools that can be used in the construction of a training plan are needs analysis; job descriptions and team roles and responsibilities; and the company's strategic plans.

NOTE

This chapter is based on deliberations conducted under two Research and Development projects for which European funding has been provided by the European Commission under its fifth framework program. The two projects are: OSMOS (IST-1999–10491): Open System for Inter-enterprise Information Management in Dynamic Virtual Environments. The consortium includes end-users: DERBi, JM AB, Olof Granlund, and leading European research centers and academia: Centre Scientifique et Technique du Bâtiment (CSTB), Information Systems Institute of University of Salford, and the Technical Research Centre of Finland (VTT) (http://osmos.vtt.fi). GLOBEMEN (IST-1999–60002): Global Engineering and Manufacturing in Enterprise Networks. The project is an international one under the IMS (Intelligent Manufacturing Systems) umbrella, and the consortium is a mix of both end-users and researchers from several countries including

Australia, Denmark, Finland, Greece, Japan, the Netherlands, Norway, and Switzerland (http://globemen.vtt.fi).

BIBLIOGRAPHY

Hannus M., and A. S. Kazi. 2000. Requirements for Distributed Engineering. In *Proceedings of ECPPM 2000: Product and Process Modelling in Building and Construction*. Lisbon, Portugal, 41–78.

Kazi, A. S., M. Hannus, and J. Laitinen. 2001. ICT Support Requirements for Distributed Engineering in Construction. In *E-work and E-commerce: Novel Solutions and Practices for a Global Network Economy*, edited by B. Stanford-Smith and E. Chiozza. Venice (Italy), 17-19 October IOS Press, 909–15.

Lipnack, J., and J. Stamps. 1997. *Virtual Teams: Reaching Across Space, Time and Organizations with Technology*. New York: Wiley.

NIST. 1993. Draft Federal Information Processing Standards Publication 183: Announcing the Standard for Integration Definition for Function Modeling (IDEF0). Available on the World Wide Web at http://www. idef. com/Downloads/pdf/idef0.pdf

The OSMOS Consortium. 2001a. Proposed Intra-company Information Process Model. OSMOS Project Deliverable (D1. 1 Iteration 3). Retrieved from: http://cic.vtt.fi/projects/osmos/d13.pdf, on October 26, 2004.

The OSMOS Consortium 2001b. Proposed Inter-company Interaction Process Model. OSMOS Project Deliverable (D1. 2 Iteration 3). Retrieved from: http://cic.vtt.fi/projects/osmos/d13.pdf, on October 26, 2004.

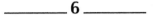

6

The Cross-Applicability of Project Management

A Vehicle for Organizational Transition in the Implementation of Multimedia Business Communications Platforms

CHERYL J. WALKER

Project management within the media industry has traditionally been more closely associated with production management, where timeline and planning efforts can range from one day for a daily newscast, to months or even years for a feature film. However, with the increasingly project-centered focus of business today, the media industry is recognizing the value of a more robust project management discipline. For example, at Disney, the need for a dual leadership role is acknowledged by having both a project manager and a director on each initiative, in order to balance both the project business objectives (on time, within budget, and according to the specifications) and the creativity/flexibility objectives.

In a related discipline, project management within the information technology/ systems (IT/IS) industry has been gaining acceptance because of the value of creating continuity and consistency in approach; however, adherence to time and cost parameters is frequently challenged because of the risks and uncertainties associated with research and development efforts. This is why iterative- and milestone-based methodologies are so popular; one only needs to focus on the costs and schedule for the next phase, rather than for the project as a whole. An additional driver for the application of project management within IT/IS initiatives is the organizational change and transition nature of these projects. With the advances in technology, there is a significant impact on business processes and individual work norms, and, therefore, a robust discipline that is capable of supporting these projects is needed. That discipline is project management.

61

The multimedia business communications industry is an offshoot of both media and IT/IS, because it draws from both of these disciplines to create a business media platform, which is capable of addressing the requirements of an increasingly global and dispersed workforce in a creative, cost-effective, and timely manner. The advances in communications platforms have had a similar impact on business practices and individual work style as that experienced by the IS/IT initiatives. Therefore, incorporating multimedia business media platforms are also considered an organizational transition effort, rather than a simple replacement-in-kind or turnkey solution. In deciding to adapt these platforms, an organization must consider the trade-off between the long-term advantages to the corporation (such as increasing individual productivity and decreasing costs) and the short-term costs/challenges of attaining buy-in for the requisite investment in technology and overcoming individual perceptions about the lack of continuity and accountability to the organization (promulgated by the increased usage of working in a virtual setting). The adoption of the new multimedia business platforms becomes an organizational transition effort, because it will have an impact on multiple divisions and alter the way in which individuals within these divisions interact.

This chapter suggests that: there is a competitive advantage, in terms of value attained through increased market share and overall cost savings, to implementing multimedia business communications forums (Webcasting, streaming media, or virtual reality) over the traditional communications channels (face-to-face meetings, telephone conference calls, and satellite networks); project management is an excellent vehicle to ensure that the modifications to business processes and individual performance criteria are effectively addressed and managed so that the organization is able to realize the productivity and profitability gains; multimedia service providers are recognizing the value-added in utilizing project management as a discipline for planning and managing the adoption of multimedia business communications platforms into their client's environments.

The conclusions derived in this chapter are generated from a literature scan of the adoption of multimedia business communications platforms over traditional communications channels by organizations and the impact this is having on their business operations. The literature review includes understanding how multimedia service providers are utilizing project management to lead these organizational transition efforts and how organizations are gaining long-term value in deploying these technologies. In addition, it is assumed that companies that deploy these technologies in a measured fashion and by utilizing a recognized discipline, such as project management, to manage this organizational transition effort are attaining sustainability and a competitive advantage. It is anticipated that the concepts of this chapter would be validated empirically in a future study that seeks to quantify the realized value (or return on investment; ROI) of project management, when applied not only to the deployment of a multimedia communications business platform, but to all other similar organizational transition efforts.

OVERVIEW: UPGRADING VERSUS ORGANIZATIONAL TRANSITION

So how does a corporation achieve both short-term profitability and long-term growth and sustainability? Corporations recognize that this balance can be achieved through staying current with the consumer's changing demands, and by deploying the latest tools and techniques to increase productivity, market position, and ROI. The adage "working smarter, not harder" has been used to justify the value of automation over manual operations and, with decreasing profit margins due to increasing competition, and escalating stakeholder expectations, corporations have acknowledged that what has led to their success today may not keep them successful in the future. Corporations seek cost-effective and timely ways in which they can either upgrade their current processes and technology or incur an organizational transition (such as moving from legacy- to client server-based systems). Although much of the process and requirements for conducting an upgrade or implementing an organizational transition are the same, the most distinctive areas in which these two efforts are significantly different are in terms of complexity, cost, and the number of people (or divisions) within the organization, which are affected.

The new advances in multimedia business communications platforms are an organizational transition. Consider the evolution of business communications. With the inventions of the telephone, the television, and the Internet (World Wide Web), technological progress has forever changed the way in which business is conducted and people interact. The Internet alone has significantly changed the face of business in the twenty-first century because of the expansive communications outreach that technology has provided. Companies are no longer confined to conducting business with those with whom they have daily face-to-face contact or who are within physical reach. Today, companies are able to cost effectively engage with individuals from all over the world in Internet time (creating a virtual 24/7 work week), and the technology exists (although not equally accessible globally) to create a virtual setting allowing for visual, audio, and real-time connectivity as well as effective business operations. With sufficiently accessible bandwidth (such as DSL, T1, wireless, and satellite), a company or individual can utilize Webcasting, streaming video, and virtual reality for business applications to create a virtual presence with their clients, project team members, management, governments, and other corporations, for day-to-day business operations, managing projects, and conducting training.

THE NEW AGE OF COMMUNICATIONS—DEFINING A COMPETITIVE ADVANTAGE

Traditionally, the company president and executive management could effectively manage their business through "management by walking around" techniques because all operations were local. However, to be competitive in today's virtual environment, management needs to find strategies and techniques to simulate that personalized touch with their employees, project teams, and clients without incurring extreme costs and family hardships by being on the road and traveling seven days a week. This can be accomplished through the new business media platforms, which allow companies to enhance their daily operations, ensure timeliness of their projects, and manage client expectations by addressing one of the key ingredients to corporate success: *effective communications.*

If we consider key business drivers metrics for corporate success to be "time-to-market" and "increased market share," then the New Age of communications ("multimedia services," which are a platform consisting of streaming media, Webcasting, and virtual reality for business applications; see appendix) becomes a competitive advantage, which can directly impact these metrics. As many companies move from regional to global markets, one of the key barriers that must be overcome is the difference in business operations and time zones. Companies who are at the forefront of utilizing these technologies to increase productivity and reduce long-term costs include Microsoft, Boeing, Cisco, Coca-Cola, General Motors, Motorola, and Hewlett-Packard.

Enhancing Corporate Communications: Cost versus Benefits

Whenever a corporation is considering a significant restructuring to the way in which it conducts its business operations, and this effort is an enhancement effort whose value will not be realized in the near term but rather in the long term, then it is imperative to consider the costs versus benefits for such an effort. If money and time were never an objective then all companies would continuously seek to enhance their operations and always have the latest and greatest technology. However, the corporation must consider the opportunity costs associated with committing funds today for a nonrevenue-generating effort. If the corporation finds that without such an enhancement they will lose their competitive edge, market share, ability to effectively interact with customers, or incur a significant decline in productivity, then these are considered significant enough that the value of investing in new technology and processes are considered not only value-added but necessary for survival and long-term sustainability.

What Are the Cost versus Benefits of Multimedia Services Compared to Traditional Mechanisms?

The New Age communication channels are definitely a long-range cost-effective and productivity-enhancing option for medium- to large-sized companies. For smaller companies, the option of leasing facilities, partnering with another company, obtaining a sponsor for the infrastructure costs, or selectively choosing to make certain messages available through this medium may prove to be the more cost effective measure. However, regardless of the size, every company should utilize the Internet and a Web presence to the greatest extent possible. For example, let us consider the overview of the costs, benefits, and drawbacks of a New Age communication channel versus a traditional mechanism.

Multimedia: Streaming Media or Webcasting: One Message $1,000–$8,000 The varied cost in streaming format/content ranges from around $1,000 (simple audio) to perhaps $8,000 (for a more complex video production).[1]

Webcasting is considered a relatively inexpensive method for communicating with large numbers of people such as customers, investors, employees, and management, because a single message can be distributed for the access cost of a local phone call (rather than satellite, teleconference, or other long distance communications services and devices). For example, when Boeing decided to move its headquarters from Seattle, it did not utilize the normal press conference forum, but rather broadcast the announcement on its Web site with a live video feed and follow-up session for the press.

Benefits

Global Reach, Cost ($1,000-$8,000 to reach an infinite number of people without additional travel requirements or utilization of teleconferencing services)

Drawbacks

Technology requirements require the target individual to have broadband access (for ease of viewing content) and Internet connectivity.

Traditional: Face-to-Face Meetings: Travel/Logistics = $312,000/year + facilities (small-sized enterprise)

(Assume three-day trip, $600 airfare, $400 lodging, $200 per diem, and $100 miscellaneous/individual)

1. 10 executives for quarterly trips (4/year) = $1300/trip = $52,000
2. 100 employees—twice a year = $260,000

- (Benefits: face-to-face communications, establishes rapport, creates synergy
- (Drawbacks: cost, coordination, logistics, and limited outreach (only the people who attend the meetings benefit from the direct communications, all others must suffice with second-hand communications).

Traditional: Telephone Conference Call = $90,000 (medium-sized enterprise)

(Assume 5,000 people participate in a one-hour conference call at $.30/minute/person = $18/person)

- (Benefits: established and proven technology, ease of access, and use worldwide.
- (Drawbacks: cost, varied time zones (inconvenience to global operations), entire company "on hold" for one hour while all participate in a company conference call, and for that time are unable to respond to customer needs.

PROJECT MANAGEMENT—AN EFFECTIVE
TRANSITION VEHICLE

Validation Process

Having evaluated the cost versus benefits of moving from reliance on the traditional-based communications platforms to multimedia-based communications forums, the corporation must now define a process or mechanism by which they can make this migration. By definition, project management is a flexible discipline consisting of defined deliverables (those tangible components or results of the project), schedule of activities, budget, risk management (identification, assessment, and response), quality assurance, communications, and so forth, that has the rigor and structure to effectively plan and manage an organizational transition effort. This type of rigor is imperative, because it takes more than installing a new technology to make it a value-added proposition. There are also numerous business processes and modifications to personal workstyles that must be addressed and implemented.

First, the company needs to define the project's ROI in the new technology and when they can expect to attain the productivity and efficiency increases. A significant measure of this value can be realized through a comparison of the alternative to this project (such as instead of being able to conduct a Webcast, everyone must continue flying to a central location for meetings). Second, the company needs to determine the impact on current productivity and time commitment of current staff if they are directed toward this project. (Note: If current staff cannot be relieved of their assignments, can this project be driven with external resources?) Third, the company needs to consider the opportunity cost, what is gained or lost when funds are directed toward this project? Fourth, the company needs to recognize that this type of effort will require more than simply purchasing new technology and installing it. It will require defining and changing day-to-day business operations and potentially restructuring the way in which people work and what is done.

It is also important to consider how technological enhancements may be cost effective and increase productivity within the company, but these benefits could be offset by a decrease in personnel interactivity and system compatibility. Therefore, when pursuing such an initiative, a stakeholder analysis is a very effective tool that can be used to determine who has a vested interest in the project, where the integration points may lie, and what potential obstacles may impede the project's progress. For example, one of the key integration points for the effective usage of multimedia business platform communications is ensuring equal access and bandwidth for all parties, across multiple countries, languages, and technology platforms. This requires both a strategic and tactical approach, which goes beyond the simple identification and installation of select technology, to encompass the environmental and stakeholder factors, which could otherwise impede success. If we assume that enhancing corporate communications is a continuous quality improvement priority for a corporation, then project management can serve as a phase-oriented vehicle for defining and implementing the discreet incremental change initiatives required in attaining this goal.

The Innovators—Multimedia Providers

Corporate communications are a classic example of "thinking globally and acting locally." A corporation realizes that their consumer base is becoming increasingly global in nature, and, therefore, their systems, processes, and people need to be able to operate effectively in a global environment. However, in reality they exist in a local setting (requiring local maintenance and updates) and must be able to operate within multiple local standards.

This is one reason why it is so challenging to stay on the leading edge of consumer needs; these needs are continuously changing on multiple fronts. The best strategy, therefore, is for a service/product provider to develop a strategic relationship with their customer base (which opens the door to both strategic and tactical planning and implementation) to assist them in identifying where the company's weak points lie. Then, having defined this market niche opportunity, the service/product provider needs to define solutions that will not overextend their research and development allocation. This becomes an ongoing process, because the consumer will have changing business drivers and needs, and if one only locks into the current needs without projecting how those needs will evolve, then what is developed becomes obsolete before it is even released. That is why it is imperative to develop tools and techniques that have open architecture, allowing for upgradeability and future expansion. Companies that have effectively combined multimedia and project management are shown below.

Sorenson Services USA[2]

- *Services*: Provides expert digital video and streaming media consulting, training, encoding, compression *and project management* to help clients integrate streaming video and audio into their web sites.
- *Value/Application of PM*: Help clients choose which streaming formats are right for them, select and implement a server strategy, advise on video production for the web, develop budgets and schedules and *then provide the project management to make it all happen.*

ALTUS Consulting Services[3]

- *Services*: Offers strategy advice *and project management* in streaming media and broadcasting undertakings.
- *Value/Application of PM*: Manage Streaming Media Projects. ALTUS performs management tasks to guarantee the smooth running of the project and to make sure that administrative and technical requirements are met.

Liberation Media[4]

- *Services*: Puts together the talents of a wide range of freelance media professionals to give clients one source for all of their media needs.
- *Value/Application of PM*: *Designated project managers* who have managed internationally touring rock bands, promoted and coordinated large concert productions, released internationally distributed record releases and managed the launch of high profile web sites that get so many hits that it would bring most Web servers (but not ours!) to their knees.

The Pioneers—Realizing the Value of Multimedia
Business Communications

The World Wide Web has expanded the productivity and collaboration of cross-functional work groups operating in virtual settings because they are no longer limited by time constraints to complete activities. In addition, it has provided an infrastructure by which multimedia services can be delivered, thus increasing the reach and timeliness of communications.

> Today, streaming media plays an increasingly important role in corporate communications at Microsoft. For example, employees can view major keynote addresses by Bill Gates and Steve Ballmer at industry gatherings over the Microsoft Internet. These and other streaming communications—many aimed at more select audiences within the company—are available for viewing at Microsoft's internal Windows Media Events site. Microsoft typically delivers about 500 internal streams daily, but live virtual company meetings (webcasting) attract up to 15,000 viewers. About 7,000 on-demand viewers log on within 48 hours of the event.[5]

- A semiconductor manufacturer went from spending $500,000 per year for onsite training of its 500 new employees and distributors to $100,000 for streamed training.
- Hewlett-Packard reaches its entire company through streaming and spends $5 million annually, streaming 150,000 hours to 70,000 people.
- A major oil company keeps up with its corporate compliance requirements through streaming to its 31,000 employees at 8,300 gas stations with one stream. Previously it had to ship 350,000 videotapes throughout the year so that each person could have their own copy of the multiple training programs.

Others may be reluctant to move toward these forums of multimedia services because they do not realize the ROI for such an effort. Although there is a considerable investment required to ensure consistency in the level of technology, in fact, this investment can realize significant gains for the company. From the Webcast "The New Economies of Scale: Utilizing Salvo in a Manufacturing and Distribution Organization," it was noted that there was a 40 percent increase in business that World Fulfillment experienced as a result of integrating their order placement systems into a customer-focused interactive Web site.[6] In addition, J. D. Edwards conducted a streaming media ROI study and determined that when meeting and other business content was available, individuals using this forum watched twenty to thirty minutes per week. The $300,000 of investment in this media service has already paid for itself in the significant reduction of out-of-pocket travel and audio conferences, and in the fourth year of this service offering, the Internal Rate of Return (IRR) is 203 percent.

THE FUTURE—CAN YOUR ORGANIZATION AFFORD
NOT TO CHANGE?

"Corporations that have traditionally spent millions of dollars on travel, training and communication increasingly are turning to streaming media to save money and to improve the processes. There are four primary areas being utilized for streaming: training, corporate communications, advertising/marketing and entertainment."[7] However, the issues of bandwidth, latency, and storage need to be addressed to ensure consistency, reliability, and quality of content access. This chapter acknowledges a need and usage of multimedia communications platforms, but broad application will still be heavily cost driven, and today the issue of security and realizing timely gains will be deciding factors.

As noted, project management can be a highly effective vehicle for transitioning an organization from their current processes, technology or business operations to a desired state. Project management has the flexibility of being a scaleable mechanism that can be applied to any size or complexity of project initiative. As has been experienced in the information technology arena, companies that have been in existence for an extended period of time generally have a heavy investment in legacy systems, and although it would be more direct and possibly simpler to replace all of the systems with current technology, it can be prohibitively expensive to do so. That is why younger companies often have a technological advantage; their systems generally already have the capacity for upgrading. This same logic also applies to a company's communications mechanisms. It is not logical to assume that we will "do away" with telephone, fax or face-to-face meetings, and in fact all three will continue to have great value. However, because company activities are becoming increasingly global, there is a need for an increased level and frequency of communications, and this drives the demand for more long-term cost advantage alternatives to corporate communications to offset the traditional communications forums. The discipline of project management can both control investment costs and help realize more readily the ROI of the multimedia business communications platforms. It is assumed that a company would have cost, schedule, and productivity constraints and therefore by necessity would need to phase in the deployment of multimedia business communications mechanisms. Project management is an ideal mechanism to approach a phased deployment strategy. Although it has not been statistically quantified in this chapter, it is expected that future studies could help define this correlation between service and application, recognizing the current technological challenges that must be overcome and the associated timing to realize gains.

As the Internet infrastructure evolves as a viable day-to-day business platform, we realize that for a business to truly prosper in this virtual forum, the technological infrastructure needs to be in place and the public must have a need to be virtualized. The future of business today lies in the application of technology tomorrow. As we have moved from an agricultural society through the

Industrial Revolution to the Information Age, technology has been our partner in progress. As a society we may have been overzealous about the viability of a dot.com world today, but the technology and infrastructure are on the way, and with the corporate (and government) initiatives to support telephony, multi-media communications and virtual operations (such as telecommuting), the demand for the infrastructure increases. Welcome to the Digital Age.

APPENDIX A: WHAT ARE MULTIMEDIA SERVICES?

Streaming Media

The traditional adage is that information is power. However, today's "power seat" resides in *the application* and *the timeliness* of that information, because the Internet has made information in itself free. Enterprise streaming media allows businesses to provide crucial information to their employees, project teams, and clients in a just-in-time manner. Previously, the only companies who could afford to "stream" their messages had to do so via a closed-circuit television network and videoconference mechanisms—a highly expensive hardware and software proposition. However one of the primary values of the streaming for-mats was to allow an individual to view the content of the message at a time convenient and suitable to them—a key advantage to a corporation that is geographically and time zone dispersed. Today, with Internet technology, this communications mode has cross-availability and is cost effective.

Webcasting

Companies have dedicated significant funds to travel and lodging because of the need to send company resources (both personnel and equipment) all over the world for face-to-face meetings. As identified previously, the alternative is a very costly satellite network that, depending on the number of meetings held each year and the number of individuals involved, could be more expensive than the significant travel funds (for instance, one mid-senior-level executive of a high-technology telecommunications firm reported that his travel budget last year exceeded his salary). However, the need to communicate and conduct meetings still exists, and the costs associated with these face-to-face meetings have in-creased. The technology to conduct Webcasts has provided businesses with a more cost-effective means to reach a greater audience base. This technology also allows the flexibility of varied location over multiple time zones. For example, in Geneva, a Webcast could be viewed after dinner (at home) while concurrently being viewed by another group in New York City at a lunch venue and in San Francisco at breakfast, from the comfort of home. Prior to the flexibility afforded by this technology, all involved had to be at the office the entire time, which could result in a twelve- to fifteen- hour workday. In addition, Webcasting allows greater audience participation in such events as virtual tradeshows and conferences, thus allowing a company to expose a greater portion of their employee base to these events while not incurring the potentially extensive associated travel costs.

Virtual Reality for Business Applications

The professional development industry (universities, long-distance course providers, simulation courses, computer-based self-training) has increasingly recognized the value of virtual reality for their business enhancement purposes for the last decade. Virtual reality has opened significant markets to small businesses seeking to provide their services and courseware to an extended audience base, allowed users access to information based on their individual schedules (rather than a pre-set time and location) at a reduced cost because of the reduction in travel and face-to-face time, and has significantly decreased the cost to universities of their traditional programs while enhancing their program offerings. For example, the University of Minnesota had already identified $500,000 in annual savings from implementing an e-business infrastructure, which significantly reduced their facilities management costs—projected at $35 million/year to maintain and manage buildings and oversee nearly $800 million in new construction and renovation projects.

NOTES

1. Arora 2001, p. 65.
2. http://sorenson-usa.com/services/.
3. http://www.altus.de/showpageen.asp?Seite=001_sm_consult.htm.
4. http://www.liberationmedia.com/libmedia/services/services_project.jsp.
5. Bloom 2001, p. 26.
6. Business Wire and Gale Group 2000.
7. Bartlett 2001.

BIBLIOGRAPHY

Arora, Anjali. 2001. Talk is Cheap. *The Industry Standard,* May 7, p. 65.
Bartlett, Michael. 2001. Companies Turn on to Streaming to Save (Industry Trend or Event). *Streaming Media West Conference,* June 21.
Bloom, M. 2001. Microsoft's Mandate. *Streaming Media Magazine,* April, 26.
Business Wire and Gale Group. 2000. NetManage Webcast Showcases Manufacturing and Distribution eBusiness Solution; Customer Case Study High Value of Web-Based Business-to-Business Processes. 28 February.
Project Management Institute. Project Management Body of Knowledge, Glossary of Terms. 1999.

7

Team Culture Communicating
= Semantics + Semiology

PHILIP HARVARD

There is nothing so permanent as change.
—Heraclitus of Greece, 513 B.C.

TEAM CULTURE

In the beginning there was silence. In the beginning there was silence because thought was not expressed with sound and forms. Then God created man and man created teams. Ever since we have been trying to understand what we mean in a team.

Team culture is not the same as esprit de corps. Esprit de corps is more a cult, rather than a cultural, phenomena. There are examples of esprit de corps throughout history when people have rallied round a charismatic leader who inspired them to work, achieve, and fight for a precise reason or cause: Alexander the Great for Victory, Caesar for Rome, Sir Francis Drake for the Queen, and Napoleon for himself. In the New World, Ralph Barton Perry's (1876–1957) Protestant work ethic paved the way, fostered, and even gave birth to team culture in a competitive market economy based on free enterprise. Perry, a highly revered American philosopher, remains the deified reference sainted by his Wasp (White Anglo-Saxon Protestant) milieu. He is remembered most for his writings, which so well portray the Gnostic mentality of this cultural sub-group of the New World. The following two Puritan principles about work have become a basis for the work ethic in the teamwork culture of North America today.

According to the British language experts, Dudley-Evans and St. John (1998), we cannot ignore culture: "we have to be sensitive to cultural differences... culture is omnipresent thus important...culture is complex and comprises different aspects such as national, professional, organizational and personal cultures ... language and culture cannot be separated." The role of culture and language is undeniable Language reflects thought (economic, social, scientific, technical, cultural as well as management thought, etc.). Language is the signifier that signifies culture in society. Montesquieu believed that meaning in life comes from *moeurs*, which are our habits or the way we live our lives therefore determining and defining our culture. For our discussion, the notion of culture is defined as being corporate, departmental, and team as well as family, ethnic, religious, racial, and national. We cannot be content in just ignoring probable cultural effects as emotional intelligence producing cultural cognition. There are undetected cultural traps hiding behind human behavior in teams. It is essential for team members to clearly identify cultural differences that can modify team communications.

The French management professor Sallenave points out a surprising cultural difference between French and American management: *Latins love titles*. For the French, the accumulation of professional power from titles is more important than the accumulation of financial remuneration within a French structure, in comparison to the same or a similar American structure. Another pertinent cultural observation concerns motivation. It is easier to motivate French employees to be against something than it is to motivate them to be for something. The other managerial cultural difference that should be mentioned concerns working relationships and workers' solidarity or unity.

The American perception of the community and the group is the opposite of the French view. Who is more important, the different individuals in the group or the group itself? A well-known example of the American priority being the group and not the individual is found in the famous quote of John F. Kennedy where he advises his fellow Americans to serve the group: "Ask not what your country can do for you but what you can do for your country." In France, Kennedy would have said the opposite. In France, the group has the responsibility to answer to the individuals that comprise it and offer them whatever they need. In other words, the group takes care of and fulfills the needs of its members. In France, social liberty abounds because individual differences are respected. In the United States, the individual is responsible for the welfare or well-being of his group or community; he must answer to the group and fulfill the needs and requirements of his group, and assumes an identity offered by his group. This explains why mass conformity abounds in the United States. Does American commercial liberty flourish at the price of sacrificing individuality? In team culture, must the individuality of team members be sacrificed for the team? This culturally explains differences in American and French ideas about entrepreneurship.

At this point, there are certain ideas of a Russian American philosopher that deserve to be evoked. Ayn Rand foresaw a mutation in professional cultures in American society. According to her, the American businessman of the future would be an artist with a keen business sense, or an artistically inclined businessman, or in her words, "artistic businessmen or business-minded artists." Time has proved her postulate to be correct. Once cinematographic success is achieved today, the first thing done in Hollywood is the creation of individual film companies by actors and actresses in order to autonomously handle, on an individual basis, business as well as artistic aspects of film making.

A pertinent example is the American actress, Jodie Foster, who is considered to be the nonconformist intellectual of Hollywood. We must also consider the opposite: Ronald Reagan. He is unique in that he changed his professional culture from a Hollywood artist to being president at the White House managing economic, political, and military affairs. Whether in Hollywood or at the White House, team cultures exist and must be taken into consideration. Because the professional cultures of team members are different, we need to understand and improve team communicating to keep up with changes in the world. Who can foresee the extent of the mutation of professional cultures in the twenty-first century?

Pushing Rand's logic even further, we can foresee a similar mutation of professional cultures even more revolutionary between business, science, technology, and the creative world of artists. Given the constant technological mutation in today's world, it is easy to apply to the twenty-first century her ideas about mutation of American professional cultures from the twentieth century. A noteworthy example is the design engineering career of the talented and innovative Raymond Lowey. This Franco-American design engineer's genius is responsible for the genesis of the twentieth-century modern look. He is recognized as being the father or creator of the new modern look called the aerodynamic line, which is often used in new technological developments. His aerodynamic lines revolutionized daily life.

COMMUNICATING

Communication skills (ability to organize thoughts and present them), interpersonal skills (ability to be with others), and social skills (simply being polite and courteous) must de developed by all team members so that team culture can be created and last long enough to become the new culture of the organization. Teams are a management tool to change employee behavior and create a new work culture. Team culture is a way of thinking and acting that favors open-mindedness and complete open communication. Complete team communication is not linear but circular, circular in the sense that it is not just one way but there is feedback that instigates adjustments to change work attitudes and work behavior. Increasing frequency of sharing information is the basis of team culture communicating. The result is change. The resulting changes in work attitudes and behavior give birth to higher quality and greater quantity of new ideas; new ideas being expressed, encouraged, developed, and accepted (see Cleland 1996). Sharing means changing. Change and sharing are the key words of team culture communicating. Electronic transmission of information is not communicating. Hence, team culture communicating suffers from technology. Today's communication technologies have become a powerful octopus. This powerful octopus of new technologies invades and depletes ethnic cultures around the world of their differences and sacrifices them on the altar of professional cultures. Hence, global professional culture clusters are developing around the planet. Every- where everyone seems to be influenced greatly by this power of new commu- nication technologies. For example, Hollywood is partly responsible for the situation in society where visual media power greatly influences and modifies attitudes, behavior, speech, dress, and social patterns around the world. Her uncontested visual power dominates as the most influential sociocultural vari- able in the world today. Does the Hollywood team impose American culture as a global norm? Does the Hollywood team offer a global cultural norm unifying the world, that in turn diminishes cultural differences, thus reducing polysemy (multiple meanings of words)? Does diminishing cultural differences reduce the probability of polysemy in teams?

Harmonizing differences between professional cultures in a team improves communicating between team members: communicating = feedback = insight = foresight = vision. Feedback offers insight when team members share informa- tion. Insight creates foresight about the future, making vision possible. Com- munication occurs more frequently and increases more rapidly in team work units as compared to the vertical hierarchy of traditional staff, office, and department organizational designs. According to Cleland (1996) there are numerous kinds of teams in an organization: reengineering teams, crisis management teams, product and process development teams, self-directed production teams, task forces and problem-solving teams, bench-marking teams, facilities construction project teams, quality teams, general purpose project teams, audit teams, plural executive teams, new business development teams and so forth and so on.

These various teams impose a multidimensional communication model that crosses over, crisscrosses, and by-passes traditional communication network systems. Cleland, proposes that successful team culture communicating in- cludes such tools as letters, memoranda, formal reports, all forms of reporting, team meetings and review meetings, management-walk-arounds, conversation, observations, listening, rumors, and gossip. Team culture can break down bar- riers by sharing information through complete, open, multidimensional commu- nicating. It allows those working in an organization to legitimately trespass hierarchical organizational barriers (authorization, rules, etc.), stakeholder bar- riers (suppliers, banks, etc.), physical barriers (walls, PCs, etc.), psychological barriers (attitudes, prejudices, etc.), and social barriers (background, education, previous work experience, etc.).

Cleland (1996) proposes that team culture communicating privileges new ideas by expressing such new ideas, by encouraging them, by respecting those who propose them, by assisting in the development and follow-up of a new idea, and by accepting different ideas. He goes on to explain how, in a team culture, everyone, as a leader, shares information, communication, feedback, insight, foresight, vision, responsibility, authority, and accountability with each other horizontally and diagonally rather than vertically. Open, complete communi- cating increases sharing and the resulting changes. Cleland has listed some of the barriers to team culture: lack of expertise and knowledge, narrow-mindedness, and office fiefdoms. They must be replaced by the right to try and then learn from mistakes made, acceptance of different ideas, and new allocation schemes of resources. Team culture requires a continuous ongoing climate of learning and acquiring new skills and knowledge allowing employees to improve their performance.

Team culture means mutually respecting and taking into consideration members' beliefs, customs, knowledge, practices, and behavior patterns. Team culture is enriched and strengthened by differences: disagreements, controversies, adversarial situations, and conflicts. Dividing differences are caused by non-expression or misunderstanding of expectations and poor communication, thus unclear roles. Expectations and roles must be communicated and confirmed regularly. Consensus, faith, loyalty, commitment, and bonding ensure the continuity of team culture. Belonging, listening, and team pride fulfill individual needs for social as well as psychological satisfaction in work. The ambiance or climate of team culture is linked to the attitudes, behavior, and feedback between team members. Cleland confirms this new work culture results in increased synergy, creative thinking, new range of ideas, new outlooks, new products, new processes, more communication, more motivation, lower costs, higher quality, fewer managers, more leaders, more pride, and more fun.

Communication inside a team is usually approached from two points of view:

- according to communication concepts relative to the "self" as an individual or
- according to concepts of communication within a team and between other teams.

Communication experts define team communication by five generally accepted characteristics: (1) conscious sharing of something in common with all members of the team(s), (2) a common objective or purpose, (3) a set of rules governing desired behavior or performance expected from all members of (a) team(s), (4) assigned roles that are stable but not static and require behavior modification to adapt to different rules of different teams, and (5) a system of reward and acceptance or corrective action when behavior and attitude are not acceptable and must be modified even rejected by the team (s).

Christopher Midler of Polytechnique (France's M.I.T.) has six steps for team communication systems in industrial projects They can be applied to team management because they give priority to team communication methods: (1) define the autonomy, the authority, and the role of the team leader and the team objective, (2) define one unique purpose for each work project of the team, (3) define the communication needs and establish communication tools that do more than just please or keep team members content, but communication tools that bring to the surface conflicts sufficiently early as to be able to resolve them without creating a crisis, (4) fight uncertainty by frequent lucid communication that maintains a transparent state of unity through mutual confidence and trust between team members, (5) maintain an evolutionary management style; at the beginning the team leader is a destabilizing team creator, in the middle of the project he is a team negotiator, and toward the end of a project he is a team fireman that rescues when and where and whomever is necessary to make it all come together, and (6) maintain an open system of communication to mobilize, act and achieve within a large parameter of actors and stakeholders.

Organizing employees and work activities into teams implies a greater professional need to communicate within a team and with other teams (figure 7.1). This need for improved team communications increases exponentially with the complexity of new technologies. Electronics, computers, telecommunications, and the resulting multiple access to information have accelerated and intensified the evolution of complexity in our society. Genelot believes complexity can be reduced by key ideas being expressed through a commonly shared professional vocabulary of key words that globally communicate necessary details. François Joivet, of the French consulting firm Eiffage, has over twenty years of experience with teams and projects. His analysis of team dysfunction has one key word: *communicating!* Like Midler, he warns us to not ignore the possible dysfunctions of teams.

The following three concepts explaining team dysfunction are directly related to communicating about objectives, decisions made, and work activities. He sees most team dysfunction as being related to invalid objectives, decision traffic jams (S.C.D. = smallest common decider), and the opposing poles of sequential and simultaneous activities. In the particular mindset of team culture, we need a communications approach to improve team efficiency. Clearer understanding of

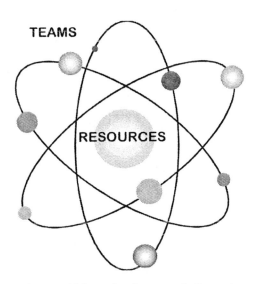

FIGURE 7-1. Team culture multidimensional communication system.

ideas behind words improves human communications in a team. What communication approach offers a universal application for almost any kind of organization with teams found in today's society? Which approach is universal enough to work for manufacturing, construction, information technology/ information systems, telecommunications, education, entertainment, publishing, law, and health care? At the end of this chapter, a team communication approach is presented based on semantics (meanings of words in audible languages of written alphabets) and semiology (meanings of objects, forms, and symbols in the visual language of the eye). It is based on common sense observations, not antidotes or miracle cures, for improving communications between teams and team members in super-crunched and ultra-complex work environments. The more crunched and the more complex the work environment, the greater the need to understand what ideas are really meant to be shared in a team above and beyond the words used by team members.

Those elements of opposition in work environments must be linked by a viaduct of transcultural understanding or, more simply, culture sharing. Such transcultural understanding must not to be confused with the overused, even abused, notion of cross-cultural communication, which is too often limited to audibly exchanging information. So our question becomes how to best explain an idea and what it really means in a team. Here it is important to admit new technologies of information and communication have increased the speed of information but they have not increased the quality nor the understanding of it.

We are overdosed with speed. Too much too fast saturates the human capacity to comprehend. So how to privilege ideas over words? Annie Sullivan and Helen Keller found a way. They were able to succeed in sharing thoughts beyond the stumbling blocks of words by appealing to a multitude of human senses when communicating: touching, smelling, feeling to understand an idea or a thought through objects and forms. We find the same idea expressed differently in the words of the Lebanese poet Khalil Gibran (1970), who richly portrayed the need to go beyond words when trying to understand the ideas words try to communicate: "For thought is a bird of space, that in a cage of words may indeed unfold its wings [ideas] but cannot fly [communicate]."

Team communicating can be improved by identifying and using key words based on semantics and semiology. Well-thought-out and well-chosen key words canalize, facilitate, organize, and furnish a succinct vision of useful precise information during the carrying out of a project in teams for everyone concerned. Those little words or linguistic phonemes composed of vowels, consonants, and syllables hide so much. The research of a little-known American pedagogue, Christine Elison, showed how much words can hide. With the risk of displeasing her native peers and homologues, she openly declared herself a disciple of the Frenchman sometimes deliberately forgotten by colleagues on her side of the Atlantic, Jean Piaget. Piaget proposed the concept of evolutionary blocks or steps of awareness and cognition in the acquisition of knowledge. Elison sought an application to create a pedagogical tool for measuring intelligence through key vocabulary word retention and usage. She revealed that a graduated sequence of word difficulty can be a more reliable indication of intelligence as opposed to the myth of the I.Q. test. Her ideas correspond to the need of reinforcing employee competence in communicating through retention and usage of common key words from professional vocabularies.

Doing work as teams on projects brings all the different actors of a company together, face-to-face, on a daily basis: engineers, accountants, salesmen, executives, and technicians. Each brings a different professional work culture to create their new team culture. Team culture is necessary in order to work together on a project successfully. Working on a project requires being able to accept and fulfill particular roles to achieve a specific objective within a certain budget before a precise deadline. Knowing the terms, jargon, and key words of the project is not just a prerequisite but a priority according to Frédéric d'Allest, honorary president of l'Arianespace (the French equivalent to NASA; +speech March 24, 1994 for the bicentennial of the Polytechnique).

Key words in common with all members of a team builds a viaduct of trans-cultural understanding spanning differences of background, education, experience, nationality, race, religion, culture, languages, among others. Therefore, team communications becomes more open, frequent, and clear so the sharing of information can provide a solid basis for a multidimensional communication system between teams and teams members. The idea here is to give priority to the analysis of opposites, not similarities, in a team culture. When differences in background, education, experience, nationality, culture, race, religion, and language are in harmony, they make a team stronger and richer by becoming unifying solidifiers not dividing differences. In analyzing differences between opposites, we discover where to find something in common or at least something similar between them. The more team members have in common, or similar, the easier it is to trust each other and have confidence in one another. Trust gives birth to confidence hence harmony.

The future of an organization depends on the harmony in the teams within its structure. Team dysfunction is due to poor communication because of unexplained differences in how we see things, think, and reason. Understanding those differences is the key to finding solutions to the dysfunctioning of a team. That which is in opposition can be harmonized through understanding the ideas of each other. Opposites cannot communicate until they identify those words that express ideas in common. Team harmony depends on establishing a common work vocabulary. Therefore, confidence and trust in a team depends on a commonly used professional vocabulary of key words clearly understood by all.

There is an increased demand for improving team culture communications in industry. The amplitude and importance of the key words as a facilitator between professionals coming from different countries and speaking several languages must be considered. More and more, employees participating in teams are confronted by professional situations where team members have different ethnic origins, different professional cultures (due to education and experience), and different ways of communicating (due to different native languages). Glen Peters, of Price Waterhouse in London, presented some very interesting viewpoints in his December 1996 article. How can we imagine the world in 2010? He proposes either a more open or an even more closed up world. In the first case of openness we see the growing importance of English as the international professional language. A more open world means birth of global professional culture clusters where everyone becomes bilingual: one's mother tongue (L1) and English (L2). I would like to introduce and add the following application of his ideas to team culture. In other words, a more open world will exist when everyone becomes bicultural, professionally speaking, by knowing one's own professional culture (C1) and by understanding the professional culture of a fellow team member (C2).

The other option foreseen by Peters is one of a world even more closed up. Such a destiny will lead to the setting up of industrial and economic barriers as well as cultural ones: protectionism and nationalism. English will experience a decline in its importance as the international professional language but will always be in vogue when seeking to communicate outside of and between most professional cultures. Whatever be the world's destiny—languages and words expressing ideas will be more important than technology. Communications, key words, semantics, and semiology are priorities for global professional culture clusters in the twenty-first century.

SEMANTICS

The importance of language and the meaning of words (semantics), in team culture communicating, can be seen by looking closely at a commonly used word in French management: *patron* meaning boss. It comes from the Latin, *patronus* or *pater,* meaning father. These words insinuate a sense of fatherly caring as a protector who takes charge of those who depend on him. The cultural influence of this semantic Latin heritage on French team management is easily recognized in the dialogue today between executive management and workers' unions during strike negotiations in France.

Medical care, retirement programs, and numerous other benefits are seen as human rights, not as a corporate benefits package offered as options or gifts to entice potential employees. Executive management in France has a moral duty, as well as a financial obligation, to care for and protect employees by taking charge of their medical care, retirement program, and other needs within the company family. For example, I had three weeks of sick leave in France for a sprained ankle, while my cousin working in the American airlines industry had only four weeks for a broken leg and arm. Both of our cases were on-the-job work accidents. Hence, we see how in the French culture, the notion of team is being responsible for the team members as individuals, whereas individuals sacrificing themselves for the good of the team is often the case in American culture.

Professional biculturalism can be defined as the ability of a professional to work harmoniously, thus effectively and efficiently, in a team on a project, with another professional not from his own specific professional culture. For example an engineer (C1) working harmoniously, thus efficiently and effectively, with an accountant (C2) becomes professionally bicultural when he begins to understand accounting and how to understand and work with accountants. The reverse is also a bicultural professional situation for an accountant (C1) working in a team on a project with an engineer (C2).

An engineer and an accountant must realize they can learn how to communicate the same idea about a need for money with different words from their professional vocabularies. The engineer can express the same idea about a need for money when he speaks the word costs, as the accountant when he uses the word budget. Acquisition of professional vocabulary is based on the understanding of ideas behind key words used by different kinds of professionals when working together in teams. A professional knowing his own professional vocabulary (V1) becomes bilingual in a team culture when he understands another team member's professional vocabulary (V2) from a different professional culture. He/she becomes a bicultural (C1 + C2) and a bilingual (V1 + V2) team member when capable of harmoniously working on the same project with other team members from various other professional cultures.

We have already mentioned the honorary president of the French space consortium l'Arianéspace, Frédérique d'Allest. He is concerned about the polysemy of key words between professionals from various work cultures using different work-related vocabularies. He gives priority to key vocabulary words. He feels that polysemy in team management can be reduced by establishing a list of key vocabulary words to be used by all professionals working on the same project. Nizard's (1996) explanation of the importance of professional vocabularies and cultures confirms a need to deal with polysemy and build a viaduct of transcultural understanding in teams. He says a professional vocabulary is (1) the choice of key words used while working and (2) the professional key slang words used to codify then decipher essential information in a team situation.

The question now to be asked is: How does technology influence professional vocabularies in the twenty-first century? First of all, we need to realize that a technologically dominated world generates fear because it threatens direct human one-to-one contact. We have been taken hostage by NTIC because these present-day technologies interrupt and diminish the need for human contact in daily life. The domineering octopus of new technologies is a definite threat to direct human contact. Human contact is essential in order to reduce polysemy in a team culture. Once again we reconsider Genelot (1994), who also adds his own warning about such influences in society. He warns us about the danger in society of an overwhelming technological complexity in the world. According to him, it has already begun with technological changes affecting our daily living habits such as computers, satellites, space travel, instant long distance telecommunications, nuclear power stations, high-speed trains like the French TGV, and so forth.

Second, we must also realize the global information market favors the use of key words reducing communications down to a minimum number of words. We have the habit of rapidly visualizing shortened versions of information and knowledge rather than taking the time to enjoy a more complete longer written version. New communication technologies favor the use of key words expressing key ideas allowing a maximum amount of information in a minimum amount of time. Daily examples of minimizing human communication to key words can be found in computer science, Internet, Intranet, Exranet, Web sites, all other highways of information, digitalization, fiber optics, CDs, laser, telephotocopiers or faxes, telephone answering machines, voiceovers and all other message-taking services. Such technological advancements increase polysemy by reducing the number of words.

The number of, and which, words are used depends on the global professional culture cluster we belong to. Speed and frequency increase polysemy between global professional culture clusters. Hence, there is an ever-increasing need for professional bilingualism and biculturalism in and between different team cultures. Team culture communication suffers from technology because technology increases the speed and amount but not the quality of communicating.

The next question to be asked is: How do we minimize polysemy between professionals working on the same team? The answer—through identifying key words of a professional vocabulary to be used in a specific work project by team members from different professional cultures. Dudley-Evans and St. John (1998), ask the same question another way: Within the interplay between language and culture, a crucial question is what does this event or statement mean to the other person? Polysemy must be a priority of team communications when team members are from different professional cultures (C1, C2, etc.) and speak different professional vocabularies (V1, V2, etc.). To simplify, for our discussion about team culture communicating, below is a definition about the polysemy of keywords from professional vocabularies:

> The same signified (idea) has different signifiers (words) in team communications for team members from different professional cultures (C1, C2, etc.) having different professional vocabularies (V1, V2, etc.).

It was logical to have adopted the terminology of de Saussure because his terms permit greater clarity and precision. The key concepts, and related ideas, of the text are the signifieds (meanings) of words used while the actual words used that do the signifying are the signifiers (signs). Explained with the more precise terminology of de Saussure: "Team culture communicating between professionals of different work cultures and vocabularies depends upon the mutual transcultural understanding of the signifieds (meanings or ideas) expressed by signifiers (signs or words)."

In a professional culture, professional vocabulary determines the degree of transcultural understanding. This is the situation when negotiating a contract. The need for transcultural understanding in such a professional situation can be seen in the breakdown of contract negotiations between British Rail and la SNCF for the construction of the Channel Tunnel. The breakdown in contract negotiations can be retraced to the semantic roots of polysemy for certain key words used in the English and French versions of the same contract. An excellent example can be found in the English term from time to time, which was used as being the equivalent to the French term: de temps en temps, meaning now and then or once in a while. Culturally speaking, the British and French ideas were not only different, they were opposite. It would have been more appropriate, in this particular situation, to use in English periodically, and in French to use a truer semantic twin, périodiquement.

The choice of words with a more similar spelling and pronunciation, as in homonymy, would have facilitated the monosemy needed to decrease the polysemy between the negotiating teams from English and French cultures. Lerat (1995), a French linguist, confirms the universality of polysemy (multiple meanings) and thus the importance of dealing with polysemy in professional situations that require speaking more than just one's mother tongue (L1) (bilingual [L2], trilingual [L3], multilingual [Lx], etc.). Multilingualism reveals the notions really shared and those which are related to culture in a language, therefore, it is necessary to see the limits of equivalencies (often due to the fact of the universality of polysemy and synonymy). In a team it is necessary to go beyond words to symbolize the different meanings in a more transparent or clearer way.

Besides vowels/consonants/alphabets, are there other more efficient symbols to use when sharing ideas between team members? Mathematicians offer a universal example. The Islamic culture gave the world symbols allowing transcultural understanding of mathematical values between professionals around the world: 1, 2, 3, 4, 5, 6, 7, 8, 9, 0. Here we can see that mathematical ideas about numeric values associated to symbols are the same for all professional cultures and professional vocabularies.

According to the French visual communication expert Bertin (1983), the mathematical language is very monosemic (one single meaning) with little polysemic (multiple meanings). Symbols other than words make mathematical ideas more transparent. Transparent team culture communicating requires the sharing of ideas (signifieds) through a shared vocabulary. Therefore, we cannot ignore the words (signifiers) that represent them. And yet team culture still needs to go beyond these words to share ideas more completely.

Dudley-Evans and St. John (1998) ask a most important question for teams: "Has the ... (team member) ... fully understood the term? If not, how ... (to) check the meaning?" It is through the signifiers and signs (words and images of all kinds) that we can identify a specific signified (idea) needed in order to understand something heard, read, seen, felt, touched, smelled, and so on, when working together in a team. Total transparency between mental lexicons of different cultures (professional or ethnic) and languages (professional or linguistic) would be a utopic Saussurrian-Barthesian paradise. A paradise or a hell, professionals working together creating a team culture must successfully carry out their work project.

SEMIOLOGY

Semiology is the scientific study about how man associates and represents meanings by symbols, objects, forms, and signs. The French word, *la sémiologie,* is translated by certain experts in English as semiotics. Yet in French, a particular branch of *la sémiologie* is called *la sémiotique.* So what are the real meanings of the ideas to be understood hiding behind these key words semiology/la sémiologie and semiotics/la sémiotique? La sémiotique studies the characteristics and roles of symbols and signs in society, whereas la sémiologie gives priority to the symbols, signs, characteristics, and roles of languages in society. One must not confuse semiotics in English with la sémiotique in French. An example of *false friends/faux amis*? To avoid polysemy in our discussion, we shall adopt a direct translation into English of la sémiologie as being semiology not semiotics. This is the case of the translation in English by William J. Berg of the title of the book, *La sémiologie graphique/The Semiology of Graphics.* This exceptional book was authored by Jacques Bertin, a famous French researcher in the field of graphics. According to Bertin (1983), when adopting a semiological approach to communicating with a system of signs, we must take into consideration two criteria: (1) the eye and the ear have different systems of perception, and (2) the meanings we attribute to signs are monosemic (single meaning), polysemic (mutiple meanings), or pansemic (universal meaning).

Everyone sees the value and admits a more rapid understanding when communicating with forms, symbols, objects. Their superior speed favors pansemic meanings of ideas in a team. As it is proposed by Dudley-Evans and St. John (1998): "We can use visuals for language work, to generate spoken or written production, and as comprehension check. . . . Visuals include diagrams, flow charts, graphs, bar and pie charts, matrices, photographs and sketches." Visuals offer a definite advantage toward increased transparency in team culture communicating. They are as important as words in sharing ideas between team members from different work cultures with different work vocabularies. They are credible tools for team communication when working together on projects. The brain mentally organizes knowledge by codifying, classifying then links it all together so that it can later be reproduced. The right side of the brain assumes the visual learning with colors, images, drawings, maps, charts, diagrams, outlines, and comparisons. The unifying central link is key words, terms, expressions, images, forms, symbols, or other types of signs that associate knowledge acquired to signifieds.

The mental organization of knowledge acquired is accomplished through a visual logic that establishes hierarchical referents by criteria that link signifieds through similarity. This means being able to see or recognize the differences in information learned, and then being able to identify these differences (similarities or nonsimilarities) with signs (words composed of letters with sounds) or images (composed of objects and forms without sounds). Can intelligence simply be the capacity to understand differences between what is similar or not?

Semiological communication of ideas responds to team communication needs between professionals of all ethnic cultures coming from different work cultures with different professional vocabularies and languages. Throughout history, there has been an ever-present need for humanity to find the means to symbolize their ideas when trying to share them with each other. Today, scientists, engineers, and managers around the world—all speaking different professional vocabularies and different linguistic languages—must work together in teams on industrial and technological projects. My research shows mutual understanding in teams can be quadrupled when giving priority to the language of the eye (images) more than to the language of the ear (words). Transcultural understanding of ideas can be quadrupled when priority is given to semiology (visual language of the eye) over semantics (audible language of sound and words). This interpretation of my research offers a potential communication approach to all kinds of teams found in the different global professional culture clusters around the planet.

Gary Ferraro (1996), professor of Anthropology at the University of North Carolina, proposes communicating as a priority for any cultural (professional or ethnic) and therefore the need to adapt ourselves to those whom we speak with. According to him, in order to better understand a foreign language, it is necessary to understand the associated cultural values and customs. His idea is supported by Dudley-Evans and St. John (1998): "A sensitivity to cultural issues and an understanding of our own and other's values and behaviors is important . . . it is vital for people to communicate effectively across borders and to bridge cultural gaps . . . [and] . . . communication requires awareness and sensitivity to the diversity of values and customs around the world."

My research quantified the probability of semiological improvements in team communications. The results of my research show Barthes' semiological language of the eye can build a viaduct of transcultural understanding. Hence differences between professionals can be harmonized when working on the same or related team projects. Transcultural understanding gives priority to ideas behind and beyond the words of traditional cross-cultural communications. Let us now consider a transcultural example of such a semiological approach to visual team communications.

CONCLUSION

Pictographic, logographic, and ideagraphic communication systems have symbolized human thought and action for centuries. Mesopotamian scribes, their Summerian colleagues, and of course the hieroglyphics of Egyptian scribes as well as Islam's numbers greatly contributed to the semiological evolution of human communications. Drawings and symbols are successful alternatives to alphabets when representing meanings of ideas and concepts.

The universal language of the eye favors pansemy-reducing polysemy while increasing monosemy in teamwork situations. Barthes' (1985) semiology is essential to team culture communicating because it gives priority to visual communicating of the eye as opposed to audible communicating of the hear and mouth. Technology has increased polysemy in society. NTIC has cursed the human race with an antihuman contact screen syndrome. Instead of looking each at other we look at screens! Team culture communicating suffers from technology because it increases the frequency but not the meaning of information.

We have been taken culturally hostage by technology because it has increased the speed and amount of information but does not increase the quality of communicating in teams. Different global clusters of professional cultures exist around the world and require everyone to now become professionally bicultural as well as bilingual. Speed and polysemy threaten team communicating between these global professional culture clusters developing around the planet, hence the need to become professionally bicultural as well as bilingual. Acquisition of professional vocabulary is based on semiological as well as semantic perceptions of key words used by different kinds of professionals when working together in teams on the same project. Team harmony is the result of professional bilingualism and biculturalism.

The global crisis of economic disequilibrium has increased the need for professional bilingualism and biculturalism between teams of different global professional culture clusters around the planet. This developing global professional culture clusters forces us to no longer think in terms of cross-cultural communicating but rather transcultural understanding permitting cross-management culturing. Keynes rejected, even twisted then inverted the accepted ideas of his day and proposed the probability of a disequilibrium between supply and demand. Should we twist then invert the key word globalization to better understand today's disequilibirum? Everything is not global and everyone is not living globally because economic equilibrium does not exist for everyone.

Today, economic disequilibrium, not equilibrium, has become the reality and increases the need to improve team culture communicating. This means, for us in the particular mindset of team culture, team culture communications must give priority to the sharing of ideas (signifieds) beyond words (signifiers) that try to represent them. Visual communication links the sense or meanings between ideas in our memory. Visuals, as a system of signs, constitutes a semiological language for sharing ideas in a team. Sharing means changing. Change and sharing dominate as the key words of team culture.

In this light, Rand's (1961) ideas about mutation of American professional cultures in the twentieth century can be reinterpreted for the twenty-first century. Mutation of professional cultures even more revolutionary between business, science, and the creative world of artists is foreseen. Cross-cultural gaps will exist even more between professional cultures as well as between ethnic cultures. Cultural differences (both ethnic and professional) affect the understanding (transparency) in a team situation.

Team culture tends to break down barriers by sharing information through complete more open multidimensional communicating: by mutual respect and taking into consideration members' beliefs, customs, knowledge, practices, and behavior patterns. Team harmony depends on establishing a common work vocabulary. Polysemy in team communications constitutes an unavoidable challenge in a changing world—a challenge even the ancient Greeks had the wisdom to understand:

There is nothing so permanent as change. (Heraclitus of Greece, 513 B.C.)

BIBLIOGRAPHY

Barthes, Roland. 1985. *L'aventure sémiologique*. Paris: Editions du Seuil.

Bertin, J. 1983. *Semiology of Graphics: Diagrams, Networks, Maps*. Madison: University of Wisconsin Press.

Caron Jean. 1997. *Précis de psycholinguistique*. Paris: Presses Universitaires de France.

Cleland, David I. 1996. *Strategic Management of Teams*. New York: John Wiley & Sons.

Cormaire, Sylvette. 1996. *Gestion de conflits interculturels dans les rencontres d'affaires: approche critiqu, note de recherche DEA*, Bordeaux: DLVP Bordeaux 2.

Cotton, David. 1988. *Keys to Management/Les clés du management*. London: Unwin Hyman Limited.

Dossier. 1987. *Design Industriel le beau et l'utile, Courrier cadre n 746*. Paris: ANPE, 35–45.

Dudely-Evans, Tony, and Jo St. John. 1998. *Developments in ESP: A Multidisciplinary Approach*. Cambridge: Cambridge University Press.

l'Expansion Management Review, various articles, Paris: Groupe Expansion Magazines.

Genelot, Dominique. 1994. *Farwell to Planning Welcome to Inventing!/Adieu à la planification bienvenue à l'invention!* Autumn, 103–9.

Gibran, Khalil. 1970. *The Prophet*. London: Heinemann.

Glykos, Allain. 1994. *Montesquieu*, Christian Pirot Editeur, Saint Cyr-sur-Loire.

Harvard, Phillip. 1998. *A cultural responsibility for the future of the human race (the renaissance of the 21st century)* presented at the 7th annual MOT International Conference, Orlando: February 16, 1998.

Heynes, Paul, and Thomas Johnson. 1976. *Towards Understanding Macroeconomics*. Chicago, Science Research Associates.

Jolivet, François. 1995. *Is Dysfunctioning Avoidable?/Peut-on éviter les dysfonctionnements?* March, 62–70.

Knowles, John. 1959. *A Separate Peace*. New York: Dell.

Lange, Claudine. 1993. *Etre ingéniuer aujourd'hui*. Monaco: Editions du Rocher.

Nizard, Georges. 1996 *Cinquante mots clés du management*. Toulouse: Privat.

Lerat, Pierre. 1995. *Les langues spécialisés*. Paris: Presses Universitaires de France.

Marion, Gilles, and Daniel Michel. 1992. *Marketing; How to Use/Marketing mode d'emploi*. Paris: Les Editions d'Organisation.

Midler, Christophe. 1995. *A Group Learning Problem/Une affaire d'apprentissage collectif,* March, 71–79.

Miller, George A. 1991. *The Science of Words.* New York: Scientific American Library, W. H. Freeman.

Narcy, Jean-Paul. 1998. *Séminaires DLVP pour DEA,* Bordeaux: Bordeaux 2, 23.10.98, notes prises pour l'étude.

Peoples and Places of the Past. 1983. National Geographic Society.

Perry, Ralph Barton. 1876–1957. *Various files of the famous professor of philosophy/dossiers divers du célèbre professeur de philosophie.* Boston: Harvard University archives— ref@elmer.harvard.edu

Peters, Glen. 1996. *Un monde impitoyable pour les dirigeants,* December, 70–78.

Rand, Ayn. 1961. *The New Intellectual/Une perspective intellectuelle nouvelle.* New York: Signet Classics—New American Library.

Sallenave, Jean-Paul. 1993. *L'Antimanagement Du sytème D à la théorie L.* Paris: Editions d'Organisation.

8

Better Project Management Through Effective Meetings Management

THEODORE H. ROSEN

M eetings are a primary activity of information sharing that can lead to future project successes. Project team meetings, one-to-one, staff–staff, manager–staff meetings, up to full project staff, face-to-face and virtual meetings, are the one set of activities that can either enhance the successful completion of a project's goals or cause the project to fail. The importance of conducting effective staff meetings cannot be overstated. The project manager has the responsibility to call, develop agenda for, conduct, and follow-up on project meetings that will lead to a successful project conclusion. The project manager also must ensure communications throughout the project are accurate and understood by all project team members.

This chapter is a discussion of answers to questions often raised about project meetings. Each answer focuses on a supporting strategy for the effective use of the meeting as a critical project management tool. The terms project manager, meeting facilitator, meeting convener, and team leader are used interchangeably; the principles of effective meetings management apply to all people who call, develop, lead, and follow-up on meetings in some official organizational capacity.

WHY ARE MEETINGS SO IMPORTANT
TO PROJECT MANAGEMENT?

Most projects where at least two team members are working toward a common goal—a meeting—require transfer of data and information sharing of experiences, collaboration on strategy, planning, creativity, and effective communications to be successful in reaching project goals. These issues are especially critical when working on virtual project teams at multiple sites around the country or the world. On virtual teams, those where attendees are not sitting in the same room, there are missing elements of face-to-face communications (e.g., body language, tone of voice, facial expressions) that can lead to disinterest in "attending" such meetings and interpersonal issues surrounding the concept of trust of unknown teammates. Without trust, missing information or holding back from sharing data from a team member can lead to less than successful project results. Making decisions with incomplete data is a problem when one is not aware of the missing data, and the reliance on other team members to help identify such deficiencies is lacking. Developing mutual trust and a sense of teamwork helps to address that problem.

Team problem solving also can improve overall project success. Architects use a minimum of three views to describe a solid object. Each view provides unique data about that object. Likewise, project problems can also benefit from multiple views of the problem where more people are working on the problem with more experience and education to analyze the problem and seek solutions.

Team problem solving occurs at meetings. Each team member brings a special view to the problem. The other team members, with their own areas of expertise, build on each others' perceptions and thoughts and, in turn, come up with new thoughts and solutions to the stated problem. The environment and team culture contributes to the team's overall success. The phenomenon known as synergy is the well-known benefit of group versus individual problem solving. It can only occur when two or more people are addressing a problem in a meeting situation. Managing this process requires expertise in group dynamics and leadership to coordinate and motivate the numerous participants to full participation in the problem-solving process.

Contemporary projects are large and involve multiple teams and task teams, each providing input to the overall project goal. Meetings are the venue at which problems get voiced, discussed, analyzed, and solved. The more people there are considering each problem, the more creative and often better solutions can be found. To reach this desired goal, an organization requires an effective meeting culture. Meetings must encourage attendance, motivate the participants, have reason for their existence, and be enjoyable to attend. Therefore, the project manager, or whoever calls meetings of more than two team members needs to be instructed in how to run such meetings to develop the culture of trust, synergy, and creativity.

Effective communications can be one primary driver for scheduling full project staff meetings. At key milestone points of a project, it might be appropriate to conduct a full staff meeting, while at other times smaller group meetings might be preferable and more productive. At full project staff meetings, announcements concerning changes to the next set of tasks can be announced and discussed, or new policies might be introduced. This is the time to communicate information that affects the entire project staff. Whatever might be the specific driver of the meeting will be uniformly communicated to the entire staff when done together at this meeting. This enables staff to ask clarifying questions about the communication and receive definitive answers. Everyone will hear the exact same answers and have opportunities to ask questions for clarification of specific issues. This process will lead to a common understanding of the issues involved.

Clear and precise communications will lead to better collaboration through the use of a common jargon and language throughout the project staff, even when team members are from different parts of the organization. Future interactions will be able to avoid many miscommunications when everyone starts out on the same path with a common understanding and language for the project.

WHAT ARE SOME REASONS FOR HAVING PROJECT MEETINGS?

Meetings are a major activity of information sharing that can lead to future project success. Recent studies have noted the importance of "storytelling" as a methodology for sharing information and, especially, experience on various projects. (A discussion of storytelling in the scope of "knowledge continuity" is discussed by Michael Kull elsewhere in this volume.) Meetings often deal, anecdotally with interpersonal issues not likely to be written down or otherwise shared. These include methods of dealing with particular stakeholders, cross-functional organizational communications, and "tricks of the trade."

Meetings create a sharing experience for team staff via the more formal "lessons learned" discussions and project evaluations at the end of a milestone for a task or the entire project's completion. They also provide the opportunity for developing creative and new solutions to problems, as well as act as training opportunities.

Celebrations of milestones are another important part of project management activities and are conducted at meetings. Celebrations give the staff markers of success, events that become historical symbols of the project's progress and goal attainment. In a meeting venue, celebrations also serve as team-building events that increase morale, trust, and camaraderie among the staff.

The Project Management Institute's *Project Management Book of Knowledge* (PMBOK Guide), 2000 edition, speaks of meetings as one of nine "Information distribution methods" (PMI, 2000, section 10.2.2.3, p. 122).

A project manager needs to address the following questions and issues in order to create an effective meetings culture and practice during a project.

DO WE NEED A STAFF MEETING IN ORDER TO CONDUCT BUSINESS AT THIS TIME?

There are five general purposes of meetings: (1) information giving, (2) information getting, (3) problem solving, (4) attitude adjustment prior/following a decision, and (5) instruction (education/training).

The first question anyone should ask when a problem arises while working on a project task, or the need to get advice on an issue arises, is: Do I need to call a meeting to work on this problem or share this information, or should I just call someone on the phone or visit their office to discuss this issue on a one-to-one basis? Too often we call full staff or task meetings to work on a problem or specific task when only one person should be consulted. Probably many project team members can recall being summoned for a meeting and the convener spoke only to one attendee while the rest of the attendees sat and listened having no real need to be there. This can be a tremendous waste of time and money. Figure 8.1 shows

---

TIME = $
What are the costs of a nonproductive meeting?

The Meeting: The regularly scheduled Monday morning meeting to "catch-up" and "keep in touch" with everyone's tasking is held without regard to neither specific needs nor requirements. It lasts about 1 hour per week. Usually there is nothing to say, and most announcements are about information sent out during the past week via e-mail. The feeling among the staff is that the organization could meet every other week, or less, for more benefits, or, if something special comes up, immediately call a meeting.

Costs:

> The meeting lasts one hour, but we calculate the total meeting time as 1½ hours: 15 minutes for stopping work and walking to the meeting and preparatory time, and 15 minutes for walking back to work from the meeting and resetting oneself back to work. (This includes rest room stops and drink refreshment activities).

> The assumption is an *average* salary of $75,000 per year for project managers and technical staff, or $73.50 per hour. (The estimate is based on $36.75 per hour with benefits, etc. loaded on).

> There are 15 people on the project staff including the project manager.

Calculations: 15 staff x $73.50 per hour x 1½ hours meeting time = **$1653.75 cost of a wasted 1 hour meeting**

Results: The feelings of the project staff were that about ½ of the meetings were a waste of time. Using that metric, **the per-meeting cost of $1653.75 grows to $42,997.50 for 26 wasted meetings per year**. That seems like a lot of money for wasted time! It does not include, however, opportunity costs associated with the value of time, and loss of project work time during the meetings. That raises the cost of those meetings even higher.

With that amount of money, a project manager could, for example, hire an administrative assistant to help out the project staff. How many other meetings are like this?

FIGURE 8-1.   The cost of meetings.

a calculation of money wasted during meetings that are nonproductive, such as regularly scheduled, full project staff meetings every Monday morning with no agenda other than informing each other of "where we are."

Sitting through many meetings that require attendance but are not useful for the attendees can also result in lowered morale and job satisfaction. The time spent at a worthless meeting is time away from the real project activities that need to be accomplished. This is especially costly for meetings that are not part of the project plan. Meetings that are built into the plan can be wasteful enough if not conducted properly, but at least they have been accounted for in the plan and project budget.

When planning a meeting, one needs to always ask: Is it necessary to call a meeting to accomplish this goal or solve this problem? The word "necessary" is probably too strong. The word "desirable" is a better concept. Consider different types of meetings or methods of exchanging information and see if it is still desirable to hold a meeting. In making this decision, we need to consider alternative approaches to accomplish the same objectives with the same impact on the project staff. What alternative communications or interactive methodologies could replace this meeting that would be more efficient and less costly yet still effectively address the issue that a meeting would address? Table 8.1 offers possible alternatives to face-to-face meetings. The alternative depends on the nature of the issue to be addressed.

TABLE 8-1. Alternatives to meetings

Purpose of Meeting	Key Issues for the Purpose	Alternatives to Meetings
Information Giving	Is that information as readily presentable in the written format without interaction?	➢ written memos ➢ written reports ➢ e-mail messages ➢ phone calls ➢ one-to-one interviews
Information Getting	Is that information as readily understandable in the written format without interaction?	➢ written memos ➢ written reports ➢ e-mail messages ➢ phone calls ➢ one-to-one interviews
Problem Solving	Is the public and enthusiastic development and acceptance of the solution important in making the solution easy to implement and succeed?	➢ Groupware ➢ Delphi type techniques ➢ Decision support center
Attitude Adjustment Prior/Following a Decision (culture issues)	Is the "sale" and opportunity for persuasion of a change or solution better when face-to-face and among co-workers?	➢ written memos ➢ e-mail messages ➢ one-to-one interviews ➢ phone calls
Instruction (education/training)	Availability of qualified teachers, trainers, coaches; number of other trainees; facilities?	➢ individual facilitation ➢ distance courses ➢ programmed/self-paced instruction (computer and written) ➢ other institutions

WHY ARE SO FEW PROJECT MEETINGS EFFECTIVE,
AND WHAT CAN WE DO ABOUT THEM?

The first response to this question might be another question: How do we know only a few project meetings are effective? Having facilitated the learning of over 1,000 students, workshop attendees, managers, and executives, and having counseled and coached, as well as seen shelves of books on business meetings in bookstores, this author feels a consensus that an effective meeting is an unreachable quest of project staff and management. It should be pointed out that the above-mentioned students are graduate-level students in programs designed for the full-time employee-student. In particular, many of the employee-students are enrolled in a project management master's degree program. They share their experiences with the classes about their own work meetings, and many say they have never attended what they consider to be an effective, well-run meeting. Many say they stopped going to regular weekly meetings, instead feigning illness, other meetings, or work deadlines (clear signs and behaviors associated with ineffective meetings). Project managers would improve team relations and meetings by asking their project team members what could be done to improve their meetings and following up on their suggestions, if reasonable.

One important factor for the success of meetings is the composition of the project team and the background of its members. Although staffing is usually addressed in the human resources office for the project team, it is the project manager's responsibility to make sure the project team is properly staffed. When initial team building and other meetings are held at the start of a new project, team members can quickly assess if others on the team seem appropriate for the job. If the perception is that the other members of the team do not seem to have the right credentials, then the team morale may suffer, and the team will not development the camaraderie and trust that is necessary for a successful project. Selection of team members is a key activity to the success of every project team.

In order to properly staff the project team, the project manager first needs to review the work breakdown structure to determine and understand what tasks and behaviors are required on the project. Knowledge, skills, and abilities (KSAs) required to perform those tasks and behaviors are evaluated, and competency requirements are determined for the project team. The human resources function within the organization is then tasked to locate either existing organizational staff or to locate external individuals who can meet those competencies for the project team. The project manager then must ensure that the people sent for placement on the team are, in fact, fully capable of carrying out the competency requirements of the job. The team selection process is a joint activity between the project manager and the human resources office and must be carried out using the most valid selection processes available.

In order to work successfully as a team, the technologies used and interpersonal relationships must be developed to encourage full participation and collaboration on all phases of projects. It is precisely at team meetings where these behaviors can be developed and carried out. Team building and development activities are usually focused on personal interactions early in the life of a team or project—during project planning activities. Project teams must be developed, motivated, encouraged, and maintained throughout the project. Team building and development activities at early project meetings will result in more effective meetings. But, to develop a team is difficult. Few managers and team leaders have the background and competencies to do so.

In the special case of virtual teams, initial team development activities to create the collaborative and sharing project culture is done most effectively in a face-to-face venue. Project staff understand how important their contributions to the project are and want to be able to trust and rely on the other team members to fulfill their roles to reach their project goals and objectives successfully. Having provided virtual team building and development activities to virtual teams in global organizations, participant team members reported to this author what they consider to be the most important elements of the developmental activities and meetings. They stated that getting to know their distant virtual team members as real people, on a face-to-face basis, was one of the most important issues of virtual team development. Establishing a culture of trust and collaboration were two critical outcomes of the virtual team development sessions. The responsibility for these outcomes falls on the shoulders of the project manager. Alternatives to face-to-face team development activities are few, namely, video-teleconferences and video-computer meetings. The critical variable is being the ability to capture the body language, voice tonality, and facial expressions (as discussed previously).

> E-mail and cell phone communications alone are insufficient. Face to face [sic] time, in-person presentations and other live activities cannot be eliminated from organizations. This goes for both internal and external communications. We have increased travel budgets for virtual/remote teams to address this very problem. (Moore 2002, entry for May 11, 2002)

The above quote records the observations of a project management student about a large multinational organization where this critical need is being addressed.

Team building for both virtual and face-to-face teams can be in the form of productive exercises to develop a team culture. Exercises that lead to more effective meetings include developing ground rules for running meetings (see a more detailed discussion of ground rules below), and activities for developing a common understanding of team leadership includes team building components such introductions of team members, breaking the team into small working groups of three to five members, and consensus building (e.g., Rosen 2000). The understanding of team leadership leads to a better appreciation of the role of the project manager and subsequent benefits to meetings and other project activities. There are many other traditional team-building activities that are useful. Many are useful for particular team needs both at the start of the project and during later phases of a project.

One critical factor for having effective meetings and overall project management performance is appropriate training for the project manager. As with other aspects of project management, understanding the dynamics of meetings, dealing with individual and group dynamics, demonstrating leadership, and establishing and maintaining individual relationships are competencies that require specific training and educational opportunities to develop. Unfortunately, top-performing staff armed only with technical experience and skills are rewarded for their experience and skills by promotion to supervisory, and, later, to managerial positions. Hence, these excellent staff members are no longer doing the staff work and are unprepared to do the key managerial activities related to effective meetings management, or other management related tasks. This sounds very much like the Peter Principle, which states that "In a hierarchy every employee tends to rise to his level of incompetence" (Peter 1972, p. 4). Peter explained:

> Each hierarchy consists of an arrangement of ranks, grades, or classes to which the individual may be assigned. If he is competent he may contribute to the positive achievement of mankind. Promotion up the ladder may remove him from this level of competence and place him at his level of incompetence.
>
> For every job that exists in the world there is someone, somewhere, who cannot do it. Given sufficient time and enough promotions, he will arrive eventually at that job and there he will remain, habitually bungling the job, frustrating his coworkers, and eroding the efficiency of the organization." (Peter 1972, p. 4)

Management development and education for the next promotion or level in the hierarchy is one type of activity and investment by the organization that can lead to more effective management of meetings. Usually, an engineer or chemist or nurse does not get involved in calling staff meetings until they become supervisors or managers. Therefore, it behooves organizations to prepare these technical people to become more focused on interpersonal skills and management competencies, including how to call, run, and follow-up effective staff meetings.

Since often the project manager has been promoted from a "technical" level in the hierarchy, education and development need to focus on facilitation skills, interpersonal relationships and behavior, leadership development, supervision skills, group dynamics, plus the usual management courses. Supervision and management behaviors may take the incumbent away from the technical issues for the first time in her/his career. The focus on the project and management is usually considered to be less technical for a manager than for a staff member. Competencies for managers have traditionally focused on those listed in table 8.2, which are common educational areas in M.B.A. programs. As part of a developmental program for up-and-coming staff, these areas would be worth the organization's investment to develop well-rounded project managers.

TABLE 8-2. Traditional management competencies

Competencies
• Planning
• Organizing
• Directing
• Coordinating tasks and people
• Staffing
• Reporting
• Budgeting

The traditional management competencies listed in table 8.2 focus on getting the task/work accomplished. One additional area for managerial development includes those skills related to interpersonal behavior and staff motivation, as mentioned previously. Research into leadership behavior has consistently found two critical behavioral variables for managerial leaders, findings that go back to early studies conducted by Iowa State University in the 1930s (Lewin 1939; Lewin and Lippett 1938; Lewin, Lippett, and White 1939). Researchers at Ohio State University and the University of Michigan found similar behaviors of effective managerial leaders. In addition to a job orientation, get-the-job-done factor, these studies identify behaviors that demonstrate the importance of having a sensitivity to subordinates, in which the manager respects the subordinates ideas and interacts in a supportive manner with them. Ohio State researchers defined this dimension as "consideration," while the Michigan researchers discussed "employee-centered" behaviors (Hemphill and Coons 1957; Bowers and Seashore 1966). Later work at the University of Texas, by Blake and Mouton, resulted in a two-dimensional theory of leadership called the "Leadership Grid" (Blake and Mouton 1985). This was built on the earlier work at Ohio State and Michigan Universities. Again, a factor analogous to the consideration/employee-centered factors was identified (Daft 1999; Yukl 1994)

The project manager or other meeting convener is responsible for conducting an effective meeting. Several key competencies are useful for more effective meetings. These include conflict resolution skills, a focus on process facilitation, and the need to support the effective meeting culture in order to exploit all creativity and knowledge inherent among the meeting participants. Effective leadership skills will motivate the participants and support the team culture unique to each project team. Team task functions, and team building and maintenance functions, include those skills analogous to the two primary leadership behavioral factors described previously.

Behaviors related to team task functions include:

- *Initiating*—proposing tasks or goals, defining a group problem, suggesting a procedure or ideas for solving a problem.
- *Information or opinion seeking*—requesting facts, seeking relevant information about group concern, stating a belief, giving suggestions or ideas.
- *Information or opinion giving*—offering facts, providing relevant information about group concern, stating a belief, giving suggestions or ideas.
- *Clarifying or elaborating*—interpreting or reflecting ideas and suggestions, clearing up confusion, indicating alternatives and issues before the group, giving examples.
- *Summarizing*—pulling together related ideas, restating suggestions after the participants have discussed them, offering a decision or conclusion for the participants to accept or reject.
- *Consensus testing*—sending up "trial balloons" to see if the participants are near a conclusion, checking with the participants to see how much agreement has been reached.
- *Energizing*—prodding/motivating the participants to action or decision, attempting to stimulate them to "greater" activity or to activity of a "higher quality."

Behaviors related to team building and maintenance functions include:

- *Encouraging*—being friendly, warm, and responsive to others; accepting others and their contributions; regarding others by giving them an opportunity for recognition.
- *Expressing group feelings*—sensing feeling, mood, and relationships within the group; sharing one's own feelings with others by giving them an opportunity for recognition.
- *Harmonizing*—attempting to reconcile disagreements, reducing tension, getting people to explore their differences.
- *Compromising*—when one's idea is involved in a conflict, offering to compromise own position; admitting error.
- *Gate-keeping*—attempting to keep communication channels open, facilitating the participation of others, suggesting procedures for sharing opportunity to discuss group problems.

The PMBOK devotes a five-page section—Section 2.4—to a discussion of "key general management skills that are *highly likely to affect most projects* and . . . are well documented in the general management literature, and their application is fundamentally the same on a project" (PMI 2000, pp. 21–24).

Structure and control of the meeting are very important in order to make sure the meeting's goals are accomplished. The facilitator can control the flow of the discussion by keeping focused. Using the following stages of discussion can help: (1) state the proposal/describe the situation/present the data, (2) present the analysis and its methodology, (3) discuss the analysis results, (4) develop solutions/possibilities/further analytic needs, and (5) decide on an outcome/next steps. We see similar stages of a discussion in courtrooms, where one must follow certain rules and procedures. However, with proper planning, information exchange, and facilitation on the part of the convener, an effective meeting is certainly possible.

Many meetings are held without any careful forethought, planning, or an agenda. The real reason for the meeting is unknown to the participants. Planning results in precise meeting objectives, why the meeting is needed, and determines what subjects are to be covered. Without an agenda, participants attend only because they are required to do so, and, without any foreknowledge as to why the meeting is being called, they also are unprepared to participate in the meeting. This results in an ineffective and unproductive meeting.

In order to establish proper motivation and staff commitment to the meeting and team, the convener must pass out a detailed agenda that will contain the information necessary to prepare the attendees for the meeting so they will be prepared to participate and be productive. Figure 8.2 shows a sample agenda template and definitions of its contents. Using the Meeting Planning Guide communicates to participants exactly what is going to happen. Prior to meeting, each participant will know date, time, location, duration of the meeting; reason for the meeting; goal/outcomes expected from the meeting; designated recorder (unless a secretary is available); attendees and how to contact them; and the agenda items and how long is allotted for each item. Minutes from the last meeting are attached.

Participants will be prepared to work toward a known goal/outcome during the meeting, know how much discussion time is available for each item, and be able to contact others who may have useful information to share or contribute prior to the meeting. They will be ready to work and not perceive the meeting to be just another waste of time.

Additional planning considerations are: availability of appropriate meeting space and technologies; time to schedule meeting—day of week, time of day, discussion times for agenda items; frequency of meetings—calendar and project plan task events.

Regularly scheduled meetings are often unfocused and do not have any goals or outcomes defined. Conveners just "play it by ear" or go around to each attendee and see if they have any items to be discussed. This is usually descriptive of many regular Monday morning meetings where the project manager wants everyone to contribute their experiences from their tasks and to learn from others. Often these are the anecdotal methods of knowledge transference, as discussed previously, and they can be quite informative. Information, as previously discussed, that would not normally be sought after nor offered in a project review meeting often is shared, and much learning occurs for later use on the project or on other projects. However, participants must be focused and encouraged to participate to make this work. When meeting participants see clear goals, they perceive the meeting to be more productive and an effective use of time. For this type of meeting to occur, there must be an established "effective

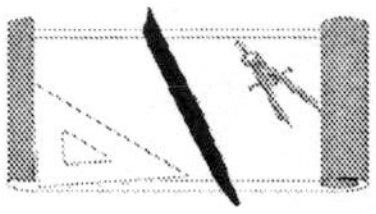

MEETING PLANNING GUIDE

Meeting Title: _____

Meeting Called By: _____

Meeting Date: _____

Meeting Times: Start - _____   End - _____

Location: _____

Purpose: _____

Desired Results/Goals: _____

Designated Recorder: _____

Attendees / Phone Numbers / E-mail Addresses:

_____   _____   _____

_____   _____   _____

_____   _____   _____

MEETING AGENDA

(time allotted for discussion)

_____

_____

_____

SEE MINUTES FROM THE LAST MEETING

(ATTACHED)

FIGURE 8-2. Sample agenda template—meeting planning guide.

meetings culture" where team members are willing to discuss any and all project activities they experience and want to hear other team members' experiences. When criticized about overscheduling these regular Monday morning meetings, the convener often says that it is necessary to keep the meeting on the team's calendar so people will be available when it is needed. The response to this statement might be: "Okay, keep the meeting on the schedule, but cancel it if there is nothing to discuss." By canceling the "regular" meeting, the convener will get the respect of the project staff for realizing the time spent at such a meeting would not be productive.

The facilitator often does not maintain order and/or stick to the agenda. No one enjoys sitting in a meeting where there is constant arguing, sidebar conversations, yelling out, or general chaos. When the manager or facilitator tries to maintain structure or order and cannot, the participants lose interest in the meeting topics and get nothing out of the meeting. Without orderly direction and facilitation of the meeting, the meeting itself becomes a victim of the chaos, and nothing is accomplished.

Meetings accomplish much more business when the facilitator follows the agenda and there are group norms or ground rules for attending meetings established when the project team first convened at the start of the project. As part of the team-building activities that occur during the first project meetings, brainstorming and establishing consensus on a list of ground rules or norms for the meetings will serve multiple purposes. First, it will get people talking with the rest of the staff. Second, this exercise will get commitment for their ideas about teamwork. Third, the outcome of this exercise will be a set of ground rules for conducting business, including meetings that will serve as a set of behavioral guidelines for the length of the project. Examples of meeting ground rules are: arrive to and start meetings on time, no sidebar conversations during the meeting, it is okay to disagree, do not interrupt the speaker, and maintain a parking lot for ideas that should be visited at a later time.

Meeting attendees/participants can negatively influence the outcome of meetings. If too few staff attend the meeting, then information to be conveyed will not be heard with a single ear. Secondary communications must follow the meeting to ensure every staff member gets the intended information. This reduces the effectiveness of the communications and renders the meeting to be of minimum value and wasteful. Staff who skip out of meetings (i.e., to take or make phone calls) or spend a lot of time outside the meeting room during a meeting, also are reducing the effectiveness of any meeting they are missing. They could miss critical information that might help them to better carry out their assignments as specified in their contracts and performance standards. They might also cause information they possess not to be shared with team members who need it.

Having the correct staff present at meetings is critical for determining the success of particular meetings. Even when the project manager follows proper meeting planning and other procedures, if the wrong people attend the meeting, then all will experience an ineffective meeting. Meetings are called to address specific issues about the project. Therefore, proper staffing at meetings means that those key team members involved with the situation under discussion at the meeting are present to lead the discussion. If a team member has noted a problem and has written it up for discussion at the meeting, that team member is there to present the issues and data to the rest of the team for analysis and decisions. If that team member's task leader presents the issues and data, then other meeting participants might feel that the presentation could be missing crucial information and an improper decision or solution would be forthcoming.

Another example would be that a statistician is needed to explain a procedure or analysis, but the only person there is the staff member who noticed the data issue. Other participants might feel frustrated in not being able to understand the task leader's interpretation of what the statistician did with the data. Lack of clarity of explanations presented at a meeting makes that meeting perceived as ineffective and a waste of time.

Additionally, there will be a lack of participation and involvement on the part of the participants and reduced follow-up on their part. If the people who have action items from earlier work to follow-up with are not present at the meeting, then the meeting should be rescheduled or new assignments made for those action items. In both instances, the staff who performed the work are best able to present the work to the meeting. These staff have the most intimate knowledge of the topic at hand and are best able to field questions and comments regarding their work.

Poor record keeping can result in a considerable waste of time and the perception of a very ineffective meeting. Included as poor record keeping are generalized instead of detailed minutes of meetings, and file copies of handouts and paper records, not electronic records. This situation results in a meeting that spends much of its scheduled meeting time arguing over what happened at the last meeting: who said what, what was decided, how the decision was reached, what the action items were, and who was in charge of which action items. This wastes time discussing those issues a second time, and has a demoralizing effect on the project staff. Poor record keeping also poses serious questions over the management of the project when auditors look for information to support project decisions and rules.

Figure 8.3 is a suggested template for recording the meeting's business and minutes. As a communications tool, such a postmeeting information sheet will give references for the staff as to what was accomplished, what decisions were made, action items and who will be working on those items for future meetings, and due dates for the action items. As noted on the last line of figure 8.3, minutes of the meeting are also attached. Historical data from the project can be easily stored and referenced should that be necessary. Discussions leading to decisions can be tracked, and a knowledge base for future projects can be built from this data regarding best practices. Audit trails are easy to follow and all project information is in one storage location. Figures 8.2 and 8.3 add to the quality and effectiveness of project communications and historical records as well as improving the quality of meetings.

Technology can play an important role in determining meeting effectiveness. For virtual project teams, it is crucial to have the proper technology for all team members to access, especially for virtual meetings. Whether it is a chat room format, video teleconferencing, Internet based, Intranet based or teleconferencing, the use of technology requires competence on the part of the users. Hardware and software instruction is always required for new users. For other meeting formats, it is incumbent that the proper equipment is available to meet

MEETING OUTCOMES RECORD

Meeting Title: _____

Meeting Called By: _____

Meeting Date: _____

Purpose: _____

Recorder: _____

ATTENDEES / PHONE NUMBERS / E-MAIL ADDRESSES:

_____ _____ _____

_____ _____ _____

_____ _____ _____

_____ _____ _____

_____ _____ _____

ACTION ITEMS / PERSON RESPONSIBLE / REPORT DATE:

_____ _____ _____

_____ _____ _____

_____ _____ _____

SEE MINUTES AND HANDOUTS OF MEETING

(ATTACHED)

FIGURE 8-3.   Sample template for recording meeting business—meeting outcomes record.

the needs of the meeting and that the equipment is functioning correctly. As part of the meeting planning process, the convener is responsible for meeting the requests of presenters and other participants. When the meeting runs smoothly, the participants have less trouble staying focused and will increase their participation.

WHAT ARE CRITERIA FOR DETERMINING EFFECTIVE MEETINGS, AND HOW DO WE KNOW WHEN OUR MEETINGS ARE EFFECTIVE AND SUCCESSFUL?

There are probably no exact methodologies for guaranteeing an effective meeting. To facilitate a meeting that is deemed effective requires an effort to control and demonstrate multiple factors and behaviors. The above discussion looked at what can make meetings ineffective and what can be done to address those issues. It takes much more than simply addressing those issues to conduct a meeting that is productive and perceived by the attendees to be effective. It takes a concerted effort by the project manager to organize and facilitate the meeting, and to motivate and lead the staff during project work outside of the meeting times.

But to evaluate organizational performance, valid performance measures are required. The most obvious is to ask the team members to evaluate the meetings and address their concerns about what they perceived to be problems affecting meetings' effectiveness. In order to measure improvement over time, it is suggested that the project manager utilize an attitude scale. This type of instrument is first given after several project meetings are held. The participants fill out the evaluation anonymously. The data from this first administration serves as baseline data from which improvement can be demonstrated. The instrument is then analyzed and discussed by the team. Then at project milestones, or every five or six meetings, the instrument is given again and the results are compared to the original baseline data and data from previous meetings. With proper analysis and graphic demonstration of the data, the project manager and team can see where improvement occurred and where there was none. Most inventories are comprised of several subscales that are more focused on identify more specific problems. Other measures of performance include:

- attendance statistics (% of staff attending),
- number of attendees who leave before formal end of meeting,
- on-time record of starting meetings,
- length of meetings,
- the number of meetings held per time period (i.e., day, week, month), and
- work deadline accuracy.

These, and others, are all clear signs and behaviors associated with ineffective meetings. Project managers would improve team relations as well as their meetings by asking their project team members face-to-face what could be done to improve their meetings and following up on their suggestions, if reasonable. All can be utilized to get feedback from the project management team. Just as with any organizational measurement, these data are used to track and continually improve meetings activities.

SUMMARY

Effective meetings can lead to improved project performance, but they require a lot of work from the project manager to make them successful. This chapter has addressed five key question areas to provide an understanding of the importance, complexity, and difficulty associated with leading project meetings:

Why are meetings so important to Project Management?

What are some reasons for having project meetings?

Do we need a staff meeting to conduct business at this time?

Why are so few project meetings effective, and what can we do about them?

What are the criteria for determining effective meetings, and how do we know when our meetings are effective and successful?

The questions and issues raised can provide guidance and "food for thought" for project managers as they plan and conduct their meetings as part of their project plan. As such, this chapter also serves to create an awareness of effective meetings management from a project management perspective.

Most important, this chapter is an attempt to make readers aware of an area of project management that is often ignored for team and individual developmental purposes. Two courses in a graduate project management master's degree program focus specifically on these key areas of team performance and management (Web site: http://www.sbpm.gwu.edu/mspm/). The program is offered in two modes of delivery: on campus and distance education, both serving full-time and part-time students, many of whom are active, full-time professionals working in project management. Often their responses to these courses concern the fact that no one ever mentioned these critical issues to them and that managing people is often identified as the most difficult part of their project work.

BIBLIOGRAPHY

Blake, R., and J. Mouton. 1985. *The Managerial Grid III.* Houston: Gulf.

Bowers, D., and S. Seashore. 1966. Predicting Organizational Effectiveness with a Four-Factor Theory of Leadership. *Administrative Science Quarterly* 11:238–63.

Daft, R. 1999. *Leadership: Theory and Practice.* Fort Worth, Texas: Dryden Press.

Hemphill, J., and A. Coons. 1957. Development of the Leader Behavior Description Questionnaire. In *Leader Behavior: Its Description and Measurement,* edited by R. Stogdill and A. Coons. Columbus: Ohio State University, Bureau of Business Research.

Lewin, K. 1939. Field Theory and Experiment in Social Psychology: Concepts and Methods. *American Journal of Sociology* 44:868–96.

Lewin, K., and R. Lippert. 1938. An Experimental Approach to the Study of Autocracy and Democracy: A Preliminary Note. *Sociometry* 1:292–300.

Lewin, K., R. Lippert, and R. White. 1939. Patterns of Aggressive Behavior in Experimentally Created Social Climates. *Journal of Social Psychology* 10:271–301.

Moore, J. 2002. Management Science 201.DE, Course Learning Journal. The George Washington University, Program in Project Management.

Peter, L. 1972. *The Peter Prescription.* New York: Bantam Books.

Project Management Institute. 2000. *A Guide to the Project Management Body of Knowledge.* Newtown Square, Pa.: Project Management Institute.

Rosen, T. 2000. Understanding Leadership for Team Development. In D. Saunders and Smalley, N. *The International Simulation & Gaming Yearbook, Volume 8, Simulations and Games for Transition and Change.* London: Kogan Page.

Yukl, G. (1994). *Leadership in organizations.* Englewood Cliffs, N.J.: Prentice-Hall.

9

Scaling the Water Cooler

Digital Storytelling for Knowledge Continuity

MICHAEL D. KULL

If you want to teach people a new way of thinking, don't bother trying to teach them. Instead, give them a tool, the use of which will lead to new ways of thinking.
—Buckminister Fuller

BEHIND THE SCENES

The metaphor of Hollywood has been applied in organizational theory to describe organizations as project-based, virtual organizations that come together temporarily to create a product and then disband. Every movie produced represents a collaborative effort of not fewer than three distinct entities. The metaphor also carries a dramaturgical connotation, one adopted at companies such as Disney that have adopted terms such as "cast," "crew," and "production" to refer to elements of organizational "performances." Today, the metaphor can be extended further through the arrival of DVD movies with their accompanying special features. "The Making of . . ." documentaries provide an inside look at the project environment behind moviemaking. These behind-the-scenes exposures of movie production reveal the same project management issues faced by project management professionals everywhere. These documentaries uncover the stories behind the story portrayed in the movie, and act as a kind of informal after-action review or lessons learned session with an important difference: these stories are captured on video.

The need to document project work applies to all industries and organizations, especially when so much consideration is given to problems of continuity and change. In the past decade these problems have led to developments in knowledge management, and more recently to storytelling as a technique for sharing knowledge. In several progressive organizations, it is now standard practice to document the knowledge gained throughout a project's life. Yet in most project environments of mainstream organizations, knowledge management practices still remain the exception. Activities that include conducting post-project knowledge-capture sessions, interviewing project staff to gather lessons learned, producing video reports on intangible assets or intellectual capital, and so on—generally receive little to no managerial attention.

Efforts by scholars and practitioners in knowledge management have provided a coherent rationale for why such activities are essential for generating repeatable success. Knowledge sharing results in the transfer of best practices across an enterprise, and knowledge creation results in new strategies for adapting to change. At the same time, recent efforts in corporate storytelling have reminded people that knowledge is far more than documents and data. Knowledge arises from the lived experiences of individuals and is rooted in the collective stories of communities of practice.

Given our culture's absorption in television and film, it seems ironic that business practices for documenting organizational knowledge rarely include video. At the same time, new digital media technologies have virtually eliminated the barriers to video production and distribution to the point that nearly all organizations can afford to produce their own "Behind the Scenes" stories and project documentaries.

Digital storytelling is defined here as the use of digital video for capturing and sharing narratives that reflect the knowledge essential for organizational continuity and innovation. It occurs in enterprises of all shapes and sizes, from small start-up firms to large government agencies. For example, when the General Services Administration wanted to capture the story behind a particularly successful partnership that involved massive logistical support for the U.S. Census Bureau in 2000, the team met to tell what happened and recorded it on video. They wanted to capture the essence of what made for a successful partnership in order to recall what was most effective and to communicate new ways of doing business. In another case, a small consulting firm wanted to capture on video the knowledge of professional services experts who specialize in biotechnology. This allowed managers of start-up biotech firms to focus more funding on the science, rather than on learning the business from scratch.

Although the intuitiveness of sharing knowledge through video may appear obvious, the issue of understanding what knowledge is truly important to capture for the organization remains problematic. The last thing a project manager needs is a staff member running around haphazardly with a video camera. In part, problems arise from difficulties in connecting organizational strategy to relevant knowledge. The word "relevant" suggests that value may be attributed to knowledge, but knowing the value of past, current, and future knowledge across changing market, technological, and social factors is an exercise in itself. Problems also arise in communicating stories concisely. In order to make a point, illustrate an example, present a specific case, or share an embryonic idea, professionals seldom resort to charts or graphs; rather, they tell stories. However, stories told by employees and experts are not easily reducible to bullet-points or spreadsheets. Moreover, knowledgeable people are often aware that their knowledge might be useful to someone else in a different context. Finally, opportunities for knowledge sharing are often serendipitous—casual conversations held in the cafeteria, accidental insights gleaned from conference attendees, chance meetings in the hallways, and dialogue around the watercooler. The essence of a useful story lies in the contextual details that are left out of formal documentation. Digital storytelling extends the reach of the storyteller and her audience in countless ways, but in ways that tend to be more "illuminating" than "enabling." That is, the technology is more effective at revealing interesting practices, insights, and beliefs than it is at capturing quantifiable data. Getting people to use video has also posed problems. Luckily, video opens up a third category of incentive—besides money and power—that organizations can use to reward employees: celebrity. Video lets individuals and project teams become famous for their star performances. Video celebrates efforts at knowledge sharing by recognizing visually the project champions who weave compelling stories of success.

The usefulness of the idea that knowledge is embedded in the collective stories an organization tells itself about itself depends on a culture that respects the past and responds to opportunities to learn from it. In an age of discontinuity, the ability of an organization to provide a sense of continuity is arguably the source of future success. While knowledge management has tried to address the problem of how to amplify collective knowledge, the tools offered by vendors tend to suggest that the solution lies in better information management. A growing divide between knowledge management concepts and knowledge management tools is exacerbated when vendors claim to offer solutions to wrongly defined problems. On the one hand, information technology implementations are often seen as the core to sharing knowledge across an enterprise. On the other hand, it is largely recognized that much of the intangible yet essential knowledge of an organization is largely implicit and uncodified in any form that is easily transferable. In other words, while research and intuition suggest that people often share critical knowledge through stories told around the watercooler, as a knowledge management technology, the watercooler does not scale very well.

CORPORATE EPISTEMOLOGY

In the 1999 movie *The Matrix,* the hero is provided a clue about the reality of his world and a choice: two pills, red and blue, each symbolizing a path before him. The blue pill will let him to return to his old life to believe whatever he wishes to believe. The red pill will allow him to stay in Wonderland and to see just how deep the rabbit hole goes. To the audience the decision is clear; if this story is going anywhere, he had better choose the red pill. When he swallows the red pill, he awakens to discover he has been living inside a dream. Choosing between alternative worldviews in knowledge management is like that choice between the blue pill and the red pill. Understanding the power of the story requires a philosophy of knowledge that is less about representing knowledge in data and statistics and more about revealing interesting perspectives.

People's stories are their knowledge. Stories express collective experiences, values, theories, and interpretations. In knowledge management parlance, storytelling conveys best practices, communicates intangible measures of performance, and helps to leverage intellectual capital. Storytelling does these things because it is a practice deeply rooted in the tribal nature of human organization. New media brings inexpensive, innovative technology to this ancient art form. Why do more organizations not turn the camera lens on their own activities and communities of practice? Unfortunately, the reason is not a simple lack of awareness or access to new media technologies. It reflects a much deeper problem in the philosophy of knowledge.

When it comes to managing information, it can be argued that organizations historically have not done even that very well, so to spend time and allocate resources to "soft" areas such as building a philosophical understanding of the nature of knowledge makes all but the most enlightened leaders squirm. Perhaps the soft stuff is the hard stuff after all. The ability of an enterprise to leverage soft knowledge and learn faster than its competitors may be the only source of sustainable advantage in the future. Yet money is poured into building information systems, not into creating environments for learning and reflection. Some organizations have devoted resources toward epistemology—questions of the nature of knowledge—and there are managers in a few enterprises, including Ford, with the word "epistemologist" in their titles. For most organizations to largely ignore this area of strategic capability because it involves talking about soft stuff suggests that perhaps there are too many blue pills in circulation.

The great idea from philosophy resurrected by knowledge management is that individual and social perspective matters more than we generally acknowledge. Thomas Kuhn pointed out that more than one interpretation can always be drawn from any set of data, and that those interpretations have more to do with an observer's paradigm than with the characteristics of the data (Kuhn 1970). "I'll see it when I believe it," is a more apt way of explaining how in making decisions, people often rely on unarticulated beliefs and gut feel when determining what knowledge is relevant to a situation. Moreover, people hold tacit knowledge and can articulate only a portion of that knowledge (Polanyi 1967). These ideas convey the same point: knowledge management is not about getting the right information to the right people at the right time; it is about enabling people to interpret what they observe and empowering them to use their judgment when confronted with the observations and interpretations of the people around them who matter.

This perspective of the world—that reality is inherently subjective and the best we can do is share our subjective beliefs with each other—is called *interpretivism*. Stories are drawn from the process of interpretation itself, so that every artifact of culture, every document, data point, theory, and consultant report do not simply furnish material for a story, they are stories. Unless a story can be constructed from data, the data are meaningless. Data such as stock indexes tell stories: stories of growth, stories of stagnation, and stories of decline. Even data considered "hard," such as the automated recording of a transaction, remains useless unless a story can be constructed of why the transaction took place and how that transaction makes sense in some meaningful context. As we begin to understand the world as an amalgam of interpretations, the deep complexity of human knowledge begins to sink in. One begins to wonder if the stuffy college professor who questioned the existence of the chair he was sitting on might actually have been on to something.

Central to the myth that information technologies alone can create and share human knowledge is the idea that if people have the right information they will make better decisions. It is assumed that managers can display omniscience by predicting correctly which information to distribute as well as to whom it should be distributed and when. Suggesting that the solution to this is to construct a repository or Web site avoids dealing with the underlying fact that people will apply different knowledge to a situation given the same information. Moreover, it posits that the quality of human judgment can be measured directly at the time of information acquisition—that there is always a "right" answer that can be derived from information.

This notion, that there is always an a priori "right" answer or a "best" way is called *positivism* or *objectivism* and is the antithesis to interpretivism. The basic tenet is that there is objective truth somewhere "out there," and it is only a matter of diligence until it is revealed. If in reviewing our actions we find that we have not discovered truth, or our knowledge seems to have been incorrect or unwise, then it must be because we did not try hard enough or spend enough money on the problem. The entire information technology industry is predicated on this philosophy, and it is arguably a main reason why so many implementations fail. Information technologies can store and retrieve numbers, text, images, and other representations, but they do not store the ability to make sense.

This philosophical discussion is foundational to the corresponding recognition of storytelling as an acceptable and valuable practice in organizations. Good stories are hard to quantify, do not store experience in the same way that computers store data, nor are they asynchronous mediums in which meaning is simply delivered to a listener like information is delivered to a desktop. Rather, stories depend on non-verbal elements and the ability of the storyteller to shape a story. Increasingly, this philosophy is backed by neuroscience and reveals that the rabbit hole is much deeper than we imagined.

Organizations are learning that it is futile to attempt to capture all the knowledge from the minds of its members, but instead should work to amplify the ability of all members to access knowledgeable people and their knowledge artifacts (e.g., documents, presentations, spreadsheets). The idea is to connect the "haves" with the "have-nots." But what does it mean for a person to "have" knowledge? What is it that a knower possesses that is so valuable? What is stored in the heads of people that cannot be captured objectively and uploaded? If we cannot capture knowledge objectively and statistically, what is it good for? How do we catch this white rabbit? The use of language such as "store," "capture," and "retrieve" perpetuates the illusion that knowledge is a tangible thing—something with an ontology that can be forced through electronic pipelines.

WHAT KNOWLEDGE DO STORIES STORE?

There is little argument that codified knowledge sharing has not served civilization. One need only look to architecture, manufacturing, and library science to see the profound effect the printing press and the Internet have had in civilization. Computers and communications make it seem natural that we should automate data and document sharing so that others may benefit from receiving this information.

But when did the word "document" become a noun instead of a verb? Today the term "document" refers to paper or the electronic simulation of paper that encode information. We rely on paper document and Web pages today because until now this was the only media readily available for representing knowledge. Video transforms the meaning of "document." People like to tell stories and listen to the stories of others. Stories provide the opportunity for people to engage their interpretive nature and gives them a way to be creative, to reshape a story to fit their experience, and to take ownership of a story in its retelling.

If the brain were a logical system, it seems there would be no need for stories. We would simply store information in memory and recall it at will when required. This remains the prevailing notion of the purpose of knowledge management. But intelligent people do not do this. Instead, they create interpretations of their experiences and those of others, check their interpretations with credible people, and revise their interpretations according to the feeling they have of the possible consequences. We term this process "experience." Research from the neurosciences supports the claim that the brain is an emotional system and the simulation of logic a kind of by-product of meaning-making through the emotions (Damasio 1994). To evaluate consequences means to place value on a future desired state. One cannot "value" something without a visceral response. Just as the brain is less a logical system than it is an emotional one, organizations, too, are not logical systems but emotional systems. That is, people do not form strategy or reinvent business processes or hire and fire without evaluating these activities against a valued future state. Value, not logic, drives organizations. Therefore, an enterprise can be thought of as a community of purpose that reflects the basic nature of people who value certain ends to band together in order to achieve these ends.

The most important organizational knowledge is reflected in the experiences of its people. Stories give a face to knowledge and lead a listener down the road that the storyteller has traveled before. Though we might be tempted to state all knowledge as value propositions, or a set of principles such as, "Our company rewards honest, open communication," this does little to convey what needs to be done. When a story is told, listeners can derive lessons for themselves. While a simple story may contain more words than can comfortably fit on the back of a business card, the cultural values assimilated will figure far more prominently in future behavior.

Stories provide a way of dealing with organizational life by embedding scripts in context. A script is a set of expectations about what will happen next in a well-understood situation. In launching a business, we might rely on a script that reads, "First, we need to get funding. Next, we need to do some marketing. Then, let's hire the right people for the job." Scripts are not rules, but more akin to narrative plots. Scripts help to orient actions and to understand the actions of others in a particular context (Shank 1990).

Context is a term used to mean that people relate what they are told to what they already know. When rules or data are presented without context, a person cannot judge their value. Without context, rules and policies can be applied inappropriately and relevant information ignored. Storytelling provides a way of presenting scripts to people so that they "get it." However, like most of human endeavor, relying on scripts is a balancing act. The more scripts a person knows, the greater her range of comfortable action in a common context. On the other hand, the more scripts a person relies on, the more limited she may become in handling novel situations or situations that are "out-of-context." Not every project experience makes a good story, but every good story marks a memorable set of scripts. Thus, it may be said that a person who learns well is able to modify their scripts when hearing or telling a compelling story. Stories allow people to interpret knowledge relevance by tapping into the value context (Gabriel 2000). In Specific,

- *Intention*—stories attribute motive to actions and identify the main actors.
- *Causation*—stories provide a connection between temporal events.
- *Credibility*—stories offer a way to evaluate the propositions of others.
- *Morality*—stories help us recognize the heroes and villains in a situation.
- *Connection*—stories define the qualities of concepts and relationships.
- *Setting*—stories explain the organization and its business environment.
- *Emotion*—stories distinguish content and create a context for value.

Knowledge is the mosaic of interpretation through the stories we tell ourselves about ourselves. One may imagine the mind not as a supercomputer that stores a multitude of scripts, but as a visual medium that both responds to the world and creates it. The knowledge management challenge then is not necessarily to catalogue and index scripts but to create environments where stories can be evoked and reenacted. While stories help organizations make sense of their projects and activities, misconceptions of the value of storytelling persist. Table 9.1 presents several of these misconceptions and how they might be reconceived through an interpretive lens.

TABLE 9-1. Storytelling: misconceptions and reconceptions

Misconception	Reconception
Stories can be separated effectively from the storyteller.	The way a story is told is essential for a listener to make meaning.
Stories contain knowledge that can be transmitted in the retelling.	Stories convey the context in which knowledge may be understood.
Storytelling is a one-way method for those who have knowledge to enlighten those without knowledge.	Storytelling is an act of meaning that depends on both the storyteller and the audience and reflects a dialectic process.
Storytelling is a "soft" skill out of place in modern business; people who advocate storytelling are usually touchy-feely types and not serious professionals.	Storytelling is a "hard" executive skill to master and essential in creating compelling business plans, launching initiatives, and learning from successes and failures.
The effectiveness of knowledge transfer through storytelling cannot be measured objectively or accounted for quantitatively.	The mainstream business community does not accept measures of the intangible benefits gained through storytelling.
Stories are generally too long or amateurish to be useful.	Rules out of context may be too abridged to be applied intelligently by professionals.

DIGITAL STORYTELLING IN PRACTICE

As organizations and communities become video-enabled, more attention will be given to the affective and intangible dimensions of management. In project management, we see more visibly that project success does not necessarily mean meeting the triple constraints of time, budget, and requirements, but rather depends far more on customer satisfaction and building relationships. A project can look "successful" on paper, but if the customer is not happy, the project has failed. Conversely, a project may be over-budget, over-time, and deliver a gold-plated toaster, but if the customer is happy and the customer returns, the project has succeeded. The intangible and contextual dimensions of trust, perseverance, intuition, and so on, can be illuminated through digital storytelling.

As more organizations adopt digital storytelling, the second-order social effects of this technology are difficult to predict, as are the cultural issues that will arise from incorporating digital video into project execution. The cultural dimensions that currently create the most debate surround three areas: privacy, accountability, and publicity.

Privacy

Digital video is an amplifying technology in the sense that management practices, good or bad, will tend to be made better or worse. If people see management as a "big brother" interested primarily in punishing people who act unconventionally or break rules that they see as arbitrary and bureaucratic, video will make things worse. The intangible benefits that accrue are linked to cultures that see video as a boon to enterprise knowledge sharing and project success. Organizations that respect individual creativity will use digital storytelling to enhance the experience of novel work. The greatest challenges come from constrains imposed by legal departments of organizations, which will generally sacrifice innovation to any legal threat, real or imagined.

Accountability

A culture that rewards creativity and sharing will also reward risk-taking and learning. This means that failure is not seen necessarily as incompetence, but as a learning investment and a form of experimentation. Traditional business culture still defines excellence as superior execution, not superior learning ability. The best learners are not necessarily the top performers, but the most improved over time. An organization that captures people's mistakes on video will need to define this practice as one that helps identify areas for improvement, not for placing blame. Mistakes will happen in any organization occupied by human beings; the trick is not to avoid mistakes but to avoid making the same old mistakes again. In this context, digital video is a tool to help individuals and project teams improve performance in a manner similar to the way football teams rely on video to improve their performance between seasons.

Publicity

Video interviewees ("talent") are notorious for being terrible judges of themselves on camera. Video professionals frequently hear talent say things like, "Oh, I sound like an idiot!" or "I look fat on video," and "No one is going to see this, right?" It is no wonder that talent are asked routinely to sign away rights to content. However, talent who want nonmonetary rewards often see digital video as a means for gaining celebrity. In addition, the production quality is not "slick"—rather, the idiosyncrasies that individuals show on camera are part of the "real" look and feel of authentic experience. If an organization rewards authenticity and expertise, style is less important than content. Experts rarely need to be trained to be passionate about their work or emphasize the importance of their specialties, projects, and key roles. Some coaching can be useful, but the guideline holds: people who know things are interesting to people who want to know those things.

Various applications of digital storytelling can improve knowledge continuity when employees enter or leave a project or organization, when important clients give feedback, when new projects are initiated, when important events are promoted, and for other innumerable applications. In addition, digital video promises to revolutionize project workflow and collaboration among project stakeholders. Table 9.2 provides specific ways to integrate digital storytelling into the project environment.

TABLE 9-2. Applications of digital storytelling for project management

Type of Narrative	What it Means	When and to Whom It Is Effective
Success Stories	Stakeholder stories that convey the core values of the organization in a context-specific and personalized manner.	To build identity, credibility, and enthusiasm in the minds of the organization's stakeholders. Stories may illustrate core values, roles, norms, best practices, belief systems, and generalized rules, and give life to the positive experiences made and shared in the course of performing. Excellent for creating cohesion.
Lessons Learned	After-action reviews that capture the practices, anecdotes, insights, emotions, and perspectives of team members. May include clients, partners, outside experts, and even family members whom the project may have affected.	Too many projects conclude without reflection on what was done, what could have been done better, and how it was perceived internally and/or how the client evaluated what was done. After-action reviews captured on video can be useful for the team for future projects, to help others in the organization benefit from the experience of the team, and even to provide insight to customers on how the organization approaches problems. Extremely effective when trying to convey that even intelligent, competent people sometimes make mistakes, and when trying to convey excitement over unconventional and innovative solutions that emerge during a project.
Yellow Pages	A member directory that includes short video clips of people discussing their expertise areas, roles, and obligations.	Useful internally and sometimes externally to personalize the organization to its members and to other stakeholders via a Web portal. When combined with competency mapping and indexing, yellow pages offer an effective means for identifying experts, team members, and internal service providers.
Champion Stories	Vignettes that offer the rationale and motivation behind an initiative launch.	Within or across organizations, champion stories can inform strategic partners and potential participants of an initiative may benefit them. Effective when the intention is to build support and attract participants.
Orientation Tours	Video narratives of the corporate sites, client sites, and other locations of interest.	When new people enter an organization, they usually go through some kind of orientation process. Video tours of various sites can provide a visual context for a new member, a new client, or a new strategic partner.

(Continued)

TABLE 9-2. (*Continued*)

Exit Interviews	Video interviews that correspond to key areas of learning and knowledge in danger of being lost after someone leaves.	As expertise walks out the door, it is becoming more and more essential to capture perspectives and information from the people who are departing. This is arguably one of the most important areas of expertise management. Video clips or images greatly improve the motivation and ability of the expert to leave a legacy.
Fireside Chats	Periodic updates by the senior managers and executives.	As part of a newsletter, broadcast, or daily communiqué to the staff to keep people informed of what is going on, why it is important, and how it fits into the strategy.
Out-takes	Humorous incidents captured on video and posted on the Intranet.	As video cameras become ubiquitous, the results can serve to shape a playful learning culture by allowing people to share funny moments with one another.

IMAGINEERING THE FUTURE

Does an enterprise need a digital storytelling strategy? Do project manager certifications need to include storytelling as a skill? In the next decade, this question will become as rhetorical as the one asked a decade ago: Is project management a definable profession? The applications of new media to project planning, execution, and communication will evolve into innovative business practices that will transform the project environment and culture. Marshall McLuhan presaged that through new media technology, the art of storytelling would resurface as the preferred mode for sharing knowledge (McLuhan 1964/1994). It brings Hollywood inside the organization.

Is knowledge management simply about getting the right information to the right people at the right time? Or is it about making meaning from our interpretations and offering useful stories to each other about what to do next? Will it be the blue pill or the red pill? Digital storytelling is made possible by and is reflective of a learning culture. In a video-enabled future, project managers will become the movie producers who shape our collective business story.

SELECTED BIBLIOGRAPHY

Bruner, Jerome. 1990. *Acts of Meaning*. Cambridge, Mass.: Harvard University Press.

Czarniawska, Barbara. 1999. *Writing Management: Organization Theory as a Literary Genre*. New York: Oxford University Press.

Damasio. A. 1994. *Descartes' Error: Emotion, Reason, and the Human Brain*. New York: Avon Books.

Gabriel, Y. 2000. *Storytelling in Organizations: Facts, Fictions, and Fantasies*. New York: Oxford University Press.

Gill, Philip. 2001. Once Upon an Enterprise. *Knowledge Management Magazine,* May, 24–28.

Kuhn, T. S. 1970. *The Structure of Scientific Revolutions* (2nd ed., enlarged ed.). Chicago: University of Chicago Press.

Kull, Michael D. 2001. Corporate Storytelling and the New Media: Bringing Hollywood Inside the Enterprise. In *Building Knowledge Management Environments for Electronic Government,* edited by Ramon C. Barquin, and Shereen G. Remez. Vienna, Va.: Management Concepts.

McLuhan, M. 1994. *Understanding Media: The Extensions of Man.* Cambridge, Mass.: MIT Press. (Original work published 1964)

Polanyi, M. 1967. *The Tacit Dimension.* New York: Doubleday.

Polkinghorne, Donald E. 1988. *Narrative Knowing and the Human Sciences.* Albany: State University of New York Press.

Shank, R. C. 1990. *Tell Me a Story: Narrative and Intelligence.* Evanston, Ill.: Northwestern University Press.

Wenger, Etienne. *Communities of Practice: Learning, Meaning, and Identity.* New York: Cambridge University Press.

10

Defense Project Management Knowledge Flow Through Lessons-Learned Systems

MARK E. NISSEN
KEITH F. SNIDER

B ecause of their large scale, technological complexity, and lengthy schedules, Defense projects present some of the greatest challenges to project management professionals. Although every Defense project is unique in certain respects, many commonalities are shared across a broad diversity of projects, and project managers may gain much by learning from one another, both contemporaneously across projects and longitudinally through time. But it is unclear how such learning should occur and what technical, organizational and managerial activities can be employed to facilitate it. Drawing from current theory on knowledge flow, we formulate a conceptual model of this phenomenon and apply it to the domain of project management (PM). Using a lessons-learned system developed by the U.S. Army for illustration, we discuss key factors that must be in place to affect project management knowledge flows for Defense systems, and we generalize this discussion to project management knowledge beyond the military and government.

PROJECT MANAGEMENT IN THE MILITARY

Any account of the development of PM theory and practice would be incomplete without acknowledgment of its history in the military setting. Aspects of national security and defense figure prominently throughout PM, from examples of ancient practice, such as Nehemiah's rebuilding of Jerusalem's walls (ca. 444 B.C.), to the origins of modern PM in the aerospace projects of the 1950s and 1960s (Baumgardner 1963; Cleland 1999).

Today, major weapon development projects in the United States continue to attract significant attention from Congress, the media, and others, mainly because of their comparatively high costs, lengthy schedules, and "high-tech" performance capabilities. These projects often embody controversial policies about appropriate means for national security (e.g., "Star Wars"). Thus, Defense PM presents particular challenges. It is a highly complex enterprise that encompasses multiple contexts—politics, business, technology, and the military—and multiple stakeholders with often competing interests (Fox 1988; McNaugher 1989).

Because of its inherent controversy, Defense PM in the United States has been the object of numerous reform initiatives. Since the 1940s, reform recommendations by the Hoover Commission, the Packard Commission, the Grace Commission, and other bodies have addressed a variety of issues, including the appropriate level of project oversight by executive and legislative officials, the professionalism of the Defense PM workforce and the proper role of the private sector in Defense PM. Considering the frequency of such initiatives, reform may well be the single defining theme of Defense PM.

One aspect of reform on which there has typically been general agreement over the years is the need for Defense PM to adopt, where appropriate, so-called "commercial practices" from the private sector. The assumption is that a business-oriented mindset, with a focus on bottom-line profitability, should replace the bureaucratic mindset that may lead to waste and inefficiency in Defense projects. Hence, many private-sector management innovations soon find their way into the practice of Defense PM.

In recent years, one of the most exciting areas of innovation emerging from the private sector has been knowledge management (KM; Nonaka 1991). Many scholars (e.g., Drucker 1995) assert that knowledge represents one of the very few sustainable sources of comparative advantage for a firm. Such assertions are supported by case studies of successful implementation of KM systems (e.g., Fulmer 1999), as well as through the popularization of related concepts such as organizational learning (Argyris 1999) and the "learning organization" (Senge 1990).

Recognizing the promise of this movement, leaders in U.S. Defense PM have begun to explore ways in which knowledge can be transferred among its practitioners. The first steps have consisted mainly of local Intranet systems for knowledge sharing in single organizations. A larger system intended to create an enterprise-wide "community of practice" (Brown and Duguid 1991) has also been developed.

We see Defense PM as an area that may benefit richly, in terms of reform and from KM, but also as one that may be particularly problematical for implementation of effective KM processes. To the extent that our exploration reveals issues associated with the relatively extreme case of Defense PM, other non-Defense professionals and scholars may gain insights into effective KM in the field of PM in general. In particular, we see much promise in current theory and practice associated with enterprise *knowledge flow* to address the importance and difficulties associated with Defense PM. The primary objective of knowledge flow is to enable the transfer of capability and expertise from where it resides to where it is needed—across time, space, and organizations as necessary. The problem is that knowledge often is not evenly distributed through the enterprise, and Defense PM—due to the factors noted previously—is particularly prone to knowledge "clumping."

This chapter addresses knowledge flow in the PM organization by applying emerging knowledge flow theory to state-of-the-practice Defense PM processes. The balance of this chapter follows with a summary of knowledge flow background research and conceptualization of a model applicable to enhancing knowledge flow in the PM organization. The chapter then evaluates this model in Defense PM through application to a PM lessons learned process developed and implemented by the U.S. Army, and it closes with conclusions that can be drawn from this study, along with suggested topics for future research along these lines.

KNOWLEDGE FLOW RESEARCH

Drawing from Nissen (2001), we distinguish the concept *knowledge* from its counterparts *information* and *data,* and summarize current theory pertaining to knowledge flow. This sets the stage for conceptual development in the subsequent section.

The Nature of Knowledge

The emerging phenomenon of KM is generating substantial attention. Miles, Miles, Perrone, and Edvinsson (1998, p. 281) caution, however, "knowledge, despite its increasing abundance, may elude managerial approaches created in 20th century mindsets and methods." In fact, knowledge is proving difficult to manage, and knowledge work has been stubbornly resistant to reengineering and process innovation (Davenport 1995). For one thing, Nonaka (1994) describes knowledge creation as primarily an individual activity performed by knowledge workers who are mostly professional, well educated, and relatively autonomous, often with substantial responsibility in the organization. They tend to seek and value their relative autonomy and often resist perceived interference by management in knowledge-work activities (Davenport, Jarvenpaa, and Beers 1996).

Moreover, substantial, important knowledge is tacit (Polanyi 1967), unstructured (Nonaka 1994), and external to the organization (Frappaolo 1998). This can greatly impede the identification, acquisition, interpretation, and application of such knowledge. Also, corporate knowledge has historically been stored on paper and in the minds of people (O'Leary 1998). Paper is notoriously difficult to access in quantity and keep current on a distributed basis, and knowledge kept in the minds of workers is vulnerable to loss through employee turnover and attrition.

Most information technology (IT) employed to enable knowledge work appears to target data and information, as opposed to knowledge itself (Ruggles 1997). This may contribute to difficulties experienced with KM to date (Lueg 2001). Almost by definition, knowledge lies at the center of knowledge work, yet it is noted as being quite distinct from data and information (Davenport, De Long, and Beers 1998; Nonaka 1994; Teece 1998). Indeed, many scholars (Davenport and Prusak 1998; Nissen, Kamel, and Sengupta 2000; von Krough, Ichijo, and Nonaka 2000) conceptualize a hierarchy of knowledge, information and data. As illustrated in figure 10.1, each level of the hierarchy builds on the one below. For instance, data are required to produce information, but information involves more than just data (e.g., data in context). Similarly, information is required to produce knowledge, but knowledge involves more than just information (e.g., it enables action). We have notionally operationalized the

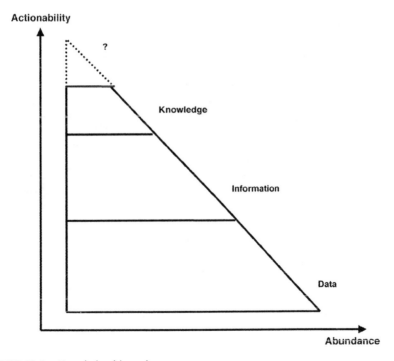

FIGURE 10-1.   Knowledge hierarchy.

triangular shape of this hierarchy using two dimensions—abundance and actionability—to further differentiate between the three constructs.

Briefly, data lie at the bottom level, with information in the middle and knowledge at the top. The broad base of the triangle reflects the abundance of data, with exponentially less information available than data and even fewer chunks of knowledge in any particular domain. Thus, the width of the triangle at each level reflects decreasing abundance as one progresses from data to knowledge. The height of the triangle at each level reflects actionability (i.e., one's ability to take appropriate action, such as a good decision or effective behavior). Converse to their abundance, data are not particularly powerful for supporting action, and information is more powerful than data. But knowledge supports action directly, hence its position near the top of the triangle.

Knowledge Flow Theory

One of the best-known theoretical treatments of knowledge flow to date stems from Nonaka (1994) in the context of organizational learning. This work outlines two dimensions for knowledge: (1) *epistemological* and (2) *ontological.* The epistemological dimension depicts a binary contrast between explicit and tacit knowledge. Explicit knowledge can be formalized through artifacts such as books, letters, manuals, standard operating procedures, and instructions; tacit knowledge pertains more to understanding and expertise contained within the minds of people. The ontological dimension depicts knowledge that is shared with others in groups or larger aggregations of people across the organization. Although this aggregation of organizational units appears arbitrary, in the enterprise context, it could clearly apply to small teams, work groups, formal departments, divisions, business units, firms, and even business alliances or networks.

Nonaka uses the interaction between these dimensions as the principal means for describing knowledge flow. This flow is roughly characterized through four steps. First, Nonaka asserts that new knowledge is created only by individuals in the organization and is necessarily tacit in nature. The first flow of knowledge is then theorized to occur through a process termed *socialization*, which denotes members of a team sharing experiences and perspectives, much as one anticipates through communities of practice. This first socialization flow corresponds to tacit knowledge (i.e., along the epistemological dimension) flowing from the individual to the group level (i.e., along the ontological dimension). The second flow of knowledge is theorized to occur through a process termed *externalization*, which denotes the use of metaphors through dialogue that leads to articulation of tacit knowledge and its subsequent formalization to make it concrete and explicit.

The third flow of knowledge is theorized to occur through a process termed *combination*, which denotes coordination between different groups in the organization—along with documentation of existing knowledge—to combine new, intrateam concepts with other, explicit knowledge in the organization. The fourth flow of knowledge is theorized to occur through a process termed *internalization*, which denotes diverse members in the organization applying the combined knowledge from above—often through trial and error—and in turn translating such knowledge into tacit form at the organization level.

Another view of knowledge flow involves the *life cycle* concept. Nissen et al. (2000) observe a sense of process flow or a life cycle associated with KM. Integrating their survey of the literature (Despres and Chauvel 1999; Gartner Group 1999; Davenport and Prusak 1998; Nissen 1999), they synthesize an amalgamated KM life cycle model as outlined in table 10.1. Briefly, the "create" phase begins the life cycle, as new knowledge is generated by an enterprise. The second phase pertains to the organization, mapping, or bundling of knowledge. Phase 3 addresses some mechanism for making knowledge formal or explicit, and the fourth phase concerns the ability to share or distribute knowledge in the enterprise. Knowledge application for problem solving or decision making in the organization constitutes Phase 5, and a sixth phase is included to cover knowledge evolution, which reflects organizational learning through time.

Both the models proposed by Nonaka (1991, 1994) and Nissen (2001) appear to have some merit in terms of describing knowledge flow. But it is unclear whether these two models are mutually compatible, and neither model is clear in terms of articulating *how* knowledge flows. Moreover, both models are silent in terms of matching knowledge-flow patterns with complex processes such as PM. This leads to the knowledge-flow conceptual development discussed next.

PM KNOWLEDGE-FLOW CONCEPTUAL DEVELOPMENT

The conceptual development discussed in this section has its focus on the *business process* as a key unit of analysis. Despite use of the word "business" in describing this unit of analysis, however, the process construct has proven to be very effective for analyzing a wide variety of enterprises, in the public (e.g., military units, governmental agencies) and private (e.g., for-profit firms, nonprofit organizations) sectors alike. Drawing from more than a decade of process-focused research and application through business process reengineering (BPR), we concentrate initially on the workflow of an enterprise, for this represents the critical activities required for an enterprise to add value through its processes.

TABLE 10-1.   Knowledge management life cycle models (adapted from Nissen et al. 2000)

Model	Phase 1	Phase 2	Phase 3	Phase 4	Phase 5	Phase 6
Despres and Chauvel	Create	Map/bundle	Store	Share transfer	Reuse	Evolve
Gartner Group	Create	Organize	Capture	Access	Use	
Davenport & Prusak	Generate		Codify	Transfer		
Nissen	Capture	Organize	Formalize	Distribute	Apply	
Amalgamated	Create	Organize	Formalize	Distribute	Apply	Evolve

Indeed, workflows have long been the focus of analysis in reengineering, but substantial integration of KM with reengineering has been observed in recent practice, as companies realize the direct connection between KM and knowledge-work process innovation (Davenport et al. 1998). In their study of more than thirty KM efforts in industry, Davenport et al. (1996) note the practice is "fundamentally change management projects." And emerging theory of knowledge creation and management has a dynamic, distinctly process-oriented flavor (Nonaka 1994). Ruggles (1998) goes so far as to suggest a primary objective of the practice is to assess the impact of KM as a process, fundamentally a proposition of reengineering.

Building on the research above, we begin to characterize a powerful interaction between the flow of work (i.e., workflow; Georgakopoulos, Hornick, and Sheth 1995) and the flow of knowledge (knowledge flow) in an enterprise. For instance, in a pilot study (Oxendine 2000; Oxendine and Nissen 2001) preceding the present investigation, the business processes associated with military intelligence were studied in the field (i.e., onboard naval warships at sea). Numerous distinct process steps, participants, organizations, and tools were identified and diagrammed to represent such processes, and the flow of work from raw-intelligence gathering to dissemination of completed intelligence products were well defined and easily traceable, as delineated in figure 10.2

Our observations and participants' perspectives suggested that such intelligence processes perform very well within a particular formation of ships—which collectively constitute a carrier battlegroup—and that local knowledge is critical to process efficacy. But negligible capability exists in terms of transferring such local knowledge from one battlegroup to another, even though any particular battlegroup typically stays only a matter of months in a given operational area.

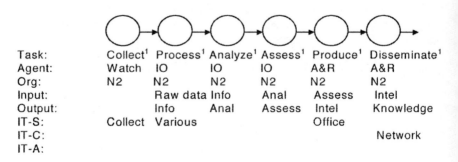

Task:	Collect[1]	Process[1]	Analyze[1]	Assess[1]	Produce[1]	Disseminate[1]
Agent:	Watch	IO	IO	IO	A&R	A&R
Org:	N2	N2	N2	N2	N2	N2
Input:		Raw data	Info	Anal	Assess	Intel
Output:		Info	Anal	Assess	Intel	Knowledge
IT-S:	Collect	Various			Office	
IT-C:						Network
IT-A:						

Acronyms:
IO: Intelligence Operations
A&R: Intelligence Analysis & Reporting
N2: Intelligence Department

FIGURE 10-2. Battlegroup intelligence process.

Through further investigation, we concluded that a different set of processes—associated with knowledge transfer—was distinct from the military-intelligence process being investigated. Whereas the same basic business processes associated with military intelligence were performed by each distinct battlegroup, separate knowledge-flow processes were needed to link each intelligence process across different battlegroups and through time. Thus, processes associated with the flow of work (e.g., military intelligence within a battlegroup) appear to be distinct from their counterparts associated with the flow of knowledge (e.g., transfer of local knowledge between battlegroups). Analytic generalization in this prior study suggested that such distinction between workflow and knowledge flow is not limited to military-intelligence processes.

A related pilot study (Espino 2000; Nissen and Espino 2000), also preceding the present investigation, examined the business processes associated with maritime interdiction at sea. This military process was similarly studied, described, and diagrammed to represent the workflow, from the search for smugglers to the boarding, search, and seizure of vessels carrying contraband. This process shares a number of similarities with its intelligence counterpart above (e.g., in terms of local knowledge being critical to efficacy), and it similarly suffers from inadequate complementary processes to transfer such knowledge between different interdiction vessels and units as they sail in and out of particular geographical regions.

In this latter study, a more general conceptualization of the phenomenon was developed, in which the respective flows of work versus knowledge are referred to as *horizontal processes* and *vertical processes*, as conceptualized in figure 10.3.

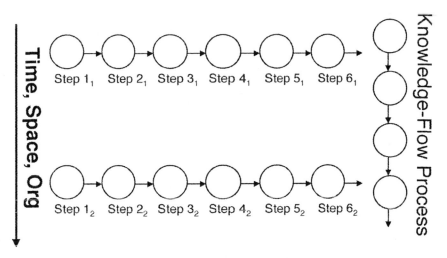

FIGURE 10-3.   Horizontal and vertical processes.

Briefly, the two horizontal directed graphs in the figure delineate separate instances of a work process (e.g., steps 1–6 as performed at different points in time, space, organization). The graph at the top of this figure represents one particular instance (e.g., performed at a specific point in time, location, organization) of this notional process, and the graph at the bottom represents a different instance (e.g., performed at a separate point in time, location, organization).

Whereas both horizontal graphs represent the flow of work through the enterprise, the vertical graph represents a complementary set of processes responsible for the flow of knowledge. As noted previously, knowledge is not distributed evenly through the enterprise, yet management is interested in performance, consistency, and effectiveness across various workflows. This requires the associated knowledge (local conditions, process procedures, best practices, tool selection, and usage) to flow across time, space, and organizations. Such cross-process activities drive the flow of knowledge—as opposed to the flow of work—through the enterprise, but it is unclear what steps, participants, organizations, and tools comprise such vertical processes. Further, it remains to apply this model of vertical and horizontal processes to the specific field of PM. This represents the content of the next section.

KNOWLEDGE FLOW PROCESS ILLUSTRATION—LESSONS LEARNED SYSTEMS

While the conceptual model from above awaits theoretical development, some organizations have implemented processes designed to promote knowledge flow across workflows. As mentioned earlier, some Defense PM organizations have implemented local KM systems, and Defense PM leaders are exploring larger enterprise-wide possibilities. Of course, with an incomplete or improper understanding of the details and interrelationships among the elements of the model presented above, leaders may choose design and implementation options that are poor fits for their organizations (Davenport 1993; Snider, Barrett, and Tenkasi 2002). As a result, valuable organizational resources may be wasted, and the intended benefits of KM may be lost.

As a way to explore the model's potential applications, this section describes one enterprise KM exemplar in the context of knowledge flow. In particular, we characterize the activities associated with PM in terms of a horizontal process (PM workflow), and we depict the complementary activities associated with a U.S. Army-developed "lessons learned system" as a vertical process (PM knowledge flow) that is used to transfer knowledge from one project instance to another. We then extend the discussion to Defense PM to address its unique issues.

Lessons Learned System Exemplar—CALL

One of the best-known lessons learned systems in current operation is the Center for Army Lessons Learned (CALL) at Fort Leavenworth, Kansas. Established in

1985 for the purpose of collecting lessons learned during simulated combat training exercises (U.S. Army 1997), over the years, its mission has expanded to encompass lessons from actual combat and other military operations (e.g., JUST CAUSE in 1989). CALL's methods include both active collections of lessons by dedicated expert observer teams as well as passive collection of lessons submitted from the field. CALL is staffed with resources necessary to accomplish a variety of lessons learned functions, including collection, analysis, processing, dissemination, archiving, and research. It publishes tailored lessons learned products in a wide variety of media, including newsletters, handbooks, bulletins, and the Internet, including both secure and public online databases.

To help understand the design features of CALL, we refer to table 10.2, which adapts Aha's (2000) characterization to group system characteristics into lesson, operational, and organizational factors. Factors corresponding to the CALL system are highlighted in boldface for reference. Lesson factors describe the "product" of the system, that is, whether it produces lessons only (pure) or includes other products such as best practices or information updates (hybrid) as CALL does. The other lesson factor describes the type(s) of processes addressed by the lesson. Technical processes usually deal with scientific, engineering, or other highly technical matters. Administrative processes usually

TABLE 10-2.   Lessons learned system characteristics (adapted from Aha 2000)

Lesson:

Content	Pure			**Hybrid**
Process Type	**Technical**	Administrative		Planning

Operational:

Access	Open		**Closed**
Formality	**Formal**		Ad Hoc
Locus	**Centralized**		Distributed
Process Relation	**Embedded**		Standalone
Acquisition	**Active**		Passive
Handling	**Rigorous**		Open
Dissemination	**Active**		Passive

Organizational:

Interpretive Context	**High**	Medium	Low
Type	Adaptable		**Rigid**

involve fairly routine procedures or decisions made by a single individual, for example, a purchasing specialist. Planning processes entail more complex and strategic matters involving multiple stakeholders. CALL focuses mainly on "tactics, techniques, and procedures" for operational forces rather than on "macro-issues" or strategic operations; hence its processes would be classified as "technical."

Operational factors describe how lessons learned systems function. Access refers to the extent to which those outside an organization may use its system. Due to the sensitive nature of military operations, clearly, CALL represents a closed system. CALL is also a formal system, as it has established procedures and processes of operation. The locus of CALL operation is centralized in that it serves the U.S. Army worldwide from its offices at Fort Leavenworth, Kansas. And the lessons learned system of CALL is embedded, because it operates in an integrated fashion during other organizational activities (e.g., as in the case of Army units conducting after-action reviews in the course of training exercises; Baird, Holland, and Deacon 1999). The acquisition of lessons in CALL is active, as Army personnel from around the world are encouraged to contribute lessons from a variety of military operations. Handling refers to the level of treatment a system gives a specific lesson after it has been generated. CALL's handling is rigorous; significant control through a review and approval process is imposed on candidate lessons before they are formally incorporated into the system. Finally, dissemination is active, as CALL includes in its process of lesson development a coordination step to solicit comments from agencies and commands that may be affected by or have interest in dissemination of a lesson.

Regarding organizational factors, interpretive context (Zack 1999, p. 50) refers to the extent to which members of an organization share similar knowledge, backgrounds, and experiences. In an organization with a high interpretive context, such as the Army, most members are likely to understand the content and significance of lessons generated by other members. The other organizational factor is how rigid or adaptable an organization is in terms of changing its "habits of action" in response to lessons learned by its members.

Knowledge Flow in Defense Project Management

Building on our experience with CALL, what can we say about lessons learned systems for PM in Defense? We formulate our ideas from examination of figure 10.3 in the context of Defense PM, which indicates some of the challenges of designing processes for knowledge flow in general and lessons learned systems in particular. Specifically, the ways in which Defense projects (horizontal processes) are separated must be understood in order to define (and design) the vertical (knowledge flow) processes to connect them.

In the United States, Defense projects are managed within each of the military services (Army, Navy, Marine Corps, and Air Force), rather than within a single organization of the Department of Defense (DoD). Significant organizational barriers thus exist between, for example, a fighter aircraft project manager in the Navy and a fighter aircraft project manager in the Air Force. These barriers take various forms, including different organizational cultures, regulations, and incentive systems (Kronenberg 1990). This organizational separation is exacerbated by competition among the services for roles, missions, and most importantly, resources (Thompson and Jones 1994). Under such conditions, there may be few incentives and structures to facilitate knowledge flow among Defense projects.

Within each of the military services, projects are separated in other ways. Separation in a technical sense occurs because Defense projects typically produce unique systems (as opposed to, for example, construction projects) with little, if any, overlap or duplication of military utility. Each project is "one of a kind" from a technical or performance view, and hence carries with it unique management challenges and risks. Projects of similar types are separated temporally; for example, recent Army attack helicopter projects have been separated by as many as twenty years.[2] In the years between such projects, tremendous changes occur in technology, in the projected employment and tactics of the system, and in the legal, regulatory, and political environment of Defense PM. Thus, temporal separation, as with technical separation, may create the perception that all Defense projects are unique. Such a perception has significant implications for the potential for knowledge flow among projects; if each project is perceived as unique, the validity and wider relevancy of knowledge created in any one project may be subject to challenge.

Clearly, then, designing appropriate processes and structures for vertical knowledge flow in Defense PM requires close attention to and consideration of not only the horizontal activities of PM, but also to the nature and extent of the separation between Defense projects. We may posit a relationship between this concept of separation between workflows and that of interpretive context mentioned earlier, namely, the more significant the separation between project workflows, the lower the interpretive context shared by practitioners in those workflows. From our previous discussion, this means that in order for lessons to be shared effectively across widely separated projects, certain characteristics such as formal and rigorous handling should be present, characteristics that require greater commitment of organizational resources. Thus, it seems clear that the resources required to enable knowledge flow across Defense projects through a lessons learned system would increase as the separation between projects increases.

This logic raises intriguing questions for any project leader facing decisions about whether and how to invest in knowledge flow processes. At what point do such investments outweigh the benefits that accrue from knowledge flow? May such investments be "saved" if the separation between project workflows can be decreased? How do the costs and benefits of knowledge flow processes compare with those of reducing workflow separation?

Obviously, answers to these and similar questions demand data that simply have not been collected. Little research has been done regarding the "return on investment" of knowledge management and organizational learning initiatives. It seems clear, though, that an integrated managerial approach to knowledge flow that considers both the horizontal flows and the vertical flows of figure 10.3 is appropriate. Knowledge flow may be enhanced as separation between workflows is reduced.

CONCLUSIONS AND FUTURE RESEARCH

Several potential topics for future research emerge from this discussion. First, the conceptual model of knowledge flow requires further development. In the context of PM, we need to identify what other vertical processes may also contribute toward knowledge flow, as the kinds of lessons learned systems discussed in this chapter represent only one of possibly many such processes. For example, PM education, training, and research also constitute vertical knowledge flow processes that serve to link workflows across several dimensions. It will be important to understand the differing contributions of each type of process and the ways they may interrelate in influencing workflows. Of course, each process will have different elements, and these must be understood so that leaders can make informed decisions about how best to design and improve knowledge flow.

Conceptual work is also necessary to investigate and develop the nature of the relationship between knowledge flows and workflows. Much of what has been presented here regarding knowledge flow represents the conduit perspective (Axley 1984), in which knowledge is seen as objects or transmissions that flow through organizational channels from a source to a receiver (e.g., from one project manager to another). Against the conduit view is the idea of knowledge as socially constructed (Berger and Luckman 1967), or put another way, as the product of interpersonal relationships. This constructivist perspective emphasizes social processes that lead to knowledge creation and sharing (Putnam, Phillips, and Chapman 1996). The implication of this view is that knowledge, rather than flowing between and among workflows, is created and modified dynamically in the "space" between workflows as a product of the social relationships among workflow members. While such a view is not inconsistent with the model presented throughout this chapter, its emphasis on social interactions certainly warrants special attention.

As another potential topic, fieldwork may be warranted to investigate practicing project managers and PM organizations to discern the extent to which such vertical processes are in place and being exploited for organizational learning. Such fieldwork can complement theory development nicely, providing an empirical basis for confirming, modifying, or refuting theoretical concepts and relationships, in addition to identifying and integrating new concepts and relationships from practice.

Sticking with lessons learned systems, one could utilize the guidelines developed in this chapter to develop and implement such a system for PM. Because the Army has considerable experience with its CALL system, this may represent a logical first organization to address in terms of implementing a PM lessons learned system. And clearly, a wealth of empirical data could be collected pertaining to the use and utility of such a system. These represent only a few potential topics for future research along the lines of this chapter. Much remains to be done and learned, and many PM professionals eagerly await this future work.

NOTES

1. This figure employs an attributed directed graph to represent the military-intelligence workflow. Each node represents a process task, and the directed edges depict the flow of work through the process. Eight attributes are used to describe each task: (1) task name, (2) role of agent performing the task, (3) organization in which the task is performed, (4) task inputs, (5) task outputs, (6) IT used for task support, (7) IT used for task communication, and (8) IT used for task automation.

2. Initial deployments of the Cobra and Apache helicopters occurred in 1967 and 1984, respectively. The Comanche, currently under development, is scheduled for deployment in 2006.

BIBLIOGRAPHY

Aha, D. W. 2000. Briefing: Intelligent lessons learned systems. Presented at the Department of Energy Society for Effective Lessons Learned Sharing, Spring 2000, Meeting, April 5. Retrieved from: http://tis.eh.doe.gov/11 /proceedings/aha400.pdf, October, 2000.

Argyris, C. 1999. On Organizational Learning, 2nd ed. Oxford, U.K.: Blackwell.

Axley, S. 1984. Managerial and Organizational Communication in Terms of the Conduit Metaphor. Academy of Management Review 9:428–37.

Baird, L., P. Holland, and S. Deacon. 1999. Learning from Action. Organizational Dynamics 27(4): 19–31.

Baumgardner, J. 1963. Project Management. Homewood, Ill.: Richard D. Irwin.

Berger, P., and T. Luckman. 1967. The Social Construction of Reality. Garden City, N.Y.: Doubleday, Anchor.

Brown, J. S., and P. Duguid. 1991. Organizational Learning and Communities of Practice. Organization Science 2(1): 40–57.

Cleland, D. 1999. Project Management, 3rd ed. New York: McGraw-Hill.

Davenport, T. H. 1993. Process Innovation: Re-engineering Work Through Information Technology. Boston: Harvard Press.

Davenport, T. H. 1995. Business Process Re-engineering: Where It's Been, Where It's Going. In Business Process Change: Re-engineering Concepts, Methods and Technologies edited by V. Grover and W. Kettinger. Middletown, Pa.: Idea Publishing, 1–13.

Davenport, T. H., D. W. De Long, and M. C. Beers. 1998. Successful Knowledge Management Projects. Sloan Management Review, Winter, 43–57.

Davenport, T. H., S. L. Jarvenpaa, and M. C.Beers. 1996. Improving Knowledge Work Processes. Sloan Management Review 37(4): 53–65.

Davenport, T. H., and L. Prusak. 1998. Working Knowledge: How Organizations Manage What They Know. Boston: Harvard Business School Press.

Despres, C., and D. Chauvel. 1999. Mastering Information Management: Part Six— Knowledge Management. *Financial Times,* 8 March, 4–6.

Drucker, P. F. 1995. *Managing in a Time of Great Change.* New York: Truman Talley.

Espino, J. P. 2000. *Innovating the United States Coast Guard Law Enforcement Detachment (LEDET) Deployment Process through Knowledge Management.* Master's thesis, September, Naval Postgraduate School, Monterey, Calif.

Fox, J. R. 1988. *The Defense Management Challenge: Weapons Acquisition.* Boston: Harvard Business School.

Frappaolo, C. 1998. Defining Knowledge Management: Four Basic Functions. *Computerworld* 3:8.

Fulmer, W. E. 1999. *Buckman Labs* (Case N9-899-175). Boston: Harvard Business School Press.

Gartner Group. 1999. The Knowledge Management Scenario: Trends and Directions for 1998–2003. *Strategic Analysis Report,* 18 March.

Georgakopoulos, D., M. Hornick, and A. Sheth, A. 1995. An Overview of Workflow Management: From Process Modeling to Workflow Automation Infrastructure. *Distributed and Parallel Databases* 3(2): 119–53.

Kronenberg, P. S. 1990. Public Administration and the Defense Department: Examination of a Prototype. In *Refounding Public Administration,* edited by G. Wamsley, R. Bacher, C. Goodsell, P. Kronenberg, J. Rohr, C. Stivers, O. White, and J. Wolf. Newbury Park, Calif.: Sage.

Lueg, C. 2001. Information, Knowledge and Networked Minds. *Journal of Knowledge Management* 5(2): 151–59.

McNaugher, T. L. 1989. *New Weapons, Old Politics: America's Procurement Muddle.* Washington: Brookings.

Miles, G., R. E. Miles, V. Perrone, and L. Edvinsson. 1998. Some Conceptual and Research Barriers to the Utilization of Knowledge. *California Management Review* 40(3): 281–88.

Nissen, M. E. 1999. Knowledge-Based Knowledge Management in the Re-engineering Domain. *Decision Support Systems* 27:47–65.

Nissen, M.E. 2001. Toward a Program of Research on Knowledge Flow in the Very Large Enterprise. Technical Report NPS-GSBPP-01-003. Naval Postgraduate School, Monterey, Calif.

Nissen, M. E., and J. P. Espino. 2000. Knowledge process and system design for the Coast Guard. *Knowledge and Process Management Journal,* 7(3), 165–76.

Nissen, M. E., M. N. Kamel, and K. C. Sengupta. 2000. Integrated Analysis and Design of Knowledge Systems and Processes. *Information Resources Management Journal* 13(1): 24–43.

Nonaka, I. 1991. The Knowledge Creating Company. *Harvard Business Review,* November-December, 2–9.

Nonaka, I. 1994. A Dynamic Theory of Organizational Knowledge Creation. *Organization Science* 5(1): 14–37.

O'Leary, D. E. 1998. Enterprise Knowledge Management. *Computer* 31(3): 54–61.

Oxendine, E. 2000. *Knowledge Management Support to Network-centric Warfare (NCW).* Master's thesis, September, Naval Postgraduate School, Monterey, Calif.

Oxendine, E., and M. E. Nissen. 2001. Knowledge Process and System Design for the Naval Battlegroup. *Journal of the KMCI* 1(3): 89–109.

Polanyi, M. 1967. *The Tacit Dimension*. London: Routledge and Kegan Paul.

Putnam, L., N. Phillips, and P. Chapman, P. 1996. Metaphors of Communication and Organization. In *Handbook of Organization Studies*, edited by S. Clegg, C. Hardy, and W. Nord. London: Sage, pp. 375–408.

Ruggles, R. 1997. *Knowledge Management Tools*. Boston: Butterworth-Heinemann.

Ruggles, R. 1998. The State of the Notion: Knowledge Management in Practice. *California Management Review* 40(3): 80–86.

Senge, P. 1990. *The Fifth Discipline: The Art and Practice of the Learning Organization*. New York: Doubleday.

Snider, K. F., F. J. Barrett, and R. Tenkasi, R. 2002. Considerations in Acquisition Lessons Learned System Design. *Acquisition Review Quarterly*, Winter, 67–84.

Teece, D. J. 1998. Research Directions for Knowledge Management. *California Management Review* 40(3): 289–92.

Thompson, F., and L. R. Jones. 1994. *Reinventing the Pentagon*. San Francisco: Jossey-Bass.

U.S. Army. 1997. *Center for Army Lessons Learned Handbook* 97-13. Fort Leavenworth, Kan.

von Krough, G., K. Ichijo, and I. Nonaka. 2000. *Enabling Knowledge Creation: How to Unlock the Mystery of Tacit Knowledge and Release the Power of Innovation*. New York: Oxford University Press.

Zack, M. H. 1999. Developing Knowledge. *California Management Review* 41(3): 127–45.

11

Project Managers' Changing Cognitive Schemata and the Achievement of Group Goals

CAROLYN R. SPENCER
TREVOR HINE

A significant risk area for project sponsors is managing unplanned change. Theorists of organizational behavior have attempted to understand the circumstances of how activity change occurs on projects and have identified the significant impact time has on activity. In the present research, leading-edge projects from six major Australian industries (telecommunications, banking and insurance, information technology, railway signaling, inorganic chemistry, and construction) were monitored at three key points through their life cycle to understand how feedback impacts on project activity through the project manager's cognition to cause change. This research takes the study of cognition into the real world setting of project management.

The project managers' cognitive representation of meaningful aspects of a project (their "cognitive schemata"), which guide activity change during the project, were investigated and the effect of feedback evaluated. Six key categories of feedback were identified, which potentially represented the foci of project-related schemata. These were validated by a panel of Australia's leading experts in project management as important indicators for project management performance. Sixteen project managers participated in the field study, where a customized methodology enabled the collection of verbal reports from project managers.

Strong evidence was found that linked the set of key schemata to the hypothesized effects of feedback. Overall, the effects were found to be general across all industries, individuals, and projects. A contrasting effect was observed where schemata were poorly developed in inexpert project managers, raising the issue of measurable differences in behavior according to project management competency. Furthermore, the findings raise issues about the strength and weaknesses of project management as an organizational tool when project managers' cognition is not addressed.

OVERVIEW

Organizations invest vast resources in projects that provide them with the flexibility to achieve innovative and strategic goals. Unplanned change is, however, a growing area of high risk due to the dynamic nature of project work and project environments. The field of project management currently attempts to explain project systems without reference to their most active and integral element: the cognition of project managers. Project management systems are therefore vulnerable to higher risk due to a lack of understanding of the circumstances that may drive or, conversely, inhibit radical or gradual change to planned activity during the achievement of group goals.

Project management theorists have over the past decade described emerging difficulties in managing projects in highly dynamic circumstances. In 1995, for example, Kreiner highlighted the challenges posed by the erosion of relevance of projects in all industries due to the effect of drifting of the project management environment during implementation. Rapid change is now of concern in numerous industries. Benamati and Lederer (2000) described eleven different categories of problems for information technology projects due to rapid change, and Huchzermeier and Loch (2001) described high risk and uncertainty in research and development projects due to change. There has, however, been very little research to date into goal-directed, group behavior in project management environments, and little from a cognitive perspective.

Theorists in project management have criticized the lack of organizational behavior models and constructs that has slowed conceptual development in this field (Shenhar 1998). In the area of group goal achievement, McGrath (1991) and Gersick (1988, 1991) have insisted on moving away from laboratory-based perspectives on group behavior, and have incorporated the effects of organizational contexts into their theories. From their observations of project groups they have developed theories that emphasize a time-based perspective on activity change during the achievement of project goals. However, their findings do not provide a complete view of what is happening in contemporary project management contexts, especially with regard to the cognition of project managers.

The aim of research described here was to enhance our understanding of the project managers' changing cognitions due to feedback, and how this changes the achievement of project group goals. The central research question of the study was: "What triggers unplanned change on group projects?" It was hypothesized that activity change on projects is triggered by a change in the cognitive schemata of project managers caused by project-related feedback arising in key areas. This central hypothesis was investigated through a study of feedback and activity change in natural project settings.

PROJECT MANAGERS' COGNITIVE SCHEMATA

Cognitive schemata are knowledge structures organized around particularly meaningful issues (Wofford and Goodwin 1994). The issues of concern to project managers during the achievement of project goals are termed the foci of their project management schemata. Schematic processing is identified in the literature as the type of information processing likely to be used by individuals pursuing group goals (Gioia and Poole 1984). Cognitive schemata have received particular attention over the past two decades within the organizational literature and have been shown by many researchers to be basic elements in information processing within organizations (Gioia and Poole 1984; Bartunek, Lacey, and Wood 1992; Walsh and Charalambides 1990).

Schemata themselves are affected by the information they process. This information is collectively termed feedback, and for the purpose of this research it was defined as "the new information received by the project manager in the natural setting of the project, and during the course of the project." Theorists generally treat an operating schema as an internal hypothesis about goal achievement and conceptualize the relationship between a schema and a specific feedback event in terms of whether the event is congruent, incongruent, or irrelevant according to the individual's expectations formed due to the schema (Hastie 1981). The structuring effects of schemata during processing have been demonstrated by field study findings, such as Lau and Woodman's (1995) observations of organizational change schemata held by students and staff of a university. It has been established, however, that individuals will frequently overlook data that do not fit with expectations according to existing schemata, and they may be led to focus erroneously on certain aspects of incoming information, which may cause irrational or inappropriate activity choices for a specific case (Taylor and Crocker 1981).

There is also an established link between individual behavior and cognitive schemata at both an elementary procedural level (Hastie 1981) and more recently, at the level of decision making in complex and dynamic work contexts (Endsley 1995). Individual behavior is the observable part of the effect of schematic processing based on an individual's cognitive schemata (Wofford and Goodwin 1994), and the various behavioral components can be termed the "schema-products." The verbal components are best collected through the tailored interview process applied in this study, since it meets the key requirement of being restricted to carefully structured and limited conditions (Wofford and Goodwin 1994).

THE GROUP GOAL ACHIEVEMENT THEORISTS

The present research was designed to provide essential information about individual phenomena underlying group behavior as observed and interpreted by McGrath (McGrath, 1991; Arrow and McGrath, 1995) and Gersick (1988, 1989).

Using quantitative methods, McGrath (1991) studied the verbal and nonverbal behavior of a number of groups and developed a theory of the interaction and performance of groups, which emphasizes their temporal patterning. His Time, Interaction, and Performance (TIP) theory is based on a broader model of *social entrainment* and proposes that all group actions involve one or another of four modes of group activity:

Mode 1: inception and acceptance of a project (goal choice);

Mode 2: solution of technical issues (means choice);

Mode 3: resolution of conflict, that is, of political issues (policy choice); and

Mode 4: execution of the performance requirements of the project (goal attainment).

McGrath proposed that the synchronization of various processes over time (and across individuals) is induced by either internal (that is, possibly cognitive) or external stimuli, and suggested that this "social entrainment" of project groups occurs to the group's external pacer, which is time.

The model developed by Gersick (1988) describes group goal achievement as a *punctuated equilibrium,* where periods of relative stability precede and follow significant change at the midpoint in the duration of a project. The concept of punctuated equilibrium was drawn from the field of natural history. Gersick audiotaped key project meetings and analyzed transcripts of the discussion. She observed that a working framework of goal achievement commenced almost immediately on group formation. Changes to that framework seemed to be triggered by members' awareness of time and deadlines around the halfway point in the time allocated. Time, therefore, was the "pacing device." A second key issue for the venture capital groups she later studied was individual expectations of events occurring in a sequence across time. An unexpected finding was that groups commenced a chosen course of action immediately after they formed. At approximately the halfway point of the time allotted to the project, Gersick observed that the groups reassess their situation and change the direction of their activity, if they believe it necessary to achieve their goals. This transition set a revised direction for phase two, based on each individual's assessment of the likelihood of achieving work goals if the current activity was continued.

There has been little critical research of the two models to date, and what has occurred suggests that Gersick had confounded individual and group level phenomena. In Seers and Woodruff's study (1997), the midpoint effect was observed, but the effect was found to occur in both individual and group tasks. McGrath and Gersick have between them identified six categories into which project activity clusters (table 11.1). These are: project inception, execution, technical issues, political issues, time and pace, and finally, event sequence. While both theorists observe behavior change in groups across time, they fail to provide an account of the processes occurring within individuals that lead them to judge

TABLE 11-1. Categories and conceptual definitions

Category	Conceptual Definition
Inception	The initiation, establishment and acceptance of project goals and plans.
Execution	Choice of the means to carry out and monitor work.
Technical Issues	The identification of techniques or procedures.
Political Issues	The identification of the actions necessary to resolve potential/actual conflicting values, preferences or interests.
Time and Pace	The temporal aspects of project work coordination involving complex issues of scheduling, synchronization, and time allocation.
Event Sequence	The individual's use of a conceptual structure of events, conditions, and outcomes that occur in a temporally sequential manner.
Other Personal/ Organizational Concerns	Other personal or contextual issues that are part of the individual's broader concern that are outside the immediate project system.

that adequate progress has, or has not been made, and fail to account for how new practices are chosen if it is judged that there is a need to change practices.

In an initial phase, our research set out to validate a set of potent project-related schemata that are distinguishable from other schemata. A second phase led to the development of an appropriate methodology, while in a third phase we collected the identified schema-products in natural project settings. Analysis of the field study data revealed how feedback in six key categories was associated with unplanned change on projects. Finally, we showed that managers coming to projects with undeveloped schemata might respond to feedback in a different way than experienced managers.

Phase One: An Expert Panel Defines the Project Managers' Schemata

The aim in the initial phase was to identify potent categories of feedback, which would impact on activity. The feedback categories needed to be potent in the sense that they were meaningful to project managers, and therefore had the potential to impact on elements of an individual's underlying project manage-ment schemata. They also had to have the achievement of project goals as their particular system focus as opposed to any other goal or objective.

A panel of subject matter experts (SMEs) was formed, and they endorsed the concepts that were most likely to be active elements of their project-related schemata from prior observations reported in the literature (Gersick 1991; McGrath 1991). Conversely, they did not endorse categories less likely to be meaningful within project management contexts—operational area categories. They then indicated what type of project feedback was most meaningful to them within these active elements. Researchers and practitioners, particularly in cognitive studies, commonly use SMEs to understand work tasks (Landy 1989; Lau and Woodman 1995; Meyer 1996). In understanding work tasks, SMEs are usually asked to assign an importance rating to tasks, since they are likely to possess well-developed or richer schemata in the foci areas. Therefore, in our study, SMEs were required to rate the importance of project-related feedback in order to identify the types of feedback that were meaningful to project practitioners, and six meaningful categories were found spanning dif-ferent industry contexts. They also thought, however, that project managers should respond to feedback from organizational and personal areas when appropriate.

The less meaningful items were drawn from operational management activities, which theoretically should contrast with the project management items. It was possible to identify items belonging to this "alternative" group of schemata since the basic premise of a project has been defined as "a set of inter-related activities, with defined start and end dates, designed to achieve a unique and common objective" (National Committee for Standards in Project Manage-ment 1996, p. 16). The group has no need to exist after achieving its objective.

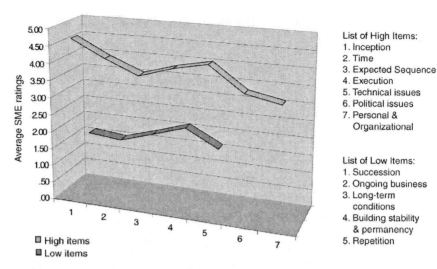

FIGURE 11-1. Ratings averaged across SMEs for organizational vs. project feedback areas.

By contrast, operational management is generally a repetitive activity where outcomes, usually commercial products, are produced by a team where the work practice evolves through ongoing improvements to efficiency (Turner 1999).

In order to ensure that the relevant categories were identified, the survey items used in this first study were a mixture of those categories identified before by Gersick (1988, 1991) and McGrath (1991), and those from the operational management literature that were expected to be less prominent in project management practice (Turner, 1999). An example of the latter alternative, more operational, schema is that for "routine/ongoing" tasks, rather than "time-limited" project tasks.

The Subject Matter Experts

The total population of Fellows (*N* = 14) of the Australian Institute of Project Management (AIPM) were the group of SMEs invited to participate in the survey. The AIPM is the professional body of project managers in Australia, and has sister organizations in the United States, Britain, and elsewhere. The ten project managers who participated had between twenty-two and thirty years of experience in project management, with the mean years of experience being 26.8 years. This population of project managers had worked in diverse industries. The average length of the respondents' projects in the past five years ranged from six months to three years.

Materials and Procedure

The four-page survey questionnaire was presented in a table format, with a column for ratings and a column for the SMEs to provide their own examples from their project experience, and to provide examples of how these led to new decisions. Respondents were asked to rate the importance of each type of feedback to their work on a 5-point Likert scale: 1 = not at all, 2 = minimally, 3 = moderately, 4 = very, and 5 = extremely. New areas and feedback types they considered important could also be added. Our group of SMEs was surveyed on two different occasions, eighteen months apart, to assess reliability of responding. A comparative analysis of the ratings provided across items when the SMEs were surveyed initially was used to identify those that were the most meaningful to them.

Results and Discussion

Figure 11.1 presents the mean response ratings for each feedback category. It shows that the mean ratings for the six categories from the literature on group goal achievement, and the broad category of organizational and personal issues, are high (see table 11.1). All these feedback categories achieved a mean rating of 3 or greater. As well, SMEs provided detailed examples of the issue categories and how the categories of feedback led to new decisions in their experience. Together, this indicates their importance to the SMEs, in contrast to the items from the operational management literature. A paired samples t test on the average ratings for project management feedback and operational management feedback indicated a significant difference between the means ($t = 11.419$, $df = 9$, $p < .01$, one-tailed). The pattern of ratings across SMEs for the group of project management items were in moderate agreement: a Kendall's coefficient of concordance indicated significant agreement ($W = .54$, $df = 7$, $p < .01$), and variability within each item was within an acceptable range (standard deviations from 0.5 to 1.0). The items referring to project management feedback were then correlated with the ratings given by the same SMEs at follow-up. A correlation was performed between SME item ratings given to the items receiving high ratings on the initial survey, and ratings on the same items by SMEs at the eighteen months follow-up. The results are presented in figure 11.2 and indicate that the item ratings given eighteen months apart were significantly similar ($r = .695$, $p < 0.01$ level, $n = 70$, two-tailed).

Thus, support was confirmed for a key set of unique project categories that were distinct and qualitatively different to other operational schemata and meaningful to project managers (table 11.1). The observed categories of activity described by the Group Goal Achievement theorists were endorsed and did contrast with the SME's ratings of items drawn from operational management contexts. Interestingly, SMEs also reported that in some circumstances they may respond to feedback from a general group of items external to the project system, termed "personal and the organizational issues." This was retained as a control category to test the hypotheses.

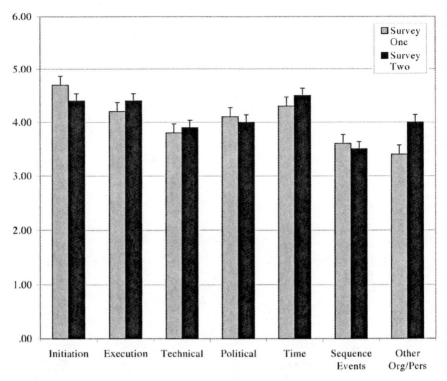

FIGURE 11-2. Ratings of the feedback areas that expert project managers attend to in order to achieve their goals.

Phase Two: Developing a Methodology Tailored to Project Management Contexts

This phase of the study was designed to develop and fine-tune the methods of data collection and coding for application to natural project management contexts, which had to meet a number of requirements. To test the central hypothesis, it was necessary to elicit and code valid data from project managers without changing their behavior. Bearing this in mind, a structured interview was identified as the primary method for exploring the products of schematic information processing (the schema-products) in the foci categories. Collecting interview text for content analysis in response to written or verbal prompts is the typical approach used in previous research to collect data on the products of individual schemata (Carley 1997). A survey-questionnaire method, while suited to some types of research contexts, was considered inappropriate for this type of context. A structured interview for face-to face delivery was optimal since it had a number of advantages over a questionnaire (ERIC 1997; Gorden, 1980). It would:

- facilitate the establishment of rapport between the interviewer and respondents and maintenance of a focus for the duration of the procedure;
- permit more complex questions to be asked by enabling amplification to occur where necessary;
- permit the lengthy data collection necessary within a structured format to enhance reliability; and
- enable the necessary collection of before-and-after data in a dynamic, but structured situation.

The interview techniques used included specific forms of verbal behavior, such as prompts like, "Can you tell me more about that?" Questions of this type would later allow the researcher to gauge influencing factors and consequent action from the material collected. This laddering style of questioning was therefore selected as the exploration technique allowing project managers to explore the ramifications of their project (Brown 1992; Eden 1988). An example would be a follow-up question such as, "What led up to that occurring?" after a project manager had mentioned a specific time-related issue that had arisen on a project. After their response, a typical further follow-up question would be, "What were the consequences of that occurring?" Since the interviewer would ask the same questions of numerous individuals in a precise manner to elicit all available knowledge on the project, the test–retest reliability of the data collected as noted below was significantly higher than for other types of approaches, for example, self-ratings to determine locus of control (Bober and Grolnick 1995), and leadership style (Wofford and Goodwin, 1994).

Using the categories identified by SMEs as a starting point, a number of interview methods were piloted through two studies, one in each of the Banking and Insurance (two project managers, average experience five years), and telecommunications (two project managers, average experience ten years) industries. The work in the first pilot project indicated that a structured interview strategy was viable, as it did not intrude on project operations. The quality of the atmosphere achieved was very good and could be scheduled at a time that suited the project managers, who secured a private room for the interview. This limited interruptions and ensured that project managers were entirely focused during the time of the interview, which gave a sense of formality to the event.

The initial pilot effort had indicated that significant modification was required to the process of content analysis, and coding the data produced, in order to improve validity and reliability. These modifications were trialed through the second pilot project, and were found to effectively improve content analysis. A coding system (table 11.2) was constructed to enable the coding of both the

TABLE 11-2. Coding categories for feedback and activity change types and operational definitions

Feedback

Operational Definition: A single ideational issue that is reported verbally in response to questions from the structured interview.

1   Feedback considered irrelevant to goals and performance.

2   Feedback related to the project that is neutral as it does not assist in evaluating performance.

3   Feedback that reflects positively on performance.

4   Feedback indicating a discrepancy between goals and performance.

5   Feedback that changes the goals/performance required, and that may have implications for likely success.

Change

Operational Definition: The amount of unplanned activity change. reported verbally in response to questions from the structured interview, occurring as a consequence of each feedback event.

1   No change.

2   Change within one activity.

3   Change in two to three activities.

4   Identifiable affect on more than three activities.

5   Identifiable affect on the planned project outcome(s).

feedback and change from the verbal reports of subjects. This led to excellent reliability ($r = .97$, $p < .001$ level, $n = 101$, two-tailed) for feedback type codes and ($r = .94$, $p < .001$ level, $n = 100$, two-tailed) for change type codes, when assessed through a cross-rating exercise, where a research assistant, who was blind to the hypotheses and research goals, randomly selected and independently coded 40 percent of all research material collected. The relatively unambiguous process of coding the raw material proved to be a strength of the overall research study.

Phase Three: The Field Study

Subjects
Of sixty potential organizations in eight industries, the five projects included in this third phase of the research were all significant leading-edge examples of the work of the industries concerned. They were selected on the basis of their commencement of a new project at the start of the research data collection phase. The subjects were therefore all available project managers working on those projects. This led to the inclusion of sixteen subjects in the field study. The project managers on one of the projects had no previous project experience. However, experience for the remainder ranged from two to thirty years. They had, on average, ten years of experience in project management. The average length of their projects over the previous five years was 1.4 years. The nature of the five projects and distribution of project managers is briefly described in table 11.3.

Procedure
A total of forty-eight detailed interviews were conducted by an experienced interviewer in three stages: at the commencement, middle (just after the midpoint of the project), and end of each project. The duration of each interview ranged from one to one and a half hours, and was terminated when all participants had arrived at a point where there were no new issues (initial interview), or feedback or change events (middle and end interviews) to discuss. The verbal protocols from the middle and endpoint interviews were then coded according to the operational definitions for feedback and change event types (table 11.2).

Results
A cross-tabulation of the frequency of occurrence of the types of feedback by the types of change appears in table 11.4. If there were no differences between the types of change that followed different types of feedback then it would be expected that cell frequencies would be homogeneous across the matrix. Inspection of table 11.4 indicates, however, that this was not the case. It can also be seen that the larger proportion of unplanned change on projects arises from discrepancy-related feedback.

TABLE 11-3.   Brief description of the five leading-edge projects that were included in phase 3, and the number and experience of the project managers

Five Leading-Edge Projects
Inorganic Chemistry Project: The setting up of new technology in Australia for odor emission analysis, which would develop a leading-edge methodology for toxic emission analysis of odoriferous gases escaping from an oil shale smelter plant (as the first paid client it was also the first project experience of the four project managers).
Rail Signalling Project: The development of Australia's first rail signalling system for a unique airborne rail link from a capital city to its major airport, using new standards and partnering arrangements. This was part of a multimillion dollar project, which won the Australian Institute of Project Management's overall award for 2001 (three project managers, average experience six years).
Telecommunications Project: The development of a coherent integrated telecommunications system in the context of a large hospital, using leading-edge technology, while maintaining essential services and overcoming a number of significant structural communications barriers peculiar to the site (two project managers, average experience of eight years).
Construction Project: One hundred million dollar development of a unique combined residential, commercial, and business property in Brisbane's CBD. This project was the first of its type with a unique legal, contractual, and title arrangements (four project managers, average experience thirteen years).
Information Technology Project: National government project for the implementation of human resource systems across Australia, using a unique partnering arrangement (three project managers, average experience 7.5 years).

The data in table 11.4 were analyzed using a chi-square (χ^2) test. A highly significant effect was observed ($\chi^2 = 280.25$, $df = 16$, 2-sided, $p < .000$). Gersick's group observations in relation to the proposed individual mechanism of schematic processing of feedback suggested time, and, "an expected sequence of events," triggered change (Gersick, 1991, 1994), while McGrath (1991)found that activity achievement clustered within four activity categories. On the other hand, we propose that time is merely one of six generic foci of the project management schemata, which emerge when change is studied across a natural cross-section of industries and projects. Further analysis therefore involved two steps. First, it had to be identified that the unplanned change effect arose from feedback in the six categories as opposed to other issues collected under the broad control category of "personal or organizational issues" (table 11.1), and second, it had to be shown that time did not exhibit a greater effect on change than any of the other categories of feedback.

The amount of change following feedback indicating discrepancies between goals and expectations or performance within the six generic categories, was

TABLE 11-4. Cross-tabulation of feedback types by change type

| Feedback | Change | | | | | |
	Type 1	Type 2	Type 3	Type 4	Type 5	Total
1. Irrelevant	6	1	0	0	0	7
2. Neutral	35	5	5	8	1	54
3. Positive	32	11	5	9	1	58
4. G/P Disc.	5	37	15	91	6	154
5. E/P Disc.	19	4	2	8	45	78
Total	97	58	27	116	53	351

compared to feedback from the control category (table 11.5). A significant difference was identified ($\chi^2 = 109.58$, $df = 1$, 2-tailed, $p < .000$). The proportion of feedback indicating a discrepancy between goals/expectations and performance that produced change was compared across the six categories. As shown in table 11.6 the difference was statistically insignificant ($\chi^2 = 4.939$, $df = 5$, 2-tailed, $p = .423$).

Analysis then turned to the timing of feedback and change through the project. The laboratory findings in the schema literature suggest a gradual accumulation of negative feedback leading to greater change in the last half of the projects (Hastie 1981). Gersick's findings suggested, however, that there would be a higher rate of change in the first half of the project due to an increase in vulnerability or reactivity to negative feedback as the project approaches its midpoint. We hypothesized, however, that there should be no significant difference in the rate of change that followed from feedback indicating performance discrepancies between the first and second half of the projects, since it was the type of feedback that was triggering the change, not an overwhelming accumulation of feedback, or the passage of time itself.

The analysis involved comparing the proportion of all types of change that occurred up to the midpoint of the project, to that which then occurred up to the end of each project, across the range of projects in the study. The analysis

TABLE 11-5. Cross-tabulation change vs. no change following feedback in the foci and control category

| Feedback | Change | | Totals |
	No Change (Type 1)	Change (Types 2–5)	
6 Foci Categories	3	194	197
Control Category (Personal/Organizational)	21	14	35
Totals	24	208	232

TABLE 11-6. Comparison of feedback producing change or otherwise across the six foci categories

Feedback	Change		Totals
	No Change (Type 1)	Change (Types 2–5)	
1. Initiation	10	29	39
2. Execution	7	33	40
3. Technical Issues	15	53	68
4. Political Issues	10	49	59
5. Time & Pace	11	40	51
6. Event Sequence	17	35	52
Totals	70	239	309

considered discrepancy-related feedback, which indicated a discrepancy between goals/expectations and performance. As anticipated, there was no significant difference between the proportion of all change that occurred in response to discrepancy-related feedback from the first to the second half of the projects ($\chi^2 = .160$, $df = 1$, 2-sided, $p < .689$), where the frequencies show that 61 percent of the change to occur to just after the midpoint and 39 percent by the endpoint, the proportion of change these feedback produced were 68 percent compared to 60 percent.

There was, however, an unanticipated midpoint effect just in the Inorganic Chemistry project. In this case, a disproportionate effect for discrepancy-related feedback existed at the midpoint, which was producing highly significant (Type 5) change. In table 11.2, there were eight instances where feedback indicating a discrepancy between performance and goals resulted in significant change that changed the project/goals (Type 5 change). All these instances occurred in the Inorganic Chemistry project and prior to the middle interview.

DISCUSSION

These findings strongly suggest that feedback impacts on a generic set of project management schemata leading to the occurrence of unplanned change on projects, and those effects are calibrated in proportion to the nature and significance of project feedback. In this study, the schema-products of cognition, which were project managers' reports of feedback and activity change, were monitored and measured in key categories of meaning. Through this investigation of project impacts, support was demonstrated for the hypothesis that activity change is driven by the effect of feedback on individual cognition. These findings enhance both our understanding and potential to better control goal-directed behavior during the management of projects, in addition to raising new issues worthy of investigation. The application of cognitive theory to project management contexts was therefore also endorsed by these results. Furthermore, the available evidence, although limited, suggests that the relatively simple conclusions noted above, have several complications that may have significant implications for project management.

The alternative hypothesis of a midpoint effect was not supported across this diverse group of project managers. This was despite the effect being evident for highly significant feedback for the least experienced project managers. The raw data indicates a larger amount of discrepancy-related feedback and therefore a larger frequency of change in the first half of the projects compared to the second half. The difference in the rate of change occurring in response to feedback is, however, not statistically significant, and therefore there is no disproportionate vulnerability to change in the first half of the projects, which includes the midpoint, compared to their second half. Our findings challenge prior findings by supporting our belief that the midpoint effect observed by Gersick and others relates to a subgroup, or portion, of all change observed on projects when a broad range of projects is monitored. The groups studied by the group goal achievement theorists met the definition of project groups; each was convened to develop a specific concrete piece of work, and the group's lifespan coincided with the initiation and completion of their special project goals by a deadline.

The groups were, however, clearly working in an unstructured manner and not applying the techniques contemporary project groups use to control project evolution and achievement of project outcomes, for example, milestone plans, project plans, cost, risk, and quality plans. They were, therefore, not representative of the naturally occurring range of project groups. This distinction, in terms of how representative the research groups were, which were studied by Gersick and McGrath, could be highly pertinent to interpreting their observations. It is proposed here that a project manager's competency in applying project management techniques to a project arises from that individual's development of project management schemata. The effect of well-developed meaning-based structures—their project management schemata—can be inferred through the application of project management competencies such as the use of the tools and techniques of project management, for example, project and resource plans.

The importance or impact on a group project that rich project management schemata may have can be demonstrated in terms of their leading the project manager to expect certain types of information representing the project situation to be available in the project system and, if lacking, lead them to facilitate development of the information. Where project managers have poorly developed cognitive schemata in applying generally accepted techniques of project management, it is proposed that their projects would be relatively unstructured. In Gersick's and McGrath's research, no reference is made in the verbal transcripts published of the group meetings to consideration of any project management method. It is therefore a reasonable assumption that those involved in the projects observed, were less skilled in the application of such techniques, and therefore had less well-developed cognitive schemata relating to the management of projects.

The observed resistance of project managers in this study to highly significant feedback from the organizational and personal systems (table 11.5) was a counterintuitive finding that could possibly be due to the combined effect of individual cognitive schemata and the aforementioned project management informational techniques for controlling the project. It might reasonably have been expected that significant feedback indicating discrepancies from all systems would lead to change on the projects. This was clearly not found to be the case during this study, where the diverse cross-section of project manager participants was designed to reduce potential error due to historical/contextual factors on any one project, which might otherwise have affected our observations. These limited, but fairly solid, findings raise questions, therefore, regarding project integration to achieve beneficial outcomes for organizations, and the use of project management as a tool by organizations to achieve their goals. Similarly, a further question arises about the potential clash between individual needs and project demands. Clarification of possible implications from this finding regarding the strengths and weaknesses inherent in current approaches to project management that do not take account of project managers' cognition suggests a need for further research.

Our findings have implications for optimizing the management of human decision making on projects through an enhanced understanding of the effect of project feedback as triggers of behavior change due to cognition, and its interaction with existing characteristics of the project managers—their schemata. Risk occurs on most projects due to reliance on a significant human decision-making component, which can currently be unpredictable. These findings raise the possibility of reducing risk, and, of optimizing costly inputs by taking into consideration the nature and operation of project management schemata.

BIBLIOGRAPHY

Arrow H., and J. McGrath, J. 1995. Membership Dynamics in Groups at Work: A Theoretical Framework. *Research in Organizational Behavior* 17:373–411.

Bartunek, J., C. Lacey, and D. Wood. 1992. Social Cognition in Organizational Change: An Insider-Outsider Approach. *Journal of Applied Behavioral Science* 28(2):204–23.

Benamati, J., and A. L. Lederer. 2000. Rapid Change: Nine Information Technology Management Challenges. *INFOR* 38:336–58.

Bober, S., and W. Grolnick. 1995. Motivational Factors Related to Differences in Self-Schemata. *Motivation and Emotion* 19:307–27.

Brown, S. 1992. Cognitive Mapping and Repertory Grids for Qualitative Survey Research: Some Comparative Observations. *Journal of Management Studies* 29:287–307.

Carley, K. 1997. Extracting Team Mental Models through Textual Analysis. *Journal of Organizational Behavior* 18:533–58.

Eden, C. 1988. Cognitive Mapping, *European Journal of Operational Research* 36:1–13.

Endsley, M. 1995. Toward a Theory of Situation Awareness in Dynamic Systems. *Human Factors* 37:32–64.

ERIC. 1997. Designing Structured Interviews for Educational Research *ERIC Clearinghouse on Assessment and Evaluation.* Washington, D.C.: Author.

Gersick, C. 1988. Time and Transition in Work Teams: Toward a New Model of Group Development. *Academy of Management Journal* 31:9–41.

Gersick, C. 1989. Marking Time: Predictable Transitions in Task Groups. *Academy of Management Journal* 32:274–309.

Gersick, C. 1991. Revolutionary Change Theories: A Multilevel Exploration of the Punctuated Equilibrium Paradigm. *Academy of Management Review* 16:10–36.

Gersick, C. 1994. Pacing Strategic Change: The Case of a New Venture. *Academy of Management Journal* 37:9–45.

Gioia, D., and P. Poole. 1984. Scripts in Organisational Behavior. *Academy of Management Review* 9:449–59.

Gorden, R. 1980. *Interviewing: Strategies, Techniques, and Tactics.* Homewood, IL: Dorsey Press.

Hastie, R. 1981. Schematic Principles in Human Memory. In *Social Cognition: The Ontario Symposium on Personality and Social Psychology* , Vol.1, edited by T. E. Higgins and M. P. Zanna. Hillsdale, N.J.: Erlbaum, 39–88,.

Huchzermeier, A., and C. H. Loch. 2001. Project Management under Risk: Using the Real Options Approach to Evaluate Flexibility in R&D. *Management Science* 47:85–101.

Kreiner, K. 1995. In Search of Relevance: Project Management in Drifting Environments. *Scandinavian Journal of Management* 11:335–46.

Landy, F. J. 1989. *Psychology of Work Behavior,* 4th ed. Belmont, Calif.: Brooks/Cole.

Lau, C. and R. Woodman, R. 1995. Understanding Organizational Change: A Schematic Perspective. *Academy of Management Journal* 38:537–54.

McGrath, J. 1991. Time, Interaction, and Performance (TIP) a Theory of Groups. *Small Group Research* 22:147–74.

Meyer, J. 1996. Retrieving Knowledge in Social Situations: A Test of the Implicit Rules Model. *Communication Research* 23:581–611.

National Committee for Standards in Project Management. 1996. *A Guide to the Project Management Body of Knowledge.* Upper Darby, PA: Project Management Institute.

Seers, A., and S. Woodruff. 1997. Temporal Pacing in Task Forces: Group Development or Deadline Pressure? *Journal of Management* 23:169–87.

Shenhar, A. J. 1998. From Theory to Practice: Toward a Typology of Project-Management Styles. *IEEE Transactions on Engineering Management* 45:33–48.

Taylor, S., and J. Crocker 1981. Schematic Bases of Social Information Processing. In *Social Cognition: The Ontario Symposium on Personality and Social Psychology,* V01.1, edited by T. E. Higgins and M. P. Zanna. Hillsdale, NJ: Erlbaum, 89–134.

Turner, J. R. 1999. *The Handbook of Project-Based Management.* Berkshire, U.K.: McGraw Hill.

Walsh, J., and L. Charalambides. 1990. Individual and Social Origins of Belief Structure Change. *Journal of Social Psychology* 130:517–32.

Wofford, J., and V. Goodwin. 1994. A Cognitive Interpretation of Transactional and Transformational Leadership Theories. *Leadership Quarterly* 5:161–86.

12

Analyzing Failure in Project Management Systems Using an Integral Approach of the Fish Bone and the Fault Tree Techniques

MAGED SEDKY MORCOS

Failure of many project management systems (local and foreign organizations) to achieve planned goals and to meet clients' expectations in finishing projects on time has been a common occurrence in the past years. This problem, which can appear clearly in international organizations working in foreign markets outside their homeland, is due to some factors impinging on the organization. These factors, if not taken into considerations as early as possible, can dramatically affect the overall performance and reliability of the project management services offered by those organizations on the long run, either with the same clients or with different ones. The major effect is that most times those organizations fail to maintain or gain more workload in those markets, which are characterized by being relatively unstable or uncertain. Top executive managers of those organizations hold the responsibility for the downfall or failures of their projects and/or their organizations.

Based on personal experience with a famous international project management company working in the Middle East, the author attempted to identify some major possible causes of such failures. These causes can be the result of external and/or internal factors. The external factors are outside the full control of the managers, however it is still their role to attempt to analyze, study, and try to predict the probability of the occurrence of such events and to try to calculate the risk associated with them as early as possible. The internal factors, on the other hand, are all factors controllable by the managers of the company or the project managers in sites, and the ones that the probability of their occurrences can be predicted or defined easier than those caused by the external ones. Both types of factors will be highlighted and addressed in detail later in this chapter.

OBJECTIVE AND FOCUS OF THE CHAPTER

In order to eliminate the causes of failure of project management organizations, managers of those organizations need a formal failure analysis to identify potential failures in project management systems and apply a method of assessment that can ensure the robustness and flexibility of their systems to cope with any environmental fluctuations and uncertainties involved in the construction industry. Reliability analysis offers the solution. Managers need to perform an overall reliability assessment to evaluate the performance of all the individual components of their system and to study the effect of their internal policies together with outside factors on the performance of the projects and their success in achieving their targets. Accordingly, this chapter focuses on the application of two reliability techniques. The first is using the Fish-Bone method and drawing its Fish-Bone Tree (FBT) as a qualitative approach for predicting and identifying sources of possible failures in the whole system. The Fault Tree Analysis (FTA) is then applied where it helps in transforming the qualitative FBT to a quantitative Fault Tree Diagram (FTD) where the values of the possible failure basic events in the system can be easily input using probability values, which give more insight to the problem and its severity.

POSSIBLE CAUSES OF PROJECT MANAGEMENT
SYSTEMS FAILURE

"All kinds of technological and organizational systems suffer failure" (Sauer 1993). Answers are needed to the question of the causes of such failure: what situations/factors inside and outside the organization and/or project affect their effectiveness and what outcomes characterize an organizational and/or project performance as failure? There is no generally agreed account of the nature of failure of organizational and project systems. Failure can be caused by a vast number of external and/or internal factors, which can interactively contribute toward the failure of the organization as a whole. These are detailed as follows.

External Factors

These external factors can arise from continuous change in political, economical, social, technological, and international factors [PESTI]. They are outside the control of the managers but need to be predicted as early as possible; hence identifying them is major step in the approach to the solution. They can be due to the existance of some areas of uncertainties in the construction industry, as they are unavoidable and very high. Undoubtedly, these uncertainties could cause disastrous impacts on the performance of the organization with its different projects. "The more uncertain and changing the environment, the more complex is the organization structure likely to be" (Pilcher 1992). In agreement to this statement, the role of top managers here has to account for the risks associated with these uncertainties while designing their management systems. Although it is very difficult to predict all types of problems, managers need to identify, diagnose, and predict their chances of occurrence as early as possible. They should focus their way of thinking on the reality of those problems caused by external factors. These PESTI factors were addressed in literature by different authors. For example, Harvey (1982) and Luffman, Sanderson, Lea, and Kenny (1991) showed how strategic managers could conduct such study to answer important questions to help them in identifying the opportunities and threats in the environment. With respect to the construction industry Porter (1980) identified five major forces impinging from the environment on construction firms. These are potential entrants, suppliers, buyers, substitutes, and industry competitors, which are more applicable to companies who construct and build but can also be considered by project management companies. Newcombe, Langford, and Fellows (1990) also identified the parameters of the environmental analysis in the form of an Input-Conversion Process-Output (ICO) model showing its usefulness in studying organizations from an open system perspective. However, an awareness of these five PESTI factors and their joint influences is important for understanding the competitive environment facing organizations working in the construction industry. They can be summarized as follows:

- *Political factors*, or governmental factors, are the main factors beyond the control of the managers in the organization. Foreign organizations of any discipline should gather as much information as they can by studying the international market where they are going to work in an attempt to prepare scenarios of political matters and to predict probability values of all bad events that can affect their progress and future performance.
- *Economic factors* affect organizations differently, as they can exert threats on its performance or provide some promising opportunities. Rate of economic growth, level of unemployment, and rate of price changes on the operation of their business and their affects on the operation of the business are samples of economic factors that managers should take into considerations before setting their long-term policies.
- *Social factors* influence the behavior of the organization in the form of employees' attitudes and behavior, as the human resources with their needs can cause threats to the strategic managers, and understanding such needs is vital. Hence, the question that needs to be answered by managers before setting their long-term policies is: What is the likely impact on the business changes taking place with respect to some social issues like health and welfare, recreational needs, education, living and working conditions, and other social changes?
- *Technological factors* can greatly influence the success and failure of the organization. For example, in the construction and engineering field, new technological developments in

engineering, new construction methods for contractors, and introduction of computers with their wide applications in business can influence the performance of the organization. Hence, the question that needed to be answered by managers before setting their long-term policies is: What impacts are the developments in the technological environment going to have on the business? These can be transportation technology, construction technology, materials sciences, mechanization, robotization, and computerization.

- *International factors* are additional factors that emerged as a result of globalization. They exert some sort of pressure on companies and forces them to follow different approaches and set aggressive polices to cope with the challenges of competition in local and foreign countries. Uncertainties increase with the development of new trends in trade, business, and project management due to the differences in corporate cultures and diversity of personnel and their perceptions. Accordingly, managers of project management organizations should realize those factors when taking jobs in international markets and take into account the uncertainties and risks involved by applying risk and reliability analysis.

Internal Factors

These factors are supposed to be in full control of the managers. They need to be identified properly and with complete honesty as early as possible. Their causing events can be predicted earlier and easier than those of the external factors. Bad design of the management systems with all their requirements of physical and financial resources either on the macro level of the organization or on the micro level of the projects is an example of these factors. Since management in its general and practical definition is the efficient allocation and utilization of the organization 5Ms—Manpower, Materials, Machines, Money, and Methods— problems can be encountered regarding any mismanagement of these 5Ms, therefore, managers should properly allocate and utilize these resources for adequately managing their projects and/or organizations. Unfortunately, from practical experience, when faced by scarce resources, managers sometimes try to put more loads and pressure on their employees. This causes a sense of dissatisfaction among employees that creates recklessness and a careless attitude. In this sense, the internal factors affecting both levels macro (organizations) and micro (projects) can be classified under the following five management problems.

Manpower Management Problems

- Culture diversity of personnel.
- Personal perception, education, and interests.
- Inexperienced staff either local or expatriates.
- No loyalty to the organization.
- No adaptation to the organization strategy.
- No clear management style.
- Communication differences.
- Wrong selection and bad training.

Material Management Problems

- Lack of supplying computer packages to facilitate work.
- Lack of providing printing and/or drawing papers.
- Shortage in supplying staff with their basic needs of materials.

Machine Management Problems

- Lack of providing employees with means of transportation.
- Lack of providing computers and printers.
- Shortage in supplying staff with their basic needs of equipment.

Money Management Problems

- Lack of supplying projects with their correct budget and staff.
- Lack of funding projects properly.
- Lack of providing financial support to projects.
- No financial support from head office.
- Mismanagement of the allocated budget among projects.
- Failure to market the services causing budget shortages.

Methods of Management Problems

- Wrong organization and/or project structures.
- Lack of conducting proper marketing research.
- Bad marketing and business development plans.
- Following old processes and procedures.
- Lack of communicating updated documents among staff.
- Exaggerating in the project management fees causing less work obtained.
- No clear identification of the scope of the work offered to clients.
- No clear understanding of what are the exact demands of clients.

The main origin of these factors, in the opinion and experience of the author, is in the lack of correct representation of knowledge and in the lack of communication among the different management levels and all participants of the projects, which is a serious sign of bad management. Obviously, considerable understanding of the organizational behavior, attitudes of employees, and functional interactions between the different departments and subsystems can reduce this problem and would help in solving problems successfully.

WHY RISK AND RELIABILITY EVALUATION OF PROJECT MANAGEMENT SYSTEMS?

By Studying and thoroughly analyzing the external and internal factors impinging on project management organizations, top managers can effectively design their management systems to reach the intended goals by using a formal reliability program at all levels of the organization. This program should begin at the early stage of structuring the hierarchical tree of the organization and/or projects and should continue to be conducted during implementation of the designed systems. Studying the reliability of process plants as in the chemical, electrical, and mechanical fields, is the role of the reliability program manager (Andrews and Moss 1993). In the project management organizations, this should be the main role of top strategic managers who—in the author's opinion— should work in a group and their decision should be a group decision. Furthermore, in order to understand the stochasiticity of the construction industry, the author suggests that strategic managers should not only apply qualitative reliability techniques in assessing the performance of their organization but quantitative risk, reliability, and management methods must also be introduced as well. Unfortunately, most studies done in reliability evaluation highlight and diagnose the problem in qualitative rather than quantitative terms (e.g., Harison 1987). Confirming the importance of introducing quantitative reliability methods, Andrews and Moss showed that reliability technology has benefited significantly from applying some qualitative and quantitative reliability techniques such as Fault Trees, Markov, and human reliability analysis. They have found many applications in process plant assessment. The shortage is, thus, addressed in the field of construction industry where the introduction of such useful techniques are still not recognized and appreciated.

TERMINOLOGY AND DEFINITION OF RELIABILITY

Before analyzing systems reliability and identifying their types of connections, it is important to give some idea of the terminology of reliability of a system and its definition. Aggarwal (1993) quoted a detailed definition by the Electronics Industries Association (EIA), that defined reliability in general terms by stating, " 'Reliability of an item (a component, a complex system, a computer program or a human-being) is defined as the probability of performing its purpose adequately for the period of time under the operating and environmental conditions encountered.' "

Similar definitions of reliability can be found in texts and articles written by a number of authors and reliability theorists including Bazovsky (1961), *IEEE Transactions on Reliability* (1970), Greene and Bourne (1972), Anderson (1975), Billinton and Allan (1983), Ang and Tang (1984), Pages and Gondran (1986), Singh and Kiangi (1987), Ireson and Coombs (1988), Cox and Tait (1991), Kececioglu (1991), Rao (1992), Ramahumar (1993), and Andrwes and Moss (1993).

SYSTEMS RELIABILITY TECHNIQUES

In systems reliability analysis there are two types of techniques: either qualitative or quantitative and their combination. Qualitative techniques mainly help in understanding the logical structure of the various modes of failure of the system and their interrelationships. They serve as the initiating procedure of a comprehensive and effective risk and reliability analyses where they are integrated for better systems' performance assessment. Some qualitative reliability techniques include: Reliability Hazard Analysis (RHA), Reliability Block Diagrams (RBD), Failure Mode and Effect Analysis (FMEA), Failure Mode Effect and Criticality Analysis (FMECA), and Common Cause Failure Analysis (CCF). For more details on these techniques, refer to texts by Andrews and Moss (1993), Cox and Tait (1991), and Billinton and Allan (1983). Quantitative reliability techniques on the other hand, allow for ascertaining the risk involved in the system's design through adopting criteria of risk measurement. This can be expressed in terms of the probability of failure, percentage of failure, expected number of failures of a component over a period of its operating time, or in terms of quantitative reliability indices used in process plants like the mean time between failures (MTBF), mean time to failures (MTTF), the average time between failures (ATBF), expected loss in revenue due to failure, expected loss of output due to failure, and so on. In this regard, the author agrees with Billinton and Allan (1983) in what they concluded about quantitative reliability evaluation: with the help of probability, reliability evaluation provides a thorough quantitative prediction of the adequate performance of the system in addition to the consistent evaluation of the relative importance of all the alternatives proposed for solving complex problems. Some of the quantitative reliability techniques include Conditional Probability Approach, Enumeration Method, and Simulation. Additionally, both techniques can be combined for playing an increasingly effective role in the assessment of systems' performances. The inductive Event Tree Analysis (ETA) and the deductive Fault Tree Analysis (FTA) are some examples of these combined types. Both methods can be referred to in literatures by Billinton and Allan (1983), Ang and Tang (1984), Pages and Gondran (1986), Cox and Tait (1991), and Andrews and Moss (1993). In the following sections, two of those reliability techniques are discussed. These are the Fish-Bone technique with its qualitative Fish-Bone Tree (FBT). The other is the versatile and effective Fault Tree Analysis (FTA) technique with its qualitative and quantitative Fault Tree Diagram (FTD).

The Fish-Bone method or Ishikawa diagram is schematic technique used to discover possible locations of quality problems. It is a cause-and-effect diagram as shown in figure 12.1. It starts with identifying causes to the problem and the effect to these causes appears at the end of the diagram. In its basic form it resembles the bone of a fish where managers identify all causes to the problem and then input them in the diagram on the branches which are considered as individual bones. They provide a good checklist for initial failure analysis. Individual causes associated with each category (branch) are tied in separate bones along that branch, often through a brainstorming process. Each bone represents a possible source of error or problem. Generally, production and operations managers use this Fish-Bone method in analyzing failure or problems in

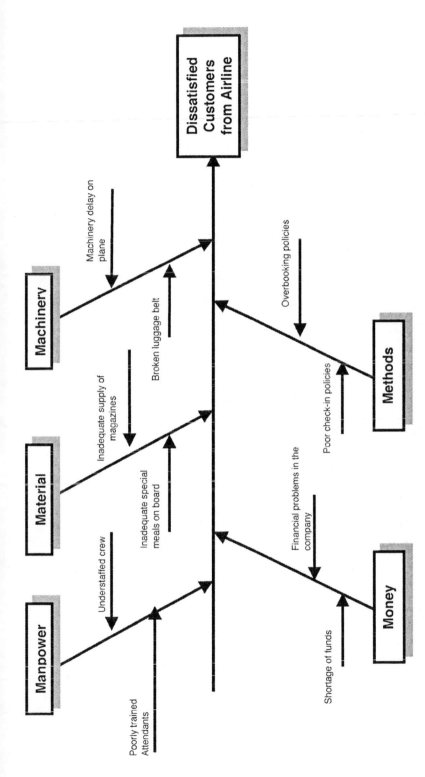

FIGURE 12-1. Example of a fish-bone tree (FBT) of an airline operator.

production and/or operations problems. For example if an airline company wants to analyze possible problems with dissatisfied customers (effect) from airline operation, managers start drawing the individual bones or causes to this effect. They can start by defining the famous 5Ms that may contribute to the occurrence of this undesired effect These five Ms are the "causes" and the "effect" is the dissatisfied customers, as shown in figure 12.1.

The FTA is a deductive method, or a top-down approach, or *effect-to-cause* diagram as shown in figure 12.2. It has received widespread attention in the risk and reliability analyses of complex systems. It is one of the most commonly used representations of system logic. The fault tree method first appeared in 1962 in the Bell laboratories and was used to eliminate several weak points in the MINUTEMAN missile launch control program. Subsequently, it spread widely in the Boeing Company in the mid-1960s. The field of nuclear power stations and aerospace industry have benefited greatly from its application and usefulness in diagnosing and detecting errors in nuclear reactor calculations (WASH-1400 1974, The Rasmussen Report). Since then, it has been extensively used as an important and versatile risk and reliability assessment technique and also for diagnostic purposes. It is considered as a qualitative and quantitative technique that is represented in the form of a top-down tree called the FTD.

FTA Concept

FTA uses a logic that is mainly the reverse of that used in event trees. While the aim in the ETA is to identify unwanted incidents following an initial event (e.g., What happens if fire is initiated in a house?), the starting point of the FTA is these unwanted incidents (i.e., What are the causes of this fire?). It is also different from the FMEA. In the FMEA the concept is to identify possible failure modes and their effects on the system's performance; in FTA, the aim is to develop a visualization structure capable of providing a simple logical relationships that can be used to obtain the probabilistic relationships and distributions between the various contributing events of a complex system. In fact, the FTA is always proceeded by the FMEA, which prepares a tabulated database essential for decomposing the failure of the system further. "As systems become more complex and the consequences of accidents become catastrophic, technique such as FTA should be applied" (Barlow and Lambert 1975).

FTA Procedure

In this method, a particular failure called the Top Event (Undesired Event) is first identified and a vertical deductive tree is constructed. In this tree, the Intermediate Events (Input Events), which are the contributing events to this top event, are connected by some symbolic shapes called the "AND"/"OR" gates. The FTD terminates with component failure events, which are called Basic (Primary) Events and whose quantitative probabilities are sufficiently known or can be

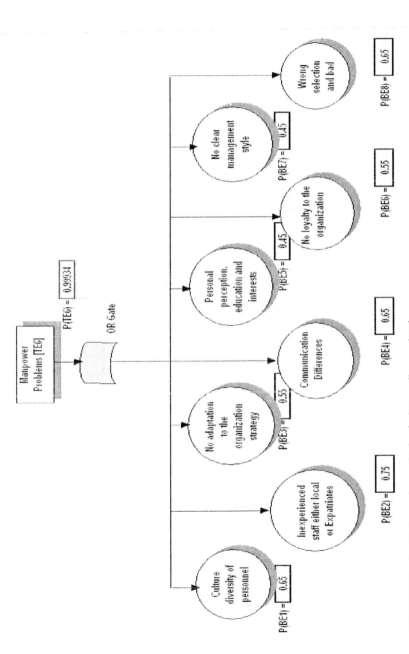

FIGURE 12-2. Qualitative and quantitative fault tree diagram (FTD).

obtained easily by direct analytical input. No further decomposition is then done. The general procedure of constructing the FTD can be summarized as follows:

- Define the Top Event (undesirable event) (e.g., failure of a system, damage to public health and environment, failure of reactor in a nuclear power plant, failure of an organizational management system, etc.)
- Construct the FTD from the Top Event to the Basic (Primary) Events.
- Decompose the Top Event to other contributing events called Intermediate Events. Logically connect these events using AND/OR Gates.
- Identify all Basic (Primary) Events to complete the procedure. The secondary events causing the basic events also have to be identified.
- Evaluate of the FTD either qualitatively or quantitatively or both. The aim is to obtain the probabilities values of the intermediate events from those of the known basic events. The Top Event probability value or distribution is then finally obtained.
- Produce a realistic picture about the overall adequacy of the system performance. Hence, effective decisions and corrective actions can be confidently taken.

One of the major advantages is that the construction of the fault tree forces the analyst to understand the behavior and performance of all parts of the system thoroughly and comprehensively, a step strongly needed for performing an effective risk and reliability assessment. Also, the promising detailed qualitative and quantitative analysis provided by FTA for assessing complex organizational performance justifies and compensates for the additional effort and expenses that can arise from its use. More detailed information and examples on using this powerful method can be found in literature, for example, Haasl (1965), *IEEE Transactions on Reliability* (1970), SIAM (1975), Billinton and Allan (1983), Ang and Tang (1984), Ireson and Coombs (1988), Cox and Tait (1991), Rao (1992), Ramahumar (1993), Andrews and Moss (1993), and Rouhianian (1993).

A PROPOSED INTEGRAL APPROACH OF THE FISH BONE AND FAULT TREE TECHNIQUES FOR SOLVING FAILURE PROBLEMS OF PROJECT MANAGEMENT SYSTEMS

The Problem

While working with an international project management organization operating in the Middle East region, the author had realized the emergence of some major problems that affected the smooth operations of the organization and caused failure in gaining more work. To analyze and assess the reasons behind such failure, potential areas of risks have to be identified and the causes of this failure have to be defined. The first investigation shows that those problems are caused either by the PESTI external factors, which are outside the control of the management, and/or internal factors, which are under their own control. However, the previously mentioned 5Ms can categorize the internal factors that can drift the company to the limit. In response to those factors that exert continuous forces on the strategic managers of the organization they have to study two main and related issues: the stability of long-term performance of their organizational management systems, and the flexibility in running the organization daily works in terms of its functions, processes, and procedures. Both studies, if done properly using reliability methods, would positively reflect on providing better and reasonable services to clients in the local market with their different demands, hence ensuring long-term sustainability and guaranteeing obtaining more workload to keep in business. Finally and most importantly, this would lead to improve the organization reputation. In an attempt to diagnose and create a reliable model to solve such problems with their different causes, the integration of both the Fish-Bone (FB) and the FTD is suggested as in the following flow chart.

Suggested Flow Chart Model and Steps for Fish-Bone (FB) and FTD Integration

The flow chart shown in figure 12.3 explains in detail the proposed integrated approach. The steps are as follows

Qualitative Steps

- Define the problem with its two causing factors: external (five types) and internal (five types) as mentioned earlier.
- Build the FB showing both factors on ten major branches. The ten problems with their causing events were listed in the part dealing with defining external and internal factors mentioned earlier.
- Transform the FBT to individual FTDs, each representing one of the major branches of the FB with its minor branches as basic events on the FTD. The problem name on the top of each major branch of the FB is the Top Event on the individual FTDs.
- Decompose each FTD to its basic events level. In this case, the author used the worst-case scenario in order to show how severe the problem could be. In terms of reliability analysis, a series type of connection of all basic events on the fish-bone branches and is represented by OR gates connection on all individual FTDs.
- Construct the Main FTD either with an AND gate or with an OR gate connecting the individual FTD Top Events to the main FTD Top Event. This connection depends mainly on how management perceives the reliability connection and the relationship between both factors. They can imagine that both factors are two connected components in a system under reliability study. Two types of reliability connection or two scenarios can be thought of by management: either *parallel connection* (best-case scenario) as it gives better results, or *series connection* (worst-case scenario) as it gives bad results.

Best Case Scenario (Not likely to happen): where management may think that external factors and the internal factors can be considered as two independent factors that

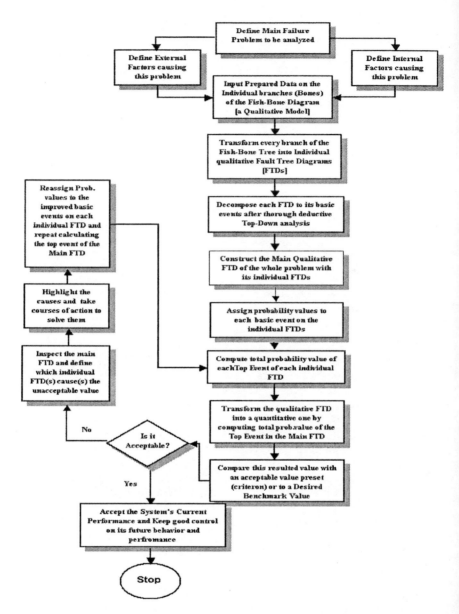

FIGURE 12-3. Flow chart of proposed integral approach of the fish-bone and fault tree diagram for analyzing failure of project management systems.

can happen separately. This can be resembled by parallel reliability connection (i.e., represented by AND gate on the FTD). In this case, both factors should happen simultaneously in order to cause effect on the whole organization or cause its failure.

Worst Case Scenario (More likely to happen): where management may think that the external factors influence the internal factors or if happened can at least affect the internal factors. This can be resembled by series reliability connection (i.e., represented by OR gate on the FTD). In this case, either factor should happen in order to cause effect on the whole organization or cause its failure.

In the opinion of the author, the second case is more likely to happen than the first case in turbulent markets, such as those existing in the Middle East, due to uncertainties in the market, high local and international competitions, scarce resources, and bad management by organizations.

- Assign probability values to each basic event on the individual FTDs. Refer to data preparation section next to see how probability values can be assigned.

Quantitative Steps

- Compute the total Probability value of each Top Event on every FTD constructed, using either the addition rule if OR gate connection or multiplication rule if AND gate connection. For example, assuming, for simplicity, the independent relationships between events, then if we have two events A and B connected by an OR gate to the Top Event then the addition rule applies where: $P(\text{Top event}) = P(A) + P(B) - P(A)*P(B)$.On the other hand, if they are connected by an AND gate, then the multiplication rule applies where: $P(\text{Top Event}) = P(A) \times P(B)$.
- Transform the qualitative main FTD to a quantitative one by computing the total probability value of the Top Event of the main FTD using the same additional or multiplication approach.

Evaluation Steps

- Compare the result to a desired benchmark criterion assigned before the study, or to an acceptable criterion set by the management of the organization, for example, a preset probability value not to be exceeded is assigned. If the calculated Top Event probability value is within acceptable range, go to step 15.
- If not acceptable, inspect the main FTD and define which individual FTD(s) cause(s) this unacceptable value.
- Highlight the basic cause(s) and take corrective actions to remedy or adjust them.
- Reassign new probabilities values to the improved Basic Events and repeat calculating the Top Event of the main FTD.

Reevaluation Steps

- Repeat the computation and evaluation steps by going to step 7 above.
- Keep repeating the process until reaching a satisfactory probability value.

- Monitor real performance of the organization and keep good control on the improved events. Repeat any of the above steps whenever the management add, change or need to assess any effect of the previous factors on the organizational future performance.

Data Preparation for Solving the Model

In order to solve any model, managers should collect data and gather information to feed the model to get better results. In our model, the main issue is how to assign the probability values of each Basic Event on each individual FTD.

Methods for Assigning Probability Values as Inputs to the Basic Events
The methods that can be used for assigning probability values can be listed as follows

- Brainstorming session among all participants in the analysis.
- Take expert opinion either from local staff or expatriate staff who live in the country for some time and know more about the country and its system.
- Guessing if the events are new to the management staff.
- Use subjectivity or intuition to predict values of probabilities.
- Conduct a detailed market analysis to get feeling about the probability values likely to occur.
- Perform good feasibility studies to prepare scenarios of expected occurring events.
- Input very high values as the worst case that can happen, then using sensitivity analysis to modify and review your inputs.

Detailed Numerical Model Solution

A detailed numerical analysis for calculating the Top Event values of all FTDs is performed as in table 12.1. By using an integral approach of the Fish-bone diagram and the FTD, and by inspecting the values shown in table 12.1, it can be deduced that solving the model numerically is very powerful and very effective. It helps in making a good comparison between the failure and success values of both scenarios: the best case and the worst case.

Findings of the Evaluation

As seen in table 12.1, and checking for the worst case scenario the P(fail of top event), represented here by the Failure of Project Management Organizations to Sustain Reputability and to Obtain More Workload in Foreign Countries, is very high approaching a value of 1.0 (i.e., P(success) = 0.0). This means complete failure. This is obvious as both factors are connected in series. On the other hand the P(fail of Top Event) for the best case equal 0.45, while that for P(success) equals 0.44. The emphasis here can be seen in the thinking approach of the

TABLE 12-1. Summary of findings and comparison between different original models

Connection	Scenario	Success / Failure Prob. Val.	If different basic events values are used		If very low basic events values are used	
			Original Model	Improv. #4	Original Model	Improv. #4
Parallel	Best Case	Success Value P(S) =	0.54697973	0.94545246	1.00000000	1.00000000
		Failure Value P(F) =	0.45302027	0.05454754	0.00000000	0.00000000
Series	Worst Case	Success Value P(S) =	0.00000000	0.00000002	0.48735949	0.67172808
		Failure Value P(F) =	1.00000000	0.99999998	0.51264051	0.32827192
		Comments on Improving original models:	Original inputs to basic events of main FTD before making preliminary good marketing and internal analyses.	Improved Best Case Scenario but no significant improvement to Worst Case Scenario.	Original inputs to basic events of main FTD after making preliminary good marketing and internal analyses.	No change to Best Case Scenario but improved Worst Case Scenario.

reliability connection type of both factors. The recommended one is to follow the best scenario connection model, that is, the parallel connection (if possible) as it gives better results in success and failure values. In order to eliminate or reduce such effect managers should try to improve the assigned probability values of all basic events on each individual FTD as they are very high as shown in table 12.1. In addition to that, they have to conduct effective market and internal analyses to eliminate the chances of occurrence of some of the external and internal factors. Performing tracking and sensitivity analysis approach as done next can help in achieving this aim.

Reevaluating and Tracking Sensitivity Analysis

In an attempt to provide managers with possible remedy actions and better solution to this problem, table 12.2 is proposed as a useful reevaluating and tracking analysis to the quantitative FTD. Five improvements (Improvement 1–5) are considered by suggesting that managers can take qualitative actions as suggested in table 12.2 by reducing the probability values of all basic events by only 0.05 (i.e., 5 percent). A sixth column is introduced where managers have to set a criterion of the minimum acceptable value of failure to those basic events (i.e., a benchmark). Also, a seventh improvement is considered where managers can imagine that all basic events are set at a constant probability of 50 percent, that is, P(Basic Events) = 0.5. If the accepted success is set at P(Success) over 90 percent, that is, they only accept 10 percent chances of failure (P(failure)] = 0.10 in this problem), then by inspecting table 12.2, one can see that the basic events of all FTDs should be reduced using Improvement 4, which is the closest value to this benchmarking where P(Failure) = 0.06 (P(success)] = 0.94) for the best case scenario, while it is not of much significance regarding the worst case scenario. Accordingly, managers have to go back the table and try to reduce those basic events to the values given in the column of Improvement 4. Doing this, managers can make a sensitivity tracking analysis to improve the whole process for better performance of this failure problem.

Findings of the Reevaluation

Ideally, managers have to work their process to reach Improvement 5, which is considered to be the excellent solution to the whole problem as the calculated P(failure) = 0.02 and hence the P(success) = 0.98, which is very optimistic and ideal for any organization. Also an interesting finding can be seen if 50 percent performance in all events is considered then the analysis produces a very bad result where P(Failure) = 0.53 and hence P(Success) = 0.47 for the best case scenario, and P(Failure) = 1.00 and hence P(Success) = 0.00 for the worst case scenario. Therefore, managers should not accept any easy 50 percent inputs to the Basic Events as this gives unexpected high failure value. As a quick summary

TABLE 12-2. Computation of the individual FTD top events and the main FTD top event for both case scenarios (best case and worst case)

Factors	No.	Individual Top Event	Succ./Fail.Prob.Val	BE1	BE2	BE3	BE4	BE5	BE6	BE7	BE8	BE9	BE10	Top Event TE
E X T E R N A L	1	Political Problems TE1	Success Value P(S) =	0.55	0.45	0.35								0.08663
			Failure Value P(F) =	0.45	0.55	0.65								0.91338
	2	Economical Problem TE2	Success Value P(S) =	0.4	0.5	0.55	0.6							0.06600
			Failure Value P(F) =	0.6	0.5	0.45	0.4							0.93400
	3	Social Problems TE3	Success Value P(S) =	0.35	0.65	0.55	0.45							0.05631
			Failure Value P(F) =	0.65	0.35	0.45	0.55							0.94369
	4	Technol. Problems TE4	Success Value P(S) =	0.55	0.65	0.35	0.65							0.08133
			Failure Value P(F) =	0.45	0.35	0.65	0.35							0.91867
	5	Intern. Problems TE5	Success Value P(S) =	0.5	0.3	0.4		0.55	0.45					0.06000
			Failure Value P(F) =	0.5	0.7	0.6		0.45	0.55					0.94000
I N T E R N A L	6	Manpower Problems TE6	Success Value P(S) =	0.35	0.25	0.45	0.35	0.55	0.45	0.55	0.35			0.00066
			Failure Value P(F) =	0.65	0.75	0.55	0.65	0.45	0.55	0.45	0.65			0.99934
	7	Material Problems TE7	Success Value P(S) =	0.6	0.55	0.5	0.35							0.16500
			Failure Value P(F) =	0.4	0.45	0.5	0.65							0.83500
	8	Machine Problems TE8	Success Value P(S) =	0.65	0.65	0.45	0.55							0.19013
			Failure Value P(F) =	0.35	0.35	0.55	0.45							0.80988
	9	Money Problems TE9	Success Value P(S) =	0.6	0.65	0.65	0.55	0.6	0.4					0.03346
			Failure Value P(F) =	0.4	0.35	0.35	0.45	0.4	0.6					0.96654
	10	Methods Problems TE10	Success Value P(S) =	0.65	0.25	0.65	0.4	0.35	0.65	0.55	0.45			0.00238
			Failure Value P(F) =	0.35	0.75	0.35	0.6	0.65	0.35	0.45	0.55			0.99762

Factors	No.	Main Top Event	Succ./Fail.Prob.Val	TE1	TE2	TE3	TE4	TE5	TE6	TE7	TE8	TE9	TE10	Top Event TE	Gate Type	Connection Type
Both	1	Best Case	Success Value P(S) =	0.086625	0.066	0.056306	0.081331	0.06	0.00657	0.166	0.190125	0.033462	0.002379	0.54698	AND	Parallel
			Failure Value P(F) =	0.913375	0.934	0.943694	0.918669	0.94	0.99343	0.836	0.809876	0.966538	0.997621	0.45302		
Both	2	Worst Case	Success Value P(S) =	0.086625	0.066	0.056306	0.081331	0.06	0.000657	0.166	0.190125	0.033462	0.002379	1.00000	OR	Series
			Failure Value P(F) =	0.913375	0.934	0.943694	0.918669	0.94	0.999343	0.836	0.809875	0.966538	0.997621			

to this reevaluation and tracking sensitivity analysis, a chart showing relative linear relationship between success and failures values of each improvement trial is produced to compare the P(Failures and Successes) values of each trial in comparison to the original current model as shown in figure 12.4. As can be seen, Improvement 5 is the best, and Improvement 4 is the closest to the minimum criterion set in column 6. Hence, managers should try to adopt model 4 and then attempt to continuously improve the performance by conducting more internal analysis and external market studies to achieve the results of Improvement 5. Going back and forth across the table, managers can obtain reliable solutions to the problem and have more control on the Basic Events causing the undesired events to happen. This tracking analysis gives them the vision and power to eliminate, enhance, and/or improve the whole structure connections, functions, processes, and procedures of the whole organization to withstand any internal or external pressures.

The above analysis shows improvement only in the best case scenario (parallel connection), while in the worst case scenario (series connection), the improvement is minimal and still total failure dominates the solution. This is obvious, as the values of probability assigned to the basic events of the individual FTDs are very high. In order to make real improvement, management would have to consider eliminating chances of occurrence of some of these Basic Events by making good marketing and competitive analysis of the country they are going to work in; based on information obtained from this good analysis, they might assign very low probability values to be used in the FTDs such as, for example, P(any Basic Event on the individual FTDs) $= 0.01$, that is, 1 percent failure value or little higher. If this is applied, a significance improvement can be made to the solution. As seen in figure 12.5, the original model shows P(F) (best case scenario) $= 0.00$ (i.e., P(S) $= 1.00$) better than P(F) $= 0.4530$ in the first approach. While P(F) (worst case scenario) $= 0.51264$ (i.e. P(S) $= 0.48736$) better than P(F) $= 1.00$ in the first approach. Similar results can be obtained for additional Improvements 1–5, thus showing considerable improvement in the outcomes. In all cases, managers should avoid using 50 percent inputs values to the basic events of the FTD as this yield very bad failure values in both scenarios as seen in figures 12.4 and 12.5.

BENEFITS OF THE PROPOSED INTEGRAL APPROACH

In assessing the reliability of complex systems as those of project management organizations working in international fluctuating and turbulant markets, an important question has to be answered by strategic managers who are responsible for the efficiency of their organization: How reliable will their organizational system be during its intended and future operating life? The answer seems not to be easy, as the forces impinging on its systems affect its operation, and the performance of the subsystems changes accordingly. Organizational managers, therefore, have to ensure that although a subsystem may fail, its

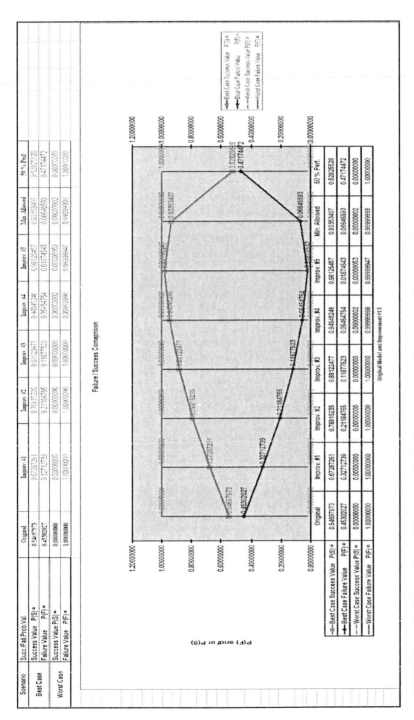

FIGURE 12-4. Tracking and sensitivity analysis for both case scenarios (best case and worst case).

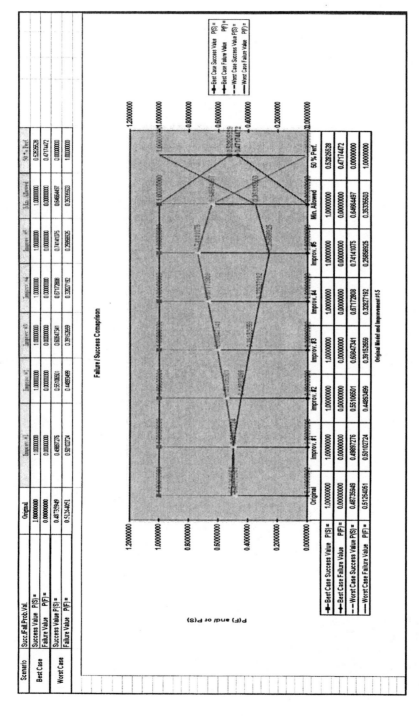

FIGURE 12-5. Improving in success and failure values of both cases (if individual FTDs basic events are assigned very small probability values [e.g. P (Basic Event) = 0.01 or similar]).

frequency of failure or probability of being in a failed state at any time is within a certain limit, and its effect on the total system is acceptable. Following the famous saying that precaution is better than curing, it is easier to predict possible chances of failing events than trying to solve deteriorating events after their occurrence—especially when other parties are involved or extensive investments are involved as in the project management practice. The FB technique, together with the FTD, can serve effectively to assess the reliability of any system. They can help put precaution measures to the system under study before problems happen. The integral approach of both techniques proved to be very effective in defining problems affecting project management organizations working in foreign markets and helped in providing a full quantitative analysis to the problem. The improvement in the system failure value can be reached by following a tracking and sensitivity analysis methodology to reduce the probability values assigned, hence, helping managers take reliable courses of action to reduce, eliminate, modify, and/or improve the whole performance of the organization management systems. Accordingly, this approach if correctly followed can improve performance of the organization and can ensure the continuous long-term success of its business either locally or internationally.

SIGNIFICANCE AND PROMISE OF GENERALIZING THIS INTEGRAL APPROACH

The significance of this work can be seen valid in the integration of both techniques that can assist managers to correctly evaluate the reliability of their project management systems and to compute the rate of their success/failure in an easy and effective qualitative and quantitative manner. The recommended integration also offers managers a method by which they can improve the structure, process, and/or procedures of their project management systems to overcome any potential failures in their system. Undoubtedly, this will improve the performance of the projects and consequently ensures good and reliable service to the clients, which adds to their satisfaction and ultimately ensures continuous existance in any market—either stable or turbulent—with reliable success and less turnovers in the long run. Furthermore, this integral approach can be used as a general reliable technique for solving complex problems. It is a very useful technique in diagnosing and defining areas of weaknesses and possible chances of failures in any system and can help managers to early predict the probability of occurrence of some major events that can hinder the success of the organization in its mission. Following the suggested flow chart steps is the road to achieve good results when analyzing complex problems in any field of application.

BIBLIOGRAPHY

Aggarwal, K. K. 1993. *Reliability Engineering.* Boston, MA: Kluwer Academic Publishers.
Anderson, R. T. 1975. *Reliability Design Handbook.* IIT Research Institute.

Andrews, J. D., and T. R. Moss. 1993. *Reliability and Risk Assessment.* Longman Scientific & Technical.

Ang, A. H.-S., and W. H. Tang. 1984. *Probability Concepts in Engineering Planning and Design, Volume II—Decisions, Risks, and Reliability.* John Willey & Sons.

Barlow, R. E., J. B. Fussell, and N. D. Sinpurwalla, editors. 1975. System Reliability and Safety Assessment SIAM. *Reliability and Fault Tree Analysis.*

Barlow, R. E., and H. E. Lambert. 1961. *Introduction to Fault Tree Analysis.* In *Reliability and Fault Tree Analysis*, edited by R. E. Barlow, J. B. Fussell, and N. D. Sinpurwalla. SIAM, 1975, pp. 7–35.

Bazovsky, I. 1961. *Reliability Theory and Practice.* Prentice-Hall.

Billinton, R., and R. N. Allan. 1983. *Reliability Evaluation of Engineering Systems: Concepts and Techniques.* Pitman Advanced Publishing Program.

Cox, S. J., N. R. S. Tait. 1991. *Reliability, Safety & Risk Management: An Integrated Approach.* Butterworth Heinemann.

Crosetti, P. A. 1970. Fault Tree Analysis with Probability Evaluation. *IEEE Transactions on Nuclear Science*, November, 132.

Greene, A. E., and A. J. Bourne. 1972. *Reliability Technology.* John Wiley and Sons.

Haasl, D. F. 1965. Advanced Concepts in Fault Tree Analysis. In *Proceedings of System Safety Symposium*, Seattle: The Boeing Company.

Harison, M. I. 1987. *Diagnosing Organisations Methods, Models, and Processes.* (Applied Social Research Methods Series, Vol. 8). Sage.

Harvey, D. F. 1982. *Business Policy and Strategic Management.* Columbus, Ohio: Bell and Howell Company.

IEEE Transactions on Reliability, R-19, 1970.

Ireson, W. G., and C. F. Coombs. 1988. *Handbook of Reliability Engineering and Management.* McGraw-Hill.

Kececioglu, D. 1991. *Reliability Engineering Handbook*, vol. 2. Englewood Cliffs, N.J.: Prentice-Hall.

Luffman, G., S. Sanderson, E. Lea, and B. Kenny. 1991. *Business Policy—An Analytical Introduction.* Blackwell Business.

Newcombe, R., D. Langford, and R. Fellows. 1990. *Construction Management: Organisation Systems*, vol. 1, and *Construction Management: Management Systems*, vol. 2, Construction Technology and Management, Mitchell-London. CIOB.

Pages, A., and M. Gondran. 1986. *System Reliability Evaluation and Prediction in Engineering.* North Oxford Academic.

Pilcher, R. 1992. *Principles of Construction Management*, 3rd ed. McGraw-Hill.

Porter, M.E. 1980. *Competitive Strategies: Techniques for Analyzing Industries and Competitors.* New York: Free Press.

Porter, R. B., and K. Carey. 1974. Stochastic Dominance as a Risk Analysis Criterion. *Decision Sciences* 5:10–21.

Ramahumar, R. 1993. *Engineering Reliability Fundamentals and Applications.* Englewood Cliffs, N.J.: Prentice-Hall.

Rao, S. S. 1992. *Reliability Based Design.* McGraw-Hill.

Rouhianian, V. 1993. Modelling of Accident Sequences. In *Quality Management of Safety and Risk Analysis*, edited by J. Suokas and V. Rouhianian. VIT, Technical Centre of Finland, Safety Engineering Laboratory, Tampere, Finland: Elsevier.

Sauer, C. 1993. *Why Information Systems Fail: A Case Study Approach.* (Information Systems Series). Alfered Waller Limited.

Singh, G., and G. Kiangi. 1987. *Risk and Reliability Appraisal on Microcomputers.* Kent, U.K.: Chartwell-Bratt.

WASH 1400. 1974. *US Atomic Energy Commission, Reactor Safety Study: An Assessment of Accident Risks in US Commercial Nuclear Plants.* Report WASH-1400, USAEC, NUREG-75/014, October, Washington D.C.

Why Project Termination Tarries

VICTOR S. SOHMEN

T he typical project is a time-bound entity conceptualized at the outset to terminate at a predetermined point in time. However, the final termination date—when the project is formally commissioned—has a tendency to be somewhat later than the date earmarked during the preexecution segment of the project life cycle. There are several reasons for this unplanned "growth" of the tail end of the project life cycle. These appear to fall under the following broad areas: *strategic, financial, behavioral, organizational, cultural,* and *operational.* As a late termination date translates into increased cost without necessarily enhancing quality, this involuntary elasticity of the project's tail has adverse economic consequences. In this chapter, the slice of linear time bracketed by the original, target termination date and actual termination date is the focus. It explores the possible causes of tardy termination under the above areas. Tentative guidelines are suggested to minimize the costly, temporal gap between the target termination date and actual project commissioning. It is hoped that this will attract empirical studies to explore the ideas presented in this chapter.

OVERVIEW

By definition, projects are *temporary* organizations, whether they produce temporary or permanent offspring. For instance, a five-year labor-intensive construction project of a suspension bridge across a major river between twin cities is meant to be a permanent product. On the other hand, a knowledge-intensive, three-month software project could result in a database program that is not expected to last more than a year before it becomes obsolete. The word temporary has a time dimension; etymologically, it is derived from the Latin adjective *temporarius,* meaning "lasting for a limited time" (Merriam-Webster 2000). The project *must* be terminated.

Whatever the nature of projects, time and timing are key constructs in their management. Unfortunately, a large number of projects are unable to terminate on time. They cost a great amount to the project owners and heavy opportunity costs to the client. Obviously, this is serious enough to deserve our focused attention. This chapter therefore looks at the problems in completing a project on the original Target Termination Date (TTD). It also suggests remedies to achieve timely termination without jeopardizing other project requirements.

THE STRATEGIC IMPORTANCE OF PROJECTS TODAY

Competitive organizations are turning their strategies into reality through innovative projects. Indeed, firms are increasingly adopting multifunctional project teams to accomplish resource-constrained tasks, solve problems, and improve efficiency (Curling 1998). This renders such firms more flexible. It makes them responsive to changing external environments and enables them to unleash their innovativeness. In business and commerce, projects represent a substantial proportion of the productive efforts of enterprises in every industrial sector (Cooke-Davies 2001).

Though projects are essentially fuelled by a structured flow of finances, they need not always be driven by the commercial motive. They may even have aesthetic and cultural impacts that last for centuries. An outstanding example is that of the illustrious Taj Mahal, built by the Mogul emperor Shah Jahan as a symbol of his undying love for his deceased wife. This twenty-two-year-long project began in 1631 and employed over 20,000 skilled artisans and 1,000 elephants. Aptly described by the Indian Nobel laureate Rabindranath Tagore as "a tear-drop on the cheek of time," this exquisitely poetic edifice in iridescent marble captures the hearts and minds of millions of admirers even today. Indeed, some projects can have a timeless impact.

In a competitive world awash with ephemeral opportunities, economic vagaries, and occasional windfalls, however, the commercial motive has become an undeniable driving force in the spawning of projects. The inexorable drive to capture new markets, outmaneuver peers, and displace rivals compels companies to launch innovative projects. The window of opportunity to deliver a unique product to market can be fleeting, and timing becomes of strategic importance to the company. In the turbulent computer industry for instance, the danger of delaying the market entry of software can be tragically real to firms in the rat race. Therefore, the necessity to complete projects as quickly as possible—within technological, financial, and human resource constraints—is becoming increasingly evident today.

REFLECTIONS ON THE PROJECT COMMISSIONING PHASE

The Commissioning Phase of the project is not only the final stage of the project life cycle, but is also in many ways an anticlimactic one. The excitement of the Execution Phase with its hectic activity and critical dependencies give way to a greater focus on efficiency; we enter a more humdrum routine of checklists, tests, troubleshooting, and meticulous documentation. The Commissioning Phase commences with completion of the first major deliverable, and finishes when the facility, product, or service is formally handed over to the client—whether internal or external to the sponsoring organization. In any event, the Commissioning Phase carries the highest stake with significant risk impact and severe consequences due to cumulative investment in the project. This is depicted in figure 13.1, where the uncertainty regarding the project outcome decreases steadily through the project life cycle, whereas the investments in the project—hence the stake—increases, reaching its highest levels during the Commissioning Phase. Further, the creativity required for activities decreases rapidly, down from the high levels occurring during the Design and Execution Phases. Similarly, we see a sharp decrease in the deployment of resources as we move toward project termination.

In this context, we need to look at the purpose of the project: to satisfy the customer with a product, facility, or service that has been contracted for delivery on time, within budget, and with satisfying performance criteria (Tukel and Rom 2001). The increasing focus by businesses on customer satisfaction has driven competition, improved quality, and fuelled innovation in the past two decades. Despite the lack of interest in the Commissioning Phase by project practitioners and even researchers in the project management area, the customer shows the

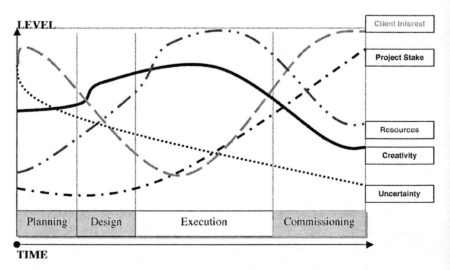

FIGURE 13-1. Client interest, project stake, resources, creativity, and uncertainty.

highest interest in the first and last phases of the project: the Planning Phase and the Commissioning Phase. At the beginning of the project, the client is interested in making sure that the stated requirements are formally planned and scoped for. At the end of the project, the client asks the question: "Will the project be completed on time and meet our specifications?" The customer's level of interest is obviously very high toward the end. Thus, both the project and client parties have a great stake in successful completion of the project—on time.

It can be deduced that of the three generic parameters—time, cost, and performance—time moves to center stage in the Commissioning Phase, with performance close on its heels. The substantial part of cost has already been sunk into the project and has largely been dealt with in earlier phases through progress payments, as well as through external stakeholders' mediation. Now, delivering the output of the project on time becomes critical for the client, especially where the timing of market entry is a driving factor of paramount importance.

Having extolled the virtue of time as a critical parameter and constraint in project management, it must be conceded that late termination may not necessarily mean project failure. Consequently, projects that are late, with major flaws and cost overruns, may find not only acceptance, but perhaps also market success (Whittaker 2000). However, this should be treated as an exception, and contingent on extraordinary market conditions. This chapter assumes that timely project termination is a critical dimension for project success and client goodwill through containing costs and maximizing post-project benefits.

The Commissioning Phase may be divided into three sub-phases: Pre-commissioning, Core Commissioning, and Initial Operations (Sohmen 1992). Pre-commissioning overlaps with the tail end of the Execution Phase, and together with Core Commissioning and Initial Operations comprise hard commissioning. This is preceded by the "soft commissioning" segment spanning the project life cycle up to the transition to hard commissioning (figure 13.2). The purpose of soft commissioning is primarily to preempt the inevitable frustrations of hard commissioning by ensuring systematic preparation and completion of long-lead-time activities. These include planning and scheduling for commissioning, various preliminary tests, and meticulous, timely documentation even during the Execution Phase. Subsequent handover to the client-operator is thus made smoother, along with efficient, timely delivery of necessary initial client-operators' training, manuals, technical specifications, and drawings.

A major problem with the Commissioning Phase is that efficiency is often emphasized over effectiveness. The project personnel see termination as the end of a tunnel, rather than as the glorious beginning of innovative change and opportunity in the environment. It is important to ensure that the linkages between the terminating project and the big picture of organizational strategy are made more visible toward the end of the project. This will enhance the morale of project personnel, sharpen understanding of the overall fit of the project with the environment, and promote effectiveness—well before commencement of the Commissioning Phase.

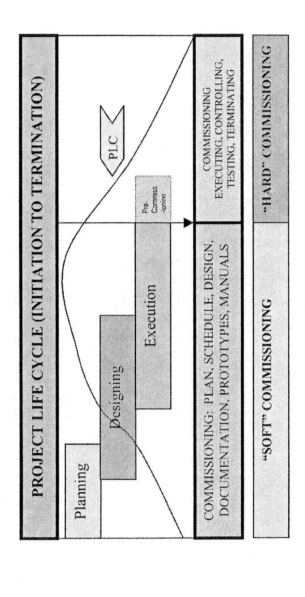

FIGURE 13-2. Commissioning management as a "Project within a Project".

PROJECT TERMINATION

Projects are a means by which organizational strategy is implemented and may often have social, economic, and environmental impacts that far outlast the projects themselves (PMBOK 2000). Yet projects by definition are time bound, and must terminate. Indeed, the substantive objective of a project is to "attain the objective" and close the project (PMBOK 2000). It is certainly important to finish well. Nobody remembers an effective start-up, but everyone remembers an ineffective project termination, the consequences of which are long lasting (Turner 1999).

Certain projects are required to finish *before* target termination to remain competitive and to get faster returns on the investment (Dey 2000). On the other hand, many projects are aborted midstream for both volitional and involuntary reasons. As for volitional motives, the business need for the project may no longer exist, and continuing the project will only produce a "white elephant" with little congruence or fit with organizational strategy. Legal problems and environmental concerns may arise, necessitating the dissolution of the project to avoid severe penalties, which may exceed any benefit from the project. On the obverse, involuntary failure of the project may occur due to insufficient financial support, poor leadership, weak front-end planning, and excessive negative impacts of project stakeholders.

It is also possible to terminate a project that has not attained all its objectives. Such projects have inflexible deadlines such as widely advertised conference dates. Whether the preparations and fine details of such projects are complete or not, the projects themselves have to terminate on the due date. This seems to be common where the deliverable is a service. Yet, not all projects are terminated in the conventional sense. There are five fundamentally different ways to terminate a project (Meredith and Mantel 2000): (1) by extinction, such as when it is no longer cost-effective or environmentally viable; (2) by addition, when it is made an external addition to the client organization; (3) by integration, when the product becomes part-and-parcel of the client or parent entity; (4) by suspension, when the project is untimely and has to be suspended or shelved; and (5) by starvation, when the project is killed by withholding financial and other resources.

FACTORS CAUSING TERMINATION DELAYS

Strategic

Project success involves strategic control of the formulated goals and the methods used to accomplish the venture. Lack of sustained support by top management can be a serious problem in maintaining the project schedule toward timely completion. Further, the project champion may have lost power in a political shakeout within the parent organization, resulting in the unfortunate demise of the project. In addition, the strategy of the company may have been altered during the project life cycle, making the project incongruous with the firm's new strategic objectives and directions. The parent organization may have thus lost interest in ensuring project success. Finally, the project in question may have negative effects on other projects being implemented in the parent organization's overall project portfolio—and therefore may be delayed, suspended or killed.

Financial

The scope of the project may be inconsistent with the company's financial strength or strategy. Thus, some companies may simply run out of money towards the end of their project due to underestimation or unforeseen inflation (Dey 2000). In this case work cannot continue, causing serious disruption of schedules and milestones. "Termination by starvation" is a variation of this, where the project is deliberately retarded and killed by choking off its financial resources. Further, changes in governmental and regulatory requirements can be costly and time-consuming.

Behavioral

The tendency of project participants to postpone irksome or difficult tasks as long as possible can cumulate along the time continuum toward the Commissioning Phase to extend its tail beyond the TTD. During the Commissioning Phase, project team members are laid off in increasing numbers. This can cause morale problems, with people losing their social contacts nurtured over the project life cycle. Those who remain through the Commissioning Phase also have the anticlimactic experience of slowdown in some aspects of the project. Finally, there is also stress built up due to anxiety about subsequent employment after project termination. The result can be depression and erratic behavior. Some of the personnel may even leave due to burnout or to seek other employment. Paradoxically, fear of unemployment may impel personnel to slow down the project progress.

Organizational

Inadequate or unwieldy project organization structure can be a problem as much time is wasted in inefficient logistics, reporting relationships, and information flows. Poor planning of the project details and slipshod scope definition can significantly jeopardize the chances of meeting project targets, including its termination date. Related to this is the all-too-common careless attitude toward planning the commissioning activities. In many cases, the termination date is arbitrarily imposed without considering all milestones, resources, and constraints. Such unrealistic scheduling increases project risk, adds cost, and jeopardizes quality. Further, poor staffing, weak responsibility matrixes, and tenuous team development cause severe morale and substandard productivity problems. Finally, incompetent project leadership can be disastrous.

Cultural

Project commissioning can also be delayed due to ethnic cultural problems that vary from time perceptions to power relationships to work ethics. The concept of time differs greatly from one culture to another. Some cultures, such as that of the United States, look at time from a linear perspective. Time cannot be "wasted" because it never comes back! On the other hand, Middle Eastern cultures treat time in a cyclical manner. This has significant implications from a project perspective. In Western cultures, hard work goes in tandem with other values such as materialism, practicality, and efficiency. Further, efficiency is measured in terms of costs and profits. Success is correlated to positive cash flows. In many other cultures, relaxing and engaging in aesthetically pleasing activities are considered important counterbalances to hard work. Efficiency is tempered with enhancement factors such as satisfaction and enjoyment, rather than with purely materialistic motives.

In some countries, contracts and business ethics are not held in high regard, and they can be violated without serious consequences. Many international legal contracts are therefore not enforceable. This can be a problem when dealing with subcontractors—and even major contractors—who become critical stakeholders in ensuring project success. At the tail end of the project, the scrupulous performance of contractors and subcontractors is vital. It is therefore important to thoroughly investigate the credentials and track records of these key stakeholders to the project, and formalize ethical controls during the bidding process itself.

Operational

Project operations include all production support activities. Operational processes in the project can be both hard and soft. Whereas the hard processes such as equipment operations are predictable and managed with scientific precision, the soft processes such as the training of the client's staff are fraught with uncertainty and complexity. The operations team of the client that takes over the plant or product may take longer than expected to learn the ropes.

Further, during the Commissioning Phase, it can be a frustrating experience to run into snags when conducting various equipment and process tests. For instance, crucial documents may be missing, and specifications and troubleshooting information may be untraceable. This is made worse by the sharp drop in resource loading during the Commissioning Phase (figure 13.1), making it difficult to get timely assistance. These bugs can introduce delays through schedule slippages for process, equipment, and program completions.

MANAGING FOR TIMELY TERMINATION

Orderly termination on or before the TTD is important to ensure client satisfaction and neat completion of the project and its final payments. It is also good for favorable publicity for the firm, for general goodwill in the community, and for repeat business with competitive clients. Frustration and panic hardly make for good public relations. Yet, timely termination of a project cannot happen by accident. It requires astute, time-conscious, and diligent management on various fronts.

Project Commissioning Management

- *Create a Commissioning Team during the Planning Phase.* The team should consist of representatives from key stakeholders: major contractors, subcontractors, consultants, and the client. The Commissioning Team should also comprise detail-oriented project players with diverse functional backgrounds.
- *Appoint a Commissioning Manager (CM—figure 13.3) to lead the team and report to the Project Manager (PM—figure 13.3).* This team leader should be detail-oriented and familiar with both the technical and administrative details of the project. "The magic of an outstanding product or a superior process is in the *details*" (Clark and Wheelwright 1993).
- Treat commissioning management as a "project within a project" (Sohmen 1992) with cost, schedule, and reporting plans (figure 13.2).
- Begin the training of the client's operations team during the Pre-commissioning stage of the Commissioning Phase.

Project Stakeholder Management

- Identify and classify project stakeholders (for, against, neutral) and analyze their respective possible impacts on the project through the project life cycle.
- Isolate and analyze stakeholders with possible *negative* impacts on the project (such as environmentalists and local competitors). Plan to counter these impacts.
- Incorporate and involve the key primary project stakeholders (including the client, labor union, suppliers, contractors, consultants, and government agencies) in the Project Plan and in every subsequent phase of the project.
- Make needed information available to the stakeholders at appropriate times, ensuring that key stakeholders clearly concur with the project objectives.

Project Risk Management

- Include stakeholders in the risk analysis criteria to forestall termination delays.
- Identify, prioritize, evaluate, and mitigate project risks early in the project.
- Make contingency plans using realistic scenarios and time-sensitive alternatives.
- Aggregate the risks after identifying them. The higher the number of risks that can be aggregated, the more marked the effect in the reduction of overall risk (Steyn 2001).

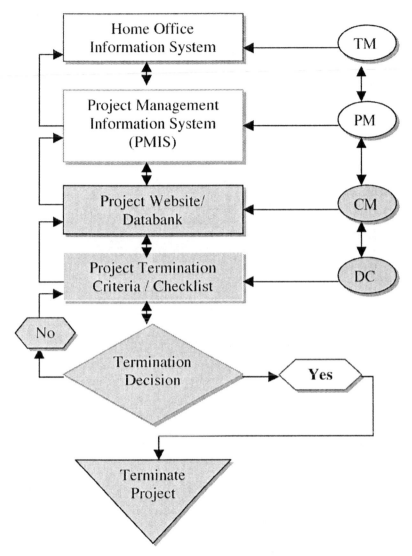

FIGURE 13-3. Commissioning decision support system (CDSS).

Total Quality Management (TQM)

- Incorporate TQM in the project scope and plan to help compress schedules while enhancing quality—the customer-focused PM's primary success measure (Tukel and Rom 2001).

- Formalize and document construction and quality standards against cost and time factors. It must be kept in view that excessive quality can delay the project and raise costs, whereas substandard quality can cause friction with the client.
- Minimize the necessity of rework by doing things right the first time—this is a matter of systematic and resolute TQM in action. Rework is wasteful because it pushes the project beyond time and budget limits (Webster 1999).
- Insist on quality in every aspect of the project, as it instills discipline, raises morale, and enhances pride in the work, while effecting long-term cost efficiencies.

Project Human Resources

- Appoint a competent project manager (PM) with an excellent track record of projects completed on time, and with favorable post-project performance reviews.
- Appoint a Commissioning Manager (CM) spearheading a composite Commissioning Team during the Planning Phase. The CM reports to the PM.
- Make plans well before the Commissioning Phase to re-deploy project personnel in other projects, or to return them to their functional departments.
- Provide adequate retraining and interim compensation until alternate employment of those who are to be laid off after project termination.

Project Planning and Controls

- Scope out the project thoroughly at the outset in the planning phase, ensuring formalization of the project objectives, scope baseline, WBS, reporting structures, and commissioning milestones. Fine-tune estimates as more accurate information comes in along with decreasing uncertainty (figure 13.1). A well-defined scope and work content provides the highest chances of meeting project targets.
- Tighten up project controls during the Commissioning Phase, with more frequent control meetings, using Information Technology and strong interdependencies.
- Streamline performance-reporting structures: status reports, progress tracking, change management, and forecasting through all the phases of the project.
- Use a Commissioning Decision Support System (CDSS—figure 13.3). Such a system harnesses the power of the computer to store, process, and communicate information across different project players and stakeholders. The CDSS also helps analyze and select from alternatives (Dey 2000). Further, it has the potential to play a crucial role in improving the effectiveness of problem solving at the working level (Clark and Wheelwright 1993).

Document Control

- Appoint a Document Controller (DC—figure 13.3) during the Planning Phase, who reports to the CM as part of the Commissioning Team.
- Deliveries of change orders, drawings, and user manuals should be marked as milestones in the project schedule and tracked by the DC.

- To avoid frustrating delays and backtracking, ensure that all manuals, invoices, patents, drawings, and other documentation in the project are trailed, indexed, approved, copied, distributed, and archived throughout the project life cycle.
- Create and update checklists of both technical and administrative details to be completed during the Commissioning Phase.

Project Time Management

- Be deliberate in deciding on the Target Termination Date TTD, as projects flounder when this final project milestone is too ambitious and unrealistic.
- Shore up project time management and optimize the Critical Path—reexamining activity definition, activity sequencing, activity duration estimating, schedule development, and schedule control. The higher the number of activities on the Critical Path of a project, the more the project duration can be reduced (Steyn 2001).
- Fine-tune WBS to increase parallel activities and to compress the schedule. Schedule all noncritical activities as late as possible, but with buffers that feed into the Critical Path, constantly monitoring them as well (Steyn 2001).
- Create an "Early Termination Date" for the project team to aim for, between 5 percent and 10 percent ahead of the TTD for the client (figure 13.4). Compress the project schedule and seek to increase parallel activities throughout the project. The best way to achieve this would be to finish as many activities as possible ahead of schedule, however trivial. The resulting floats (Late Start to Early Start) will snowball into an aggregate "buffer." However, the extra labor deployed and provision of incentives to contractors and subcontractors to meet this Early Termination Date would offset any cost savings from early finish (see S-Curves).

Project Culture Management

- Insist on culturally sensitive project leadership.
- Incorporate a diversity policy throughout the project.
- Build trust and transparent relationships among diverse players.
- Provide rich socialization to build and maintain project morale.

Project Communication Management

- Redesign communication systems to eliminate gaps or blind spots, aiming for richness of connectivity, fluidity, and transparency of communication.
- Employ computerized data warehousing for easy access to information by all parties involved, at least in "read-only" format, with proprietary access for key personnel to make changes and updates.
- Set up discussion forums on the project Web site/Intranet to enable both synchronous and asynchronous project communication around the clock.
- Arrange periodic discussion sessions to resolve bottlenecks and conflicts.

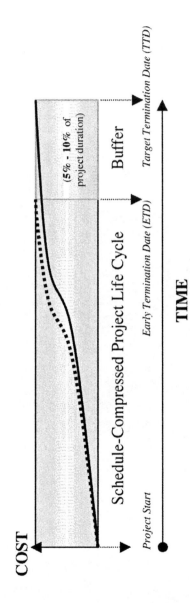

FIGURE 13-4. Early termination date.

SUMMARY AND CONCLUSIONS

Timely and orderly project termination capstones project success. To significantly increase the chances of meeting the TTD, the following are recommended:

- Appoint a detail-oriented CM to spearhead a Commissioning Team in the Planning Phase, with both administrative and technical skills, and reporting to a PM with culturally sensitive leadership skills.
- Formalize and plan the Commissioning Phase as a "project-within-a-project"—with its own cost, schedule, reporting criteria, meetings, milestones, and staff loading— during the project Planning Phase. Appoint a DC.
- Develop a CDSS with a computerized database to track, analyze, compile, duplicate, and archive project manuals, drawings, and reports throughout the PLC, not only during commissioning.
- Create an Early Termination Date to provide a buffer of around 5 percent to 10 percent of the PLC, ahead of the TTD. Constantly compress task schedules by finishing discrete activities early to accumulate sufficient float to achieve the Early Termination Date. Use TQM techniques, giving incentives to suppliers, contractors, and subcontractors to steer the project to remain within the TTD.
- Build and sustain high morale throughout among project personnel (especially during the Commissioning Phase), maintaining fluid and transparent communications.

Little dedicated research has been conducted to explore the reasons for delays in the termination of projects. Once the project is thoroughly scoped, it is reasonable to aim for and achieve control of every phase and milestone. Timely project termination can be achieved only if delays are not allowed to accumulate through the project phases. This chapter has looked briefly at strategic, financial, behavioral, organizational, cultural, and operational reasons for tardy project termination. These ideas need to be empirically tested. For example, completed projects could be examined in three diverse industries (e.g., computer, automobile, and petrochemical) for causes of termination delays. What are the factors that could be controlled *within* the project? What potential problems need to be controlled from *outside* the project? What are the weighted impacts of stakeholders? Have they helped or hindered project progress? How can project personnel be motivated to work concertedly toward timely project termination? These could be investigated in depth for new insights. This effort would be well worth it, for there is much at stake when companies fail to launch their facilities, products, and services in a timely manner in an unforgiving, competitive environment.

BIBLIOGRAPHY

Clark, Kim B., and Steven C. Wheelwright. 1993. *Managing New Product and Process Development: Text and Cases.* New York: Free Press.

Cooke-Davies, Terence J. 2001. *Toward Improved Project Management Practice: Uncovering the Evidence for Effective Practices Through Empirical Research.* Leeds, U.K.: Leeds Metropolitan University.

Curling, David H. 1998. Globalization of the Project Management Profession. http://www.pmforum.org/docs/prof2col.htm.

Dey, Prasanta Kumar. 2000. Managing Projects In Fast Track: A Case of Public Sector Organisation In India. *International Journal of Public Sector Management* 13(7): 588–609.

Meredith, Jack R., and Samuel J. Mantel. 2000. *Project Management: A Managerial Approach.* New York: John Wiley & Sons.

Merriam-Webster's Collegiate Dictionary and Thesaurus. 2000.

PMBOK. 2000. *A Guide to the Project Management Body of Knowledge.* Newton Square, Pa.: Project Management Institute.

Sohmen, Victor. 1992. Project Commissioning: Factors for Success. *Proceedings of the First World Congress on Project Management and Cost Engineering.* Orlando, FL.

Steyn, Herman. 2001. An Investigation into the Fundamentals of Critical Chain Project Scheduling. *International Journal of Project Management* 19:363–69.

Tukel, Oya Lemeli, and Walter O. Rom. 2001. An Empirical Investigation of Project Evaluation Criteria. *International Journal of Operations & Production Management* 21(3): 400–416.

Turner, Rodney J. *The Handbook of Project-Based Management.* Berkshire, U.K.: McGraw-Hill.

Webster, Gordon. 1999. Project Definition—The Missing Link. *Industrial and Commercial Training* 31(6): 240–45.

Whittaker, John. 2000. Reflection on the Challenging Nature of Projects. In *Projects as Business Constituents and Guiding Motives,* edited by Rolf A. Lundin and Francis Hartman. Kluwer Academic Press.

14

Project Management in the Engineering and Construction Industry

JOHN A. KUPRENAS

INTRODUCTION TO THE INDUSTRY

Characteristics

Construction is big business. The projects are large with individual projects are typically worth millions of dollars. Large projects are worth hundreds of millions of dollars if not billions of dollars. The industry employs large numbers (5 percent of the workforce in the United States) and makes up a large portion of gross national product (GNP; 8.1 percent of the U.S. GNP in 1997) (Gould and Joyce 2001). The industry influences everyone's lives in that it produces the infrastructure and buildings in which we live and work.

Although construction is arguably the most visible of all industries, it is not well developed from a project management point of view. Only in the last forty years has project management of the design and construction process has begun to be widely used. Difficulty in development and effective utilization of a project management body of knowledge for the industry is a result of the inherent peculiarities within the industry. Some of these peculiarities include:

- Although design elements are standardized, most projects are "one of a kind."
- Project design is based on site characteristics (geography and climate).
- A large portion of design process influenced by physical conditions (material availability, equipment availability).

- A large portion of the construction process is influenced by physical conditions (labor skill and climate).
- Labor is hired on a project basis.
- Tight profit margins created by competitive procurement processes provide little room for innovation and research.

Within the industry, projects are characterized by their type/nature of work. First, work can divided into public and private sector, with about 30 percent of the work falling on the public side. Second, work can be divided by type. Four main types of construction exist—residential, building, heavy civil, and industrial. Each type of construction has its own attributes with respect to technologies and processes. As such, designers, constructors, and even managers to a certain extent, tend to categorize themselves into these groups. Table 14.1 shows the characteristics of each type of construction (Barrie and Paulson 1992; Gould and Joyce 2001).

Project Lifecycle and Responsibilities

The life cycle of a construction project can be defined in many ways depending on the project and the motivation for the project. In simplest form, a project has five phases as shown in figure 14.1. The figure also shows the parties involved in each phase of the process and the approximate cost breakdown spent on each phase. Given the unique nature of every project, these phases may blur and overlap depending on project type, constraints, and delivery system. Figure 14.1 shows the activities, cost, and time typically associated with each of these phases.

TABLE 14-1. Types and characteristics of construction

Type	Market Share	Characteristics	Typical Projects
Residential	30% – 35%	Mostly private sector finance Labor and materials intensive Low technology Demand instability	Single family homes Apartment buildings High-rise condominiums
Building	35% – 40%	Public and private sector finance Labor and materials intensive Higher complexity	Retail (small to large) Commercial office Government facilities
Heavy Civil	20% – 25%	Mostly public sector finance Equipment intensive Engineering requirements	Dams Tunnels Bridges Pipelines
Industrial	5% – 10%	Mostly private sector finance High level engineering expertise Labor and equipment intensive Utilizes unique contractual arrangements for consideration	Refineries Process plants Mills

	Typical Activities	Typical Cost (as percentage of total project cost)	Typical Duration (as a percentage of total project duration)
Predesign	• Go-no decision for project • Establish total project cost(+/- 30%) • Establish Project Financing and Risk • Define project program or function • Select designer(s) and award contract(s)	1%- 10%	5% to 25%
Design	• Finalize total project cost (+/- 10%) • Establish desired quality • Establish Project Milestone dates • Produce plans and specifications	5% to 40%	10% to 40%
Procurement/Bid and Award	• Finalize project sequence • Identify special conditions for the project • Select constructor(s) and award contract(s)	1% to 10%	5% to 10%
Construction	• Construct project based upon plans and sepcifications • Clarify project uncertainties • Negotiate changes to contract • Inspect quality as construction work progresses	40% to 85%	50% to 90%
Closeout and Occupancy	• Prepare as-built documents • Test project systems • Train facilitiy staff • Create punchlist of quality deficiencies to be repaired • Close construction and design contracts	5% to 20%	5% to 20%

FIGURE 14-1. Phases of the project life cycle.

Many individuals contribute to the entire design and construction process. Common to most any project are the following:

- Owner—individual or group for whom the project is to be built; may or may not finance construction; defines basic project parameters;
- Designer—architects or engineers or team who translates vision of owner into plans and specifications to be built;
- Project/Construction Manager—professional third party who assists all team members to ensure project meets objectives; typically under contract to the owner;
- Inspectors—professional third party (often public-sector employee) who checks that work put in place is installed per plans and specifications and within design codes.

Responsibilities of the parties vary with size and type of project. A responsibility matrix is created on many projects to define specific responsibilities of all project parties (in conjunction with professional services contracts).

Current Trends

Like any industry, the design and construction industry has evolved based on research and trends. Past trends/research in project management that have impacted industry include computerized cost and schedule controls, and development and recognition of the professional construction manager/project manager as a required project delivery team member. Recent trends within the industry include:

- Specialization—Market-driven demand has designers and contractors looking to specialize in a niche. While not a new concept, emerging markets in today's technology-driven construction have made specialization a profitable choice for some firms. As such, designers and construction contractors increasingly have narrow expertise. In addition, in order to compete in such niche markets, large firms have begun to consolidate smaller specialty firms in order to acquire their expertise. This phenomenon is particularly true in the project/construction management industry.
- Green/sustainable building—Sustainable development is a new trend within the industry by which organizations seek economic development approaches that also benefit the local environment and quality of life. It has become an important guide to many organizations that have discovered that traditional approaches to planning and development are creating, rather than solving, societal and environmental problems. Where traditional approaches can lead to congestion, sprawl, pollution, and resource overconsumption, sustainable development offers real, lasting solutions that will strengthen our future. Green building is closely related to sustainable development. The resources required for creating, operating, and replenishing the current infrastructure are enormous, yet the resources available for such activity are diminishing. To remain competitive and to continue to expand and produce profits in the future, the building industry has now begun to focus on the economic and environmental consequences of its actions. This need is driving the building industry to develop and market products and processes that are more environmentally and

economically viable—called green building. Note that when used, these products and/or processes may result in higher initial project costs, but with lower long-term operational costs (financial and environmental; U.S. Green Building Council, 2002).

- Web-based project management tools—Online project management tools for the design and construction industry centralize information from project conception to completion, allow building owners, architects, engineers, construction managers, general contractors, and subcontractors to coordinate and manage immense amounts of information online. They are typically hosted online and are available on a subscription basis. Key features include Multi-project, Multisite, online project collaboration, purchasing, cost control, document management, field administration, project Web sites, and extensive reporting, all within a secure environment. Potential benefits center on communication with all information available to all parties at any time. Additional benefits include time savings in the physical moving of project correspondence as compared to fax or mail and the ability to use complex computer programs to create four dimensional models to study project problems, to assist in project decision making with incomplete information (case-based reasoning, influence diagrams, neural networks, and knowledge-based systems), and to conduct risk analysis of project cost and schedule.

- Management of entire project life cycle (Program Management)—While the concept of a project management professional overseeing the construction phase of a project is well established, a recent trend toward program management of the entire project delivery process (from inception to completion) has recently evolved. Program management involves multiple projects; it is the development of a comprehensive program for the design, development and implementation of a large-scale multi-project facilities program, generally occurring over several years. Program management services may include traditional project management services (management of a project(s) from the planning and design phase through closeout and occupancy) and construction management services (management of the bid and award, construction, and close-out phases of a project(s)). In addition, multiple project (program) tasks such as condition assessments, facilities master planning, implementation planning, master program schedule, program budget and budget control system, cash flow analysis, project prioritization, management information system, would possibly be included in program management responsibilities in the design and construction industry.

- Lean Construction—Lean Construction is a production management-based approach to design and construction project delivery. Lean production management has caused a revolution in manufacturing design, supply, and assembly. Applied to design and construction, Lean thinking changes the way work is done throughout the delivery process. Lean Construction extends from the objectives of a lean production system—maximize value and minimize waste—to specific techniques and applies them in a new project delivery process. As a result:

The facility and its delivery process are designed together to better reveal and support customer purposes. Positive iteration within the process is supported and negative iteration reduced.

Work is structured throughout the process to maximize value and to reduce waste at the project delivery level.

Efforts to manage and improve performance are aimed at improving total project performance because it is more important than reducing the cost or increasing the speed of any activity.

"Control" is redefined from "monitoring results" to "making things happen." The performance of the planning and control systems are measured and improved.

- The reliable release of work between specialists in design, supply and assembly assures value is delivered to the customer and waste is reduced. Lean Construction is particularly useful on complex, uncertain, and quick projects. It challenges the belief that there must always be a trade between time, cost, and quality (The International Group for Lean Construction 2002; Lean Construction Institute 2002).

PROJECT MANAGEMENT IN THE SECTOR

Project management tools in the construction industry have evolved with the sophistication of the management forces and the increased use of computers on the project. In general, cost- and schedule-control tools the design and construction industry uses are consistent with the tools used within the project management profession. Tools used for quality control are generally reactive (i.e., plan review of design documents for code compliance/errors and omissions and inspection of completed work for defects).

Quality of the completed construction work ideally begins within the design phase. A designer will produce a set of construction documents consisting of a set of plans (graphical layout and details) and specifications (item performance standards). The builder of the project will prepare submittals for the designer to review that include detailed descriptions and specifications of how work will be installed and manufacturers' literature as to component specifications. Onsite inspectors then assure that materials and equipment installed are per approved submittal documents within the intent of the plans and specifications. Design phase quality improvement measurements include constructibility reviews of the plans and specifications and modeling of project buildings, features, and site coordination in order to attempt to reduce construction phase changes (potential cost and schedule changes). In addition, in most countries, the design and construction industry is heavily regulated by public building officials, who ensure structural and fire safety of all buildings and projects through plan reviews and onsite inspections.

Cost and schedule project controls in the construction industry are used to identify and correct for deviations from project objectives during the course of the project. Controls are established for various dimensions of project (design or construction) performance; typically for cost (or another resource) and time. Actual performance is compared to target performance to identify a variance in any of these dimensions. These variances are signals to project managers of the potential for negative impacts on the project. Project managers act to assure performance meets project objectives, usually through conforming performance to plan, or occasionally through modification of the plan, as in recovery plans (PROJECTmagazine 2002).

Some projects have begun to use management tools beyond cost, schedule, and quality control. An increasing awareness of the need for training of project managers has risen within the last five years, and many public-sector organizations within the United States have established project management groups with separate civil service classifications for project managers.

Some organizations (public and private) have begun to use partnering in the design and especially construction phases of a project. Partnering is a semiformal management process developed to improve the area of team communication. In partnering, all of the project delivery parties agree from the beginning (either in the design or construction phase) in a formal structure to focus on creative co-operation and teamwork in order to avoid adversarial confrontation. Working relationships are carefully and deliberately built based on mutual respect, trust, and integrity. The partnering approach is based on the idea that partnering can provide the basis for participants to reorient themselves toward a "win-win" approach to problem solving and can foster synergistic teamwork. A facilitator or project manager will lead formal and informal sessions in this process, beginning with a one- to three-day session(s) that involves all the key players, including the main contractor, subcontractors, and professional consultants meeting together as the starting point for the partnering process. During the partnering workshop, a project charter is developed to formalize the shared objectives and the teamwork and communication principles. Once the partnering session is completed, a partnering coordinator or project manager is given the responsibility to keep the partnering on track and champion the process through to the successful completion of the project (United States Army Corps of Engineers 2002).

Although partnering may not resolve all the problems encountered in the construction process, it does create a framework for conflict resolution, improved communications, reduced litigation, and cost containment on potential overruns. Unlike construction documents and contracts found in the project manual, partnering agreements are not usually binding. Therefore, many unfulfilled promises are often made during partnering sessions, and project managers must still manage the design and construction process.

Despite large cost and schedule consequences of poor management, as well as potential safety problems, application of the other project management tools and processes used in other industries (especially quality control, work flow, and numerical analysis) stems not from a lack of knowledge, but rather from inherent difficulties within the industry such as nonuniformity of the project delivery process; site/location variations for every project; unique nature of most projects (structure and systems); transitory workforce; low bid process for most all public-sector construction work; and traditional industry perceptions/mentalities not geared toward process improvement.

PROJECT MANAGEMENT BEST PRACTICES/IMPACT
OF PROJECT MANAGEMENT

Many diverse groups within the design and construction industries continue to advance the state of the management practice in the design and construction industry. The American Society of Civil Engineers (ASCE), Project Management Institute (PMI), and Construction Industry Institute (CII), and hundreds of other industry groups worldwide, also sponsor research and sponsor conferences on management practices and research. In addition, much applied management research (especially in areas of project controls and contracting) is conducted by government groups. Other government groups sponsor more theoretical strategic research (such as National Science Foundation). Individual public-sector organizations and individual designers or contractors also often conduct case studies and research to solve particular management problems or project delivery difficulties. In addition, several universities have design and construction research institutes funded by local and national industry groups and federal research grants.

Best Practices and Success Factors

Best practices studies form the basis for much project management research in the design and construction process. Several researchers have published valuable project management best practices studies. Most assessment of the best practices takes the form of identification of actions or processes that, when utilized, increase the likelihood of project success (typically defined as cost and schedule conformance). These actions are identified as Critical Success Factors (CSF). Work by Might and Fisher (1985), Pinto and Slevin (1987), Savido et al. (1990), Jaselskis and Ashley (1991), Parfitt and Savido (1993), Anderson and Tucker (1994), Heath, Scott, and Boyland (1994), Chua, Kog, and Loh (1997), and many others have successfully created comprehensive list of management factors that, when present, increase the likelihood of design and construction project success (subdivided based on project phases, project parties, and project delivery technique). Table 14.2 shows an excellent compilation of project management best practices for the design phase (Anderson and Tucker 1994).

Impact of Project Management

Some research has recently begun to try to identify the value of project management to the design and construction process. Work by Kuprenas (2000) provided an analysis of over 270 completed municipal facilities, stormwater, sewer, and street design, and construction projects within a large public-sector design and construction organization in order to assess the impact of the use of a project management processes and tools on design phase cost performance. The only project management performance measure for the 272 project data set was

TABLE 14-2. Critical success factors for design phase activities

Project Aspect	Success-Related Factor
Project Characteristics	Political risks, economic risks, impact on public, technical approval authorities, adequacy of funding; site limitation and location; constructability; pioneering status; project size
Contractual Arrangements	Realistic obligations/clear objectives; risk identification and allocation; adequacy of plans and specifications; formal dispute resolution process; motivation/incentives
Project participants	PM competency; PM authority; PM commitment and involvement; capability of client key personnel; competency of client proposed team; client team turnover rate; client top management support; client track record; client level of service; capability of contractor key personnel; competency of contractor proposed team; contractor team turnover rate; contractor top management support; contractor track record; contractor level of service; capability of consultant key personnel; competency of consultant proposed team; consultant team turnover rate; consultant top management support; consultant track record; consultant level of service; capability of subcontractors key personnel; competency of subcontractors proposed team; subcontractors team turnover rate; subcontractors top management support; subcontractors track record; subcontractors level of service; capability of suppliers key personnel; competency of suppliers proposed team; suppliers team turnover rate; suppliers top management support; suppliers track record; suppliers level of service
Interactive Processes	Formal design communication; informal design communication; formal construction communication; informal construction communication; functional plans; design complete at construction start; constructability program; level of modularization; level of automation; level of skill labors required; report updates; budget updates; schedule updates; design control meetings; construction control meetings; site inspections; work organization chart; common goal; motivational factor; relationships

design phase cost performance data. Design phase cost performance is defined through a cost performance index (DCPI) computed as:

$$DCPI = ACDWP/BCDWP$$

where BCDWP is defined as the budgeted cost of the design work performed, and ACDPW is defined as the actual cost of the design work performed. In the study, the BCDWP for all projects was based on preestablished budget templates—historical estimates of dollar costs (expressed as a percentage of estimated construction cost) for every task/element required in the design of a project.

Given a constant level of quality and schedule performance, Kuprenas (2000) found that the process of a design team meeting frequency was found to be statistically significant in reducing design phase costs with the mean DCPI reduced by meeting more than time per month as compared to than meeting less than one time per month. Similarly, given a constant level of quality and schedule performance, the process of written reporting of design phase progress more than one time per month resulted in a lower mean DCPI (with marginal significance) than reporting less than one time per month. The use of project manager training and the use of a project management-based organizational structure were found to be processes that do not create a statistically significantly lower mean DCPI by their application. Kuprenas noted that future research should also investigate how schedule and quality performance of design phase work can be measured, and whether the use of project management processes can also have a similar positive influence to these measures.

Several studies by Ibbs and Kwak (Ibbs and Kwak 1997; Kwak and Ibbs 2000) attempted to determine the financial and organizational impacts of project management. A study of project management processes used by thirty-eight different companies (in four industries) across six project phases and eight project management knowledge areas used to create a five-step Berkeley PM process maturity Process Maturity Model. Their research found that there was an association (not statistically proven) between an organization's project management maturity and its ability to execute projects effectively and that there was an association (not statistically proven) between an organization's project management expenditures and its ability to execute projects effectively. Most important, their work provided and assessment method for the effectiveness of project management efforts and allowed the differentiation of performance enhancements based on use of management processes/maturity and to allow managers to measure their return on investment for project management (PM/ROI). Recent unpublished work by Ibbs et al. has begun to examine better methods to collect detailed cost, quality, and customer service data across six project phases.

Work by Pocock (Pocock, Hyun, Liu, and Kim 1996; Pocock, Liu, and Kim 1997; Pocock, Liu, and Tang 1997) found direct improvement of project performance with improved project integration. Pocock et al (1997a, 1997b) defined a measure called degree of interaction (DOI) that is used to measure the extent of interaction of designers, builders, and project team members during all project phases. In a study of thirty-eight public-sector projects, a statistically significant correlation was found between DOI and project performance (measured as less cost growth, schedule growth, and modifications/changes). Work by Brown and Adams (2000) measured the effect of a formal project management program to the building process across time, cost, and quality outputs for fifteen case study projects. Their research found that the use of project management did not improve the efficiency of the building process. Brown and Adams, however, attribute the lack of results to deficiencies in the project management tools used in the study. They argue defining project management benefits beyond traditional operation measures (time, cost, and quality) is essential to recognize the benefit of project management.

Given the tremendous size of the design and construction industry and ongoing pressure of delivering projects for less money in less time, research in project management will undoubtedly continue. As our research evolves from best practices into process studies and quantification of impacts, it is essential that a strong research network associated with key design and construction industry organizations continues to evaluate research results and to ensure the professional application of project management on design and construction projects of all types and sizes.

BIBLIOGRAPHY

Anderson S. D., and R. L. Tucker. 1994. Improving Project Management of Design. *Journal of Management in Engineering* 9(3): 35–44.

Barrie, D. S., and B. C. Paulson. 1992. *Professional Construction Management.* New York: McGraw Hill, 7–12.

Brown, A., and J. Adams, J. 2000. Measuring the Effect of Project Management on Construction Outputs: A New Approach. *International Journal of Project Management* 18:327–35.

Chua, D. K. H., Y. C. Kog, and P. K. Loh. 1999. Critical Success Factors for Different Project Objectives. *Journal of Construction Engineering and Management* 125(3): 142–50.

Gould, F. E., and N. E. Joyce. 2001. *Construction Project Management Professional Edition,* Upper Saddle River, N.J.: Pearson Education, Prentice-Hall, 2–14.

Heath, T., D. Scott, and M. Boyland. 1994. A Prototype Computer-based Design Tool. *Construction Management and Economics* 12:543–49.

Ibbs C. W., and Y. H. Kwak. 1997. *The Benefits of Project Management—Financial and Organizational Rewards to Corporations.* Upper Darby, Pa.: Project Management Institute.

The International Group for Lean Construction (IGLC). 2002. Web sitehttp://cic.vtt.fi/lean/.

Jaselskis E. J., and D. B. Ashley. 1991. Optimal Allocation of Project Management Resources for Achieving Success. *Journal of Construction Engineering and Management* 117(2): 321–40.

Kuprenas, J. A. 2000. Impact of Communication on Success of Engineering Design Projects. *Project Management Research at the Turn of the Millennium: Proceedings of PMI Research Conference.* PMI, Paris, France, June.

Kwak Y. H., and C. W. Ibbs. 2000. Calculating Project Management Return on Investment. *Project Management Journal* 31(2): 38–47.

Lean Construction Institute (LCI). Web site What is Lean Construction, http:// leanconstruction.org.

Might R. J., and W. A. Fisher. 1985. The Role of Structural Factors in Determining Project Management Success. *IEEE Transactions on Engineering Management* 32(2).

Parfitt, M. K., and V. E. Savido. 1993. Checklist of Critical Success Factors for Building Projects. *Journal of Management in Engineering* 9(3): 243–49.

Pinto, J. K., and D. P. Slevin. 1987. Critical Factors in Successful Project Implementation. *IEEE Transactions on Engineering Management* 34(1): 22–27.

Pocock, J. B., C. T., Hyun, L. Y. Liu, and M. K. Kim. 1996. Relationship Between Project Interaction and Performance Indicators. *Journal of Construction Engineering and Management* 122(2): 165–76.

Pocock, J. B., L. Y. Liu, and M. K. Kim. 1997a. Impact of Management Approach on Project Interaction and Performance. *Journal of Construction Engineering and Management* 122(2): 411–18.

Pocock, J. B., L. Y. Liu, and W. H. Tang. 1997b. Prediction of Project Performance Based on Degree of Interaction. *Journal of Management in Engineering,* ASCE 13(2): 63–76.

PROJECTmagazine. November 2000. Earned Value Management, http://www. projectmagazine.com/nov00/evm1.html.

Savido, V., F. Grobler, K. Parfitt, M. Coyle, M. Guvenis, and M. Coyle. 1990. Critical Success Factors for Construction Projects. *Journal of Construction Engineering and Management* 118(1): 94–111.

United States Army Corps of Engineers. 2002. Partnering Web site, http://www.hq. usace.army.mil/cemp/c/partner.htm.

U.S. Green Building Council (USGBC). 2002. http://www.usgb.org/aboutus/index.htm.

15

Project Management During the Reconstruction of Kuwait

RALPH V. LOCURCIO

In the aftermath of Desert Storm, the U.S. Army Corps of Engineers undertook the challenging task of reconstructing the basic infrastructure of the state of Kuwait to reestablish life support systems sufficient to guarantee the safety and security of the postwar populatzion. The Kuwait Emergency Reconstruction Operation (KERO) may well be a model for the future international aid; namely, U.S. military assistance to Third World countries, followed by nation assistance to restore civil infrastructure, establish internal security, and enable political reform.

What follows is a description of the project management activities utilized in Kuwait with implications for similar projects wherever they may be conducted. What is significant for the engineering profession today, considering the growth in the practice of project management, is an account of the major management decisions that governed operations in Kuwait with a commentary on the effect these decisions had on the success of the overall recovery project. This chapter reviews the following subjects as they were applied during the KERO operation. These are considered to be core elements essential to the success of any project management process: project environment, planning, organizing and staffing, contracting, project management process, logistics, budget control, political factors, and leadership and partnership.

PROJECT ENVIRONMENT AND BACKGROUND

All projects exist within a context or a social environment that influences the management decisions of the project team. In truth, the project's ultimate purpose, in most cases, is to serve this context by providing design, construction or manufacturing services that improve upon the condition of the environment. The Kuwait recovery was no exception and we will, therefore, begin with a description of the situation and conditions that underlay the need for the KERO project and the desired outcomes.

During the Iraqi occupation and the resulting Gulf War, more than 90 percent of the Kuwaiti population of 1.2 million fled to Egypt, England, and other safe havens. Anticipating extensive devastation from the Iraqi occupation and the resulting Gulf War, the emir of Kuwait needed to rebuild the country as quickly as possible to reestablish normal government operations and to guarantee the safety and security of his citizens. Consequently, the emir formed a government committee known as the Kuwait Emergency Recovery Program (KERP) to manage reconstruction operations. With functions similar to the Federal Emergency Management Agency (FEMA) in the United States, this committee was headed by Dr. Ibrahim Al Shaheen, who was later named a national minister. Dr. Shaheen's task was to restore the civil infrastructure of Kuwait, that is, the municipal services and government functions, to a condition that would support the returning population of Kuwait in peace and safety after the war.

After considering several private contractual options, Dr. Shaheen advised the emir of Kuwait to ask President George H. W. Bush for recovery assistance from the U.S. Army Corps of Engineers, with all costs to be reimbursed by the government of Kuwait. The Corps had extensive experience in natural disaster recovery operations and recent experience with several major disasters, such as Hurricane Hugo and the San Francisco earthquake. Additionally, the Corps had a thorough working knowledge of the Middle East and the region's construction environment and business culture. Dr. Shaheen and his advisors assumed that this experience, and the Corps professionals who had accomplished those recovery operations, could just as successfully apply their expertise to the devastation wrought by a military disaster in Kuwait. They were correct.

On January 14, 1991, as the air attack began and plans for the ground attack to liberate Kuwait were being finalized, the Corps signed a $46.3 million Foreign Military Sales (FMS) case with Kuwait to begin the process of assistance. The Corps launched the recovery operation from its Transatlantic Division Office in Winchester, Virginia, formerly known as the Middle East/Africa Projects Office, which was to provide command, control, and logistical support throughout the operation. The recovery task force, dubbed the Kuwait Emergency Recovery Office (KERO), was organized in the Virginia office of the Corps' Transatlantic Division and later moved into Kuwait from a staging area in Dhahran, Saudi Arabia, following the liberation of Kuwait in February 1991. Once in Kuwait, KERO operated under the local direction of the Defense Reconstruction

Assistance Office (DRAO), which, in turn, reported to the Department of Defense and the U.S. Ambassador to Kuwait for guidance and direction.

The KERO team entered Kuwait on March 4, 1991, and began operations almost immediately. In the 300 days following liberation, this team, which averaged 140 U.S. and sixty Kuwaiti professionals, placed over $550 million in repair work through contracts with major U.S. and foreign construction firms. Working seven days a week and an average of twelve to fourteen hours per day, they surveyed, repaired, and restored major infrastructure systems and facilities. The scope of operations included repair of the national network of 5000km of 300KV electrical distribution lines, substations, water mains and pumping units, the highway network, sanitary mains, two seaports, the international airport, more than 150 public schools and over 850 public buildings, including police, fire, medical service facilities, ministerial headquarters, and some defense facilities. The details of the scope and magnitude of this operation have been reported in several accounts of the national and international media and will not be repeated here. A complete historical account of the Kuwait Recovery is provided in the *After Desert Storm, The U.S. Army and the Reconstruction of Kuwait*, by Dr. Janet McDonald, published by the Department of the Army in 1999.

PLANNING FOR THE RECOVERY OPERATION

Planning is one of the most important steps in conducting a successful project, no matter how large or small. A well-defined plan can save time, money, and team morale. No project can really succeed without a comprehensive plan to outline the key milestones and events that guide the day-to-day operations of the project team. In our daily lives, none of us would begin an expedition into unknown territory without a road map. That would be a foolish and costly adventure. Similarly, a project, by definition, is a journey into the unknown, and the project manager is the leader of that expedition. Therefore, it is the project manager's most fundamental responsibility to define the vision, or destination, for the project and to identify clearly the route the team must take to achieve success. Once under way, he must then make decisions to adjust the plan for unforeseen problems that arise along the way. This is a leadership rather than an engineering function, and although a project manager must be competent in the technical aspects of his project, his most important role is as the leader of the project team.

Unfortunately, although I do not have statistical proof, I would say that generally only about 25 percent of all projects begin with a documented plan prior to the start of operations. Lacking a formal directive to do so, many project managers launch into their duties without taking time to formulate and publish a written plan. Their reasons for this failure are numerous. Some of the most common are: no time, no funding, no need, no information, and perhaps the only understandable reason, no training.

In general, project managers are action-oriented individuals who like to see results. Many feel that they do not need to slow down to plan out what they already know. Most would probably argue that upper management overworks them, and, therefore, they are too busy to follow all the steps that textbook project management procedures recommend. They cut out seemingly unimportant steps, like publishing a plan, to meet deadlines and trim cost. Another frequent argument is that the project budget that was sold to the client by marketing or management did not include any billable hours for planning. Therefore, the project manager's only recourse is to somehow make time for planning through after hours work or by reducing team budgets. Finally, some project managers would argue that there is too little information available at the beginning of the project to formulate a definitive written plan, and once that information is available, the plan would be counterproductive because the project is too far along. Thus, planning is frequently viewed as a waste of time and energy.

None of these arguments is acceptable. Perhaps the only defensible, but still unacceptable, argument is no training. Many, in fact most, project managers come by their titles not because they have the requisite training and qualifications in project management, but rather, because they have survived the ordeal of completing a project without major incident. In reality, every poll that I conduct at the beginning of a project management training session produces the same result, fewer than 10 percent of the attendees, most of them experienced managers, have not had any formal training in project management. In short, many who wear the mantle of project manager simply do not know what the key elements of a sound project plan are, or that sound management operations always begin with a good plan.

In the case of the KERO project, the team had only forty-five days to begin the operations, precious little time to prepare for such a monumental undertaking. Funds were extremely tight at the outset, and risk was high. No one had asked for a plan prior to funding or supporting the operation, and lastly, there was absolutely no information on which to base a definitive plan: no scope, no site plan, and no summary of damages to be repaired. No one could expect the team to develop a sound management plan with so little time and information.

Despite these impediments, planning for the Kuwait Recovery began in Washington, D.C. on January 16, 1991. This was, coincidentally, the same day that the air campaign began, initiating military operations in the Gulf War. The first stage of planning dealt primarily with the task of gathering sufficient information to determine the scope and nature of the engineering tasks that would be required to restore the civil infrastructure in Kuwait once military operations had ended. As noted earlier, the Kuwaiti government had signed a contract with the United States to provide funds in the amount of $46.5 million to accomplish the repairs within ninety days. The Kuwaiti government would then have the option to either extend or terminate the operation. No further information was available or given.

Given such a tremendous task, and so little information, it would seem impossible to develop a plan for project operations. However, I would argue that a lack of information is no excuse for a lack of planning. In fact, it may be the most convincing argument for conducting a comprehensive planning cycle.

When faced with a paucity of information about the future we have only to rely on three sources for our inspiration: (a) our experience, (b) our training, and (c) our imagination. In the case of the Kuwait operation we first looked to the only other definable recovery operation of a similar nature, The Marshall Plan for wartorn Europe following World War II. Unfortunately, the scope of the Marshall Plan was several orders of magnitude greater than the Kuwait recovery, and the time available to cull through the many volumes of historical information prevented any detailed study of that operation. On the other hand, the experience that the Corps of Engineers had recently had with recovery from several natural disasters in America was directly applicable to the scope and magnitude of the Kuwait operation. The experience gained by Corps personnel would prove invaluable Finally, KERO team leaders would have to use their imagination to develop a "notional" scope of recovery operations for Kuwait, and it was against this "notional" scope that operations were planned. The results of these assumptions are summarized in figure 15.1.

Initial planning was begun in Winchester, Virginia, with a team of approximately twenty individuals who had both overseas and natural disaster experience. This team made several crucial decisions early on. First, operations would be divided into an "emergency" phase and a "recovery" phase. During the

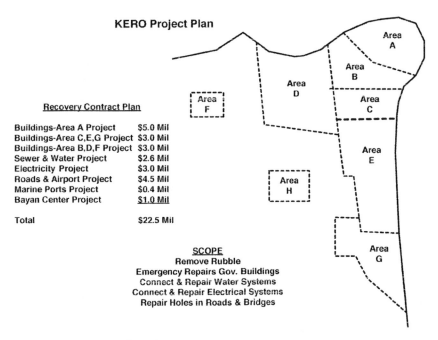

KERO Project Plan

Area A
Area B
Area D
Area F
Area C
Area E
Area H
Area G

Recovery Contract Plan

Buildings-Area A Project	$5.0 Mil
Buildings-Area C,E,G Project	$3.0 Mil
Buildings-Area B,D,F Project	$3.0 Mil
Sewer & Water Project	$2.6 Mil
Electricity Project	$3.0 Mil
Roads & Airport Project	$4.5 Mil
Marine Ports Project	$0.4 Mil
Bayan Center Project	$1.0 Mil
Total	$22.5 Mil

SCOPE
Remove Rubble
Emergency Repairs Gov. Buildings
Connect & Repair Water Systems
Connect & Repair Electrical Systems
Repair Holes in Roads & Bridges

FIGURE 15-1.   KERO project plan.

"emergency" phase, Civil Affairs military units and Kuwaiti government teams would address critical life support and security issues while the KERO team catalogued the damage to civil infrastructure. In addition, contractor teams would be mobilized, equipped, and moved to Kuwait to conduct specified emergency tasks, such as debris removal, to reopen the city's roads and remove hazards. During this emergency phase, teams of Corps volunteers from KERO would organize to identify and define the scope of specific recovery projects.

Using Corps' procedures, the KERO teams would prepare an individual Damage Survey Report (DSR) and cost estimate for each potential project. The DSR would define specific elements to be repaired at each site and establish a budget for that project. These procedures are identical to those used routinely during Corps' natural disaster recovery operations. The DSRs would then be aggregated into a repair program by Damage Assistance Groups (DAGs), which were organized by function: roads, electricity, buildings, and so on, and assigned to a KERO project manager for prioritization and direction. These project managers were functionally aligned with a Kuwaiti ministry that had responsibility for that function, that is, the KERO project manager for roads worked directly with the Ministry of Roads as his client. During the subsequent "recovery" phase, contractors would be hired to execute the repairs defined by these individual DSRs (figures 15.1 and 15.2).

Similarly, a decision was made to model the KERO organizational structure on a typical Corps' project office that might be used for natural disaster recovery operations. Corps personnel were familiar with this organization and the associated lines of authority and procedures, all of which had proven to be effective in the past. Subsequently, a detailed logistical plan, which is described later, was developed based on this organizational model. At the same time, several contracting models were investigated. However, due to a lack of information, no firm decisions were reached about the specific contracting vehicles to be used. Rather, these decisions were postponed until further research could be accomplished.

During this same period, an advance party of eight experienced managers was deployed to a staging area in Dhahran, Saudi Arabia, where they co-located with the Corps' engineering elements that were servicing the infrastructure needs of Operation Desert Shield, the build up of combat forces prior to the ground attack into Iraq. This advance party was given the task of gathering information and formulating a specific plan of action for the recovery operations.

After several weeks of meetings between Corps' and Kuwaiti officials, planning efforts in Washington began to bog down. The greatest reason for the slowdown was the voracious and frequent demand for detailed briefings by multileveled Washington bureaucracies. These agencies were demanding detailed information about operations that had not yet begun and second-guessing assumptions for those plans. The second reason for the slowdown was the fact that there simply was not enough accurate information in Washington to make meaningful plans. In effect, the team was trying to plan an operation by remote

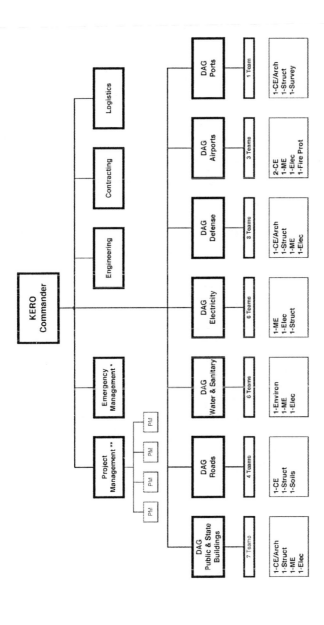

FIGURE 15-2. Damage assessment operations.

* Provides primary direction during "emergency" phase
** Provides primary direction during "recovery" phase

control and with second-hand information, a dangerous practice. The best information, scarce as it was, was to be had at the front lines, as close to the area of operations as possible. In this case, that location was Dhahran, Saudi Arabia. And it was for this reason that the commander of the Corps office responsible for control of the project made an important decision, he sent the KERO commander, who was also the project manager for the overall operation, forward to Saudi Arabia to complete the plan. There he would be far away from the bureaucratic tangle, and closest to the best sources of information about the project.

On arrival in Saudi Arabia, the project manager met immediately with the advance party to assess the status of their planning efforts. To his surprise, no plan had been formulated, and very few decisions had been made. This raises a very important point that will be repeated over and over again in this, and any meaningful discussion of project management: project management is first and foremost a leadership activity! That is to say, it is an activity that establishes the vision, the justification, and the parameters for success of the operation and, most importantly, provides the decisions necessary to define and schedule the tasks necessary to move the project forward, and then to make adjustments for any obstacles encountered. Without this direction and focus, which can only be provided by a leader with the requisite competence and authority, no meaningful progress will be made. This is precisely what was happening in Saudi Arabia. There was no onsite leadership, no decisions had been made, and so no real planning had been accomplished.

The project manager's first action on his arrival was to assess the status of planning and to meet with the client's representatives, in this case the U.S. Ambassador and the officials of the Kuwaiti government, to clarify the scope and timing of KERO responsibilities. Once again, it was immediately apparent that there was very little information available about the actual damage to the infrastructure. Therefore, the advance party had to postulate a worst-case scenario and devise a flexible plan that could be implemented prior to the end of hostilities and then expanded or contracted depending on the actual situation once the team entered Kuwait.

To accomplish the recovery task, the KERO team had to break down the overall scope, "Repair Kuwait," into manageable elements. First, the scope was divided into distinct work sectors, some functional and some geographical. Although comprised of a series of related work items, each defined by an individual DSR, these sectors were each considered as a single "project," which would be accomplished through a separate contract. Correspondingly, a project manager, whose only function was to ensure the success of that sector, would be assigned to manage each sector. For example, road repairs throughout the country were defined as a project. One project manager would direct this roads project, and the work would all be accomplished under one construction contract. Similarly, all domestic water and sewer lines, and related pumping equipment, were considered as one water and sewer project. All electrical work, power plants, distribution lines, and substations were defined as the electrical project, and so on for each component of the civil infrastructure. A separate budget was devised for each of these projects, and ultimately, a unique contract was written and a separate contractor was selected to accomplish all related construction. This very simplified procedure emphasizes the principle of clarity and unity in project operations. Only *one* project manager, *one* budget, *one* contract, and *one* contractor were assigned to each element of the civil infrastructure. Consequently, in a rapidly moving and changing environment, the number of variables was reduced to a minimum, and the chances for success thereby increased (figures 15.1 and 15.2).

As an added measure of control and management, each of these project sectors was aligned with the corresponding Kuwaiti government ministry responsible for the management and operation of that sector. For example, the KERO project manager for the roads project worked directly with the Kuwaiti Minister of Roads. Similarly, the KERO manager for the water and sewer project worked directly with the Minister of Water, and so on. These ministers were the "clients," who ultimately accepted the work delivered by the individual project managers and, therefore, each project manager responded to only *one* client, an ideal situation.

Government buildings, however, were handled a bit differently. Because there were over 1,100 government buildings in all, spread out all over the country, a slightly different method of organization was needed to break the task down to manageable proportions and guarantee simplicity of operations. In the case of government buildings, the country was subdivided into geographical, rather than functional, sectors; each of these sectors was designated a project. By this method, they could mobilize one construction contractor per geographical sector, thereby avoiding any potential problems associated with dividing the work among competing contractors in a given area. Similarly, this would keep the contract administration and budget operations separate for each sector. For example, the Central Business District (CBD) was designated Area A. All government buildings within that sector were assigned to one contractor and one project manager. Similarly, areas B, D, and E were grouped into one contract and assigned to one project manager. A single budget was developed for all work in each sector, and one contractor was hired for construction operations. In all there were five geographical sectors allocated to government buildings as shown on the project plan in figure 15.1.

Essentially, the two diagrams in figures 15.1 and 15.2 define the initial project plans for the reconstruction of Kuwait. By way of review, I will cover several notable features of these plans. First, the plans were simple and clear. The entire scope of operations, or vision, was well defined and procedures were established to clarify details and overcome obstacles as the work progressed. This plan was published for all members of the KERO team, reviewed at progress meetings, and used to brief all incoming personnel throughout the life of the KERO operation. Second, the plan broke the work down into individual tasks, each of which was to be managed by a single project manager whose responsibility it was to ensure the success of the project(s) assigned to his sector. This allowed each project manager to focus his attention on a clear set of priorities and to serve as an advocate for the success of his sector. Finally, each project manager was assigned to one client, in this case a Kuwaiti ministry. This gave each client a single point of contact for information and control. Project managers were instructed to become completely familiar with the culture and mission of their ministry so that they could make informed decisions on project features, trade-offs, and schedule, just as if they were the clients themselves. By this means, the client was assured of a constant flow of information, complete understanding of the intended outcome for each project, and, therefore, complete control of his operation.

ORGANIZATION AND STAFFING

In the case of the KERO operation, there was not much time to organize, staff, and train the initial task force of approximately 140 Corps employees, all of whom were experienced volunteers from various districts and divisions who would rotate to Kuwait on a three-month cycle. To minimize the dysfunction and confusion caused by an unfamiliar organizational structure, a decision was made to create a small "district-like" office for the Kuwait recovery. In short, civilian or military volunteers from any Corps organization would be able to arrive in KERO and "recognize" the working environment with little training and only situational orientation. KERO used two variations of a district organizational structure, each suited to the particular operation at the time, but both employing a common headquarters structure that did not change.

During the initial emergency phase of the recovery, KERO field offices were set up according to Corps Emergency Management practice. Labeled DAGs, each group had a variable number of assigned Damage Assistance Teams (DATs), depending on the mission of the group (figure 15.2). As mentioned earlier, DAGs were aligned with specific Kuwait ministry offices: buildings, roads, airport, electricity, water and sewer, ports, defense, and so on, according to prewar Kuwaiti management conventions. Adoption of these conventions simplified the interface with the host nation, as leaders and volunteers from these Kuwaiti ministry offices were readily available to work with KERO. Additionally, this organization allowed Kuwaiti volunteers to work directly with their parent ministry. This structure was used for about forty-five days while DSRs were being completed and contractors were mobilizing. Actual construction during this time was minimal; however, more than 1,200 DSRs and associated cost estimates were prepared. These reports later became the basis for all future budgets and recovery work orders.

During the subsequent recovery phase, when construction management became the dominant operational consideration, a more conventional Corps project management structure, with traditional resident offices to manage contractors in the field, was adopted to ensure that project delivery and contract administration were accomplished according to the Corps' procedures and quality standards (figure 15.3).

Following the same practice used during the emergency phase, project managers were assigned to coordinate work with the responsible Kuwaiti ministry officials. Project managers were tasked with developing a work program for each ministry to control all projects and funds for that ministry from concept to turnover. For example, all roads projects constituted "the Roads ministry program," which was the responsibility of one project manager. The project manager established project priorities, developed project and program budgets, decided project scope, features, and quality standards, monitored progress through all technical phases (design, contracting, construction), reported on the progress of each project and the entire program, and supervised eventual project turnover.

Once into the recovery phase, these ministry work programs were organized along functional lines under the direction of a resident engineer, as shown in figure 15.3. Resident offices were responsible for construction management, contract administration, modifications, and claims resolution and budget control for all assigned programs.

The KERO technical divisions handled the more specialized areas of the project development cycle: The Engineering Services Department handled analysis,

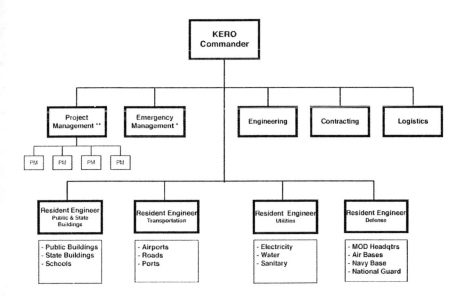

* Provides primary direction during "emergency" phase
** Provides primary direction during "recovery" phase

FIGURE 15-3. Construction operations plan.

design, estimating, specifications, value engineering, and field consultation. Contracting handled contract preparation, solicitation, review, award, small business administration, and coordination. Other professional elements, such as legal, safety, and audit, were also present on the KERO team to round out the professional package and ensure timely project completion. These divisions reported directly to the commander to ensure complete independence of their operations and timely reporting if problems arose. Additional technical and administrative functions were managed in the United States at the Transatlantic Division office (figure 15.4).

All of these decisions proved to be correct and advisable for future operations, but there were a few problem areas. For example, the conversion from DAGs to resident offices revealed that new roles and responsibilities had to be sorted out in real time under intensive operational pressure. Also, different skills were needed to staff the resident offices. Whereas the DAGs used personnel with design experience, the resident offices needed personnel with construction and contract administration experience. Similarly, the decision to rotate field-level engineering professionals every three months was a difficult, but workable, staffing concept. On the other hand, the rotation of key leaders such as deputies, division chiefs, resident engineers, the chief of project management, the resource

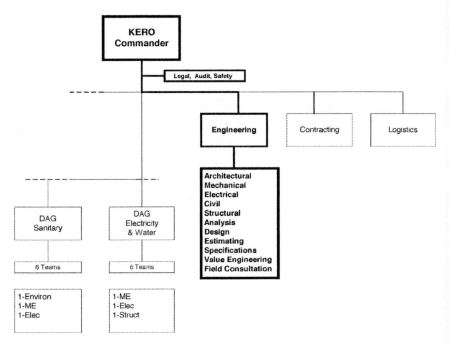

FIGURE 15-4.   Engineering operations.

manager, or the property book officer on the same three-month cycle proved extremely disruptive. For the future, these key personnel should be selected for the duration of the operation, or not less than a six-month tour with a guaranteed overlap of at least one week.

THE PROJECT MANAGEMENT PROCESS

In 1991, the Corps of Engineers did not have a formal system of project management as part of its operating procedures. Instead, projects were traditionally managed from within the functional discipline that had the largest share of the work. For example, if a project had a preponderance of mechanical engineering, a project manager from that department was selected to lead the project. Under this approach, the project management function was decentralized with little or no central control of project operations. As a result, clients had to deal with a variety of managers and processes to gain control of their projects.

This method of managing projects was an adaptation of older organizational models developed during the "industrial age" of manufacturing. As manufacturing management grew during the early twentieth century, similar functions were grouped into departments for the sake of efficiency and ease of management. It made good economic sense to have one manager specialize in a given functional area. As such, each manager became an expert in his specialty and consequently was able to optimize both quality and productivity in that area. Quality was checked at the end of the process, and adjustments were made to overcome errors and defects and improve the efficiency of the process as a whole. Over time, repetitive errors were eliminated and the manufacturing process guaranteed product quality. This seems to work well for mass production of similar products such as automobiles, refrigerators, and the like. However, this form of management is not well suited to the design of "unique" products such as buildings or water systems, which are one-of-a-kind, very expensive, and not mass produced. The obvious problem with this decentralized management is that no one manager has responsibility for the entire project. Even worse, the customer has even less influence over the development of his project, and no one knows how it will turn out until the project is completed and all of the funds are expended. When dealing with such large, one-of-a-kind products, this industrial form of management is disastrous. Errors cannot be corrected in the next item off the assembly line and often result in expensive legal battles between the customer, the designer, and the contractor.

Around the time of the Kuwait operation, the Corps of Engineers had been considering a new, more customer-oriented, form of organization for project management. Under this new system, project managers would be given responsibility for the entire project development cycle, centralized and assigned to a separate department reporting directly to the leader of the organization. This new system of organization was expected to improve several important features that were lacking in the former system. First and foremost, it would provide direct and unfiltered communications about project status to the commander or director who had the power to correct errors immediately. Second, elevating the project managers within the structure would give them greater visibility of the entire life cycle of project development and, therefore, the ability to detect errors along the way. Next, the new organization would give project managers authority equal to other department heads, which added considerable power to their opinions in discussions with functional managers. And finally, and most important, this new organization provided a "single point of contact" to the client. In other words, the project manager would be the one person in the organization who was both authorized and responsible to interact with the client and make decisions about all of his projects under development. This would give the client unprecedented control over his project(s).

Although the Corps of Engineers had not formally adopted this new management system, KERO managers decided to implement it on a test basis, as shown in figure 15.5. Under this arrangement, all project managers in KERO were assigned to a department of project management, which reported directly to the KERO commander. Within the project management department, individual

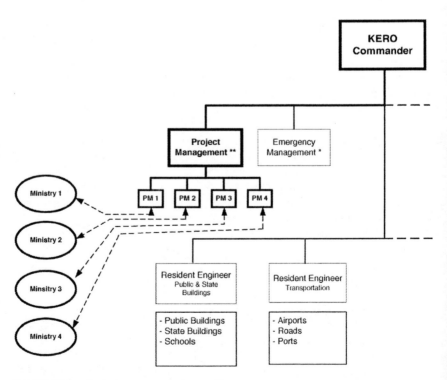

FIGURE 15-5.   Project management operations.

project managers were assigned to each Kuwaiti ministry to provide a single point of contact for all projects in that ministry. Each project manager was completely responsible for ensuring that the scope, cost, quality, and schedule of all projects met the needs of his assigned ministry. Consequently, the client had only one person to contact within KERO to gain complete knowledge of all his projects. Similarly, all functional elements in KERO were directed to look to only one project manager for decisions concerning projects for a given ministry.

In addition, the project managers were instructed to serve as advocates for their client's projects. They had to understand the mission, operations, and culture of the ministry well enough to know how each project served the needs of that ministry. With this insightful knowledge they were able to make intelligent decisions about project features or trade-offs throughout the life cycle of project development, thereby reducing errors and saving time and resources. Within KERO, they were empowered to control all variables associated with their projects to ensure that outcomes met their client's objectives.

CONTRACTING

Speed, and later, control were the driving forces in all KERO contracting operations from the outset. KERO staffers planned for a forty-five-day competitive emergency contract award cycle to be executed from Saudi Arabia. They were eventually forced to utilize a ten-day contingency plan when the war ended more quickly than expected. Working nearly around the clock, and without specific knowledge of the conditions in Kuwait, the KERO staff and their Kuwaiti counterparts completed necessary project scoping, solicitation, prequalification, and proposal evaluation actions to award eight cost plus letter contracts worth approximately $25.4 million. These letter contracts would be employed on a task order basis to execute individual DSRs as quickly as possible. Each task order would then be definitized after mobilization and converted to a fixed price, once the actual scope of the repair mission was known (figure 15.6).

To divide the work among the contractors, Kuwait projects were organized into either functional or geographic work areas according to prewar work management conventions. These work areas became the geographical or functional scope of the contracts. Consequently, the eight contracts were divided as follows: general building repair (in three areas of the city), all road repairs, all sewer/water pipe repairs, all port surveys, and all electrical repairs. A target cost estimate was assigned to each contract, and the remainder of the funds was held in reserve. Later, as needs became known, several additional program areas, such as hospitals and communications facilities, were added. Funds for these areas were supplied from these reserves with the approval of the KERP. Eventually, additional funds were provided from the augmented 1991–1992 budget request. Since KERO contract scoping was aligned with prewar ministry functional responsibilities, the KERO management structure was perfectly aligned to partner with Kuwaiti officials during recovery operations (figure 15.5).

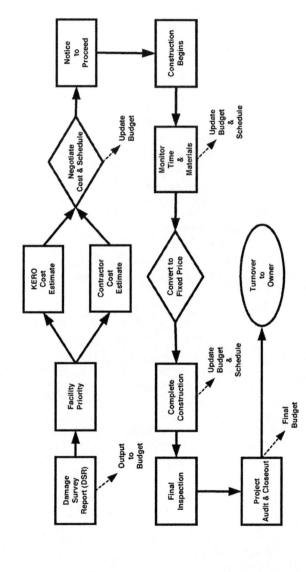

FIGURE 15-6. Contract operation.

These letter contracts were essentially cost plus instruments. Therefore, a precise method of controlling and documenting the flow of work to the contractor was required once construction operations began. As described earlier, the original DAGs were converted to standard Corps' resident offices for contract control and administration once mobilization was complete and construction had begun in earnest. For the purpose of passing specific work requirements to the contractors, the DSRs, and associated cost estimates prepared during the emergency phase were converted into work orders. These documents, which resided in the project database, were reviewed by project managers and adjusted to define the exact scope of repair work. The work orders were then provided to the Engineering Services office, where the original cost estimate for the work order was reviewed, and corrected if needed, using the Corps' newly automated M-CACES process. This extremely valuable tool allowed detailed estimates to be developed quickly and accurately, sometimes overnight. It also allowed the Corps to adjust the unit cost of labor and materials in accordance with changes in the market values of these items as time passed. These work orders, detailed cost estimates, and record of negotiations were incorporated into a contract modification that served as the plans and specs during construction. Ultimately they, in conjunction with daily construction management logs for time and materials, became the basis for final negotiations with the contractor on the cost of each work order. As the KERO operation neared completion these documents were audited to verify that no over/under payments were made (figure 15.6).

As the operation matured, some larger projects were advertised individually to enhance competition and encourage participation of both U.S. and Kuwaiti small businesses. However, after several months of operations, this conversion to individual competitive contracting was extremely difficult with the limited KERO staff. By this time, over $100 million had been spent in cost plus contracts, with well over 150 modifications to the original eight contracts in progress. In addition, the time required to formulate, advertise, and award a competitive, fixed-price contract in the uncertain universe of bidders that was available in Kuwait was both risky and time consuming. Consequently, for speed and control, eight basic contracts, each covering a specific area or function, was increased with work orders added as negotiated modifications to the original contract.

The system of dividing the country into work areas (figure 15.1) performed reasonably well during the early stages of the Kuwait recovery and served to keep the contractors separated geographically. However, in future operations, if time and staffing are sufficient, this geographical orientation could possibly be discarded after a brief period of construction to allow more competition within each area. Additionally, more general contractors should be employed during the mid- to late stages of the recovery, also to enhance competition. That is, if the projected workflow and funding is sufficient to justify the additional contractor mobilization costs, which must be borne by the host. If more contractors were available, competition for individual work orders would have resulted in greater cost efficiency. As a rule of thumb, each general contractor operating in an international setting must foresee a potential workload of $50–$100 million to justify his mobilization costs. In the case of Kuwait, the contracting operation was initially sized for a $50–$100 million horizon based on the best information available at the time guidance from the government of Kuwait was received. The eventual $300–$400 million workload could not have been forecasted accurately enough to justify the risk of opting for additional mobilization. In fact, a plan with as many as ten major contracts was considered at one point, but the option was discarded because the cost of mobilization would have consumed an inordinate percentage of the funds available for construction.

Another method of contracting worthy of consideration is "job order contracting." This method awards an indefinite delivery type contract to a general construction contractor based on competitively bid fixed unit prices for a list of desired construction activities. Later, actual quantities are specified in the field via "delivery orders" generated from DSRs or similar documents. The unit prices are fixed on award, except for out-of-scope work that is negotiated as a modification. This is an attractive method of contracting in such situations because it offers fixed pricing as well as flexibility in scope and quantity of placement.

The restrictions in this case are twofold. First, the considerable up-front work involved in preparing the unit price contract specification for solicitation, award, and administration is time prohibitive unless this data is already available and computerized from prior work in the region. Typically, a job order contract can have as many as 20,000 line items for unit price bidding. Therefore, it requires some previous experience with contracting in the area. Second, as with other fixed-price contracting, the method presumes at least general knowledge of scope and the cost and availability of materials, labor and other factors that mitigate the risk of a fixed-price bid. In the case of Kuwait, even if the voluminous specification could have been prepared and distributed in time, it is doubtful that contractors would have accepted the considerable risk of a fixed-price contract given that virtually all pricing factors were unknown.

In retrospect, it appears that some form of cost plus contracting is inevitable in such an operation. The instrument must be flexible enough to shape the work to the scope as it becomes known, responsive enough to meet the urgent requirements of the crisis, and yet controllable to minimize risk and ensure cost efficiency. Staffing plans must consider these factors and allow for adequate contract supervision, administration, and most certainly, one or more audits.

The role of auditors very early in the contract scenario cannot be overemphasized for any cost type contract. While engineers are supervising contract execution, the auditors can work with the contractors to shape the allowable range of contract overhead to suit the work environment. They will also specify the level of cost and pricing data required to eventually support the contractor's costs in the final negotiations. The sooner these parameters are established the more efficient and continuous will be the flow of modifications, negotiations, and eventual contract close out.

LOGISTICS

Engineers are not logisticians, and even great and dedicated engineers cannot do a day's work, let alone several months of intensive work in a hostile environment, if they cannot eat and sleep properly. The valuable database previously mentioned depended on computers, generators, copiers, paper, cartridges, and spare parts on a daily basis or it would not have worked and its benefits could not have been realized. In short, the success of an operation of this magnitude and duration revolves around the efficiency and effectiveness of its logistical plan.

The KERO planning team, working with Transatlantic Division, had to assume that nothing would be available for use in Kuwait, except perhaps a building shell for shelter. Since KERO was an ad hoc temporary organization that did not exist prior to this operation, there was no equipment organic to KERO, and no property book. Further, since all costs were to be borne by the Kuwaiti government, new equipment would have to be purchased on short notice with Kuwaiti funds and subsequently turned over to Kuwait on completion of the mission. Everything needed to sustain KERO operations for at least thirty days—from vehicles to copiers to personal products to food and water—had to be purchased in Saudi Arabia in the same ten-day period during which the original contracts were awarded, and loaded on leased semi-trailers for the journey to Kuwait. A complete list of all functions managed by the Logistics staff is shown in figure 15.7.

The most startling and memorable example occurred when a KERO purchasing agent walked into a Nissan showroom in Dhahran on January, 18, 1991, and purchased sixty-two Nissan Patrol 4x4 vehicles on the spot for immediate delivery because they were the only suitable and available vehicles in Dhahran. The expression on the Nissan dealer's face was indescribable. Miraculously, despite such hasty actions, the skilled logistics staff forgot virtually nothing in over 4,000 line items of materiel that were purchased.

As a result of this effort, the KERO team was able to conduct self-sustained operations almost immediately on arrival. However, since even the best planned operation is never perfect, a rapid resupply base must be available to replenish critical items that cannot be found locally, or to satisfy new requirements that develop as the operation matures and changes. The Transatlantic Division, KERO's parent organization in Winchester, Virginia, provided this support, using military and commercial air cargo resources through a sister office in Dhahran, Saudi Arabia, where the staging had occurred.

Two aspects of this logistical tale deserve special consideration in nation assistance operations. First and foremost, the equipment utilized by the team was host nation property and had to be treated as such. Accountability, maintenance and repair, and the general condition of host government property, especially on turnover, are all key components of the image of quality performance that the KERO team sought to leave on completion of the operation. I might add that this

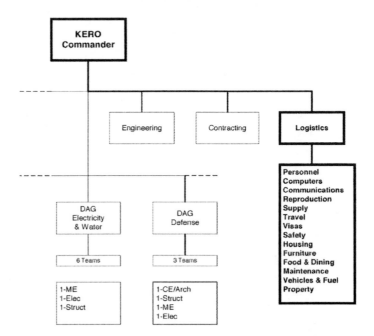

FIGURE 15-7. Logistics operations.

was a part of the vision for the KERO operation established by the commander. In his vision statement he made it clear that the reputation of the Corps and the U.S. Army was at stake, and, therefore, delivery of a quality product in a professional manner was an essential element of success. Similarly, the host government did not want to be viewed as having engaged a "rag-tag" outfit to reconstruct their country in full view of their own population, their Arab sister states, and the world media. From the client's viewpoint, both of these factors would be seen as indicators of the weakness of the Kuwaiti government, its economy, and their ability to quickly recover from the Iraqi invasion. Translated into day-to-day KERO operations, this meant strict attention to the condition of equipment and rapid attention to repairs, housekeeping, uniforms, and the like.

Another logistical consideration that deserves careful attention is the cost of doing business. Again, notwithstanding the crisis environment, the recovery operations must be sufficient to produce quality projects, but without extravagance and in keeping with U.S. and host nation government practices. In the KERO operations, the target was to hold pure overhead costs to less than 10 percent of all expenditures. KERO engineering salaries were charged to projects as direct costs wherever possible. Consequently, actual overhead costs came in around 8 percent. This figure includes the salvage value of approximately $2 million worth of vehicles and equipment that were ultimately returned to the Kuwaitis. The final overhead figure, without mobilization equipment, was around 7 percent.

BUDGET CONTROL

When KERO began work, there were no operational governmental agencies in Kuwait to accomplish the normal budgeting actions necessary to fund a large-scale national reconstruction program. Within forty-five days, KERO had exhausted the original $46.3 million and was in need of additional funding authority to continue contract operations. A process had to be developed for obtaining additional funds at the appropriate time (figure 15.8).

Extremely cost conscious, as any host nation or sponsor can be expected to be in such a situation, the Kuwaitis requested a monthly accounting of all funds. In addition, they asked for a complete financial summary prior to approving any additional funds. An efficient method of managing and displaying project information and funding status had to be developed quickly. Similarly, KERO's more than 1,200 DSRs served to inventory, record, quantify, and cost the damage, however a flexible system of managing this voluminous information was needed. Using standard software packages and lap-top computers operating on generator power, KERO engineers developed and implemented a computerized project database within days of arrival in Kuwait. A substantial achievement, this database allowed field engineers to add or modify project information as field work, estimates, or construction was added or completed. This gave project managers a consistently accurate information base and the capability to manipulate the data as required to prepare budget documents and reports in minimal time.

To develop the augmented budget request, the project managers arranged the survey data contained in the computerized DSR database into sector programs and presented to the appropriate ministry officials for decisions on priority, timing, scope, and so on. KERO project managers soon found that they had more accurate and timely information on the status of facilities than did the ministry officials, who were unable to respond quickly to such requests due to a lack of time, staffing, information, facilities, and the like. This is a normal circumstance in any disaster situation, because the responsible government officials are likely to be a casualty of the disaster themselves. Working feverishly, KERO project managers took it upon themselves to prioritize the DSRs and develop a line-item repair program for each ministry based on their acquired understanding of the ministry's function and the known damage. The project managers presented these programs to the respective ministry authorities for approval. Once approved, the programs were incorporated into a nationwide KERO repair program and presented to the KERP central committee. Once approved by the KERP committee, this reconstruction budget, which totaled some $212 million, was sent to the Ministry of Finance for funding (figure 15.8). Using this procedure, the entire budget formulation process for 1991–1992 was accomplished in little more than one week.

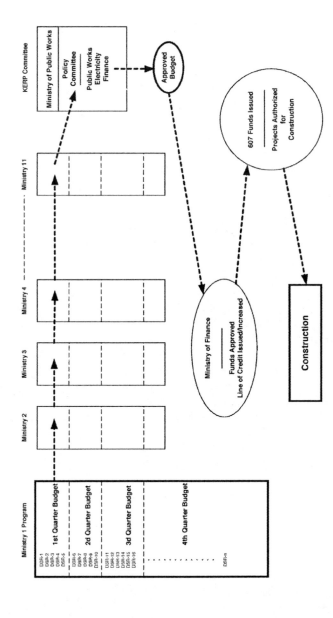

FIGURE 15-8. Budget control.

It took about one month for the ministry of Finance to act on the budget. Later, the KERP committee reserved the authority to adjust funding among programs, but allowed KERO some flexibility in moving funds within a ministry program, provided the committee was notified. This process was summarized and reviewed at biweekly meetings with the KERP committee, which also served to monitor progress and add or delete projects.

In addition, written progress reports were sent to each ministry on a monthly basis. These timely and accurate reports covered all projects in the ministry and ensured that the Kuwaiti officials were never at a loss for information about the status or funding for their projects. This frequent and comprehensive communications program was a key element in gaining and maintaining the confidence of the Kuwaiti government throughout the operation, and its importance cannot be overemphasized.

To stay abreast of the extremely fast-moving project operations and funding transactions, it was necessary for KERO to hold internal in-process reviews (IPRs), or Project Review Boards, on a weekly schedule. Again, the data that formed the basis for these reviews emanated from the project database, which was manipulated to form project management summaries, bar chart program schedules, key project fact sheets, and other management documents. This same automated system of reports was used to inform headquarters, the ambassador, Kuwaiti ministers, and other interested parties on project status and KERO operations in general.

Several salient features of the budgeting operation should be noted for future operations. First of all, a computerized and flexible project management database was needed from day one. The KERO team elected to use a simple spreadsheet program to develop this system. These spreadsheets, which could be manipulated by the project managers themselves, were extremely flexible and allowed KERO managers to quickly arrange data in user-friendly formats. This seemingly trivial feature saved a tremendous amount of time and enabled project managers to demonstrate convincingly their control of project operations and costs. Second, KERO task force engineers, who were more versed in project details than the host government officials, were prepared to develop and defend project priorities, budget requests, and subsequently to advise the ministries on how to proceed. Finally, continuous and open communications between KERO project managers and their clients was the key to good working relations and credibility.

POLITICAL FACTORS AND PARTNERING
WITH THE HOST NATION

There is no question that such an operation has political overtones at all levels that must be carefully managed. Working in an overseas environment, engineers must deal with vast cultural differences that, in spite of the unbridled goodwill exhibited by all participants, could easily result in disagreements and lasting misperceptions. After all, aside from the immediate humanitarian relief, the only lasting benefit for U.S. national interests is the goodwill and close working relationships generated by the work management process. These are political and humanitarian rather than engineering or construction products.

The first and foremost consideration for a lasting professional image is the quality of construction provided. Early on, during the heat of the crisis phase, there was tremendous political pressure to conduct only emergency repairs to facilities so that limited funds could be spread over many project areas and substantial progress could be demonstrated. Experience has shown that for all but the smallest repairs to facilities, this crisis attitude, which tolerates lesser quality, will subside long before the completion date of the work. Consequently, in the postcrisis environment, the user may no longer recognize, or accept, such crisis or emergency scoping as quality construction, and he will complain bitterly that he received shoddy work. Therefore, the standards chosen for repairs must be sufficient to stand the test of quality over time. When such questions of hindsight do arise, and they will, they need to be resolved immediately, on the ground, with the customer, and if at all possible, in his favor, rather than through long drawn out administrative appeals. This is especially true for major programs that affect large groups of citizens, as these projects justifiably and expectedly receive close scrutiny and media coverage. Here, a strong, involved, and active public affairs officer can ensure balanced coverage of the work so that such problems are properly explained in the media and do not receive undue attention.

A corollary of the above concerns project "selectivity." All projects do not have equal value in light of the culture and the political and national security objectives of the host population. The same is true for the U.S. population that will undoubtedly view the assistance effort from our own national interest and priority base. Finally, progress will undoubtedly be reported by a critical and skeptical media. Consequently, every project in the Corps program must stand the test of having a clear humanitarian purpose and content. It must appear equally beneficial to an observer in rural America as it does to someone in the poorer neighborhoods of the host country. The logic and value of each project must be obvious, because these observers, who shape political decisions and rate our performance based on public opinion and perception, will not understand or consider the intricacies of a complex approval process.

As a general rule, U.S. personnel should always be assigned to projects that afford the "highest and best" use of our resources and that reflect the maximum positive image and the least risk, politically or otherwise, to our government and our personnel. Private contractors working directly for the host government should recommend projects that do not meet this criterion for construction. Close cooperation with the U.S. ambassador and his staff will serve to provide the political sensitivity necessary to properly screen projects.

In general, projects acceptable for U.S. government construction will meet this standard and suffice for the host nation. Projects that support major population segments, versus those that satisfy the goals of special interest groups, are usually acceptable. Planners should beware of cultural differences and the attitude that "it's their money, they can do what they want with it." Citizens of the host country may readily accept certain practices, such as the use of government labor to work on private projects as one of the privileges or prerogatives of high office. Such practice may even be sanctioned legally, but they would never be condoned or understood by the U.S. citizens supporting your operation and such situations should be avoided. For example, work on residences, especially ornate facilities, VIP facilities, and so on, should be avoided unless there is an overriding and unmistakable social value to be gained. In Kuwait, for example, KERO never succeeded in explaining the reconstruction of a former palace for use as the site of replacement offices for the Kuwaiti government because of the ornate nature of the facilities and the connotation of the title palace to the U.S. population. By contrast, reconstruction of the national parliament building involved very special and expensive construction and furnishings. But since the overriding value of providing a necessary and suitable facility for the return of democratic government to Kuwait, it was universally acceptable to both U.S. and Kuwaiti citizens; the project was instantly hailed as a great and successful work.

A second consideration for those in charge of nation assistance efforts is the political question of who is in charge of the recovery effort. Clearly, the host nation must be in charge and U.S. elements must keep this steadfastly in mind. This is not as trivial a matter as it might appear because many engineering judgments, which we make routinely and frequently without asking, are driven by our cultural imperatives and habits, both of which may not be valid in the host nation. For example, Americans value time more than money as a general rule, especially in crisis situations. Therefore, we are likely to condone high cost in a disaster recovery situation. Let's fix the damage quickly, right? Eastern cultures are much more patient. Cost is valued as more important than time, and this difference can cause major disagreements and the misperception that Americans are not good managers.

LEADERSHIP AND PARTNERSHIP

In the case of Kuwait, the host nation managers were adamant about having a partnership with the Americans. They wanted to share decisions, no matter how long that took. This stemmed from their need to feel, and to be seen by their citizens, as if they were directing their own recovery. A second factor, though unspoken, was their sincere desire to learn the American way of managing such a program so that they could do it themselves if necessary. This true partnership was relatively easy to achieve in the case of field engineering activities where Kuwaiti volunteers were assigned to KERO and worked on project teams with their American counterparts. These engineers worked side by side throughout the entire recovery operation and shared every experience, good and bad. In this way, the Kuwaitis and the Americans developed mutual understanding, respect, and trust for one another, and this was the basis for the true partnership that was formed. That is not to say that there were not any problems. A conscious effort was made to ensure that both Kuwaiti workers and Americans followed the same rules and practices, but there were still many differences in work practices, compensation, privileges, housing arrangements, and so on, all of which were potential areas for discord. However, because a basic partnership had been achieved, these differences could easily be discussed and resolved as each case arose.

At the managerial level, the partnership was equally important but much harder to achieve because of the complexity of the manager's role, the fact that they did not work side-by-side, and time constraints. The individuals involved had to make a concerted effort to include their counterparts in any and all decisions pertaining to the recovery program. This usually necessitated a time delay to participate in additional discussions; however, this time was well spent as it avoided later misunderstandings and delays during construction. In fact, in almost every case where managers failed to achieve a consensus on policy prior to construction, there were misunderstandings and delays during the critical, and more costly, construction cycle.

Finally, the task force commander can also expect considerable attention to all of the above concerns from higher headquarters and the U.S. Congress. These agencies will all require current and accurate information to fulfill their responsibilities and to answer constituents' questions. Consequently, a comprehensive, rapid, and preferably automated reporting system must be developed early on. In the case of Kuwait, both Transatlantic Division and the Defense Reconstruction Assistance Office (DRAO), utilizing automated reports from the KERO database, dealt directly with these agencies to provide accurate information, answer queries, and relay sensitivities to KERO. This allowed KERO to concentrate on engineering and construction activities rather than external coordination.

The above are questions of leadership rather than managerial or technical acumen. As mentioned so often in this chapter, it falls to the project leader to establish the parameters for success of the project. Perhaps more important, it is up to him to transmit those values throughout his organization and to infuse his subordinates with the will and the passion to excel in all aspects of project operations, including partnership and politics. In addition to these political and partnership concerns, the task force or project leader serves as a role model for all who observe his conduct. There is no escaping the fact that the leader of an organization sets the moral tone for his subordinates. If he is coldly efficient in his interactions with subordinates, that pattern will be reflected in the subordinates' relationships with each other. If he exudes enthusiasm and a positive attitude about the project's purpose and potential benefit to society, the workforce will be similarly motivated to overcome all obstacles to achieve success. Great motivation is a tremendous morale multiplier. It is the adrenaline of workforce behavior, enabling employees to achieve cheerfully what otherwise might have been unheard of levels of performance. On the other hand, if the leader is cheerless and negative in the conduct of business and in his dealings with subordinates, constantly criticizing them or complaining about his superiors' lack of judgment or failure to provide resources, he will similarly create a negative attitude among his project team sapping their physical and mental power and crippling his project.

LESSONS LEARNED

To sum up the Kuwait experience in a few words is difficult. There were so many lessons learned that this chapter can only scratch the surface. Certainly, the impact of positive leadership on team performance should be at the top of the list. In addition, several more general observations deserve to be mentioned.

First of all, as an intergovernmental operation, the Kuwait recovery project was a tremendous success. The humanitarian spirit of the participants easily bridged the cultural and professional differences and paved the way for close cooperation and good working relations between the Americans and the Kuwaitis. What resulted from this cooperation was the prospect of a long-term relationship based on trust and goodwill, which is probably more important than the operation itself. Of paramount importance to these excellent working relations was the responsive and accountable support of the engineering management structure in KERO. Budget documents and funds accountability were precise and convincingly accurate. This is of cardinal importance to the establishment of trust with the host nation. Second, a true and honest partnership in all engineering decisions eliminated the potential misunderstandings that could easily have delayed construction and undermined the completion of key projects. Finally, free and open communications with all parties ensured that both U.S. and Kuwaiti government officials, and their constituents, understood exactly what was happening as the recovery progressed. In the end, the Kuwaitis were satisfied with the outcome of the operation and thankful to the Americans for their very timely and professional assistance.

The Kuwait recovery was satisfying and professionally exciting for all who had the opportunity to participate. As an intergovernmental experience, it holds a promise for future application not only in the aftermath of a conflict, but potentially as an instrument of foreign assistance. The security, political stability, and goodwill that resulted from the timely restoration of the civil infrastructure in Kuwait cannot be overemphasized and warrants serious consideration as a conflict management or conflict reduction tool for future nation assistance operations.

16

Different Approaches in Managing Complex Construction Projects

Experiences of International Project-Management

WILCO TIJHUIS

R ealizing construction projects within an international scope means in many cases the rising of conflicts. This is especially the case when looking at the impact of differences between countries regarding their approach of the construction and procurement practices, the solution of claims, and so on. But when companies are acting across their own national borders they have to be aware of the serious implications that can arise out of several of these conflicts.

This chapter describes results of experiences in the construction industry, which were part of a large partly participative research project in which the experienced practical situations and case studies were used for analysis and optimization of project management attitudes in construction process. Several Dutch and German parties participated in these projects. The role of the "unwritten" rules and practical experiences inside the project management approach of these processes are decribed, illustrated with a case study. It ends up with conclusions and recommendations.

OVERVIEW

Efforts for improving construction processes in construction industry nowadays usually starts only when there are quite a lot of difficulties with which to cope. The need for raising efficiency, for example, is a continuous item, but in fact only becomes an actual theme on the agenda's from managers when companies do really start to get in a loss. This attitude not only seems to be a sign of disease in the construction industry, but is also actual in a broader area of industry. The Latham Report (1994) started for the U.K. construction industry a discussion for improving the process regarding trust, money, and the team approach( ). But the research of the commision seemed to be especially initiated while there were really problems going on in U.K. construction industry: lack of trust, several claims, and so on. So, the signal function of "critical" incidents or moments into economy and/or industry is quite evident for starting efforts for business improvement.

In the same scope there could be seen an increasing influence from the opening of the national borders within Europe: cross-national research into industry, international comparisons of business systems, special marketviews, for example (European Commission 1993; Cooke and Walker 1994; Garaventa and Pirovano 1994; PCA 1994). All of them with one main goal: making people and organizations aware of the possibilities and risks when entering the European and/or global construction market. Apart from the fact that it was and is a good and prosperous job for several parties in the field, there are also organizations and especially for parties that do not really profit from it—companies with "old-fashioned" ways of thinking and acting, nonimproved business processes, and so forth. Still, the "threat" of the globalizing economy should become for them a real stimulus for starting improvement of their business. Or at least, they should try to do it.

This chapter focuses on aspects related to improving the business process within construction firms that already act abroad, especially those firms starting to act in the obvious difficult German construction market just after the breakdown of the Berlin Wall in 1989. In fact, they used the critical incidents that arose during their efforts for improving themselves. And that turned out to be a right decision, although it took a lot of effort and money to reach the goal of establishing an efficient and profitable business abroad, with stable foundings into the market (Tijhuis, 1998). And that is just opposite of the more famous "hit-and-run" approach, but one that many stakeholders with with a long-term scope have to deal with regarding the short-term scope of their shareholders.

CONSTRUCTION ACTIVITIES ABROAD: SPREADING RISKS BY USING NEW CHALLENGES

Being active in the construction industry always means a more or less cyclic business. Influences of economic activities in general are quitely well felt within the construction industry, therefore acting as an indicator for a nation's state of economy. The quantity of produced cement per inhabitant, for example, is a well-known indicator of the health of the construction industry, since cement is a strategic product in the construction industry, but one that is rarely exported.

Examples of these cyclic processes can be seen throughout the world: decline and growth of, for example, construction activities in the Docklands/London, in

Berlin/Brandenburg, and in Amsterdam/region (*Der Spiegel* 1995). Thus, being in many cases the engine of the local/regional industry, the construction business is quite dynamic, but within more or less cyclic periods.

This dynamic and cyclic characteristic of construction business especially plays a role when starting activities abroad: In what period of the business-cycle is the construction industry? Generally, companies enter the market when there is a "boom" coming up. But what to do when the market is slowing down, or even when there comes a recession or even a crisis?

As can be seen nowadays into the Asian markets, the recession has caused enormous losses in the construction industry and elsewhere: Contractors cannot be paid anymore, and financial guarantees have broken down due to the inflation of currency rates, and there are increased threatening situations for the people at the worksites. And these risks do not exist only in developing countries but also in developed countries (Wells and Gleason 1995).

Therefore, companies who want to reduce the risk for specific recessions throughout their markets have spread their activities througout several markets and throughout several regions and/or countries. Thus, introducing new challenges (including risks) due to becoming active in the "unknown" regions (e.g., foreign regions abroad), gives reduction for the risk of a complete recession in the total scope of activities of the company. But as it is in much cases, especially when starting in foreign markets, the lesson of "knowing someone in the market is better than having market-knowledge" is very representative for such specific situations (Tijhuis and Maas, 1996). However, doing business always means accepting risks. One has to know to what extent these risks can be tolerated.

A VIEW ON THE GERMAN MARKET

When looking to a comparable booming market in Germany into the early 1990s, there has been an enormous growth of construction activities since the opening of the Berlin Wall in 1989. The reunion of both East and West parts invented a need for modernizing the old, modest former East German-built environment. Added to the new established regulations, the so called "Einigungsverträge" (Münch Von 1990), specific subsidizing programs were established to stimulate the needed investments into the construction environment.

But these new programs also incorporated a certain risk. By introducing quite generous opportunities for getting funds for building investments, construction prices, especially the price of land, were rising quite strongly during several years. Projects came with high prices, but were still quite affordable because of the subsidy programs. Thus, these developments did not stimulate the cost efficiency of the German construction process, which had already been pointed out as a quite costly and inefficient process (Syben et al. 1996). Although European construction processes differ quite from each other (Cooke and Walker 1994), the chairman of the German commission for reduction of construction costs and regulations in German housing industry stated in 1994: "It appears that there is nobody in the whole German construction-process, whose way of working is especially focussing on reduction of construction-costs" ("Eigentlich ist im ganzen Bauablauf niemand anzutreffen, dessen Handeln ganz oder nur vorrangig auf Kostenersparnis ausgerichtet ist") (Lammerskitten 1994).

By mid-1995 it appeared that the situation was not as positive as it seemed: High prospective rent rates could be achieved, return on investments collapsed while the price levels in general were decreasing, procedures for redeveloping sites took too long, and the uncertainty for success for those highly sophisticated projects became quite strong (*Der Spiegel*, 1995) These developments led to a collapse of the market in about 1996/1997. The reunion of the former East and West Germany appeared to become too costly, leading to a strong crisis as a reaction to the strong (expected?) growth in the past circa five years. And just in a period during which the other parts of Western Europe reached a quite strong economic growth.

Recently, the more or less cyclic development of the German market led to the need for highly cost-efficient construction projects such as housing. This increases the need for improvement of the quite fragmented German traditional construction (production) processes. These development may stimulate the growth of the construction industry again, but with less possibilities for subsidy programs, thus, making the construction industry and market strong in itself.

PARTICIPATIVE ACTION RESEARCH INTO GERMAN CONSTRUCTION INDUSTRY

As pointed out above, the cyclic development of the German construction market led to an interesting opportunity. Due to increased construction activities, companies from abroad became interested into these Markets. These included some Dutch companies. Some of them were quite succesful, but a lot of them failed. In several cases it pointed out that the lack of experience and their "pure technical" approach caused a lot of failures, many resulting in the filing claims. They more or less failed to focus on other important dimensions, including culture and project organization, when acting abroad. The mutual influences between the three stages of action (contact/culture, contract/project organization, and conflict/technology) pointed out to be of eminent importance for becoming succesful (Tijhuis, 1996). In figure 16.1 these relationships are represented schematically.

The research therefore focused on the experiences within several Dutch and German companies. The research method is related to Spradley's method of participative action, which means that by being partly active into organizations, the focus on the real practice becomes quite clear (Spradley 1980). Geertz stimulates this approach when doing research into different cultures, as it also was in

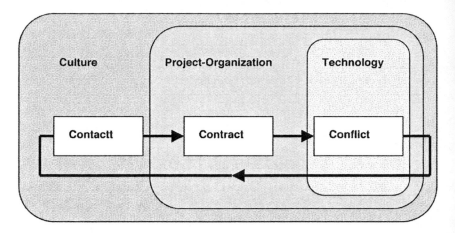

FIGURE 16-1. Schematic view on the system of relations (Tijhuis 1996).

this project. He wrote: "If you want to understand what a science is you should look in the first instance not at its theories or finding and certainly not at what its apologists say about it; you should look at what the practitioners of it do" (Geertz 1973). In fact, one is acting then like "a third culture man," as Sanders described it, focusing processes and organizations from inside, and then just taking back a step outside and vice-versa (Sanders 1995).

Doing the research during a period of four years (1993–1996) gave a lot of information, just from the inside of projects and processes. By coupling these experiences and data back to theory and an expert panel outside, it resulted to a realistic view on actions and reactions inside construction processess.

THINKING, SAYING AND WRITING: A CASE STUDY

Introduction

During the four-year period several cases were being studied. The use of documents and written and nonwritten regulations related to the quite fragmented way of organizing the construction process caused difficulties. In one of the case studies, a brief indication is given of some of the situations encountered during the total research period.

The Project

One of the projects was a large housing site in the Berlin region; about 350 houses were to be developed and built, including infrastructure. The houses were of a two-storey type, with a saddle-roof, built in several series but with specific options for the different clients. The focus within this part of the case study was on projects for private clients. During a total approach of the construction-process it is necessary on the one hand to integrate project's specifications and client's wishes as soon as possible, but on the other hand to stay flexible as long as possible, for example, in the case when houses are not completely sold yet, or being sold during construction process.

Integrated Views versus Fragmented Practices

During the entire preparation and construction process there can be seen a quite traditional approach within the German construction process. The architect still plays the major role not only for the design, but also for the management of the process. Although several alternatives are coming up nowadays (e.g., *Generalunternehmer, Generalübernehmer, Bautaktverfahren*), the traditional approach stays quite stable. In addition to that, there can be seen a large influence of a very important regulation: The "Bauhandwerkergesetz." This regulation (an official law) prohibits contractors from participating in the total approach of the construction process unless they possess certain specific certificates (e.g., "Meisterbrief"). These certificates are based on a certain level of craftsmanship and specialization, which is quite difficult to get as a generalist. Therefore, a lot of the contractors in the German market are typical specialized parties, in a rather small size. When these parties seek to do a total project, they have to reorganize themselves into joint ventures. So, by using each other's strengths and competences, projects should be carried out more easily, and with less failure costs (e.g., due to better coordination possibilities). But that is not quite easy to do, as each party has its own specific needs and wishes.

The integrated approach, therefore, is quite difficult to reach inside such a fragmented market structure. This is being pushed also by governmental means, while the public clients have obliged themselves to use the "VOB— Verdingungsordnung für Bauleistung" (VOB, 1997). Within this set of standard contractual regulations, projects should be divided into specific work packages (the so-called "Losen" or "Teil-Losen"). These work packages should be tendered separately, which should lead to a more efficient construction process. However, as pointed out during several investigations, the initial costs for construction in the tendering phase may be lower, but the indirect cost of failures and claims by unsatisfied clients and other parties, due to, for example, coordination problems, are rising quite high. This leads to an unexpected high level of total construction costs, added to unsatisfied clients and other parties involved.

However, for the mentioned housing project, the construction process was being carried out by a combined Dutch/German general contractor, active as a project developer combined with construction tasks: So, they integrated the whole construction process, including the management of the design phase and additional financial arrangements and risks.

Role of the Client

For the housing-project, the private clients in the whole process could be divided generally into two categories regarding their goals and motives:

> Clients especially stimulated by several interesting financial opportunities. They were obliged then to let their properties to others. The motives of these clients were more or less based on "investing into square meters for reducing income-taxes."
>
> Clients who were investing in properties for their own use. These clients had motives stimulated by, for example, a need for more space, other quality demands, a better environmental living.

In general the different approaches could be distinguished for the both described categories of clients (a) and (b) as follows:

> Quite "uninterested" clients; they only bought to reduce their income tax.
>
> Very anxious clients; they particularly seemed to look for getting an opportunity for claims to be paid by the contractor.

These differences introduced an enormous lack of trust, especially by category (b). Small differences in delivered specifications, for example, "were blown up to enormous proportions," thus leading to a real struggle, as it seemed, not with the goal "to solve the problem," but especially for "searching who's guilty." This led to possible claims to be paid by the accused party, which in general are quite often the contractors and subcontractors involved.

Results

During the analysis of the different situations it became clear, that in the (German) construction market, thinking, saying, and writing does not necessarily mean the same. It often seems that a private client does not say what he is thinking about the real project goals, but in relationship to the written record he often writes precisely down his thoughts, not only in a protocol, but often quite unexpectedly afterward by putting a claim on the accused party. In this way, the culture influences are quite strong, and they become increasingly "part of the deal" within the construction industry, as Tijhuis described (Tijhuis 2001). But it should also be clear that these influences led to an increasing risk of "culture costs," being one of the failure aspects within the construction industry and its project management. And these costs of failure can rise quite high!

CONCLUSIONS AND RECOMMENDATIONS

The mentioned lack of trust, which is not only typical for the German situation, looking, for example, to the British situation (Latham 1994) and the Dutch situation (Nijpels 1992), seems to be one of the main barriers for good collaboration between parties. But the differences between the goals of parties in construction still play an even more important role, not leading to the expected quality but to conflicts. So, do (sub)contractors really understand their clients? Is there a (mis)match between common goals? And which goals are focused on?

By using tools for improving the communication process and adapting the usual ways of communication and culture, a stronger reduction of the costs of failure within construction contracts can be reached (Tijhuis and Lousberg 1998). And remember this also: To understand and recognize your clients abroad, you at least must be able to understand and recognize your clients at home.

BIBLIOGRAPHY

Cooke, B., and G. Walker. 1994. *European Construction—Procedures and Techniques.* London: Macmillan Press Ltd..

European Commision. 1993. *SECTEUR—Strategic Study on the Construction Sector—Final Report—Strategies for the Construction Sector.* Epsom, Surrey, U.K.: W. S. Atkins International Limited.

Garaventa, S., and P. Pirovano. 1994. *L'Europa dei progrettisti e dei costruttori—Procedure e operatori delle costruzioni in Francia, Italia, Regno unito e Republica federale tedesca;* Architettura collana diretta da valerio di battista; Masson S.p.A; Editoriale ESA; Milano.

Geertz, C. 1973. *The Interpretation of Cultures.* New York: Basic Books.

Lammerskitten, P. 1994. *Kommentar. Bundes BauBlatt* 9(September): 640; Ed.: Bundesbauministerium für Bau- und Wohnungswesen (BMBau); Bonn.

Latham, M. 1994. *Constructing the Team.* Final report of the Joint Government/Industry Review of Procurement and Contractual Arrangements in the United Kingdom Construction Industry. London: HMSO.

Münch Von. 1990. *Die Verträge zur Einheit Deutschlands—Einigungsvertrag mit Anlagen/ Wahlvertrag/Zwei-plus-Vier-Vertrag / Partnerschaftsverträge.* Verlag C. H. Beck; 2. Auflage, 1992; Munich.

Nijpels, E. H. T. M. (ed.) 1992. *Bouwen in Europese competitie—Voorwaarden voor verbetering van de concurrentiekracht van het grootbedrijf in de bouw.* Commissie Nijpels, Ministerie van VROM; 25 Junes-Gravenhage.

PCA. 1994. *Comparison of Production Engineering and Site Management, and Their Potential of Adaptation in France, Germany, Holland and Finland—Comparaison de la conception et de la conduite de la production sur chantier, et de leurs potentialites d'adaptation, en France, Allemagne, Hollande et Finlande.* Paris: Plan Construction and Architecture (PCA); F. Pierre, M & C Methodes et Construction, Paris; Tijhuis W., and G. J.Maas, University Centre for Building Production (UCB), Eindhoven; Syben G., and K. Stroink, Hochschule Bremen; Laurikka P., and T. Alanen, VTT Technical Research Centre of Finland, Tampere.

Sanders, G. J. E. M. 1995. Being a Third Culture Man. *Cross Cultural Management: An International Journal* 01.2(1): 5–7; MCB University Press.

Spradley, J. P. 1980. *Participant Observation.* New York: Holt, Rinehart and Winston.

Syben, G., et al. 1996. *Integration and Disintegration of Roles and Actors: The German Contracting System Under Change.* London: Hochschule Bremen and Le Groupe

Bagnolet, c/o G. Winch, Bartlett School of Graduates Studies, University College London; PCA—Plan Construction and Architecture, Paris.

Tijhuis, W. 1996. *Contractors in Projects or in Conflict?—Lessons from International Collaboration* (published as a book in Dutch: *Bouwers aan de slag of in de slag?—Lessen uit internationale samenwerking*). Ph.D. thesis, Eindhoven University of Technology, Faculty of Building and Architecture, Eindhoven, The Netherlands; Berlin, Germany; WT/Consult BV, Rijssen, The Netherlands.

Tijhuis, W. 1998. *Connecting Marketing to Construction Process: The Impact of Internationalization.* Paper presented at the 1st International Construction Marketing Conference— Opportunities and Strategis in a Global Market Place; 26–27 August; proceedings, edited by C. N. Preece, Leeds: Construction Management Group, School of Civil Engineering, University of Leeds, 141–48.

Tijhuis, W. 2001. *Culture in Construction—Part of the Deal?* Proceedings of workshop; CIB-TG23, 'Culture in Construction'; Edited by: Dr.ir.Wilco Tijhuis; 22nd and 23rd May 2000; Published January 2001; publication nr.255; CIB, Rotterdam; University of Twente, Enschede.

Tijhuis, W., and G. J. Maas. 1996. *Project Development in Germany: Example of a Way of Working.* (paper CIB-W92). Proceedings of conference North Meets South—Developing Ideas, edited by R. Taylor, 592–601. University of Natal, Durban, 14–17 January 1996, Durban.

Tijhuis, W., and L. Lousberg. 1998. *TQM and Procurement in Construction Projects: How to handle Quality in Contractual Relationships.* Paper presented University of Twente, Enschede; Inbo Consultants BV, Woudenberg; Conference: Total Quality Management in Construction—Towards Zero Defect; 24–27 November; proceedings edited by Th. C. Haupt et al., Peninsula Technikon in association with Fedsure Group; Cape Town, 25–36.

VOB. 1997. *VOB für Praktiker—Kommentar zur Verdingungsordnung für Bauleistungen—mit graphiken, Urteilen und Praxistips.* W. Beck and N. Herig. Stuttgart: Richard Boorberg Verlag.

Wells, L. T., and E. S.Gleason. 1995. Is Foreign Infrastructure Investment Still Risky? Developing Countries Are Courting Investors. Is It Safe to Say Yes? *Harvard Business Review*, September–October, 44–55.

Wie von selbst—Der Spekulationsrausch in Berlin ist vorbei—Viele Bürotürme stehen leer, den Markt droth der Kollaps. *Der Spiegel* 21.

——— 17 ———

Railway Project Management

Framework and Examples

FRANK T. ANBARI

In the formulation and implementation of organizational strategy, a railway needs to integrate carefully the following two goals to enhance its competitive position: improvement of its current services and the processes of delivering these services to its customers. Examples would include improvements of track, electric traction, communications and signals, and reservations systems. Planning and introduction of new services, processes, and technologies enhance its effectiveness, efficiency, and customer satisfaction. Examples would include extending rail service to new areas, major rehabilitation of existing rail lines, implementation of centralized electrification and traffic control, and development of new software for reservations, commissary and crew management. The first goal can be pursued as part of business systems improvement, quality, and Six Sigma initiatives in the enterprise. The second goal can be carried out as a coordinated portfolio of projects and programs, guided to their completion by project management methods and tools.

This chapter discusses the following:

- A brief overview of business systems improvement and service quality.
- A framework for managing railway projects.
- Examples of selected railway projects accomplished by the National Railroad Passenger Corporation (Amtrak) over the period of twenty-five years to modernize and enhance its services in the northeast corridor and national operations throughout the United States.

The framework and examples are applicable to many other organizations, particularly those in the railway industry.

BUSINESS SYSTEMS IMPROVEMENT AND SERVICE QUALITY

Definitions

Quality in the railway industry can be defined as providing services that meet or exceed the expectations of the customer, fit his/her needs, and improve continually to enhance the satisfaction of the customer. Quality management can be viewed as the management of a total system that transforms external and internal inputs into services to the customer and has a feedback mechanism to ensure that the output is consistent with the definition of quality presented above. This approach allows the analysis of various elements of quality while maintaining a view of the entire system.

Business Systems and Service Quality Improvement

Business systems and service quality improvement are carried out within the overall system of quality planning, assurance, improvement, and control. Railway quality management can be viewed as a system consisting of the following elements:

> *Input:* consists of physical, human, and conceptual resources, available internally or obtained from external suppliers. Such resources may include right-of-way, property, material, rolling stock, rail maintenance equipment, computer hardware, labor, management, software, methods, knowledge, and experience.
>
> *Process:* transforms inputs into services, and consists of the following elements:
>
> - improvement of the services provided to the customers
> - improvement of the processes used to provide these services
> - innovation in the services provided to the customers
> - innovation in the processes used to provide these services
>
> *Output:* consists of service(s) and good(s) such as on-time performance, clean cars and facilities, fresh food, express package delivery, and accurate billing.
>
> *Feedback Mechanism:* consists of the total information used by the management team to ensure that the services provided meet the quality objectives set forth in the definition of quality presented earlier.

Quality improvement includes definition of the process under consideration, identification of the key variables affecting its quality, collecting relevant data on these variables over time, analyzing these data, and undertaking process improvement activities based on facts associated with the overall process and the system within which it operates.

Quality Improvement Initiatives
and the Six Sigma Method

The above functions have generally been carried out as part of organizational initiatives such as Total Quality Management (TQM) and Continuous Quality Improvement (CQI). These initiatives and their tools were widely implemented in railway organizations in the 1980s and early 1990s, and resulted in many useful accomplishments in these organizations. As used, these initiatives often aimed at what was called the "low-hanging fruit." Many organizations had such improvement opportunities. The problems that were targeted had occurred as a result of historical developments in these organizations. Certain activities were performed for specific reasons, and they continued to be performed well after their value diminished or disappeared completely. To improve these processes and eliminate the nonvalue-added activities, TQM and CQI aimed primarily at empowering individuals and teams to discuss these issues within their own areas or across organizational boundaries. The tools of TQM and CQI were heavily oriented toward communications, brainstorming, and simple data analysis.

By the mid-1990s, however, most organizations that adopted TQM and CQI ran out of low-hanging fruit. The problems and opportunities that needed to be tackled next did not lend themselves easily to simple data analysis; they required more investment in resources and time than what was considered appropriate in these initiatives. Significant business results were no longer achievable through TQM and CQI, and organizational commitment to these initiatives came to an end.

In the meantime, the Six Sigma management method continued to grow and thrive, from its initial development by Motorola in the 1980s, to its widely advertised adoption by GE in 1992, to its adoption by many other powerful organizations since that time, including organizations in manufacturing (such as GE, Boeing, DuPont, Kodak, Toshiba, and Seagate), service, banking, and railways. The results have been very impressive.

The Six Sigma method appeared to be the next logical step, since it cured the deficiencies of TQM and CQI by including:

- clearly measured financial results, which ensured sustained commitment to the initiative by senior executives,
- additional, more advanced data analysis tools focused on customer concerns, which ensured problems were properly analyzed, and
- project-driven organizational structure and use of appropriate project selection, evaluation, and relevant project management methodology and tools, which ensured that Six Sigma projects reached their objectives successfully.

The philosophy of the Six Sigma management method focuses on better understanding of changing customer requirements, improving business systems throughout the organization, and enhancing the financial performance of the organization. It is used to improve the organization's products, services, and processes across various disciplines, including operations, engineering, marketing, sales, service delivery, finance, and administration. It is achieved through understanding the underlying processes, and reducing or eliminating defects and waste. The Six Sigma management method integrates profound knowledge of the process, engineering, statistics, and project management. It results in substantial improvement of quality and delivery, reduction of cost, development of robust services and processes, enhancement of competitive position, and sustained competitive advantage through continual improvement of all business systems in the organization.

The Six Sigma management method is more comprehensive than prior process improvement initiatives and can be summarized as follows:

$$\text{Six Sigma} = \text{TQM and CQI} + \text{Stronger Customer Focus} +$$
$$\text{Additional Data Analysis Tools} + \text{Financial Results} + \text{Project Management}$$

Quality improvement can be achieved only on a project-by-project basis. Therefore, effective management of process improvement and Six Sigma projects is essential to the success of business systems and service quality improvement efforts. Knowledge of the relevant tools of project management is vital to that success.

MANAGING RAILWAY PROJECTS

Definitions

A railway project can be defined as a temporary endeavor that integrates human, physical, and conceptual resources to create a new service(s), achieve a unique objective(s), or deal with a specific problem(s). It is usually conducted across traditional departmental lines using required staff expertise. Its objectives may be to build a new maintenance facility, develop a new application software, improve the quality of an existing service or system, and similar objectives. The project team is selected from different units of the organization, or from the same department, and may include contractors. Resources may be committed full time or part time to the project, which has a defined starting point and a defined finishing point. When project objectives are attained or abandoned, the project team is reassigned or released.

The management of a railway project can be viewed as the management of a total system that transforms inputs into outputs and has a feedback mechanism to ensure that project output is consistent with project objectives. This approach allows the analysis of various elements of the project while maintaining a view of the entire system. The system consists of the following elements:

Input: consists of physical, human, and conceptual resources such as right-of-way, property, material, equipment, hardware, labor, management, software, methods, knowledge, and experience.

Process: transforms inputs into outputs.

Output: consists of good(s) and service(s) such as a rehabilitated railway line, a new computer installation, or an improved trip time.

Feedback Mechanism: consists of the total information used by the project manager and project team members to ensure that the output meets the goals and objectives set for the project.

The quality management and the project management systems are conducted within an environment that includes various internal and external continuing forces. In the first category are departmental objectives, company goals, organizational structure, union agreements, financial position, priorities, policies, and procedures. In the second category are customers, vendors, competitors, alternate modes of transportation, technology, government, and the community.

Elements of Railway Project Management

The process of managing a railway project consists of the following elements, which are consistent with the areas of knowledge published by the Project Management Institute in *A Guide to the Project Management Body of Knowledge, PMBOK Guide, 2000 Edition,* with some adjustments:

- Scope management, which involves the planning, monitoring, and control of project scope consistent with the objectives of the project. Scope management calls for specific evaluation of the initial scope and subsequent modifications, to ensure compatibility of the scope with other project parameters and with overall project objectives.
- Time management, which involves the planning, scheduling, monitoring, and control of the time element of the parameter of the project. Time management stresses the importance of the periodic evaluation of the impact of actual progress on the completion time of the entire project, or its components, as well as the potential impact of the time element on other project parameters such as scope, cost, and quality.
- Cost management, which involves resource planning and cost estimating of the project, as well as subsequent collection, organization, and analysis of actual cost data to attain project cost objectives. This effort includes consideration of scope, schedule, equipment cost, material procurement, labor cost, contracts cost, and overhead, to generate cost estimates and time-phased budgets. It includes periodic assessment of project cost performance, which may use specialized techniques such as the earned value method, cost variance analysis, performance indexes, trend analysis, and forecasting tools to decide on preventive and corrective action. Cost management emphasizes the importance of periodic evaluation of actual expenditures and commitments as compared to budget and to physical accomplishments. It further underlines the impact of the cost parameter on other project parameters, and the relationship between the project and the outside environment.
- Quality management, which involves the assurance of the completion of the project within the standards required by the user and established professionally. This effort includes consideration of performance criteria, tolerances, standards, requirements,

and specifications established for the project, in terms of operability, reliability, availability, maintainability, flexibility, and safety of the project. It includes implementation of measures of quality of design and conformance, inspection, testing, training, building quality into the process and the project, trial testing project, user training, and final user acceptance. The recent emphasis on quality management and Six Sigma method highlights the importance of the continuous evaluation of quality during the implementation of a project and on its completion, as well as the relationship between the quality element and other project elements.

- Human resource management, which involves the strategic, long-term, broad view of resources in the organization. It encompasses the application of current knowledge of human behavior and leadership in the project environment and the application of resource allocation tools to minimize conflicts resulting from unbalanced or unrealistic work loads. When handled effectively, it results in a committed, creative, and effective project team, having a clear understanding and acceptance of assigned tasks. The effective management of human resources is the key to productive project teams and efficient management of physical resources such as material, equipment, land, and capital.

- Communications management, which involves the formal and informal interactions of individuals and groups in the project team, across organizational lines, downward, upward, laterally, and diagonally. It includes active listening as well as sending written, electronic, verbal, and nonverbal messages, such as project reports, analyses, and presentations. Communications management needs to be evaluated in terms of its objectives of disseminating project directions and problems in a timely and efficient manner to support effective decisions and coordinated actions by the project team.

- Procurement/contract management, which involves the planning and control of physical and human resources obtained through contractual arrangements to meet the objectives of the project. This covers procurement planning, consideration of various types of contracts and contractor selection, contract cost and risk management, contract administration, postcontract evaluation and closeout. Procurement/contract management needs to be evaluated in terms of meeting its objectives of completing, accepting, and closing the contract as an integral part of the total project management system.

- Risk management, which involves the identification of risk factors associated with the project and management of these risks throughout the life of the project. This includes the systematic identification of various risk factors associated with the project, the analysis of their probability and impact, the planning and implementation of a response system to avoid, mitigate, reduce, transfer, share, or retain these risks, and monitoring these and other emerging risks to enact the response system, as appropriate, when risk warning signs or triggers are observed.

EXAMPLES OF SELECTED RAILWAY PROJECTS

Since their early days, railroads have played a major role in the growth and economic development of the United States. During the first half of the twentieth century, railroads continued to grow and prosper. However, their prominent position in the United States started to decline in the 1950s and 1960s as a result of many changes in the market environment in which they operated. These changes included the development and expansion of competitive modes of transportation, including the interstate highway system, automobile transportation, intercity busses, trucking industry, and air transportation. Competitive forces, management decisions, and other factors resulted in deferred railroad maintenance and ultimately deterioration of railway systems, particularly railroad passenger service.

The Railroad Passenger Service Act of 1970 created the National Railroad Passenger Corporation (Amtrak) to contract with various railroads for providing crews and operating facilities for rail passenger service. The U.S. Railway Association designated the densely populated Northeast Corridor (NEC) from Washington, D.C. to Boston, Massachusetts, for acquisition by Amtrak. That acquisition of most of the NEC by Amtrak in 1976 resulted in the company providing national operations and NEC service, as well as having ownership, and responsibility for maintenance of the region. Amtrak passenger trains, various commuter trains, and freight trains use the NEC heavily.

Starting in 1977 and during the next twenty-five years, Amtrak accomplished numerous major projects to modernize and enhance its service in the NEC and its national operations. Examples of selected projects carried out by Amtrak include: the Northeast Corridor Improvement Project, the Northeast High-Speed Rail Improvement Project, high-speed train service, and management information systems and application software development.

Northeast Corridor Improvement Project

The Railroad Revitalization and Regulatory Reform Act of 1976 authorized the Northeast Corridor Improvement Project (NECIP). To provide passengers in the railroad corridor from Washington, D.C. to Boston, Massachusetts, with dependable high-speed train service, the U.S. Congress NECIP. The project was started in 1977 and substantially completed by 1985, at a cost of $2.5 billion. The project accomplished improvements in track structure, route realignment, electric traction, communications, signals, bridges, tunnels, fences and barriers, stations, and service facilities.

Cost
The cost of NECIP components was distributed approximately as follows ($ millions):

Route realignment	70
Track structure	809
Bridges	255
Electric traction	298
Signaling and traffic control	391
Communications	9

Fences and barriers	21
Grade crossing elimination	16
Stations	195
Service facilities	148
Tunnels	31
Program management and systems engineering	280
	====
Total	2,500

Project Management Organization

The Federal Railroad Administration (FRA) of the U.S. Department of Transportation (DOT) directed NECIP. The FRA was responsible for the overall planning, control, and management of NECIP. DOT contracted with Amtrak for NECIP construction work through the FRA. The consortium of engineering consulting firms of DeLeuw, Cather/Parsons (DC/P) and other consultants provided engineering design, configuration management, and program management to NECIP, under contract to the FRA. Amtrak, the owner of the NEC, and the operator of passenger trains through it, became also the prime contractor for its improvement. Project progress could affect current service to the public by Amtrak and others using the NEC, as well as future operations of Amtrak. Therefore, the project had to be planned, scheduled, executed, and controlled very carefully. Amtrak formed a project management organization (PMO) in Philadelphia starting in 1976–1977 to implement the requirements of the contract with FRA and to direct the project. Amtrak forces and subcontractors accomplished all construction work of NECIP. Amtrak's NECIP PMO developed, installed, and subsequently integrated cost collection and production reporting systems. The PMO managed NECIP and reported on it monthly to Amtrak's board of directors and to the FRA. Among the main objectives of the PMO were to accomplish technical and contract requirements on time, within budget, safely, while maintaining current operations.

Four Amtrak divisions in the NEC were responsible for operations and construction work: Baltimore, Philadelphia, New York, and Boston. Division management was fully involved in setting production and cost objectives. Amtrak labor gangs, from multiple disciplines, accomplished construction work under union contracts. The size of each gang varied from under ten workers to more than one hundred workers. Some were division gangs that worked on project elements within their division. Others were designated as system gangs and accomplished their work throughout the NEC. Certain portions of NECIP work were subcontracted to appropriately selected contractors.

Results

The NEC serves more than 100 million passengers per year and is the most heavily used passenger train corridor in the United States. Amtrak and several commuter and freight railroads use the NEC (United States General Accounting

Office; GAO). The NEC has become Amtrak's most cost-effective operation and an invaluable major component of the transportation infrastructure in the northeastUnited States.

On completion of NECIP, Amtrak's Metroliner trains were able to travel between New York and Washington at speeds of up to 125 miles per hour. Amtrak's conventional trains and other commuter trains ran at lower speeds. However, the significant improvement of the infrastructure in the NEC benefited freight train and commuter train service as well. Amtrak carried a significant percentage of all nonhighway travelers between New York and Washington, and intermediate points such as Trenton, Philadelphia, Wilmington, and Baltimore (Southeast High Speed Rail corridor; SEHSR).

Northeast High-Speed Rail Improvement Project

The Northeast High-Speed Rail Improvement Project (NHRIP) was designed to upgrade Amtrak's NEC between New York and Boston, at a cost of about $2 billion (Amtrak Office of Inspector General). It was initiated to bring the New York to Boston segment of the NEC up to the same level of performance as the New York to Washington, D.C. segment. As such, it could be considered a continuation of NECIP.

NHRIP was a combination of rail infrastructure improvements and rolling stock acquisition. It extended electrification east of New Haven to Boston, rebuilt interlockings and terminal tracks to permit higher train speeds, upgraded bridges, modernized signal systems, and purchased twenty high-speed electric train sets named the *Acela Express*. These infrastructure improvements and introduction of the Acela Express service allowed train running speeds of up to 150 miles per hour along certain stretches of the NEC. This resulted in significant reductions in trip time between New York and Boston, and improved trip time between New York and Washington. NHRIP allowed reduction of trip time for Amtrak's conventional trains and other commuter trains, and provided the operating capacity to support reliable intercity, commuter, and freight operations. By the end of 1999, the entire NEC was electrified to Boston, and other infrastructure improvements were substantially completed.

High-Speed Train Service

Amtrak acquired twenty new high-speed tilting trainsets, which could run at a top speed of 150 miles per hour (240 km/h), using the improved track. The NEC has many curves, especially north of New York. Between New York and Boston, the track makes the equivalent of over eleven full circles! This dictated the choice of a tilting train, to allow higher speeds in curves without causing passenger discomfort (Acela Express, Web pages). To achieve this, tilt signals are calculated by a master tilting controller that tells the mechanism when to activate and the amount of tilt needed to reduce lateral acceleration. (Wilson 1996).

Alternatives and Selection

Amtrak announced the award of a competitive contract in March 1996 to a consortium led by the Canadian firm Bombardier that won with its design, the high-speed tilt train contract, originally given the marketing name "American Flyer." Alstom, maker of the French TGV, joined bombardier, which holds exclusive rights to the TGV technology in North America. The Bombardier design was chosen over two other tilt train proposals from competing bidders. The competitors were the ICE train, proposed by a consortium led by Siemens, maker of the German ICE train sets, and the X2000 proposed by ABB, maker of the Swedish X2000 train sets. Both train sets were demonstrated in the NEC in 1993.

Bombardier's experience with North American railcar construction and attractive financing package were factors in the selection. The train sets were largely built on U.S. soil, as stipulated in the contract. Most of the manufacturing was performed at Bombardier's plants in Barre, Vermont, and Plattsburgh, New York. Alstom furnished some components made in France. The STV Group designed and built three new maintenance facilities for the train sets. The U.S. Congress specifically mandated the timing goals as a condition for providing funding, and Amtrak's contract with Bombardier specified large financial penalties if the performance guarantees were not met.

Branding and Service

Amtrak unveiled the Acela brand in 1999. The name, conceived by the New York branding firm IDEO, was intended to reflect a combination of acceleration and excellence. The Acela brand was used for other Amtrak services in the NEC, such as the Acela Regional. The Acela Express name replaced the marketing name American Flyer, previously used by the Bombardier consortium (Acela Express, Web pages).

The Acela Express service began in December 2000 after some delays caused by technical and safety issues. During the summer of 2002, all Acela Express train sets were temporarily taken out of service due to safety concerns. After safety inspections and fixes were implemented, they were returned to full service in the late summer of 2002.

Management Information Systems, and Application Software

Several other projects were developed and implemented to improve operations and enhance service. These projects included development of several software applications such as train and engine crew management, train provisioning, labor assignment, reservations, Internet booking, self-service ticketing, and financial systems. Training on various systems and methods was conducted throughout the company. These projects helped establish an environment that enabled effective management of the modernized railroad in the United States.

CONCLUSIONS

This chapter provided a framework for the formulation and implementation of organizational strategy in the railway industry. It stressed the importance of business systems improvement and service quality. It presented a framework for managing railway projects and programs to introduce new products and services. It gave examples of selected railway projects accomplished by Amtrak over a twenty-five year period to modernize and enhance its services in the NEC and its national operations throughout the United States. Business systems improvement, careful implementation of appropriate projects, and management support systems are important ingredients for success for railroads and other organizations.

BIBLIOGRAPHY

Acela Express. Retrieved from: http://www.amtrak.com/servlet/ContentServer?pagename= Amtrak/am2Route/Vertical_Route_Page&c=am2Route&cid=1080772074490&ssid= 134 on October, 2004.

Amtrak. http://www.amtrak.com/trains/acelaexpress.html. Retrieved on October 26, 2004

Amtrak Office of Inspector General. http://www.amtrakoig.com/officeofaudits.html. Retrieved on October 26, 2004

Anbari, F. T. 1980. An Operating Management Control System for Large Scale Projects. *Decision Sciences Institute, Ninth Annual Meeting, Northeast Regional Conference,* Philadelphia.

Anbari, F. T. 1992. Quality Improvement and Project Management in the Railway Industry. *COMPRAIL 92 International Conference,* Alexandria, Virginia.

Project Management Institute (PMI). 2000. *A Guide to the Project Management Body of Knowledge (PMBOK Guide).* Newtown Square, Pa: Project Management Institute.

Southeast High Speed Rail corridor (SEHSR). http://www.sehsr.org/reports/time2act/ actchapter5.html. Retrieved on October 26, 2004

Train Web. http://www.trainweb.org/tgvpages/acela.html. Retrieved on October 26, 2004

United States General Accounting Office (GAO). http://www.ont.com/~mobdaldm/ ga00495.htm. Retrieved on October 26, 2004

Wilson, J. 1996. American Flyer. *Popular Mechanics.*http://popularmechanics.com/science/ transportation/1996/11/new_bullet_train/print.phtml. Retrieved on October 26, 2004

─── 18 ───

The Management of Railway Construction and Upgrade Projects

A Study of the Experience in Greece

JOHN-PARIS PANTOUVAKIS

The European Union (EU) and Greece budgeted 5.04 billion euros for the construction and upgrade of the national railway network. The project, which is the largest in terms of budget single construction project in Greece today, started in 1996 and is expected to be completed by 2008. It entails the upgrade of the basic railway network backbone of approximately 450 miles to achieve speeds of 125 miles per hour and the refurbishment of the 400 miles secondary lines to assist urban development. Electrification of the basic backbone and telecommunications and signaling for the greatest part of the network are also planned. The management structure, project management model and experiences of the railway construction management company of Greece (ERGOSE S.A.) will be presented in this chapter.

OVERVIEW

Greece is a European country participating fully in the EU and the European Monetary Union (EMU). ERGA OSE S.A. (ERGOSE for short) is the company formed in 1997 to take over the management of the Greek Railways Investment Program, and in particular to manage the projects cofunded by EU's funds. ERGOSE is affiliated with the Greek Railway Organization (OSE in Greek) in that the latter is the sole shareholder of the former.

In parallel with forming ERGOSE, a project manager was hired to participate in the planning and formation of the new organization. His position was integrated into the company's organizational structure. The takeover of the projects from OSE started in July 1997 and was completed in December of the same year. The aims of the Greek Railways Investment Program are fully in line with the EU transport policy as expressed in the White Book for transport issued by the EU in 1993 in which the development of the European Railways is given high priority. All the projects of the program will become part of the trans-European networks of high-speed railways, combined transports, and conventional trains.

As a result, the European funds contributed to the realization of the program are substantial. The Community Support Framework (CSF), the Cohesion Fund (CF), and the European Regional Development Fund (ERDF) fund the program. A budget of 3.8 billion euros has been approved for the period 2000–2006 by the 3rd Community Support Framework (3rd CSF) and an additional budget of 1.24 billion euros by the 2nd Cohesion Fund (2nd CF), for a total of 5.04 billion euros.

It is ERGOSE's objective to complete projects in the most technically and economically sound manner and at the same time to gain from liaison with the project manager by adopting new management methods and know-how. This will enable the company to become a marketable project execution arm of OSE capable of expansion through offered services to other countries (e.g., those of the Balkan Peninsula). In order to achieve these goals, ERGOSE applies modern project management techniques. ERGOSE staff, both Greek and internationally experienced engineers, are developing the necessary know-how and experience in the railway project sector.

More specifically, the main means for achieving the company's goals are:

- A modern organizational structure adjusted to the needs of the projects.
- Qualitative and quantitative methods of site supervision.
- Use of up-to-date project monitoring and administration methods.
- Installation of a quality assurance system of ISO 9001 certification.
- Implementation of modern design and construction criteria and specifications.
- A management information system (MIS) covering all major company's activities.
- Standardization of drawings, designs, and tender documents.
- A policy of continuous education and development of the company's personnel.
- Implementation of an appropriate environmental policy to minimize the environmental impact of the projects.
- Establishment, maintenance, and application of a health and safety system.

Realization of OSE's Investment Program will result in the updating of Greek Railways, which in turn will yield journey time reduction, an increase in the average speed of the trains up to 125 miles per hour, improvement in passenger comfort (achieved through the use of slab track instead of the traditional ballast, and the procurement of new rolling stock), a reduction of maintenance and operational costs, and an improvement in operating conditions.

On principal routes, the time gains are summarized in table 18.1.

The result expected from the whole development effort is a substantial increase in the market share of railways in the total passenger and freight transport market in Greece. The transfer of large volumes of traffic from road to rail presents major socioeconomical and environmental advantages as railways, specially electrified ones, pollute less, consume comparatively less energy, provide the safest form of transport, and create a decongested traffic environment wherever they operate. The management structure, project management model, and experiences of ERGOSE S.A., the railway construction management company of Greece, will be presented in this chapter.

BRIEF DESCRIPTION OF THE TRANSPORTATION SECTOR IN GREECE

The particular characteristics of Greece should be taken into consideration in understanding the upgrading program of the transportation sector. This factual data will be discussed briefly in this paragraph. Greece has a large number of dispersed inhabited islands that require air and sea connections. People and goods can only be transported to these islands by a combination of ferryboats and cars. Railway connections to the islands are impossible.

The Greek mainland is characterized by mountains that traverse the country from north to south and to its northern part from west to east. These natural obstacles combined with the general layout of the mainland impose the selection of a linear model to ground transportations (roads and railways). The basic road network in Greece follows a T-shape backbone whereas the railway network only covers the central and eastern part of the country. Greece is situated in the southeastern border of Europe. As such, its inter-European transportation potential is limited, however, it offers a comparative advantage for combined ground—sea transportation between Europe and Asia or Europe and Africa and as an air-transportation junction.

Regional development in Greece is characterized by two major cities (Athens, the capital city, in the south and Thessaloniki, the second biggest city, in the

TABLE 18-1. Time gains of principal routes

Route	Journey Time Before the Upgrade	Journey Time After the Upgrade
Athens – Thessaloniki	5 hours 45 min	3 hours 50 min
Athens – Korinthos	1 hour 50 min	50 min
Athens – Patras	3 hours 35 min	1 hours 50 min
Palaiofarsalos – Kalabaka	1 hour 40 min	50 min

north) where the greatest part of the population and of the economic and production activities are located. Tourism is concentrated mainly in the islands.

BACKGROUND, RATIONALE AND TARGET OF THE UPGRADE PROGRAM

The Greek Railway Network has a total operational length of 1,500 miles. The main railway lines are:

- Piraeus—Athens—Thessaloniki—Idomeni/Promahonas: This is the main railway line traversing the country from the main port of Piraeus (approx. six miles from Athens) and the capital city Athens in the south to the second largest city of Thessaloniki and the northern borders (Idomeni/Promahonas). More than 60 percent of the passengers and around 30 percent of the freight Thessaloniki—Alexandroupolis—Ormenio: This is the northern line traversing the mainland from West (Thessaloniki) to the East (Alexandroupolis/Ormenio) and connecting Greece to Asia.
- Athens—Patras: This is the southern line connecting the capital (Athens) to the Patras port. This is the only available railway line connecting Greece to the West (Europe). The railway line is of metric width (i.e., the distance between the rails is one meter–as opposed to the normal width, which is 1.452 m).

The above main railway lines are complemented by a network of secondary lines: Inoe—Halkida (thirteen miles), Larissa—Volos (twenty-five miles), Palaiofarsalos—Kalabaka (fifty-one miles), Thessaloniki—West Macedonia (Edessa, Florina, and Kozani), Patras—Kalamata, and Korinthos—Kalamata.

Prior to the upgrade program the operational railway network in Greece was incompatible as the distances between the rails were different (approximately 30 percent of them were metric, and 70 percent of them were normal width), and the majority of the network was nonelectrified. There was also a lack of modern passenger facilities, freight complexes, links to the main ports for the transportation of cargo, and links to the airports. These facts, coupled with aging rolling stock and a high percentage of accidents (four times higher than those in Western Europe), had led the railway transport to a decline.

In response to the above situation, the rationale of the upgrade project was formulated by the Hellenic Railway Organization (OSE) as being the: upgrade of the railway infrastructure to reduce transportation times; provision of access to airports and ports; considerable reduction of operational/maintenance costs through the construction of new railway lines, the procurement of modern rolling stock, and the installation of new telecommunication and signaling systems; andprovision of efficient railway services to areas with small commercial interest to assist urban development (the government will subsidize these lines). The target of the upgrade project can be stated as being the increase of the railway market share to justify the investment and the effective contribution toward the achievement of the national economic goals.

DESCRIPTION OF THE RAILWAY CONSTRUCTION
AND UPGRADE PROJECT

The strategic objective of the investment program currently being progressed by ERGOSE, is to guarantee to OSE the necessary railway infrastructure that, together with suitable rolling stock, will enable the organization to fulfill its passenger and goods transport obligations both nationally and internationally in the context of the European Railways Network. The program comprises the upgrading of the main railway lines Athens—Thessaloniki—Idomeni and Athens—Patras to provide services of a high level comparable to those provided by the railways of other European countries. Improvement on the remaining feeder lines of the network should also have a positive effect on regional development within Greece. A graphical summary of the whole upgrade and construction project is shown in figure 18.1. All major locations are shown in this map.

The Modules of the Project

Upgrading the Main Railway Line Athens—Thessaloniki
The project includes:

- Upgrade of the sections Athens—Inoe (eight bridges, installation of signaling) and Inoe–Tithorea.
- Construction of a new double line on an alignment permitting high speeds in the sections Tithorea–Lianokladi (thirty-four miles including the Kallidromo tunnel), Lianokladi–Domokos (thirty-five miles) including 2.5 miles of tunnels and 5.5 miles of bridges, Evangelismos–Leptokarya (twenty-two miles) including the tunnels of Tempi and Platamonas (six miles) and the bridge of Axios river and the section Leptokaria–Plati–Thessaloniki.
- Installation of modern automatic signaling system in sections with a total length of 105 miles.
- Construction of grade separated crossings between road and railway line.
- Construction of the Thessaloniki port 6th pier link.
- Electrification of the entire line Pireas—Athens—Thessaloniki.

After the completion of the projects, 87 percent of the Athens—Thessaloniki 315-mile route will have double line while the whole route will be electrified. The total budget is 232 million euros. The project as a whole will be delivered in 2008, but the various sections will be released for operations gradually, thus providing earlier journey time gains.

Upgrading the Line Athens—Patras
The project entails the construction of a new sixty-five-mile railway line for the section Thriassio Pedio—Korinthos—Kiato. The entire crossings road—railroad will be grade separated, and the line will be supplied with a modern automatic

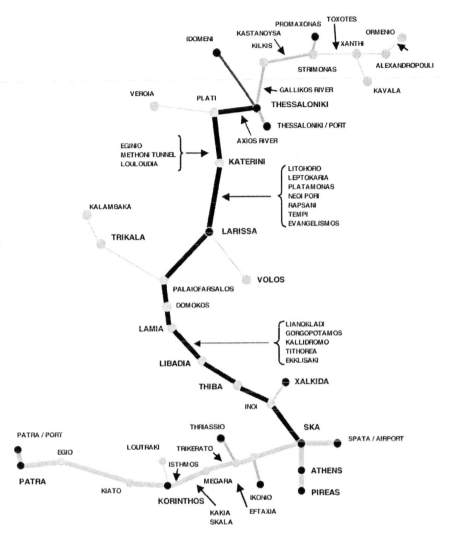

FIGURE 18-1. Graphical summary of the railway upgrade and construction project.

signaling and telecommunications system. To minimize environmental impact on the region, the major part of the new railway line is being constructed parallel to the new Athens—Korinthos highway.

The substructure of the above section is being built to accommodate a double standard gauge line providing speeds up to 125 miles per hour. In the first phase, the line to Korinthos will be meter gauge, connected to the rest of the Peloponnese network. The project includes 5.3 miles of tunnels, fifty-one over- and underpasses, and ten new railway stations. In this way the journey time will be substantially reduced for the route Athens—Korinthos but also to/from Patras and Kalamata as well as other regions in Peloponnese.

The total cost of the project is approx. 64.75 million euros and is estimated to be completed by 2004 (substructure, superstructure, telecommunication, signaling–the section Athens—Thriassio with electrification). This project also includes the infrastructure works of the high-speed railway section Kakia Skala (5.3 miles). Because of the particular features of this area, this project is considered as one of the most difficult to construct in Greece. The railway line will be built simultaneously with the new highway, while retaining the existing railway line as well as the old National road. The project also includes seventy miles of railway line for the section Kiato—Patras. Currently it is in the design phase. The total cost has been estimated to 92 million euros and the expected completion date is 2007.

Thriassio Pedio Complex and Link to Ikonio Port

This project consists of construction of a modern freight complex in the area of Thriassio Pedio in which all railway freight services, currently spread in facilities all over Athens will be concentrated. The concentration of these facilities in one area in the city limits of Athens will bring environmental and land planning benefits for the Greater Athens area. The Thriassio Pedio complex will include a marshalling yard, a freight terminal, customs, a container terminal, rolling stock repair and maintenance workshops, warehouses, and other facilities.

The new freight center will cover approximately 450 acres. Its completion will greatly improve the organization of OSE's freight activities. It will increase the volume of OSEs freight transport and accelerate the marshalling activities. If the link to the port of Ikonio in connection with the envisaged development of combined and container transports is also considered, the importance of the project is profound for OSE and the national economy as a whole. The total cost of the Thriassio Pedio project is 36.80 million euros, including the link to the existing network and its completion is forecasted for 2005. The railway link to Ikonio port entails the construction of a new eleven-mile single standard gauge line. The total cost is 16.36 million euros and the project includes 3.3 miles of tunnels and various cut and cover and bridges. The project is expected to finish by 2005.

Construction of the Athens Suburban Railway

The project aims at the development of a suburban railway system for the metropolitan area of Athens. It entails the construction of twenty-seven new railway stations (including three big ones at Athens, Pireas, and SKA), the electrification and signaling of the lines, the connection to the new Athens International Airport and the existing Metro systems, and maintenance facilities. The budget of the project has been estimated to 136.10 million euros.

Upgrading the Secondary Lines

The program also includes the upgrading of 400 miles of secondary lines and, more specifically, the upgrade of the Peloponnese network, the upgrade of the line between Palaiofarsalos—Kalabaka, Larissa—Volos, Inoe—Halkida Thessaloniki—Idomeni, and Thessaloniki—Alexandroupolis—Ormenio.

Major Projects

Signaling

The signaling project entails the installation of a train control system for bi-directional traffic with remote control capacity and train describer. The project includes the signaling of eleven stations and 105 miles of double line, with two central traffic tenters (CTCs), one in Thessaloniki and one in Larissa. The budget of the project is 11.47 million euros and is expected to be completed by 2003.

Electrification

Electrification of the railway line Pireas–Athens–Thessaloniki (315 miles). The power supply system will be with overhead line 25 KV/50 Hz single–phase. The project includes 700 miles of catenary, 16,500 poles, 12 substations, 2 CTC (in Athens and Thessaloniki). The budget is 34.08 million euros and its completion date is envisaged for 2008.

Kakia Skala

Located after Megara, with a budget of 8.86 million euros and is expected to be completed at the end of 2002. It entails the construction of two tunnels of a total length of 2.5 miles, four bridges, 2.75 miles of substructure and local deviations.

Kallidromo

New double track high-speed railway line of twelve-miles length located near Lamia. The project includes two parallel tunnels of 5.6 miles each (the longest railway tunnel in Greece and one of the longest in Europe) and various bridges. The budget is 138 million euros and its completion date is envisaged for 2006.

THE FUNCTIONS OF ERGA OSE S.A.

Time and Cost Planning

Managing a project is a continuous and constant process, from the feasibility study to the completion of construction work. When planning a project, time and cost parameters are taken into consideration; during construction, many of these parameters change, resulting in slippage between planning and execution phases. Given the special character and uniqueness of each project, it is virtually impossible to avoid this variance. Efficient project management, therefore, should focus on minimizing this variance, an objective, which can only be achieved by implementing active and efficient time and cost control, comprising basically the following elements:

- The management of the construction contracts without deviations (with the exception of the objectively inevitable ones) from the contractual requirements, price, time schedules, specified construction quality, work site safety conditions and the legislated environmental regulations.
- The check and control of the designs, which are, prepared within the framework of the design contracts.
- The undertaking and maintenance of the overall responsibility for the good progress and the right contractual handling of the individual projects and construction contracts via frequent or even continuous presence of the site supervisors on sites. Site supervisors also keep the final responsibility for the accurate application of the designs in the project.
- The complete coverage of all the provisions of the relevant legislation on public works in the project.
- To face and manage all contractual matters, according to legislation on public works and the company internal arrangements.
- The approval and possible adaptation of the designs so that the technical problems associated with their application are solved in the best possible way.
- The collection and processing of available time and cost data to produce a realistic and accurate project plan so as to substantially decrease the possibility of schedule and cost variance, which is crucial to the project.
- The preparation of time and cost reports to various receivers (ERGOSE, OSE, Ministries, EU, etc.)

Design

The design departments are mainly active in controlling and supervising design execution from the date of assignment to their completion and final takeover. The activities entailed include:

- The preparation of sound and constructible designs (initial or supplementary), and mainly, the preparation for the execution of similar designs by third parties prior to their contractual assignment and their check and approval along with their modifications, in all design stages; that is, from the initial conception for the necessity for a specific design study till its final acceptance These designs have to be compatible with the general environmental requirements as well as with the health and safety requirements of the ERGOSE Safety Management System. The completeness of these designs shall exclude the possibility for contractual changes except of the objectively inevitable ones.
- The responsible confirmation to the company administration for the correctness and the accuracy of the designs. The approval of interim and final designs.
- The preparation of the technical section of the bidding documents for the projects and the equipment/materials purchase, while guaranteeing the completeness of these documents.

- The follow-up and check of the design application with the due diligence during construction.
- The participation in the establishment and application of uniform design specifications.
- The time monitoring of design elaboration.
- The commentary on and the control of changes to approved designs proposed by a construction contractor.

Expropriation

This involves a number of procedures required to enable ERGOSE to acquire the land needed for projects. Expropriation declarations are managed and paid by ERGOSE on behalf of OSE. The following stages apply: completion of property diagrams and tables, declaration of the expropriation (Government Gazette), review and finalization of the cadastre, determination of the prices for compensation relating to the expropriated properties, enforcement of the expropriation by depositing the compensations in an escrow account.

Tendering

This is a public bid procedure resulting in the selection of a contractor who has the capability of executing a project or a procurement contract in a timely, technically and economically sound contract. Stages are as follows: completion of tender documents, tender announcement, bid execution, completion and signing of the contract.

Construction

The following are the main activities of construction:

- Site reconnaissance and mapping.
- Quality control of the materials used.
- Quantitative and qualitative control of the project under construction.
- Design review, investigation of the design assumptions, adjustment to the ground conditions, as well as modifying and adding to the design wherever required.
- Correct and accurate implementation of the project's approved design.
- Observance of environmental implications (borrow pits, noise, etc.).
- Cooperation with public sector companies (PPC, TC, etc.).
- Cooperation with Ministry of Public Works, forest department, archaeological department, and local authorities.
- Cooperation with OSE.
- Regulation of vehicle traffic.
- Monitoring and updating of physical and financial progress indicators.
- Observance of health and safety regulations during construction of the project.

Superstructure Material Procurement

The sector for procuring and controlling materials includes all the activities related to the procurement of materials for ERGOSE's projects, that is, production of an annual procurement plan; announcement of procurement bids; execution, judgment of the tenders and evaluation of suppliers; completion of procurement contract; monitoring of chosen supplier regarding fulfilment of contractual obligations (qualitative, quantitative, and procedural); and acceptance of procurement and termination of the contract.

Quality Assurance System

ERGOSE is committed to implementing a quality assurance policy for the services rendered to its client, OSE. This is achieved through the application of a quality management system, which ensures that the services provided to OSE: satisfy the specified requirements, incorporate the required degree of expertise and care, provide a viable basis to facilitate continuous improvements, and comply with the regulations and statutory requirements in force. The two main components of ERGOSE's Quality Assurance System are the quality manual and the core procedures

The Project Quality System ensures that ERGOSE's project management services achieve the aims of the company. ERGOSE has already applied for certification of the Project Quality System through a third-party certification body (Lloyds) in accordance with ISO 9001. The certification was completed in mid-2002.

THE MANAGEMENT STRUCTURE OF ERGA OSE S.A.

Organization Chart

Figure 18.2 depicts the organization chart of ERGA OSE S.A. that follows the matrix approach. ERGOSE's organization consists of five main divisions:

- *General Management* incorporating the General Manager and his office (Legal Advisor, Technical Support Agency, Administration Support Agency, Safety Technician and Company's Doctor), a Board of Experts and a Technical Council (for advice, consultation, and second-level decision making on various technical topics) and the Supervising Authority Office (for decision making on contractual variations based on the proposals of the design and construction managing departments and the consultation of the Board of Experts and the Technical Council).
- The four *Design Directorates* (Underground Works, Infrastructure Works, Railway Works, Railway Systems, and New Projects Design) coordinated by the Railway Systems Directorate.

  The *Underground Works Directorate* deals with the design and engineering of the projects concerning tunnels, "cut and cover," type works, excavation ditches deeper than five meters.

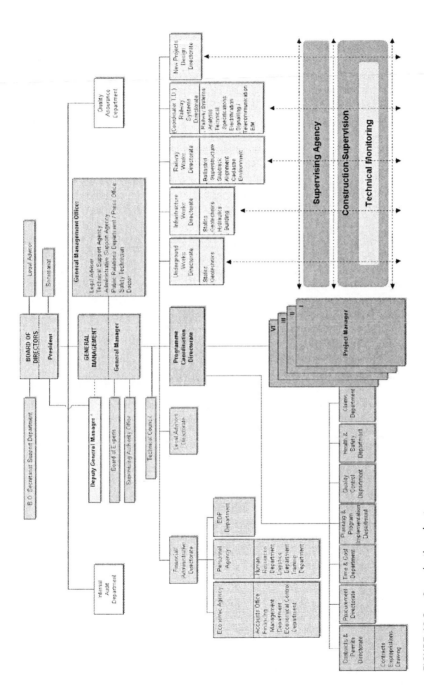

FIGURE 18-2. Organization chart.

The *Infrastructure Works Directorate* deals with the design and engineering of the projects concerning the infrastructure for the construction of railway lines, earthworks, bridges, overpasses, drainage projects, buildings, and so forth.

The *Railway Works Directorate* deals with the design and engineering of the projects concerning classic superstructure of railway lines, fixed superstructure, alignment and surveying works, environmental/archeological, and city planning matters.

The *Railway Systems Directorate* deals with the design and engineering of the projects concerning railway electrification, signaling, telecommunications, telecommand and central control of the railway system, and electromechanical works.

The *New Projects Design Directorate* deals with the location/recording of the relevant need and the necessary preparatory work for the execution of new project designs from the stage of their conception to the delivery of new design requirements to the competent Design Directorate(s). Also, in cooperation with the other Design Directorates, deals with the preparation of the annual design execution plans.

- The four *Project Management Directorates* (I through IV) dealing with:

The management of the company construction contracts in terms of time, cost, quality, and safety.

The check and control in cooperation with the Design Directorates of the designs and their appropriate application on site.

- The *Program Coordination Directorate* assisted by the Contracts and Permits Directorate, the Procurement Directorate, the Time and Cost Department, the Planning and Program Implementation Department, the Quality Control Department, the Health and Safety Department, and the Claims Department, is dealing with:

The coordination and program management of the whole Investment Program without deviations from the specified technical requirements, the overall program schedule, its approved budget, the intended quality, the general environmental requirements and the requirements of the ERGOSE Safety Management System. The Program Coordination Directorate maintains the exclusive responsibility for the timely, effective and meeting the quality criteria, completion of the program.

The maximization of the absorbance of the funds available for the program needs.

The fastest possible "transfer" for use to OSE of parts of the program, which can operate autonomously prior to the program completion.

The timely planning to commit the necessary funds as well as the planning of the required resources and the necessary actions (e.g., human resources, organizational restructuring, etc.) for the successful implementation of the program.

The frequent monitoring and recording of the program physical progress to the ERGOSE Administration and through it, to external authorities (OSE, Ministries, EU).

The timely forecast of major difficulties, which could cause delays in the program evolution.

The location of interfaces between individual projects, between contracts and also between organizational units, which would possibly cause friction and delays, and the elimination of the negative factors.

- The *Financial and Administration Directorate* is responsible for organizing, managing, and cocoordinating a number of the so-called Support Functions (besides Legal Services, which is a separate organizational unit), in order to work efficiently in cooperation with the Directorates and Departments of the Company Technical Sector to achieve the company's policies, strategy, and goals, set by the top management.

In cooperation with the Department of Program Planning and Implementation and the Finance Directorate, it takes care of ensuring the unhindered funding from European and national sources through OSE, as well as with its participation in the Committees of Funding, to be aware of all funding issues stemming from the general administration of projects.

ERGOSE's organization also includes three independent departments: Internal Audit (auditing all the operations and activities of the company's organizational units) and Quality Assurance reporting directly to the Board of Directors through ERGOSE's president of the board, and Legal Affairs reporting to the general manager.

Human Resources

There are 300 people (including the project manager's staff) working for ERGOSE. More than 75 percent of ERGOSE employees are college graduates, and about half of them are engineers. The company's personnel can successfully deal with the special requirements of the projects managed by ERGOSE, as they have long national and international experience as well as a fair degree of specialization in such areas as long railway tunnels, railway stations, electrification, and signalling. The Personnel Agency, reporting to the Financial/ Administration Directorate is responsible for administrating and coordinating the procedures relating to the rights and responsibilities of the staff as stated by the valid work law, the company procedures, and the company work regulations.

The principal targets/duties of the Personnel Agency are:

- Personnel management (advertising of job vacancies, organizing the process of candidates evaluation, in cooperation with the Finance and Administration manager, submission to the General Directorate for approval of matters of hiring new personnel or termination of employment and coordination for the smooth introduction of the newcomers to the company.
- The creation and administration and periodic update of personnel files (with seminar certificates, medical certificates, family status statements, evaluation reports, and loans-advance payments given to personnel).

- Monitoring and control of the staff leaves of absence, illnesses, "out-of-office work," and overtime work in accordance with the work regulation and the Core Procedures Manual, and the correct and timely update of payroll statements and of other archives (for example a record of leaves of absence) that should be kept according to the work regulations.
- Informing the staff on salary matters and preparation of monthly payroll statements and individual payroll receipts.
- Responsibilities of cocoordinating and organizing the procedures used in personnel evaluation and incorporation of the evaluation outcomes into the process of determining the salary levels, in accordance with the top management's guidance.
- Coordination and preparation of the annual training program (general directions).
- Coordination and timely coverage of the Directorates and departments operational needs, in cooperation with the Procurement Directorate in purchase orders for consumables, furniture, and equipment and services, securing and managing of those equipment-material that have not been handed over for use, responsible for the organization and maintenance of the interior areas of the central offices.
- Monitoring and administration of the personnel Group Insurance Contract.

TIME SCHEDULING AND CONTROLLING

The project's work breakdown structure (WBS) is primarily geographical and is expressed by the term "Project Groups." In a second stage, the WBS is analyzed in sections of line (ready for use), which are included in the above-mentioned grouping of Project Groups.

- *Project Group* 1 contains all the projects located in the railway line Athens–(Korinthos)–Patras and the remaining Peloponnese network, excluding all those projects concerning the suburban railway (connection line Pireas–SKA–Athens International Airport).
- *Project Group* 2 covers all the works between Athens and Evangelismos on the main railway line Athens–Thessaloniki.
- *Project Group* 3 is dealing with the section Evangelismos–Thessaloniki–Alexandroupolis, as well as the section Palaiofarsalos–Kalabaka, which are located in Central and Northern Greece.
- *Project Group* 4 concerns all the works of the Athens Suburban Railway, that is, the railway line Pireas–SKA–Athens International Airport.

All electrification, signalling, and telecommunication projects are incorporated within the Project Groups 1–4. However, the electrification works of Athens–Thessaloniki line are considered a "special" Project Group, due to the fact that the construction contract covers geographically Project Groups 2 and 3.

Procurement of superstructure materials is considered a "special"» group, of which the time-schedule is based on the materials supply (on Time) for Groups 1–4, and each work package corresponds to a specific type of material (e.g., ties [sleepers], turnouts, rail, ballast).

Time schedules are grouped by Project Groups. More detailed grouping is given by line sections, "Work packages" and activity categories, which are also shown in a geographical order and are broken down to design, implementation, land acquisition, and to all major phases necessary for the completion of the work package. Finally, time schedules concern only those projects that are included in the Investment Program of OSE and have been transferred to or are going to be implemented by ERGOSE, excluding those that have remained under OSE responsibility.

There are five types of schedules: Time Master (Group) Schedule, Time Monitoring Schedule (per section of line), Time Monitoring Schedule (per work package), Time Monitoring Schedule (per activity category), and Time Detailed Schedule.

Master Schedule has been designed to present an extremely compacted overview of all line sections, work packages and activities for each Project Group. Short description per Master Schedule may assist for primary understanding. Additional information is available in the introduction of the following monitoring and detailed schedules. Time Master Group Schedule has been designed in order to summarize the whole Project Group by one bar activity.

Time Monitoring Schedule (per section of line), is grouped by Project Group. Each section of line is shown by a horizontal bar, summarizing all design and construction activities. Project Group 1 contains all projects located in the railway line Athens–(Korinthos)–Patras and the remaining Peloponnese network, excluding all those projects concerning the suburban railway (connection line SKA–Spata Airport). The sections of this group are: (1) SKA–KIATO, (2) KIATO–PATRA, (3) THRIASIO: TMK & DEPOT, (4) THRIASIO COMPLEX, (5) RAILWAY CONNECTION WITH IKONIO PORT, (6) PATRA–PYRGOS, and (7) KORINTHOS–MILI.

Project Group 2 contains all projects located in the railway line between Athens and Evangelismos of the main railway line Athens–Thessaloniki.

The sections of this group are: (1) ATHENS–INOE, (2) INOE–TITHOREA, (3) TITHOREA–LIANOKLADI, (4) LIANOKLADI–DOMOKOS, (5) DOMOKOS–EVANGELISMOS, and (6) INOE–HALKIDA.

Project Group 3 contains all projects located in the railway line between Evangelismos–Thessaloniki–Alexandroupolis and between Palaiofarsalos–Kalabaka. All of them are in Central and Northern Greece.

The sections of this group are: (1) EVANGELISMOS–THESSALONIKI, (2) THESSALONIKI–IDOMENI, (3) THESSALONIKI–STRIMONAS–PROMAHONAS, (4) STRIMONAS–ALEXANDROUPOLIS, and (5) RAILWAY CONNECTION WITH THESSALONIKI PORT.

Time Monitoring Schedule per work package is grouped by Project Group and sections of line. Each work package is represented with a bar summarizing all design and construction activities.

Work packages are subsections of either line sections or separate works sections and their structure serves the better monitoring of the time schedule.

Time Monitoring Schedule per activity category has been designed to give a summarized overview of the main activities of each project, that is design, land acquisition, tendering, and construction. Each work package is represented with a horizontal bar that summarizes each of the above-mentioned activities. In this type of schedule, previous month–time forecast is also presented, for comparison reasons.

Detailed Schedule separates all processes at least to a level, where interfaces of the responsibilities of organizational units exist, for example, the structures designs are separated from the respective alignment designs, the design elaboration activities are separated from the design approval activities.

As far as the design is concerned, the work breakdown structure is applied into various kinds of design. Concerning the implementation, such breakdown is also applied respectively. Furthermore, in major projects, which are in progress, a further analysis into detailed construction activities is performed.

PROGRAMMING THE PROJECTS

Tunneling

In the past two decades, the volume of the underground works has quadrupled, and it is anticipated to increase further in the immediate future. This is particularly true in the field of railway transportations, where new routes include more and longer tunnels than in the past. There are two principal factors resulting in these new characteristics. First, the requirements for high-speed corridors limit gradients and curvature and thereby impose rigid geometric alignments that are unable to follow the natural contours of the land. Second, the contemporary tendency to respect the environment during construction of infrastructure projects imposes the adoption of technical solutions that minimize the effects on the environment.

In Greece these factors are further intensified by the ground's highly irregular morphology.

- Identifying the operational and alignment requirements (speed, radii, gradients, environmental assessments).
- *Feasibility study* to check whether the work is feasible from a technical and financial point of view.
- *Geological and geotechnical investigation.*
- *Selection of construction methods* such as excavation by a Tunnel Boring Machine (TBM) or by the "New Austrian Tunnelling Method" (NATM) depending on soil conditions and tunnel parameters.
- *Design Phase.*
- *Tendering and start of construction work.*
- *Site supervision* by ERGOSE including time and cost monitoring, quality control, safety checks, survey control.
- *Documentation* of the project.
- *Additional work* such as ventilation, lighting, trackwork, signalling.
- *Opening of the tunnel to traffic.*

Bridges

- *Identifying the operational and alignment requirements* (speed, radii, gradients, train loads, passenger or mixed traffic, environmental assessments).
- *Environmental study* to investigate the effects on the environment.
- *Preliminary design* to define the kind of structure, material construction methods (from technical and economical points of view), quantities, and cost estimate.
- *Geological and geotechnical investigations* to define the ground and ground water conditions relating to the static calculations (soil conditions, permissible pressure, elasticity module).
- *Land acquisition.*
- *Tendering procedure* (specification, bill of materials, technical descriptions, time schedule, bid evaluation. and tender award).
- *Construction.*
- *Site supervision* by ERGOSE including time and cost monitoring, design checking, quality control, safety checks, survey control, checking the interfaces to other works (trackworks, electrification etc.).
- *Documentation* of the project.
- *Acceptance.*
- *Opening of the bridge to traffic.*

Trackwork

- *Define design parameters and requirements for alignment* (minimum radius of horizontal curves, maximum cant, travelling comfort, maximum gradient, radii of vertical curves).
- *Design alignment* to satisfy the above requirements.
- *Geotechnical study* to establish what type of substructure and drainage is required.
- *Environmental study* to demonstrate an environmentally friendly alignment.
- *Define track parameters* for operational requirements such as type of rail, type and spacing of ties (sleepers) and fastening, specification of ballast.
- *Cross-section profile* to ensure sufficient ballast for track stability and enough space for staff safety.
- *Coordination of design with signalling and electrification* regarding positioning of track circuits and catenary/pole positioning.
- *Tracklaying* in the following sequence: bottom ballast, ties (sleepers), welded rail, top ballast, ballast regulation, tamping and consolidation, distressing of rail to prevent buckling, grinding of rail to ensure smoother riding on curves.
- *Testing* by ultrasonic examination of the railhead to ensure no metallurgical defects and track geometry-recording car to ensure the appropriateness of horizontal and vertical track layout.
- *Staff safety* by training and certification of all railway staff and future contractors to ensure their safety on a high-speed railway.
- *Public safety* by education of the public national network TV and in schools about the dangers of a high-speed railway.
- *Open to revenue service.*

Electrification

- *Power study* to define the power requirements, the number and the sizing of four substations.
- *Land acquisition* for substations.
- *Environmental study* to demonstrate the environmentally friendly construction and operation.
- *Interference study* to identify measures necessary to prevent interference to telephone and signalling installations caused by electric train operation.
- *Design of power substations and catenary.*
- *Discussion with Greek Public Power Corporation (DEH)* about delivery of electric power.
- *Start of construction* on site.
- Construction of foundations.
- Erection of poles, mounting of cantilevers.
- Wiring (placing the catenary).
- Erection of substations.
- *Supervision* of construction work by ERGOSE.
- *Testing of installation* after completion.
- *Training of personnel,* implementing new rules, working instructions, safety regulations, etc.
- *Start of revenue service.*

Signaling

- Capacity requirements, determine the traffic to be accommodated in terms of speed and number of trains.
- *Technology to be used,* determine type of safety interlocking, train location method, location and number of control rooms, and degree of automation.
- *Procure contracts,* for supply, installation, and maintenance of each portion of the overall system.
- *Building work,* modify or construct new buildings for control rooms and equipment housings.
- *Cable route,* construct trackside troughs and install cables for power, control, and indication.
- *Trackside erection,* install trackside equipment, signals, train detection devices, and point operating machines including foundations and access ways.
- *Safety interlockings,* manufacture and test equipment to implement the safety requirements for each location and connect to trackside equipment.
- *Traffic management system,* manufacture and install central control point(s) and connect safety interlockings and communication links.
- *Supervision by ERGOSE,* ensure compliance with designs and trackside equipment locations, safety implementation, documentation, and costs.
- *Test and commission,* each component must be tested for correct operation, then all the components are connected together and tested as a whole.
- *Training of staff* in the handling of the new equipment. Finally, the contractors provide a warranty maintenance service for a period after commissioning.

New Stations

- *Define use of the station* based on the anticipated number of passengers (depending on population, nature of the location, quality of train service, and competition).
- *Sizing of the station building* to satisfy the above requirements economically.
- *Access to station* to provide suitable facilities for passengers arriving or leaving by car, taxi, public transport, or on foot.
- *Define track layout* to accommodate nonstop trains passing through at high speed, platform tracks for stopping trains, tracks of sufficient length to accommodate the longest freight trains and signalling overlaps, sidings for defective vehicles and track maintenance machines; allow sufficient space between tracks to accommodate signal posts and electrification poles; determine size and type of turnouts consistent with actual train speed.
- *Fencing* to prevent trespass and ensure safety of public.
- *Platforms* designed of length sufficient for the longest trains, width sufficient for passenger circulation and safety, height above rail level consistent with train design and to prevent passengers from stepping on the tracks; footbridges/subways designed to enable passengers to cross from one platform to another safely.
- *Construction* of buildings, platforms, footbridges/subways, drainage, approach roads, fencing, trackwork, signalling, electrification.
- *Training of personnel* regarding new rules (for high-speed operation), working instructions, and safety regulations.
- *Open to revenue service.*

DISCUSSION

On top of the difficulties involved in managing a project of this size, a number of other factors influence the management performance. These factors are:

- *Legal framework*: Construction legislation in Greece proved inefficient for a project of this magnitude. Several procedures that need to be followed are bureaucratic and lengthily, therefore imposing time restrictions on the execution of the project (e.g., objections by potential contractors, lack of strict regulations for the delivery of quality designs, etc). There is a change toward a more flexible legal framework lately, but its value has still to be evaluated in practice.
- *Archaeology*: A number of sites of historical value have been discovered. The archaeology department in Greece has proved incapable of respecting the tight time limitations of the project.
- *Public utilities*: Public water and electricity authorities impose delays on the project due to their time-consuming processes.
- *Quality of designs and lack of design standards*: Much of the foundation work that should have been undertaken before the realization of this project was never performed. As a result, designers lack the experience and the state lacks the standards to check the designs. The problem plays a profound role in construction delays, compatibility issues between different sections of the same railway line, etc. Special attention has been given lately to the subject; however, there will be some time before the results can be harvested.

- *Project management procedure*: Project management practices in Greece are rather basic. The function is considered as an overhead rather than a necessary tool for the appropriate completion of a project. Contractors tend to underestimate it and ERGOSE lacks the necessary know-how and techniques to enforce improvements. The legal framework for the subject is complete but rather vague when it comes to real-life implementation. The result is that different contractors use their own systems (i.e., breaking down of activities, estimation of time durations, etc.) that mean that ERGOSE is facing problems of aggregating the data contained in different project schedules.
- *Project management information standards*: Although the latest versions of commercially available project management software are used, the lack of standards in project management practices has created several problems in storing, analyzing and reporting on crucial information. A major effort has started over the past year to design and implement an integrated MIS. The results are expected in about a year's time.

The major conclusions are that the legal framework, archaeology (a major concern in Greece), cultural aspects (of labor, contractors, managers, etc.), project information management (gathering, organizing, storing, and reporting of information), and the quality of designs play a profound role in construction project success.

19

Improving Project Management with the Analytical Design Planning Technique

SIMON AUSTIN
ANDREW NEWTON
ANDREW BALDWIN

M any complex projects are late, over budget, and do not meet the original objectives set by the customer. These projects traditionally suffer from a poorly conceived development program that focuses on deliverables and not the underlying process involved in creating the end result. In an increasingly competitive market, where speed of delivery is a prerequisite for sustained success, planning and managing processes and their inherent complexity becomes essential. Current construction project planning practice is typical of project management applied to development processes and takes little account of the interdisciplinary, iterative nature of the design process. The typical approach to planning design, when combined with work packaging devised to suit the construction process and other such influences, leads to a severely compromised design process.

This chapter describes the Analytical Design Planning Technique (ADePT), a project planning methodology, and its associated software PlanWeaver,[1] which helps to overcome these problems by providing a logical, structured approach based on information flow rather than the production of design deliverables. It takes account of the iterative nature of design and can enable fully coordinated, integrated design solutions to be developed within both budgetary and time constraints.

WHAT IS THE PROBLEM?

In recent times there has been a growing understanding of the importance of effective design management to facilitate coordinated design within budget, and to ensure the smooth running of the project. Construction industry customers are seeking major reductions in the cost of buildings, which can only be achieved by closer integration between the design and construction functions in the product cycle, as has occurred in other engineering sectors (such as the automobile and manufacturing industries). A key aspect is the capability to plan and manage design efficiently, taking into account the iterative nature of the process and changing needs of the customer and contractor.

Current practice in the planning and management of the design process is focused on the design deliverables (e.g., drawings, bills of quantities, and specifications) that are listed at the start of each stage of the design process. The tendency is then to plan the design process backwards from the date when these deliverables are due to be released to the customer or contractor. Typically a master program is produced by the project manager (which includes global activities and milestone) and distributed to the leader of each design team, who then plans their work within the framework of the master program. This approach assumes that design information is made available and communicated between the project participants as required, either informally or formally via drawings and design review. Experience shows that this is often not the case and that design should be planned around information flow, rather than deliverables, if a coordinated and effective solution is to be found. Network analysis and critical path methods are the generally accepted methods for the planning and scheduling of production work on large- to medium-sized projects, but they are inappropriate for design management because of its ill-defined and iterative nature. Design managers now need equivalent tools to help them plan, manage change and integrate their role with the customer, contractor and other parties.

ADEPT OVERVIEW

The ADePT methodology shown in figure 19.1 and associated PlanWeaver software have been developed over the last seven years to help overcome these problems to facilitate more effective design planning and management of building projects. However, ADePT is well suited to a broad range of problem solving and has recently been applied to diverse projects such as lubrication systems and aero engines as well as buildings. Detailed descriptions of the main stages of the ADePT methodology are given elsewhere (Austin, Baldwin, Li, and Waskett 1999a, 1999b, 2000). PlanWeaver delivers the ADePT methodology in five stages.

Understand the Process—Produce the Process Model

The first step is to produce a robust model of the process under consideration. Each component of the process needs to be captured and compiled. The models can be uniquely developed or (more usually) based on a general model, modified and tailored to the specific need of the application and the project team's standard notation. PlanWeaver assembles a model of the process making all

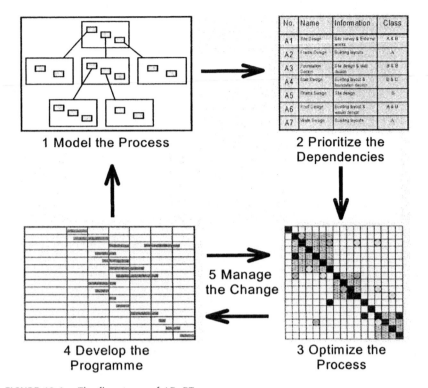

No.	Name	Information	Class
A1	Site Design	Site survey & External works	A & B
A2	Frame Design	Building layouts	A
A3	Foundation Design	Site design & slab design	B & B
A4	Slab Design	Building layout & foundation design	B & C
A5	Drains Design	Site design	B
A6	Roof Design	Building layout & roads design	A & B
A7	Walls Design	Building layouts	A

1 Model the Process

2 Prioritize the Dependencies

5 Manage the Change

4 Develop the Programme

3 Optimize the Process

FIGURE 19-1. The five stages of ADePT.

participants more aware of the information flows and dependencies between different disciplines.

Refine the Process—Prioritize the Interfaces

The activities represented in the process model are used to drive an information dependency table. This lists the activities and gives their dependencies a priority rating—critical to the calculation of the optimum sequence of tasks. Once complete, the sequence of activities is reorganised to minimise the amount of iteration within the process.

Optimize the Process—Streamline the Interfaces and Activities

The information dependency table is used to create the project's dependency structure matrix. Tasks are listed as both row and column headings, forming a matrix. Each row displays all the information inputs required to complete the task; each column displays all the information outputs to be provided for other tasks. In PlanWeaver, the matrix highlights which information exchanges involve iteration and which do not. Some iterative loops could be eliminated, others may be minimised, so that the process is as efficient as possible.

Develop the Program—Integrate External Constraints

The optimized matrix is then delivered as a program or delivery schedule by linking the PlanWeaver to a project programming software application such as MS Project, Primavera, or PowerProject. This program can then be reviewed and integrated with the procurement or other related projects. If changes are needed, they can be simulated in PlanWeaver and a revised, integrated project program produced, highlighting critical decision points and potential risks.

Monitor the Project Process—Manage
the Inevitable Change

ADePT and PlanWeaver can then be used throughout the project, allowing team members to examine the impact of changes (e.g., alterations to the specification, or late completion of activities) and hence make informed, shared and auditable decisions on the most effective way forward.

STAGE 1: MODELLING THE PROCESS

Prior to formulating the process model in the first stage of the ADePT methodology, existing models of design and modelling methodologies were reviewed. This enabled a set of requirements to be established regarding the modelling technique. The model was then produced with a proprietary computer-aided software engineering (CASE) tool.

Modelling Technique for Design

The modelling methodology must be capable of representing both the tasks and dependencies which gives rise to the complexity within any process. The prevalent model of building design in the United Kingdom is the RIBA Plan of Work for Design Team Operation (RIBA 1973). This sets out the details of work to be carried out by each profession during each stage of the design process, but does indicate their interdependency. Sanvido and Norton (1994), and Karhu, Keitilä, and Lahdenperä (1997) also adopted the IDEF0 technique to model the building design and construction process at a high level. Data flow diagrams (DFDs) are another recognized modelling technique applied, for example, by Austin, Baldwin, and Newton (1996) to model the architectural, civil, and structural engineering elements of the detailed design stage. The process protocol is a new generic process map for design and construction developed through U.K. government-funded research (Cooper et al. 2002).

A range of modelling methodologies has been examined to identify one that is most suited to representing information flow, including DFDs, IDEF techniques, entity relationship diagrams, hierarchical plus input-process-output diagrams, Jackson diagrams, object-orientated modelling systems, and Petri nets. Each of these techniques has advantages in modelling certain types of activity or data. IDEF0 was identified as the most suitable technique to produce a model of design for use in the wider context of the ADePT methodology. Each activity in the process transforms an information input into an output, and the internal mechanics of that transformation are not modelled (figure 19.2a). Each activity can be hierarchically subdivided to show finer detail on another diagram, ensuring a single diagram does not become too cumbersome.

The review found that although the some enhancements could be made to the notation for the purpose of the ADePT model where there is little benefit from representing process controls in the model. Also, activity mechanisms (architect, civil engineer, etc.) show nothing other than the discipline to which the activity belongs (which is already defined by the hierarchical structure of the model). We therefore chose to distinguish between the inputs from the same discipline, from other disciplines and from external sources (such as the customer, a regulating authority or an earlier stage of the design process) since these different types of information flow require different management priorities (figure 19.2b). Computer-aided software engineering tools such as System Architect enable balanced IDEF0v models to be constructed automatically and distinguish the different types of information input in their reporting facilities.

Building Model Features

The building model has a hierarchical or work breakdown structure (figure 19.3), the first level of which subdivides the process into design undertaken by the professional disciplines and then breakdown into systems of the building, subsystems and components. In other project management applications the process can be divided by function or system.

The model describes the process in a generic manner, and consequently it represents the design of a typical building and its systems. The project planning of a particular building will entail some manipulation of this general model to produce a project-specific process map. Redundant sections will have to be deleted, some added and others altered (for instance, some information flows will need to be reviewed to account for the location of components in the building).

A key finding of the application of ADePT on building projects is the highly generic nature of the building design process. Despite the unique nature of each product, the first three project applications found that over 90 percent of the required process was contained in the general model (table 19.1). The same will apply to many other types of project.

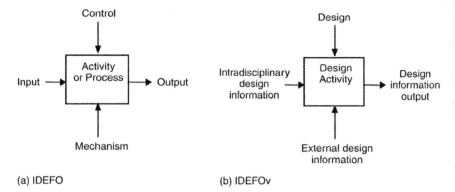

(a) IDEF0   (b) IDEFOv

FIGURE 19-2.   IDEF0 and IDEFOv notation.

STAGE 2: PRIORITIZING THE INTERFACES

The classification of information within a matrix is a subjective exercise. A three-point scale of classifications is used in ADePT, which is based on the strength of dependency of information, sensitivity of activities to changes in information, and the ease with which information can be estimated within the building design process. To determine each information classification, a subjective judgement must be made that takes account of how sensitive the receiving activity is to the information and how easy it is to estimate the information accurately. The resulting classification is given a rating of 3, 2, or 1 (from 3 = high to 1 = low). The philosophy is that weak dependencies will not cause feedback because an accurate estimate can easily be made, and therefore the size of iterative loops can be reduced and the design process clarified.

STAGE 3: OPTIMIZING THE PROCESS

Scheduling Iterative Work

Management of a complex process such as design is influenced by contract procurement, the expertise of the customer, and the structure of design team, and encompasses information exchange management and quality management. However, the fundamental activity in the project management of design is the planning and control of work. In current project management practice, design is planned by the same techniques as production, mainly network analysis. However, network analysis techniques and tools were designed to represent sequential processes and cannot deal with a process containing iteration, such as design (Austin et al. 1996). This results in the unwanted omission of logic or information links between activities. In building design, this problem is particularly prevalent when considering information exchanged between design

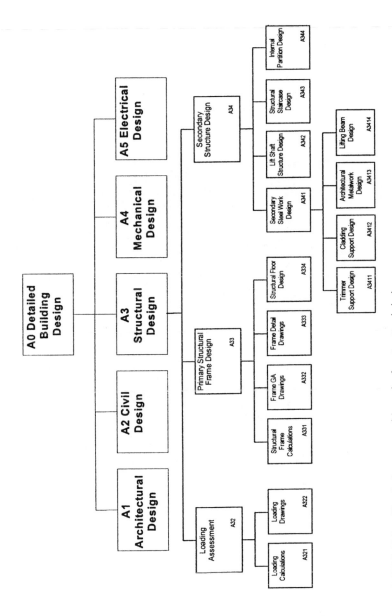

FIGURE 19-3. The design process hierarchy for structural design.

TABLE 19-1. Results of applying ADePT to three building projects

Project		A	B	C
Description		Pharmaceutical Laboratory	Railway Terminal	Office Development
No. of Design Tasks	Deleted	207	261	242
	Added	35	36	6
	Total	410	357	346
No. of Tasks in Each Discipline	Architecture		51	
	Civil Eng.		9	
Common to All Projects	Struct. Eng.		26	
	Mech. Eng.		91	
	Elec. Eng.		104	
Proportion of Model Common to All		69%	79%	81%
No. of Data Flows		2406	2804	2656
Hours to Generate		16	20	12

disciplines because of the disparate manner in which they undertake their work and its planning. In the 1960s, Steward developed a theory that a complex problem such as design could be solved more efficiently by representing the interrelationships between activities in the form of a Design Structure Matrix (Steward 1965) or Dependency Structure Matrix (DSM). DSM analysis forms the third stage of the ADePT methodology and involves analysis of the design activities and information dependencies in the process model in order to find an optimum sequence.

How a DSM Works

Figure 19.4 shows a matrix for a very simple design problem that contains twenty activities, listed arbitrarily down the left-hand side of the matrix. The same activity order is also maintained across the top of the matrix. The activities are undertaken in the order listed within the matrix, starting from the top. A mark in the matrix indicates that the activity in the row is dependent on the activity in the columns. In the assumed order of activities, a mark below the diagonal shows that an activity is dependent on information that has been produced by a previous activity, whereas a mark above the diagonal indicates that it is dependent on information that has yet to be produced. The latter can be overcome by making an estimate or assumption about the information that is as yet unavailable and then verifying the estimate once the information has been produced. For example, in figure 19.4 it can be seen that Task 3 depends on some information from Task 13 that at the time has not been undertaken.

If this information is estimated, Task 3 can be carried out and in due course Task 13, following which the estimate can be verified. It may be that the activity dependent on the estimated information (Task 3) has to be redone if the original estimate was not accurate, resulting in an iterative loop of design activities. In this case it involves at least eleven tasks (3–13), but possibly up to seventeen, as task 13 in turn requires an estimate of information from task 19 (hence the shaded block of tasks).

Optimizing the Sequence

The need to make assumptions or estimate information and then carry out activities more than once results in the process being inefficient. We can reduce the need for estimates and therefore iteration within the process by reordering the activities within the matrix so that the marks are below the diagonal or as close to it as possible, thus producing the optimum sequence (figure 19.5). This maximizes the availability of information and minimizes the amount of wasteful iteration and rework. It can be seen that the sequence is altered and that fifteen activities contribute to three iterative blocks, the largest containing nine tasks. In this improved order the estimate of the information for Task 3 will only involve the reworking of two tasks. Optimizing a matrix identifies the interdependent

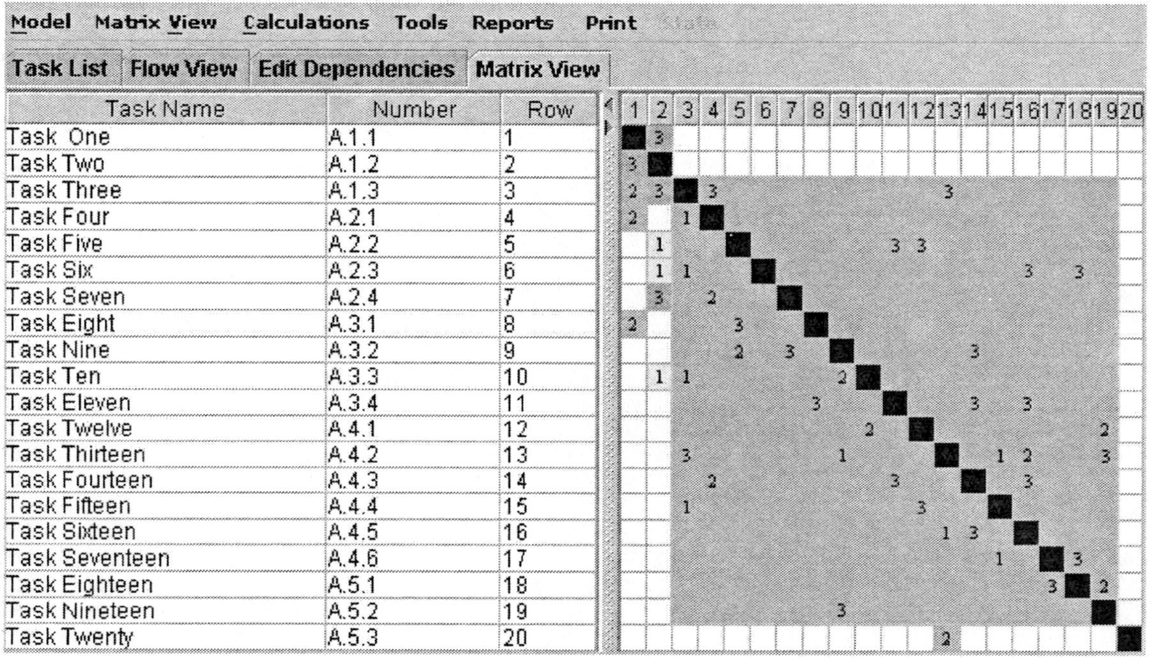
Model
Matrix View
Calculations
Tools
Reports
Print
Task List
Flow View
Edit Dependencies
Matrix View
Task Name
Number
Row
Task One A.1.1 1
Task Two A.1.2 2
Task Three A.1.3 3
Task Four A.2.1 4
Task Five A.2.2 5
Task Six A.2.3 6
Task Seven A.2.4 7
Task Eight A.3.1 8
Task Nine A.3.2 9
Task Ten A.3.3 10
Task Eleven A.3.4 11
Task Twelve A.4.1 12
Task Thirteen A.4.2 13
Task Fourteen A.4.3 14
Task Fifteen A.4.4 15
Task Sixteen A.4.5 16
Task Seventeen A.4.6 17
Task Eighteen A.5.1 18
Task Nineteen A.5.2 19
Task Twenty A.5.3 20

FIGURE 19-4. An example of a simple DSM.

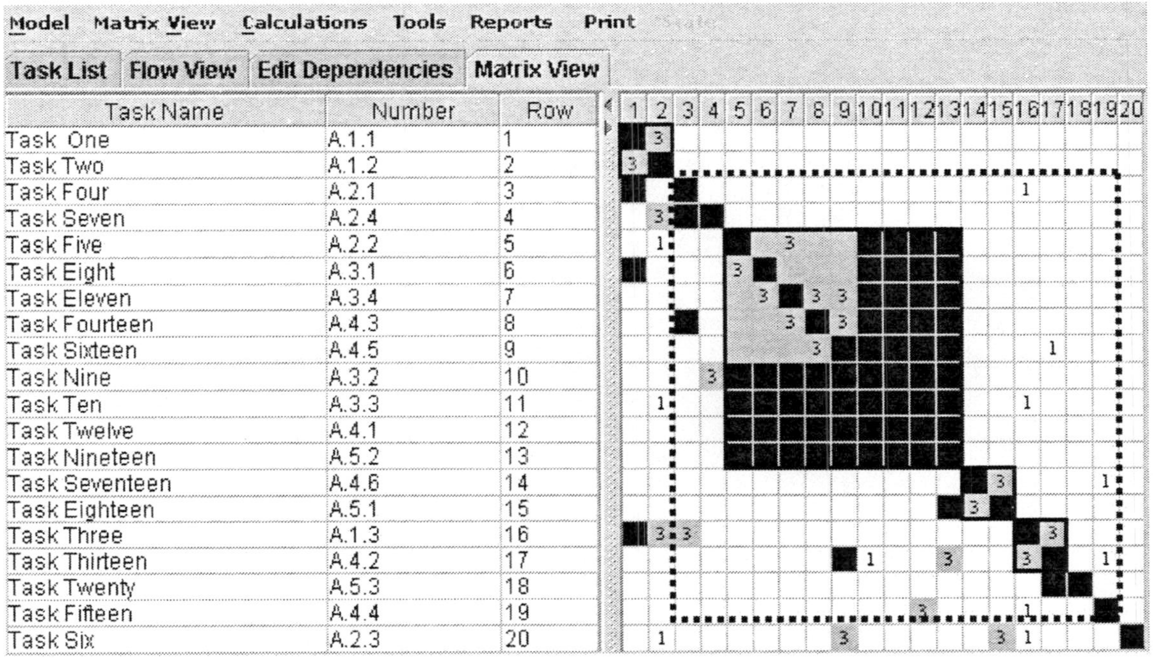
Model Matrix View Calculations Tools Reports Print
Task List
Flow View
Edit Dependencies
Matrix View
Task Name
Number
Row
Task One A.1.1 1
Task Two A.1.2 2
Task Four A.2.1 3
Task Seven A.2.4 4
Task Five A.2.2 5
Task Eight A.3.1 6
Task Eleven A.3.4 7
Task Fourteen A.4.3 8
Task Sixteen A.4.5 9
Task Nine A.3.2 10
Task Ten A.3.3 11
Task Twelve A.4.1 12
Task Nineteen A.5.2 13
Task Seventeen A.4.6 14
Task Eighteen A.5.1 15
Task Three A.1.3 16
Task Thirteen A.4.2 17
Task Twenty A.5.3 18
Task Fifteen A.4.4 19
Task Six A.2.3 20
1 2 3 4 5 6 7 8 9 10 11 12 13 14 15 16 17 18 19 20

FIGURE 19-5. Optimized example matrix.

activities that are within an iterative block and the block's location in the overall order.

Reducing Concurrency and Rework

Although the initial optimization of the matrix can eliminate wasteful iteration, at no cost, most complex processes still present large blocks of interrelated activity that would benefit from further reduction in size. This can be achieved by making a decision instead of an assumption, so that specific information flows no longer causes feedback. This is done by changing the classification to a low strength (i.e., a 1). Figure 19.6 illustrates where the dependency of Task 11 on Task 8 is to be declassified, with the result shown in figure 19.7 where the largest block of interrelated activity has only five tasks. Overall, considerable progress has been achieved in breaking the problem down, at the cost of one declassification.

How can such a downgrading of what was a critical information input be justified? The answer is that any decision will be at a price—such as an over-estimate by a designer or an early choice by the customers—but one that is worthwhile because of the benefits of making the size of a block smaller. These could include: reducing the number of tasks that must be undertaken concurrently, making the management of the process easier, getting stage sign-off of completion, and reducing risk and scope for rework.

A second, important question then arises. In real problems, the scale of the process, and hence DSM, is much larger than illustrated here—usually hundreds of activities. The blocks of interrelated tasks are also large, and it is difficult to identify which of the information flows to declassify (to 1). Two tactics can be applied: (1) an informed decision is made by experts in the project team who satisfy themselves that it is reasonable and appropriate, or (2) a powerful function of the PlanWeaver software is applied that identifies these declassifications that have the greatest effect on reducing the size of the block and hence scale of iteration. Although the second approach (which is automated) is very attractive, it could lead to totally inappropriate decisions. Therefore in practice a sanity check (first approach) is still required, and hence a combination of the two tactics is recommended by the authors as the preferred way of streamlining complex processes.

STEP 4: DEVELOPING AN INTEGRATED PROGRAM

Scheduling the Process

For the DSM to be a means of controlling the process, the information it contains must be represented against a time scale. In the fourth stage of ADePT the optimized matrix is linked to proprietary planning software to produce a program for the activities. This process raises a number of issues. Conventional

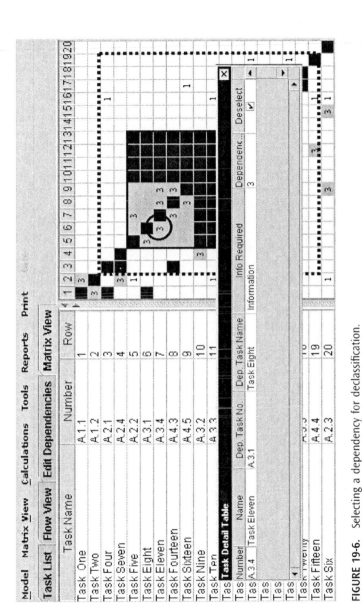

FIGURE 19-6. Selecting a dependency for declassification.

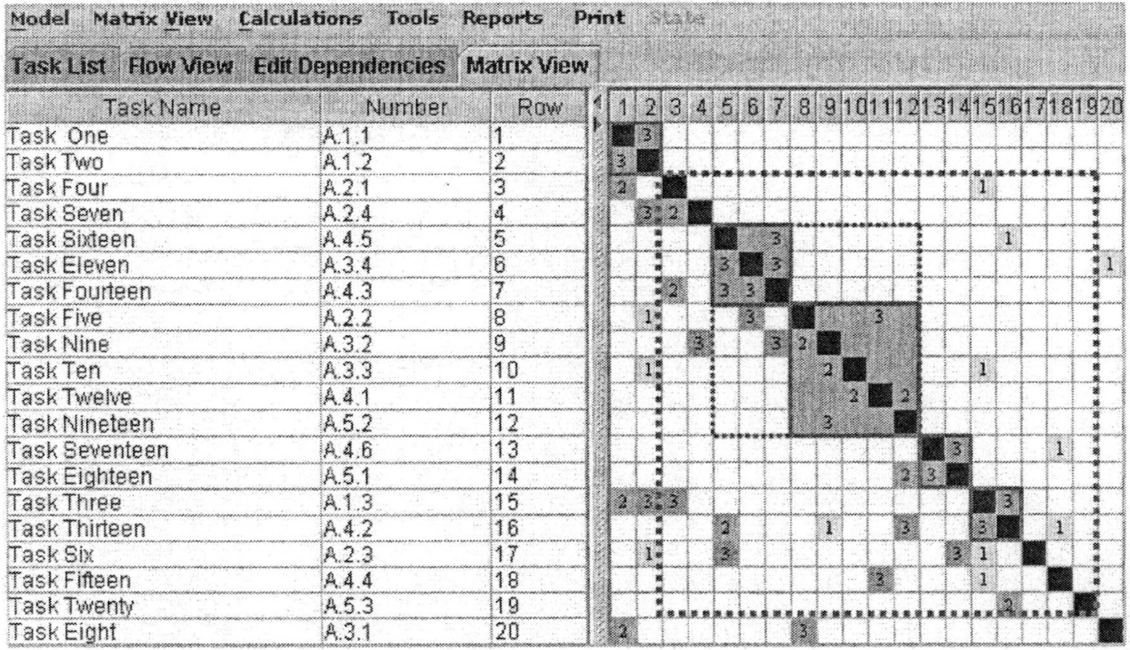

Model
Matrix View
Calculations
Tools
Reports
Print
Task List
Flow View
Edit Dependencies
Matrix View
Task Name
Number
Row
Task One A.1.1 1
Task Two A.1.2 2
Task Four A.2.1 3
Task Seven A.2.4 4
Task Sixteen A.4.5 5
Task Eleven A.3.4 6
Task Fourteen A.4.3 7
Task Five A.2.2 8
Task Nine A.3.2 9
Task Ten A.3.3 10
Task Twelve A.4.1 11
Task Nineteen A.5.2 12
Task Seventeen A.4.6 13
Task Eighteen A.5.1 14
Task Three A.1.3 15
Task Thirteen A.4.2 16
Task Six A.2.3 17
Task Fifteen A.4.4 18
Task Twenty A.5.3 19
Task Eight A.3.1 20
1 2 3 4 5 6 7 8 9 10 11 12 13 14 15 16 17 18 19 20

FIGURE 19-7. Result of declassification.

project management software represents sequential processes and does not allow elements of work containing iteration to be scheduled. Thus, feedback is not identified, resulting in coordination failures and rework both during design development and in production. With PlanWeaver the optimised sequence is linked into existing planning software, such as Microsoft Project and Primavera, where durations and resources are added. The output from the DSM is entered in a way that incorporates the iteration within the process. This is done by grouping tasks that form a block under a rolled-up activity and removing interrelationships from within the loop so that they can be programmed to occur in parallel. The group's relationships with previous and subsequent tasks remain. The overall duration of the group of tasks must allow for the necessary information exchanges necessary to achieve coordination.

While the end result, a bar chart, looks the same as that of conventional systems, it must be stressed that way you get there with ADePT is very different. Full account has been taken of the process' complex, interdependent nature, which is ignored by systems based on the critical path method that can only analyze sequential activities.

Integration with Construction

So far we have considered the design process in isolation, and it is now time to deal with the inevitable constraints. Among the greatest is a conflicting sequence required during production. In current practice, design is largely programmed to release information to suit the construction stage. The proposed approach is fundamentally different in first producing an optimal program to suit design, which is then modified as it is integrated with a procurement and construction program. This initially involves the addition of tender dates, tender periods, and other exchanges with contractors to the program, and then the determination of the procurement work package (WP) to which each design task contributes information. Having established the tender dates of each WP on the procurement program, the design program can, where appropriate, be rescheduled to ensure that these dates are met, a process that means reducing the duration of some WP designs.

This rescheduling can be achieved by either changing the duration of some tasks, with corresponding allocation of resources, or by changing the sequence of tasks and fixing some information dependencies that as a result move above the diagonal in the DSM to avoid potential iteration. Proposed changes to the optimal design program during its integration into a project program can be reviewed to establish the ease with which task duration and resources can be reallocated, and the most suitable pieces of information to estimate and fix. Also, the additional cost incurred through overdesigning some elements of the building can be compared to the costs of extending the duration of the corresponding work packages.

The DSM functionality in ADePT can be used to consider the implications of on the design process and to resolve pinch-points and scheduling conflicts. In figure 19.8 it can be seen that both the design and the procurement processes in

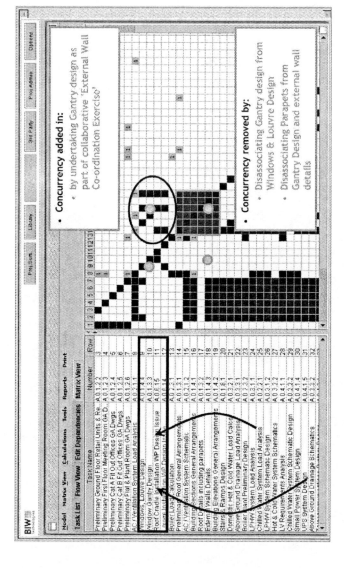

FIGURE 19-8. Impact of procurement on the optimized DSM.

question have been moved to a position in the matrix that permits an acceptable project sequence to the procurement process.

This allows designers and construction personnel to review the feasibility in undertaking design in a suboptimal way. In this case, design cannot be carried out in this manner, and a compromise was considered that allowed the conflict to be resolved.

Integrating the Supply Chain

A further area where designers need to work together is in the coordination of work between design stages, thus ensuring that adequate design development is undertaken in each discipline to provide the required cost certainty and confidence to the customer that the project will be successful. This will provide a means of identifying the timely introduction of suppliers into the design process, a benefit that is already being seen from the implementation of ADePT. This subject and the concept of Design Chains are explored fully elsewhere (Austin et al. 2002).

STEP 5: MANAGING CHANGE

A major problem during the design process is a failure to deal effectively with variations, the cause of delays and associated cost increases as the design progresses and construction is undertaken. The graphical nature of a DSM allows the impact of changes and variations to be envisaged quickly and easily. This can be achieved simply by moving tasks within the matrix (usually down the order) to simulate them being undertaken following the change. The tasks that must then be reexamined are clearly indicated by the matrix. This is a particularly useful feature where the work of one design discipline is affected by the decisions of another, or where the design in general is delayed by the decisions of the customer.

Consider a situation on a project in which an activity that has already been undertaken has to be repeated again much later in the processes because of customer induced change or change in specification. This situation is shown in figure 19.9a in which Task 7 has to be repeated again much later in the project than would be ideal. By manipulating the position of this task in the matrix to a position which is commensurate with the activities already completed, it is possible to see the potential impact on the design process by such a change. Critical dependencies now appear above the diagonal which need to be considered along with their impact on the dependent tasks that may also be affected by the change, The DSM will not tell you how to resolve the problem, but will inform managers to the areas of potential concern within the process.

The technique provides the project manager with guidance as to the areas of design that require particularly careful planning and control. It also helps to organize teams, tackle design in a focused way, and identify and control changes in the design. As such, the technique provides a means of improving the undertaking and management of the design process.

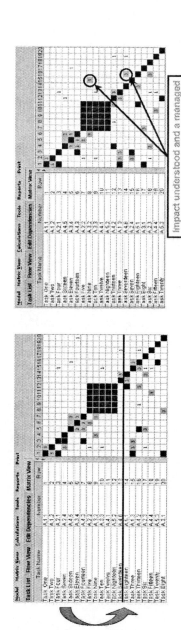

FIGURE 19-9. Understanding the impact of changes within the DSM.

MANAGING THE WAY TEAMS WORK

The integration of stages of a project and team members within each stage requires not only changes to the way a project is managed, but to the way the team members behave and interact. Where the design team may be colocated or expected to develop the design through a series of workshops, this suggests a change to the way complex coordination is approached. The blocks of inter-dependent design activity require a concerted management effort, rigorous review strategy and a strong link to the customer's decision making and approval processes. They also highlight where a concurrent, collaborative working strategy is appropriate for the design team members, who must liaise closely in all decisions, understand each others' design requirements and constraints, and have confidence in each others' commitment to the achievement of a common aim. The fulfilment of these ambitions can be encouraged through the co-location of members of the design team or, where this is impractical, via the implementation of effective electronic communication techniques.

These working practices cannot be applied without changes to the culture in the design team and project in general, but the identification of coordination issues through DSM analysis provides an opportunity for project management to plan and control the related activities effectively. The testing of ADePT has shown that there are a range of methods for planning, undertaking and managing these areas of design, and that the appropriate method is a function of the project nature, design issue (scale and complexity), team structure and program.

As such, when determining an approach to planning and management of these issues, they need to be examined in their own right. However, the identification of these issues, and the implication of re-addressing heavily interdependent sections of design following their completion, means that the matrix can be used as a guide to the timely review and approval of design.

APPLICATIONS

ADePT and PlanWeaver can be used in many different industries and scenarios. The following are just a couple of examples of where applications have been undertaken to date.

Product/Service Development

PlanWeaver was proven and used to demonstrate potential improvements in the development process for new engine lubricant systems. The technology:

- produced the first detailed, coordinated, cross-departmental schedule the project team had used,
- identified clear overlaps of responsibility across a number of departments,
- identified clear interfaces between departments (cutting indiscriminate dissemination of information and reducing the departmental silo mentality), and

- identified mechanisms to streamline the overall project program while increasing predictability of completion for market launch.

Design Planning

From the construction industry (e.g., design and construction of hospitals, laboratories) to the automotive or aerospace industries (e.g. development of power units for large commercial aircraft), PlanWeaver has been used on many projects to produce more effective and efficient design processes. The learning taken from these projects include:

- demonstration that an improved design sequences could be achieved without compromising construction and manufacturing processes, nor end date;
- design solutions that would stand a greater chance of being properly coordinated, with less resultant defects, as collaboration opportunities are identified and programmed to occur (interdependent blocks);
- an increase in design team efficiency being realised as release of information for procurement was streamlined into natural clusters and also to match the construction sequence;
- reduction in potential for a major surprise(s) to project completion as a result of a coordinated design and procurement program; and
- increased predictability of programs achieved from more realistic program and increased buy in from the design team; and
- reduction in project risk by explicitly identification of design compromises and assumptions.

PlanWeaver should not be seen as a threat to designers, and should be sold as a method to help designers' influence their own delivery process, rather than have it imposed.

BENEFITS

ADePT and PlanWeaver can help organizations in many areas. Specific benefits include:

greater predictability of timescales and costs in the development and delivery processes;

shorter lead times and timescales;

lower costs;

greater cross-team visibility—all activities and responsibilities are visible, so it is easy for participants to understand what needs to be done, when, and why. By showing everyone how their specific role contributes to the big picture, they become more aware of the consequences of their specific actions;

improved complex processes—by automatically rescheduling the sequence of activities to reduce the number of iterations involved, the overall process is improved;

earlier identification of information needs—teams can highlight activities where information will not be available in time; and

better contingency planning and risk management—teams can undertake what-if analyzes to model differing scenarios and determine the most appropriate management responses, and the information requirements to achieve different specific outcomes can also be modelled.

The ADePT methodology provides a powerful, yet simple means of understanding the interdependencies between tasks in complex processes. It offers a means of illustrating to the customer or customer, designers and constructors, the importance of a timely release of information, appropriate quality of information and information fixity based on collaborative decision making. It also ensures that the appropriate information is exchanged between members of the project team and that the problem of information overload is minimized. By providing a logical, structured approach to planning based on information flow (rather than the production of deliverables) that takes account of the process' iterative nature, ADePT can enable fully coordinated, integrated solutions to complex projects.

NOTES

1. ADePT and PlanWeaver are registered trademarks of Adept Management and BIW Technologies, respectively.

BIBLIOGRAPHY

Austin, S., A. Baldwin, B. Li, and P. Waskett. 1999a. Analytical Design Planning Technique (ADePT): An IDEF0v Model of the Detailed Building Design Process. *Design Studies* 20(3): 279–96.

Austin, S., A. Baldwin, B. Li, and P. Waskett. 1999b. Analytical Design Planning Technique (ADePT): Programming the Building Design Process. *Proceedings of Institution of Civil Engineers; Structures and Buildings* 134(May): 111–18.

Austin, S., A. Baldwin, B. Li, and P. Waskett. 2000. Analytical Design Planning Technique (ADePT): A Dependency Structure Matrix Tool to Schedule the Building Design Process. *Construction Management and Economics* V01.18: 173–82.

Austin, S., A. Baldwin, and A. Newton. 1996. A Data Flow Model to Plan and Manage the Building Design Process. *Journal of Engineering Design* 7(1): 3–25.

Austin, S., A. Baldwin, J. Hammond, M. Murray, D. Root, D. Thomson, and A. Thorpe. 2001. *Design Chains—A Handbook for Integrated Collaborative Design.* London: Thomas Telford.

Cooper, R., et al. 2002. The Design and Construction Process Protocol, www.processprotocol.com.

Karhu, V., M. Keitilä, and P. Lahdenperä. 1997. *Construction Process Model: Generic Present-State Systematisation by IDEF0.* Research Notes 1845, VTT, Finland.

RIBA. 1973. *Plan of Work for Design Team Operation.* London: Royal Institute of British Architects, RIBA Publications.

Sanvido, V. E., and K. J. Norton. 1994. Integrated Design-Process Model. *Journal of Management in Engineering.* September/October.

Steward, D. V. 1965. Partitioning and Tearing Systems of Equations. *SIAM Journal on Numerical Analysis* 2(2): 345–65.

20

Using the EFQM and Balanced Scorecards to Design Information System Strategy

ALLEN WOODS

DEFINING INFORMATION NEEDS

The developer of a management information system faces many difficulties. They include technical issues such as the transfer of raw data across operating systems and hardware platforms. Perhaps the hardest task is the identification of the key facts that a manager needs to know in order to plan effectively. In our opinion, one of the main issues to address in identifying key facts is communication. From the perspective of the Information Systems/Information Technology (IS/IT) system designer, there are two communication issues. The first is that traditionally, the skills surrounding IT/IS system design are seen as something of a black art best left to the professionals in the field. Equally, the IT/IS professional has often been found lacking knowledge of the detail of how an organization works. This has situation leads to software systems being technically proficient, but not what the business user wants or needs. The second communication problem is the passage of company policy from the board room to the shop floor in a form that everyone in an organization can understand and relate to. Using the automotive industry as an analogy, the chief executive officer of a car company may wish to capture an additional 10 percent of market share, and so make an extra £100m profit. But that may mean very little to the worker on the shop floor; he or she may not know what term "market share" means or what £100m looks like but, he or she does know that they have to make ten or eleven axles to the required quality standard.

In order to be effective, good coordinated information systems must cross the barriers outlined above. While technicians are quite capable of conquering the technical problems associated with software design, understanding the aims of business is often a different matter altogether. The essence of the problem is that no two organizations plan exactly the same way, and many organizations simply do not have a structured planning method in place. The inability to describe, in a structured way, how an organization works is not confined to any one industry or business sector.

Good IS/IT systems on the other hand should be designed and constructed using sound engineering principles. The IS/IT practitioner has a whole host of methodologies available to assist him or her. One of the more frustrating aspects of system design is the reconciliation of a controlled software development process with the chaotic world of normal business operations.

What is needed is an approach to business planning that is structured, but flexible enough to cover most business situations. Ideally any such approach should not require specialized knowledge (aside of course from an understanding of the methodology) but with a structure that could be overlayed on, or combined with, the structured analysis methods used by IS/IT system designers.

STRUCTURED MANAGEMENT PLANNING

Planning is about coordination, the control and management of all available resources to complete any given task. Everyone plans at some stage in their lives for one thing or another. Planning requires forethought and detailed knowledge of the task in hand. Successful planning also needs an element of luck.

In business, there are a number of general management planning tool sets and methodologies available. Many of them concern themselves with describing the way a particular business or activity is measured, typically in terms of financial efficiency. For example, Activity Based Costing (ABC) is used by management and financial planners to determine the most cost-effective use of resources using the relationship between activity and expenditure as the means of assessment. There are other management planning techniques, such as the Critical Path Method (CPM), that are time based and still more that are based on peer comparison. A second issue with the use of measurement techniques is that many organizations do not coordinate the activity of measurement within the concept of the business plan. Benchmarkers will go and do benchmarking, and make reports accordingly; time managers will plot critical path lines but may ignore benchmarking evidence and so on.

One of the keys to successful planning is the accuracy and timeliness of information, on the basis that "if you cannot measure it you cannot manage it." Accuracy and timeliness depend on cohesion. The key tool in today's world for improving information delivery from raw data is the organization's IS/IT infrastructure. Therefore, soundly structured, business-driven IS/IT systems that reflect business-driven information needs must improve business efficiency.

THE EUROPEAN FOUNDATION FOR QUALITY
MANAGEMENT MODEL

The management planning techniques described earlier are of course valid, but they are also task-specific and require some form of specialized knowledge to implement. Fundamentally, there is a need for a top-level methodology that can encompass other management planning disciplines on a framework basis, but would have the scope to take in activities that are not normally monitored. The European Foundation for Quality Management (EFQM) Model is an approach that may meet the requirement. In essence, the EFQM consists of a series of assessment criteria supported by survey questions that can be used to analyse the status of an organization in a holistic way. The beauty of the EFQM is that it addresses issues across a whole host of topics from core business activities to more abstract matters like an organization's impact on society.

The guiding principle of EFQM is continuous review and, through review, improvement. The EFQM can be used globally, but it can also be used on a single department or business function. The key to its utility however, is the structure to general business analysis it brings. Furthermore it is a framework that has been designed to be used in any or all business planning situations in much the same way that information system designers use SSADM or Yourdon.

One of the products of the application of the EFQM is a list of business objectives. The objectives produced as part of an EFQM analysis are based around the concept of improvement on the current situation. Assuming the desire to improve on the "here-and-now" any objectives defined as a result of considered analysis, are bound to be based on a clear understanding of what constitutes success or failure. Objectives should by definition have an aim or target against which success can be determined. If there is an aim, then there must be a series of steps that needs to be taken beforehand in order to meet them. By default, these steps are overview process definitions.

The measurement technique applied to a particular objective is of course dependent on the nature of the task. An objective-based approach to planning built on sound structured analysis would also give some indication as to the best measurement technique to apply, whether it be ABC or shareholder value or whatever.

LINKING THE EFQM MODEL TO KEY DOCUMENTS

In order for the EFQM or any other analysis technique to be seen as relevant, those doing the analysis and those being analyzed must be able to relate the analysis results to the way they work and their position in the organization structure.

In our experience there are usually documents available that are designed to pass the management message to its workers. The most common documents are "Vision" and "Mission" statements. Some organizations go to great lengths to make sure that these documents were scattered liberally throughout the work place in an attempt to communicate principles and intentions. Very often Vision and Mission are based on the results of management experimentation of a number of standards-based initiatives such as the ISO 9000 or SIGMA 6. Organizations tend to put a lot of the effort into producing Mission and Vision statements, but for many this is wasted effort for the following reasons:

> Mission and Vision statements are often full of lofty principles and ideas but were couched in language that is not simple and direct.
>
> Second, and perhaps more important, there is no link that individual workers make between them and the Mission/Vision statements that have a direct impact on their role or status.

Vision and Mission statements are, potentially, extremely powerful tools for focusing an organization's efforts to succeed. In order for the Vision and Mission to work, they must form an integral part of an organization's business plan. A good definition of Vision and Mission should allow any organization member to relate the two statements clearly to what they do. The military's use of the term "Mission" is an example. At all levels in the chain of command, the "Mission" is a clearly stated, achievable objective, often broken down into smaller tasks that themselves can be broken down to localized "Missions."

A proposed structure for linking key documents to business analysis and scorecards is illustrated in figure 20.1. The purpose of each element in the structure is as follows:

- The *Charter* statement refers to an organization's history, its core activities, and its reason for being. On a fundamental level, if you do not know your core values and have no sense of history, it is difficult to describe where you want to go and how you are going to get there.

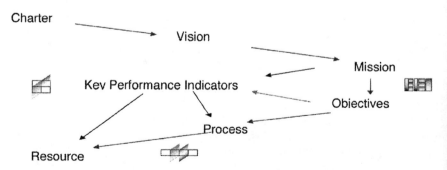

FIGURE 20-1. Linking the EQFM and key documents.

- The *Vision* statement should be a description of the long-term aims and aspirations of an organization. Having a clearly stated vision provides the terms of reference for strategic planning. The Vision statement should be written in such a way as to be able to identify an immediate Mission.
- The *Mission* statement should describe short-term achievable aims. The Mission statement should be the basis for operational planning.
- *Objectives*, based on the Mission, should describe how that mission is to be achieved. Out of clearly defined objectives will come processes and performance measures. The definition of performance measures will determine the data that needs to be collected at process level and delivered as information to managers.
- The identification of *Processes* will also identify the most appropriate *Resources* to complete a task. Allocating performance measures and resources to a process should mean that any resource should be able to make a clear link between itself and the organization's Mission and Vision statements.

Having established the link between an analysis technique and key documents there remains a need to select a suitable method of determining whether or not the organization is succeeding in meeting its Vision and Mission requirements.

PERFORMANCE MEASUREMENT

In the United Kingdom over the past five or six years, there has been something of a sea change in the way both central and local government account for the way that money is spent. One of the aims of the changes in accounting procedures has been to try and identify the "whole cost" of any given product or service. For instance, a vehicle has its initial purchase cost, but other associated costs include insurance, fuel, a driver, and so on. As a result of the whole cost approach to accounting, many organizations have found themselves forming the opinion that judging things from a solely financial viewpoint misses much of the intrinsic value of a product or service. Intrinsic values (reliability, down time, etc.) should form part of the whole cost concept. For example, one particular piece of machinery may cost £1000.00 to buy and an alternative machine £1500.00. On the face of it the first machine is cheaper by £500.00. But, ease of use, maintenance, and other factors may be much lower for the more expensive machine and, therefore, have a greater impact on long-term budget planning.

Whole cost, therefore, should be about collecting data to establish "best value," which in turn has implications for overall performance measurement. To establish best value there is a need to define performance criteria for all manner of products, services, and activities and to establish a correlation, where appropriate, between finance and other more intrinsic measures.

Measuring aspects of the value of an item generates problems of its own. Three of them are:

- to define suitable measures or indicators of performance that can be used to identify success or failure,

- to group any such indicators logically for reporting purposes, and
- to collect the relevant data on which to objectively measure that performance.

Other factors in performance measure definitions that should be considered include:

- A poorly defined performance measure can lead to bad behavior and bad relations between managers and workers.
- If a performance measure has tolerances attached, then those tolerances can be used to identify best practice and apply it elsewhere, or remedy failure.
- Tolerances also provide the means to define change within the base measure that most resources can achieve.
- Defining performance measures is a subjective process and related closely to the core activities of the organization they are designed to support.

THE BUSINESS BALANCED SCORECARD

In our opinion, a suitable method for grouping performance measures has been described by Professors Kaplan and Norton of the Harvard Business School. Their seminal work *The Balanced Score Card, Translating Strategy into Action*, describes a "scorecard" approach in which indicators are grouped into business quadrants or perspectives. Typically, a scorecard has perspectives that are concerned with finance, learning, effectiveness, and efficiency (Figure 20.2).

Using the scorecard, it is a relatively easy exercise to logically group performance measures and the data associated with them. Further, the scorecard approach makes it easy to identify a correlation across business perspectives. For example, if an organization has a training budget of £50K, then there should be some related increase in the number of trained staff who, in turn, should have a measurable impact on efficiency and effectiveness. If the training purchased does not impact on other measures, then that training is probably a waste of time and money.

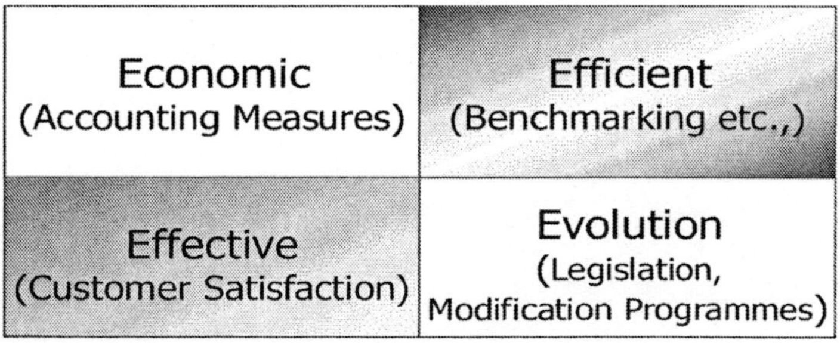

Economic (Accounting Measures)	Efficient (Benchmarking etc.,)
Effective (Customer Satisfaction)	Evolution (Legislation, Modification Programmes)

FIGURE 20-2. The balanced scorecard.

In principle, an organization could have one scorecard that can be used across all levels of its hierarchy. In practice, like objectives, it will be more likely that as complexity grows, there will be a number of scorecards that are linked to the organization's structure. The scorecard takes care of data delivery, in as much as if an organization element has a scorecard, any information needed to support that card must be delivered to the department concerned. Data collection is another matter. The place, at which data is collected to support a performance measure, should be at the lowest process level or step at the point at which a measurable transaction takes place. For example, data related to what a customer spends on a given product should be collected at the point of sale. Using a series of objectives and scorecards that cascade through an organization, it is possible, from sound business principles, to design a business-driven IT/IS infrastructure.

COORDINATED INFORMATION SYSTEM STRUCTURE BASED ON EFQM ANALYSIS AND BALANCED SCORECARDS

Assuming an organization implements a balanced scorecard approach to data collection and delivery, founded on a consistent analysis methodology, such as that provided by the EFQM then, in effect, it will be following the same systems design disciplines taken by IS/IT systems analysts. The information plan will therefore have two key advantages: it will be based on clearly defined business objectives, and it will have a structure that can easily be mapped by IS/IT system designers into their own analysis methods.

At the lowest level of the infrastructure is the data collection or feeder systems. These systems are designed to allow workers and managers alike to collect the raw data. It should be noted, that the feeder systems, and indeed any element of the structure outlined in this section includes not only computer systems, but other reporting mechanisms, too.

At the next level, are the management information systems (MIS). MIS provide day-to-day operational management information. They contain a summary of the masses of data held by the feeder systems. Feeder systems will probably be designed around the relational data model, while the MIS will probably be built around concepts associated with data warehousing. The MIS should be supported by "drill down" capabilities to the feeder systems, providing the means for managers to examine detailed raw data if required.

At the top level are decision support systems. Decision support systems could be based on correlation of scorecard cross perspective links to identify and plots (say) spend against improvements in efficiency. The aim of top-level systems is to provide decision support for senior management. Decision support systems could incorporate artificial intelligence, complex statistical analysis, and so on. Top-level systems should also have some form of drill down capability to the data warehouse provided for MIS systems.

CONCLUSIONS

One of the major problems with IS/IT design is a communication gap between the IS/IT practitioner and the general business community. The communication problem is exacerbated by the lack of a general structured business analysis technique that can be mapped into IS/IT disciplines and the limited knowledge within the IS/IT community about how business works. It is the proposition of this chapter that the EFQM and the business balanced scorecard, properly linked to key corporate documents like Mission and Vision statements is one way of dealing with these communication issues.

Proper application of the EFQM and the balanced ccorecard will not of themselves produce a detailed system specification. What they will do, however, is enable managers to define what they need to know, when they need to know it, and where data is to be delivered in the form of information. The information requirement, based on performance measures supported at process level, delivered through the medium of the scorecard should be capable of reporting on progress against objectives, but with clearly identifiable links to the organization's structure, mission, and vision.

BIBLIOGRAPHY

Web Addresses

The following Web sites may be of use to readers of this article:
www.efqm.org. The European Foundation for Quality Home Site.
www.bscol.com. The Balanced Score Card Collaborative Home Site.
www.balancedscorecard.org. The Balanced Score Card Institute.
www.schneiderman.com. Arthur Schneiderman is credited with building the first balanced scorecard.

Further Reading

Kaplan, R. S., and D. P. Norton. 1996. *The Balanced Scorecard, Translating Strategy into Action*. Cambridge, Mass.: Harvard University Press

_____ 21 _____

The Changing Project Management Requirements in the Communications Industry

DAN P. ONO

OVERVIEW

In today's business environment, especially in the communications industry, whether it involves voice, data, networking, video or voiceover Voice over Internet Protocol (VoIP), have become more urgent. These imperatives include substantially compressed schedules for every project, reduced budgets, the need for much greater flexibility for changes, and, most significantly, larger numbers of project interfaces, which make today's projects much more complex for the project manager. Today's projects, typically, are comprised of numerous subprojects from multiple disciplines. Additionally, many of today's projects include international locations, which add additional complexity, when dealing with the differing customs, cultures, and the varying legal requirements of the international locations. A heightened political environment exacerbates these complexities.

Many of today's communications projects represent the client company's business and financial lifeline or provide functionality essential to the client's business viability. Additionally, projects have been increasing in size and scope for a number of years, primarily, due to an ever-expanding scope to include additional components of the client's business. Many of today's projects are focused on improving the effectiveness and efficiency of the existing infrastructure of businesses that are desperate to improve their bottom lines.

All of these pressures focus directly on the project managers, be they professional or ad hoc. In order to meet these additional requirements, project managers need to be able to look at all aspects of their project management processes. All of the above combine to make successfully managing projects a greater and different challenge than in the past. To be successful in today's project environment, the integrative project manager has to be able to skillfully balance the traditional fundamentals of project management with the tools, personalities, and changing requirements of the new world of business.

This chapter addresses the integrative project manager versus the functional project manager. Although, there are many applications of the skills needed to be a successful integrative project manager that apply equally to the functional project manager, the integrative project manager, typically, has a pure project management function and is not, necessarily, a technology expert in any of the functional areas of the project. The integrative project manager is responsible for the proper integration of the schedules, budgets, time lines, and the scope of the project. He or she is also responsible for the integration of project reporting, the project public relations program, and communications to management and the public in general regarding the project.

UNDERSTANDING THE PAST, SO THAT WE CAN EXCELL IN THE PRESENT

Where We Were

Many of today's ad hoc project managers are not interested in the way project management has been done in the past. They quote many different reasons for taking this position. Among these reasons are:

- The methodology and principles do not apply to today's projects.
- The methodology is too slow.
- The methodology is too restricting and inhibits creativity.
- The methodology takes too much work, often disguised as I do not have enough time (Unspoken: My time is being taken up by problems on my project).
- The functional groups do not want to use the methodology or software.
- I do not know how. This is often disguised in many different forms including some of those identified above.
- I want to use a different methodology (most times, the project manager's own ad hoc methodology).
- I do not have time to be trained on the methodology (another version of I am too busy solving project problems).

Unfortunately, this view totally ignores the fundamental of learning from experience and learning from the mistakes one makes, or even better that someone else makes. The whole objective of a professional methodology is to avoid repeating the same mistakes over and over again with each new project manager. Although progress can still be made, its speed is greatly reduced by this mentality.

Many of the companies in the communications industry are still going through an evolutionary process similar to the one the construction and aerospace project management disciplines had to live through. Companies in the multiple communications technology areas, voice, data, networking, and video, and their supporting media disciplines (wireless, wire, fiber optics, satellite, etc.) are in various states of this evolution. This evolution ranges from initial corporate recognition of the need for project management to understanding the sustainable competitive advantage project management can provide a business entity.

Among the major steps of this evolution include the following characteristics:

- identifying a need for better project delivery,
- recognizing the need to hire more qualified project managers,
- establishing internal organizations that specialize in project management,
- recognizing the need for formal project management training,
- recognizing the need for defined and documented project management processes,
- understanding the components that comprise the development of a group of professional project managers,
- understanding the benefits to the corporation and to its customers created by possessing a self-sustaining group of professional project managers,
- the need for executive support for formal project management,
- understanding the appropriate placement of the project management organization within the corporate hierarchy,
- recognition that project management is a profession and making professional project managemeent a part of the company's culture, and
- the ability to leverage project management into a sustainable competitive advantage.

The speed of the progression through these steps has been, at times, painfully slow. In many corporations, the sluggish speed at which this evolution has taken place was exasperated by a continuous turnover in senior and middle management. Oftentimes, this turnover would cause a regression in the evolution as the new senior management would have to experience the same project failures and frustrations that their predecessors experienced before recognizing the need to improve their project execution capability and allowing the evolution to progress—again. This characteristic of senior management changes continues to occur in many companies, thus impeding the progress of professional project management. This characteristic will not be overcome until project management becomes part of the company's culture, just like sales, marketing, financials, and legal are part of every company's culture.

There has been a lot of documentation created from large amounts of work, mostly trial and error, and research done in order to provide a solid basis for the progressive improvement in professional project management methodologies and principles. Awareness and knowledge of this work is essential to building successful project management processes and professional project management organizations in the present and in the future.

EXCELLING IN THE PRESENT

Where We Are Now

Many project managers are technology experts with minimally developed project management skills. This is most notable in the newer technical areas such as data, networking, video, and voiceover IP. As with the more mature industries of construction and aerospace, most of the initial projects in each of these new technologies are small in size. The provider company's first project managers are, typically, senior technicians from within each of the individual technologies. Additionally, as each company begins to recognize the need for project management, they perpetuate the problem by looking for project managers with a technology versus project management background.

Most of today's project managers do not have any formal education in the field, or they have taken just a few project management classes. Unfortunately, many of these classes are advertised as three- or four-day wonder classes, which allege to make a student proficient at professional project management on completion of the course. Even worse, some corporate leaders send their project managers to a project management software class such as Microsoft Project and believe that they have "trained" project managers. With these perceptions in many corporations, most project managers have learned the hard way by learning while they are managing projects. Unfortunately, this means that their project management knowledge is limited to their own personal experiences, and they will experience many common errors.

In many companies, the need for professional project management is recognized by only a few of the company's executives, if any. Most still believe that they can take their most technically able engineers and make them project managers. While this can work for functional project management and for small projects, these technical experts in general, cannot execute accurately on the larger integrative projects. Consequently, many of the largest and most important projects are late and/or finish with reduced scope and/or are over budget or some combination of these common project failures. Also, when delivered many of these projects do not achieve initial project acceptance, which adds to the time and cost overruns of the project as well as poor customer satisfaction.

Many projects become a painful experience for all involved, the project manager, the project participants, and the project stakeholders, because of poor project delivery in one or multiple areas of the Triple Constraints. The cause for these failures often lies in the lack of project infrastructure on the project, which causes poor project communications, misunderstandings, misinterpretations, and many missed commitments.

Since the perception of the project's stakeholders, owners, and team members is so critical to today's project success, managing the internal as well as the external political environment has become essential on every major project. Unfortunately, most project managers have not been trained in recognizing and managing this area. Typically, today's project management organizations do not have a defined comprehensive professional project management program that is consistent over time. Consequently, project performance improves on an individual project manager basis versus an overall project management group improvement.

In many of today's companies, success in the project environment means a promotion out of the project management field, thus making mediocrity in project delivery a self-sustaining process. This is caused in part because no career path is defined for the professional project manager. The quickest way to begin experiencing project success is to assemble a centralized core of credentialed professional project managers experienced in successful integrative project management. The criteria for selecting this group of employees is a balance between demonstrated ability in integrative project management as well as within the technology. When selecting candidates, a perceived equality in the qualifications of candidates should go to the candidate with more professional project management credentials and successful integrative project management experience.

Consistent successful project delivery across multiple project managers is achieved by having a structured professional project management infrastructure focused on a centralized group of professional project managers. This infrastructure needs to be constructed with building a self-sustaining successful professional project management organization as the primary objective. By self-sustaining, we mean that at any point in time, this infrastructure has project managers in various stages of development; that is, mature senior project managers who can take on any project, project managers who are managing ever larger and more complex integrative projects, project managers who are managing their first small integrative projects, and project managers who are still building their project management philosophies and establishing their early project management credentials such as attaining basic project management education certificates and industry project manager certifications like the Project Management Institute's "PM Professional" certification and are, typically, assistant project managers or managing functional portions of projects.

As illustrated in Attachment 1, most areas of this infrastructure can be implemented simultaneously.

LEADING INTO THE FUTURE

Where We Need to Go

The fundamentals of modern project management remain critical to professional project management and consistent success in project delivery. In order to meet, the additional requirements of future projects, the project management organization needs to be able to look at many aspects of its processes, project infrastructure, and environment:

- What has been successful in past and why?
- What has not been successful and why?

- Identify any differences between the current set of projects and their environments and past projects and environments.
- Be knowledgeable about what methodologies and techniques need to be updated.
- Understand and leverage the advances in project management software.
- Understand and leverage the changes in the interpersonal relationships on projects.
- Understand and manage the political characteristics involved with the future's business environments.
- Maintain and update the project management infrastructure and environment reflected in Attachment 1.
- Ensure that the documented project management process is updated annually with the lessons learned from the past year. This is the only way that lessons learned are truly institutionalized into the project management organization. The project management process thus becomes the corporate memory for the project management organization.
- Understand what areas of project management that development work is being done within the project management profession. Such as today's focus has become collaboration and risk assessment on all kinds of projects. These new risk methodologies do not require the expensive and laborious assessment processes of the past.
- Constantly search for qualified personnel to feed the professional project management organization. Build a buffer of preinterviewed candidates to add new headcount or fill vacancies caused by attrition or promotion. Do not be caught settling with whom you have time to interview.
- It is critical to create a professional project manager career path. It has been our experience that for each level of project management that is in the career path, a project managerPM has a tendency to stay in the project management organization for another two to three years. We have always tried to create at least four levels of project managers: Project Coordinator, Senior Project Coordinator, project manager, and Senior project manager. Obviously, the specific titles are not critical, but should be reflective of the position in the organization as well as be a title that the project manager will be proud to carry.
- It is up to the project management director or leader to ensure that the project managers get full and progressive recognition for their successes. Unfortunately, company executives typically hear about projects only when they are in trouble. These executives need to be aware of projects that are being executed, accurately, while the projects are in progress. The more frequent positive exposure for the project managers, the sooner project management will become an accepted requirement for every corporation.
- Every aspect of the Environment for Lasting Success needs to be dynamic so that it can change with the environment surrounding it. The project managers need to create and own portions of the Environment, such as the project manager's Qualification Matrix as well as the Project Management Process.

SUMMARY

The creation of a successful project management organization has to be approached just like the execution of an integrated project. Attachment 1 illustrates fourteen areas in the project manager's environment that need to be addressed to create the infrastructure that he or she needs to thrive, grow, and produce consistently successful project delivery across many projects and over a lengthy period of time. It should be apparent that this is not easily or quickly done. Our experience has shown that establishing the infrastructure can take more than two years if practicing project managers are doing most of the work. If a staff group is assigned and dedicated to carrying out the tasks required, the time frame can be reduced significantly.

The development of a group of professional-level project managers takes even longer, because this requires doing projects. Our estimates of time frames for the evolutionary steps needed to create this professional project manager are:

- Two years to complete the education and training program. The deliverables for this program included attainment of a Master's Certificate in project management from a major university, PMI Certification Preparation, which, typically, resulted in PMI certification. The training program included what we labeled as Practitioner training courses, taught by practicing project managers or consultants with extensive project management experience. We chose this combination of education and training because we wanted to have a cross-section of academic and practitioner instruction.
- During the two years of the education and training programs, the project managers would be doing mostly second-person project management work such as helping on large projects as assistant project managers or managing functional units or small areas of major projects. Each assignment was chosen to ensure wide exposure to the individual styles of multiple Senior project managers. These assignments would be relatively short in duration (three to six months), so these junior project managers had the opportunity to work with a large number of Senior project managers and the various aspects of the projects. This philosophy served multiple purposes: these new project managers were under the protection and tutorage of Senior project managers whose project management approach was consistent with the direction of the organization, and the new project managers were protected from an early failure that, potentially, could end their careers. This approach, ultimately, protected the client and the project management organization as well because it minimized project breakdowns.

We believed that it would take another two years for each project manager to develop sufficiently his/her own individual style, work out the kinks in that style, and, finally, gain confidence in that style. During this period, these project managers would be doing their own progressively larger projects, or managing large portions of mega projects. Another two years of managing large projects would provide enough empirical data for these project managers to become Senior project managers. The project managers would have to be successful at each level to continue in the progression. The system was flexible enough to allow a portion of these project managers to stay at one of the lower levels of the project management progression if they so desired.

Fundamentally, an approach needs to be developed, documented, implemented, and maintained for a relatively long period of time, at least six years. If this is not done and the project management program is changed with each new project management executive, or if project managers are allowed to create their own processes on an individual basis, the organization will never mature past the ad hoc stage of project management and will never contribute to the corporation up to its potential. The entire project management environment needs to maintain the ability to be dynamic or it will lose its support and vitality.

ATTACHMENT 1

Attachment 1 illustrates and describes the requirements to achieve professional level of project management skills at the group level and the environment to ensure lasting success. The model is divided into two distinct categories. The first relates to the human aspects of the professional project manager, and the other relates to the process aspects of the professional project manager. The human aspects include the following:

Top personnel: The quality of the personnel must be at a high level, since these people will need to command the respect of their peers on the project.

Basic Education/Training Program: The difference between education and training is that education consists of high-level project management methods and principles in a general sense usually taught by a recognized university. Training takes those high-level methods and principles and puts them into a specific application, such as a traditional voice application, a voiceover IP application, software development application, or data networking application.

Continuing Education/Training Program: In order to facilitate continuous improvement and maintaining a leading-edge process, a continuing education and training program needs to be created and executed. This program needs to build on the basic education and training program to maintain some form of consistency in the fundamentals of project management that the company's management wishes its organization to follow.

Project Management Mentorship/Coaching Program: In order to facilitate both a positive change in behavior toward the production of the desired project management deliverables as well as to support the building of the project manager's confidence in the skills needed to produce those deliverables, a structured mentoring and coaching program needs to exist.

Career Path and the Compensation Plan: These two plans complete the professional project manager profile in the human resources area. Both should be constructed to stimulate and motivate improvement in project management skills based on documented successful project delivery. The chief objective (of both plans) should be to provide the ability to retain successful experienced project managers within the project management organization.

The following are the process-oriented portion of the Environment for Lasting Success

Standardized Process/Tools: The adoption of a standard set of project management tools as well as a single project management process provides the ability for the entire organization to improve simultaneously. Without a standardized process, each project managerwill improve to different levels, at different speeds, and in different areas. These standardized processes allow the organization to provide backup and/or assistance to each project manager with a minimal briefing, since all will already be familiar with the project management process and the deliverables required by that process.

Project Management Qualification Matrix: The Project Management Qualification Matrix is a tool to provide an objective basis for the determination of a project manager's qualifications. The quantification of the credentials and project performance is achieved through the use of a series of different objective matrixes: the Education Matrix, the Training Matrix, the Use of Professional PM Tools Matrix, and the Project Performance Matrixes. Each matrix contributes qualification points based on performance levels to a master matrix. This quantification of the project manager's qualifications is useful in salary grade determination, outlining a career path, and demonstration of the organization's differentiating qualifications during Request for Proposal responses.

Compatible Business Processes and Management Philosophy: These two business characteristics are significant components of the Environment for Lasting Success (figure 21.1). Many aspects of these components are not directly under the control of the project managers, so the group leader needs to take responsibility for ensuring these processes and philosophy, and that the project management processes are compatible with each other.

National or International Professional Project Management Certifications: These certifications are provided by the project management industry's professional organizations. Examples of these types of organizations are the PM Institute in the United States, the Australian Institute of Project Management in Australia, The International Project Management Association in Europe, and the Association of Project Management in the United Kingdom.

While the attainment of the project management knowledge required to pass these certification tests is the main goal of the education andtraining program, the attainment of these certifications is beneficial to the project manager, the project management organization, and the company, and should not be overlooked. These credentials provide a means of differentiating a company's project managers from its competition's. Since most vendors say the same thing, the potential customer cannot differentiate between vendors in the important implementation areas. Choices in RFP situations are made by the ability of a vendor to differentiate themselves from their competition. Having these certifications, having project management educational credentials, and having a documented project delivery process provides a vendor with the ability to differentiate itself in many of the key areas relating to the ability to implement, successfully.

Project Evaluation Review Process: This is a process that provides the organization a valuable training and learning tool. This process is designed to provide current project benefits as well as the typical process auditing information. The

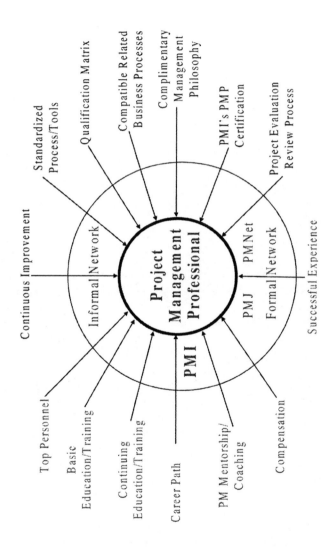

FIGURE 21-1. The project management professional and the environment to insure lasting success.

attainment of both of these objectives is achieved by conducting the project review process with a group of project management experts as the project nears conclusion of the Planning Phase. At this stage there is still time to correct any deficiencies in the planning before the beginning of the execution of the project plans. Our project managers have told us that this is the best possible learning environment, since project management process and principles are applied directly in their own project environments thus creating a direct correlation between the project management principles and a project that they are familiar with.

Formal and Informal Networks: These networks serve to provide the project manager with another means of support and continuous improvement. The formal project management network is generally created by the organization and consists of designated coaches and mentors as well as senior peers within the group. The informal networks are comprised of project managers and other project management experts outside of the immediate project management peer group and are often from outside of the company. This network is usually created by attending professional project manager functions such as PMI's local chapter meetings or by attending professional project management conferences and other functions. PMI's *Project Management Journal* and other project management publications, also provide the project manager with access to sources of the latest techniques and methodologies.

Creating Competencies: a Specific Project Management

Evidence from the Telecommunications Sector

FRÉDÉRIC FONTANE
PATRICE HOUDAYER
HERVÉ MATHE

OVERVIEW

The convergence process associated with the rapid growth of the Internet and online services has spawned new market structures and new roles for economic players. Underlying this evolution is the fact that few of the current market players have the competencies to cover the whole value chain in a converging environment. As a result, the advent of major players in the sectors affected by this convergence will inevitably, at different levels, entail partnerships of varying degrees, thus creating new networks.

The term convergence presently designates the bridging of the telecommunications, audiovisual, and computer industries. However, the relative difficulty in precisely defining the concept raises the question of whether there are different levels of convergence. The main problem is to determine whether convergence represents the existence of a single support for several services or the simultaneous existence of several supports that offer the same service.

Procuring a strong position in this emerging industry therefore involves the creation of partnerships between organizations. In other words, for a given economic player, a recurrent process must be implemented over time, whose objective is to bring some players to collaborate over the short term and thus create a unique product or service. The player's goal is to implement a project of creating competencies to enable it to adapt to this new environment.

The chapter begins with identification of key success factors for a competency creation project. Then, we specify the different factors involved for a specific economic player, namely telecommunications operators, showing the importance of these factors to define where the project starts and ends to decide who must be involved in the review and approval process. In the third section, we test whether these factors truly create competencies in order to know how these factors define what the customer (in our case a telecommunication operator) expects from the project. The final section concludes that, even though the converging environment studied leads to organizational interdependence, it is possible to manage a project that generates competencies.

IDENTIFICATION OF KEY SUCCESS FACTORS
FOR IMPLEMENTATION OF A COMPETENCY
CREATION PROJECT

The starting point of our research is an evident observation: nowadays, most companies admit that it is necessary to permanently adapt to an environment that is evolving quickly and increasingly turbulent in terms of technology, commerce, regulations, sociology, and culture.[1] The converging environment linked to the development of the Internet is a good example of this necessary adaptation for the players concerned. We have mentioned in the overview that to adapt to this converging environment, competency creation projects must be put in place. Classic project management confirms that the coordination and leading of a project group, comprised of individuals from different horizons, are key success factors.[2] Heck (1996) conducted an empirical study of these two factors at Microsoft. Nonetheless, our objective is not to foster collaboration between people from different horizons, but rather between organizations with differing composition, in order to create a product, service, process or plan.[3] We begin by generically identifying the factors that condition collaboration in such projects.

To this effect, we have chosen to adopt the Resource Dependency theoretical framework. In this theory, efficient adaptation to the environment for a player is identical to managing the requirements of interest groups on whose resources and support it depends. Therefore, companies must acquire and develop resources that they do not fully control, that is, that are managed by other organizations in their environment. An efficient organization is consequently one that satisfies the demands of its environment which support it and in turn conditions its survival. Therefore, the Resource Dependency theory proposes identifying the dimensions of this environment and their relations by means of a model developed by Pfeffer and Salancik (1978).

We have adapted this conceptual model by focusing on a single type of relation among the economic players: interdependence. We contend that a competencies creation project for a specific player involves configuration of a network of knowledge. Figure 22.1 presents this conceptual model. With regard to the abundance of resources and interconnectivity, interdependence with external and/or

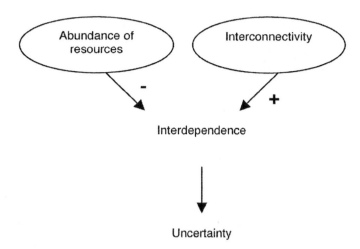

FIGURE 22-1. Model of dimensions of the environment.

other organizations can be evaluated by a company's activity. This approach is a prerequisite for the estimation of external demand. Indeed, an efficient organization will meet this demand according to its dependence. It must therefore estimate the pertinent groups that can supply or assign critical resources or activities. In addition, Pfeffer and Salancik (1978) note that two structural characteristics of the environment condition the interdependence of the economic players. The greater the interconnectivity (i.e., the number of networks and links between organizations), the higher the interdependence. Moreover, the interdependence rises in direct proportion with the scarcity of resources. The convergence phenomenon increases interconnectivity (creation of partnerships) and its technological trajectory tends to rarify the available technological resources. Thus, interdependence among the organizations is reinforced.

In order to satisfy new requirements (adapt to digital convergence), an organization must enlist support from external groups and/or other organizations in its environment. In return, the external groups expect actions from the organization. Among the factors that condition organizational interdependence, identified by Pfeffer and Salancik (1978), we have retained the following factors:

1. Factor 1: firm's awareness regarding demands made;
2. Factor 2: extent of resources;
3. Factor 3: possibility of obtaining a resource the organization lacks;
4. Factor 4: nature of external control over resources.

As our objective is to foster collaboration between organizations from different horizons in order to create a product, service, process, or plan, we have identified four key success factors that make available collaboration in projects for creating new competencies. In our view, these key success factors are not the ones that the customer will use for judging the acceptability of final deliverables. But they give ideas to establish risk limits, identify organizational constraints and project priorities.

LEVEL OF ORGANIZATIONAL DEPENDENCE IN THE TELECOMMUNICATIONS SECTOR

As mentioned in the overview, the term convergence is used to designate the bridging of the telecommunications, audiovisual, and computer industries. Significant changes are presently taking place owing to the implementation of Transmission Control Protocol/Internet Protocol (TCP/IP) technologies in each of these sectors. Such changes are not in themselves proof of convergence, but they underline the homogeneity of the technique applied that can serve as a base for development of convergence. Therefore, given the emergence of the Internet, our objective is to identify and qualify the level of dependence of an organization set: telecommunications operators.

Awareness and Criticality of Demands Made on Telecommunications Operators (Factors 1 and 2)

The Internet represents a rupture with the methodologies of the telephone industry, particularly considering information in the form of datagrams.[4] Datagrams use protocols such as TCP/IP in a selective environment that mainly consists of a large number of interconnected Local Area Networks (LAN) and personal computers. The Internet is thus a major issue for conventional telecommunications operators because it is a complete opposite paradigm to that of the past. Whereas traditional networks are highly hierarchical and secure, the Internet has arisen from a federation of IP networks.

Historical operators must resolve a strategic problem: networks that have proven their worth are now obsolete. After a century of investment in construction of infrastructures that route local communications, operators are now facing an unprecedented growth of data transmission. Telecommunications operators are aware of new demands that are made on them and the importance of integrating new technological resources linked to the Internet in their operations.

Obtaining and Controlling Internet Resources (Factors 3 and 4)

By nature, technological resources linked to the Internet are located and obtained by very different ways. In a constantly evolving world such as the Internet, research is a determining factor. Conventional operators in internal research and development (R&D) are not all starting from the same position, but they generally orient their R&D toward aspects of information content, information exchange platforms, transmission networks, and terminals. These internal research axes draw on academic research upstream of complex and very specific problems emerging from the Internet world, which differ greatly from conventional research performed by R&D centers of conventional telecommunications operators. These university relations allow the research center of a telecommunications operator to benefit from very specific technological advances that assist it in developing its product and/or service.

A similar situation applies to young innovating firms, whereby operators can foresee opportunities other than those of internal customers within their group. Startups also enable operators to target a different market and thus promote its expertise more broadly. In the telecommunications sector, it is useful to distinguish "networks" startups from "services" startups. Networks startups, for example, increase bandwidth or administer bandwidth so as to offer greater speed of access and navigation on the Internet and eventually guaranteed service quality. IP/telephone gateways and security mechanisms are additional niches for networks startups. In contrast, services startups develop new uses or harness the Internet to transform traditional activities. Startups have twofold expectations of telecommunications operators: support for development and the commercial leverage effect. For networks startups, research centers and telecommunications operators offer an opportunity to rigorously test their innovation and validate their technical offering. Beyond testing, networks startups can expect an operator laboratory to co-develop a new product or service and to promote, if applicable, this initiative jointly with international standardization authorities or on the market. Startups also expect from an operator a sign of technical or commercial recognition (such as acceptance of an experiment), which will enable them, by means of particularly aggressive external communication to achieve significant progress in raising awareness and meeting investors' expectations. Services startups expect from telecommunications operators a commercial leverage effect vis-à-vis their customers. They are also aware of their weaknesses in terms of the operators' investment capacity in a technical infrastructure (hosting and transmission). They seek partnerships with operators to enable them to promote their edge or originality in marketing without having to assume substantial investments to deploy their solutions. This upstream cooperation is also advantageous in that it enables the operator during the joint testing, experimentation and development phase to enhance the innovation of the functionalities it considers worthwhile.

Changes in modes of cooperation with industrial players in the telecommunications sector are also perceivable. To capture the network dimension of the Internet paradigm, collaboration with manufacturers of telecommunications equipment is vital. Indeed, an innovation in a service offering is heavily contingent on the technical evolution of systems, which comprises two essential components: the technology of components and software technology. Inversely, a new product will find a market only if it is associated with a service or a line of services.

Moreover, given that the first principal service required to position a company on the Internet market is that of access, it is natural that operators turn to suppliers of access (or access providers), who provide the final customer with access to a network. The importance of customer contact underlies the acquisition by conventional operators of an Internet Service Provider (ISP) already present on the market, which has been a regular occurrence for the past five years.

At the level of an economic player, we assume that this process of qualification of key success factors is an important step to identify subprojects and assignments needed to meet the goal of the project: creation of new competencies. In the next section, we show that it is possible to quantify a specific factor and test which variable the team project has to mobilize.

CREATION OF COMPETENCIES AND LEVEL OF DEPENDENCE

We will test whether obtaining and controlling resources (factors 3 and 4) allow the creation of competencies to adapt to changes in the environment.

Factors Related to Obtain and Control Resources

Obtaining and controlling critical resources, as a response to the nature and the technological environment, can be measured by R&D investments and multiplicity of technological alliances. This multiplicity implies to identify the type of technological alliance and/or the way to choose equity-based governance modes (joint venture, acquisitions or minority investments) to structure technological collaboration.

Factors Related to Creation of Competencies

Based on Nicholls-Nixon (1995), we believe that the creation of competencies can be evaluated by the number of patents held in the new technology domain, the number of products based on new technology on the market, and the reputation of the company in the new technology sector. We have retained the number of patents because it translates an aptitude to master a new technological domain by proposing original solutions. The number of products reflects the capacity of a company to systematically apply all forms of organized or scientific knowledge to practical tasks. Lastly, we have added the measure of technical expertise of the company, which corresponds to the judgment of the industry of a particular player.

MEASUREMENT FACTORS

In the case of telecommunications operators and the emergence of the Internet, we consider that the creation of competencies, namely a measure of the extent to which a company succeeds in acquiring the tools, expertise, and knowledge related to a new technological paradigm, can be determined by: the number of patents that the company holds related to IP technologies (PAT), the number of products developed on IP technologies that the company possesses on the market (PRO), and the company's reputation or expertise in the domain of the Internet (EXP). The factors related to obtaining and controlling resources for telecommunications operators can be measured by:

- The intensity of internal R&D related to the Internet measured by the proportion of total R&D expenses allocated to IP technologies. The data pertaining to the intensity of internal R&D have been aggregated over two time periods 1989–1993 (RDI1) and 1994–1998 (RDI2).
- Intensity of alliances (TALL) is measured by the total number of alliances created by an operator.
- The distinction between different contractual forms of an alliance have led us to introduce: the number of licenses (LIC), the number of research contracts (CONTRD), joint ventures (JV), the number of acquisitions (ACQ), the number of minority equity investments (MEI), and the number of R&D partnerships (PARD).
- Use of equity-based governance modes (joint venture, acquisitions, or minority investments) is measured by the frequency of use of equity alliances over two time periods, 1989–1993 and 1994–1998, in the following cases: alliance based on an interval of knowledge between the partners (FIN1 and FIN2), alliance of R&D collaboration (FCOL1 and FCOL2), alliance of R&D collaboration related to downstream activities (FRDC01 and FRDC02).

Data Collection

The selection of the sample integrated a number of constraints. By its nature, this research could retain only telecommunications operators that have sufficiently large international activities in a proprietary communication network, that is, a set of infrastructures capable of routing voice communications at a standard rate of quality for the telecommunications world (99.99 percent), along with R&D activities. The presence of at least one R&D activity implies that the company size is relatively large, notably to carry out research in the IP domain apart from research concerning fixed telephone systems. As a result, the sample was limited to companies whose sales in 1997 were higher than $1 billion. The data analyzed in our study are taken from the design and administration of a questionnaire that contains a set of quantitative and qualitative independent variables that define relations with a quantitative dependent variable (creation of competencies).

STATISTICAL ANALYSIS METHOD

Because of the small sample size, we have used nonparametric methods to determine the independent variables that have a significant effect on the dependent variables. To this effect, we will use two statistical techniques: the Wilcoxon test and one-factor analysis of variance (ANOVA). The operators have been characterized as having high creation of competencies if at least two of the following dependent variables, namely PRO, BRE, and EXP, were above the respective median of each of these variables. In the opposite case, the operators were characterized as having low creation of competencies.

RESULTS AND DISCUSSION

Table 22.1 presents a summary of the results obtained by the different methods.[5] If the level of internal investment in R&D effectively promotes the creation of competencies of a telecommunications operator, it is interesting to note that only investments in internal R&D for the period of 1994–1998 have a significant effect on the three measures of creation of competencies. Internal R&D investments for the period of 1989–1993 have a significant effect only on one measure of creation of competencies, the expertise of the operator. This can be explained by a short TAT (Turn Around Time) in the Internet domain. For example, the Japanese company NTT perceived the importance of the Internet in late 1994. One and a half years later it launched OCN, its information transmission network (Internet Service Provider) and thus increased the number of subscribers from 1.5 million in late 1995 to 8.5 million in late 1996.[6] This relatively short "commercialization" time explains why some operators who had not invested heavily in internal R&D for the period 1989–1993 are nonetheless characterized by substantial creation of competencies, particularly owing to investments in internal R&D for the period 1994–1998.

The total number of alliances signed by an operator has a significant effect on the three measures of creation of competencies. However, this result should be qualified by considering the results of the organizational forms of these alliances, which allow identification of different conditions or organizational arrangements having shaped the development of a new technical network. We can thus observe that telecommunications operators that have created competencies have a higher number of alliances in three of the six types of alliances that we have retained: LIC, PARD, and ACQ.

The variable (LIC), as shown in the variance analysis of this factor, has no significant effect on the variable (PRO). This result is due to the fact that these licenses cover software package aspects, and are used as a development base for services. In fact, we have decided to consider the variable (PRO) as reflecting the purely technological dimension of development on all types of telecommunication infrastructures. It should also be noted that the ACQ variable had no significant effect on the PRO variable. This result is logical given that most acquisitions by telecommunications operators involve ISPs.

Operators characterized by high creation of competencies have a greater number of PARD (mainly with computer manufacturers and telecommunication

TABLE 22-1.   Summary of statistical analyses for creation of competencies

Determinants of Creation of Competencies	Wilcoxon Test	Measures of Creation of Competencies		
		Number of Patents	Number of Products	Degree of Reputation
		PAT	PROD	EXP
Internal R & D				
Intensity of internal R&D				
RDI1	H_1	ns	ns	+
RDI2	H_1	+	+	+
Technological Alliances				
Variety of alliances				
TALL	H_1	+	+	+
Type of alliances formed				
LIC	H_1	+	ns	+
CONRD	H_1	ns	ns	ns
JV	H_0	ns	ns	ns
ACQ	H_1	+	ns	+
MEI	H_0	ns	ns	ns
PARD	H_1	+	+	+
Management Mode of Alliances				
Knowledge interval between partners				
FIN1	H_1	+	+	+
FIN2	H_1	+	+	+
R&D collaboration				
FCOL1	H_1	ns	ns	+
FCOL2	H_1	ns	+	+
R&D collaboration and downstream activities				
FRDCO1	H_1	+	ns	+
FRDCO2	H_1	+	+	+

suppliers). This finding is quite logical, considering that convergence around transmission of a digital signal necessarily calls for the bridging of industries, usages and networks.

In contrast, the variable (CONRD) did not have a significant effect on the measures of creation of competencies. In fact, most research contracts were signed between 1997 and 1998. Some cover specific developments that will engender patentable innovations in the months to come. In other cases, they consist of partnerships for five- or ten-year fundamental research programs aimed at developing new architectures, protocols, and applications for high-speed, next-generation networks, new technologies for interconnected personal computer interfaces in networks or software solutions for large-scale network systems.

Furthermore, we did not find a significant relation between creation of competencies and the number of joint ventures (JV). In our opinion, this situation is particular to the telecommunications sector and to strategic movements it has experienced since the 1980s. The telecommunications sector has witnessed an incredible number of agreements, particularly in the United States, obliged to form these alliances owing to a segmented market. Nonetheless, the failure of numerous attempts has compelled partners to be more rigorous with regard to the composition and objectives of their alliances. Joint ventures in the telecommunications domain have thus gravitated considerably toward the union of forces to conquer a particular clientele or specific geographic zone. In fact, this type of alliance is more prevalent in downstream activities (distribution and commercialization) than R&D. For example, the joint venture Global One created by France Telecom, Sprint, and Deutsche Telekom proposes a purely commercial IP offering (Global IP). In the area of R&D, other types of agreements have been put in place between these three partners. The research laboratory of France Telecom, operating in Silicon Valley since 1997, has signed a research partnership agreement with Deutsche Telekom Advanced Solutions (DTAS), a subsidiary of the R&D branch of Deutsche Telekom, located in Palo Alto, California. Furthermore, France Telecom signed a research contract with the research and development center of Sprint (Advanced Technology Labs) and the University of California at Berkeley for development of transactional software solutions.

In addition, we did not find a significant relation between the creation of competencies and the number of collaborations with startups. This counterintuitive result is explained by the fact that risk capital companies developed by telecommunications operators have been, from the start, designed and managed as classic risk capital corporations with the mission of financing young companies whose growth potential is expected to generate solid financial performance. The few operators that created risk capital structures have mainly focused on financial returns to the detriment of integration of technical advances.

Lastly, the final analyses confirm that in a situation where an operator and its partner possess the same internal level of technological expertise regarding what is to be exchanged, the learning prerequisites are low. The operators therefore do not need to establish strong organizational arrangements associated with equity management modes to facilitate the technological transfer. Yet the change in technological paradigm has propelled most operators into an asymmetric position in relation to the internal technical expertise on technologies to exchange, thus increasing the learning prerequisites.

CONCLUSION

As we have underlined in our introduction, the converging environment linked to the development of the Internet push players concerned to assume a recurrent process: a project of creating competencies. The scope of this project is to bring some players to collaborate over the short term, thus to create a unique product or service. In order to implement a project of creating competencies, we have identified, based on the Resource Dependency theory, four key success factors to achieve the project. We have shown the nature of these factors for a specific economic player: telecommunications operators. In this case, our empirical research shows the positive impact of these factors on the project goal. Obviously, we do not suggest a specific methodology for this type of project management, but we capture and specify, through these factors and their positive contribution to the project, some key elements of project management: resources, risks, subprojects. For example, we hope that our contribution will help executives to identify key issues in the development of mobile applications.

NOTES

1. See Erkki K. Laitinen (2000).

2. For a detailed review of project group dynamics, see Sivathanu and Rao (2000).

3. By composition, we are referring to variables such as size, duration of history, and objectives.

4. Packet of data that circulates in a TCP-IP network. The IP datagram consists of the address of the source computer, that of the destination computer and data, in compliance with the Internet protocol.

5. For each of the independent variables, we obtained: the hypothesis examined by means of the Wilcoxon test that cannot be rejected (h_0 indicating that independent variable considered is distributed in the same way in groups 1 and 2; and h_1: indicating that the independent variable considered has significantly lower values in group 1 than in group 2). The value of the coefficient of significance resulting from an ANOVA associated with each independent variable in relation to each dependent variable (in the case where the coefficient of significance is below the critical threshold level of $\alpha = 0.05$, it is noted as +, in the opposite case, it is noted as ns).

6. Source: Kiyohisa Ota, director of Merrill Lynch's Japan research team.

BIBLIOGRAPHY

Heck, Mike. 1996. Team Manager Boosts Exchange. *InfoWorld*, October 14, 99.

Laitinen, Erkki K. 2000. Long-Term Success of Adaptation Strategies: Evidence from Finnish Companies. *Long Range Planning*, December, 805–30.

Nicholls-Nixon, Charlene. 1995. Responding to Technological Change: Why Some Firms Do and Others Die. *Journal of High Technology Management Research* 6(1): 1–16.

Pfeffer, Jeffrey, and Gerald R. Salancik. 1978. *The External Control of Organizations, a Resource Dependence Perspective*. New York: Harper & Row.

Sivathanu, Pillai A., and K. Srinivasa Rao. 2000. High Technology Product Development: Technical and Management Review System. *International Journal of Technology Management* 19(7–8): 685–98.

23

Agile Project Management Methods for IT Projects

GLEN B. ALLEMAN

The difference between failure and success is the difference between doing something almost right and doing something right.

—Benjamin Franklin

A gile project management methodologies used to develop, deploy, or acquire information technology systems have begun to enter the vocabulary of modern organizations, much in the same way lightweight and agile manufacturing or business management processes have over the past few years. This chapter is about applying Agile methods in an environment that may be more familiar with high ceremony project management methods—methods that might be considered heavy weight in terms of today's Agile vocabulary.

High ceremony projects are those based on formal or semiformal project management methods, ones like Prince2.[1] PMI's PMBOK,[2] or processes based on the Software Engineering Institute's Capability Maturity Model.[3] These methods are traditionally associated with organizations that operate in software engineering-centric business domains. These domains view software activities as an engineering process, rather than a creative process based on the skill of individuals or small teams.

Organizations with mature processes often define their activities in a formal manner, applying methods with rigor and monitoring the processes and results carefully. These practices are usually constructed over time and evolve through direct experiences—either good or bad. Many times, they follow the formal structure of the underlying business process. It is common to talk about Agile methods for modern project management processes in the context of a set of lightweight activities used to manage the development or acquisition of software. These activities include requirements, design, coding, and testing processes based on a minimal set of activities needed to reach the end goal—a working software system.[4]

Although some of these Agile development methods address the management aspects of software projects—people, processes, and technology—they are primarily focused on coding, testing, and software artifact delivery.[5] Applying the concept of agility to the management of a software project is a natural step in the evolution of software development. One important question to be asked though is how can these minimalist approaches be applied to traditional project management activities? What project management process simplifications are appropriate for a specific problem domain?

Are all lightweight and agile project management process steps applicable to specific problem domains? If not which steps are applicable to which domains?[6]

WEIGHT VERSUS AGILITY

In the information technology project management literature, lightweight is often defined as not heavyweight, which is a tautology. Over time, lightweight has been superseded in the trade press and literature by the term Agile. Lightweight and Agile are not interchangeable words, however. This distinction is not well understood by many Agile proponents, so some clarification is needed here before we proceed.

Lightweight describes the weightiness of the process and its artifacts, the amount of potentially nonvalue added artifacts produced by a specific process. This weightiness can be attributed to the undesirable consequences of the process, artifacts that do not provide benefit to the outcome. This weightiness can also be attributed to the misapplication of a specific process. Agility describes the behavior of the participants and their ability to move or adjust in new and possibly unforeseen situations. Much like an overweight boat, airplane, or athlete, the undesirable weight needs to be removed in order to increase the efficiency of the vehicle. This is a standard best practice in many engineering disciplines. One problem with this analogy though is that anyone suggesting a specific methodology is over weight must answer the question: If a project management method were properly applied, in the proper domain, to the proper set of problems, with properly trained participants, would it be considered overweight and produce undesirable consequences? The usual answer is no, of course not. If everyone were doing their job properly, in the proper engineering, regulatory, and contractual environment, then the results would be accepted by all the participants. This is the definition of a tautology.

The problem of Agile project management methodology selection is compounded by the behaviors of the method as well as the behaviors of the participants using the method. In addition, the appropriateness of the method for a specific problem domain remains an issue. Making a process lightweight by removing activities or artifacts is most likely inappropriate and a possible source for project failure without careful consideration of the consequences.

PROJECT MANAGEMENT FRAMEWORK

According to the Software Engineering Institute (SEI), a methodology must posses certain attributes in order to meet the requirements of being called a methodology.[7] Another framework for methodologies is the Software Engineering Body of Knowledge (SWEBOK) that contains the knowledge development methods to be used by any professional software engineer.[8] For the moment, we will focus on the SEI's description of the software project attributes (figure 23.1).

Both, describes how these attributes could be related in an Agile project management method.[9] This structure is a process pattern view of project activities.[10] This approach focuses on the communication and people-centric aspects of project management. Agile project management can be built on this framework.

THE AGILE SOFTWARE DELIVERY PROCESS

Agile processes emphasize both the rapid and flexible adaptation to changes in the process, the product, and the development environment.[11] This is a very general definition and therefore not very useful without some specific context.

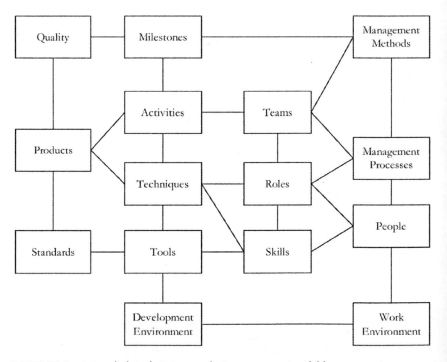

FIGURE 23-1. Interrelations between project management activities.

Before establishing this context, Agile processes include three major attributes, they are:

- Incremental and Evolutionary—allowing adaptation to both internal and external events.
- Modular and Lean—allowing components of the process to come and go depending on specific needs if the participants and stakeholders.
- Time Based—built on iterative and concurrent work cycles, which contain feedback loops and progress checkpoints.

Common Problems with All Software Projects

The National Software Quality Experiment has been conducted each year since 1992. Table 23.1 shows observations recurring over the years.[12]

The Problem of Change

Change is continuous in the business world, at all levels within an organization or marketplace. Change by itself is not the problem. The world is always changing. It always has been changing. It always will be changing. Businesses and the processes they use have always had to adapt to this changing world. Often changes in the past have occurred incrementally. When a radical change took place, the next change event was slow in coming. While there has always been uncertainty in business, it was usually not significant or sustained.

The problem in today's world is that change is no longer incremental or even linear. Radical nonlinear changes occur in the normal course of business. The pace of change is not only increasing, sustained uncertainty is now commonplace. Dealing with this new nonlinear change environment is the goal of Agile methods.

Ready for Agility?

All organizations face problems that can be addressed by Agile methods, but not all companies are ready for the radical ideas needed to become an Agile organization. Agility is still an emerging topic and is at the stage where it is not possible to buy an off-the-shelf solution that has been shown to behave in the same manner as heavier weight processes.[13] Elements of agility can certainly be found in many processes, but as the saying goes—*one swallow does not a summer make.*[14]

The introduction of an Agile process should only be undertaken by organizations that are risk aware if not risk averse. Organizations that need answers and concepts that are fully developed and result in a solution that can be implemented with little risk should carefully examine Agile processes before jumping in. The irony is though—there is no such process that can deliver a fully developed plan resulting in a fully developed project or product, let alone one that can be deployed without risk.

TABLE 23-1. National software quality experiment results

Common Problem	Consequences
Software product source code components are not traced to requirements.	Software product is not under the control and the verification procedures are imprecise. Changes cannot be managed in a controlled manner.
Software engineering practices are not applied in a systematic manner.	Defect rates are unacceptable.
Product designs and source are managed in an ad hoc manner	The understandability, maintainability, and adaptability of the product is negatively impacted.
The construction processes for the product are not clearly defined.	Common patterns of the processes are not exploited.
Rapidly changing code base has become the norm.	The code base services the only the short-term benefits and mortgages the future where traceable baseline requirements, specifications, and design artifacts are the foundations of success.

The Forces Driving Agility

Software acquisition and deployment are generally driven by a need to solve a specific problem, to do things better, to modify or improve a business or technical process. The software development process community has two schools of thought regarding the outcome of these efforts: things are getting better, things are getting worse. This conflicting set of opinions adds more confusion to an already confusing question of—are we actually improving the outcome of the software by improving the management processes?

A few years ago, methodologies and processes were the domain of academics. The methodology zoo has grown however and at the same time become focused on the commercial aspects of selling these methodologies to anxious managers, developers, and stakeholders. This selling process has, in many cases, overtaken the rational application of these methods of specific problem domains.

PRACTICAL AGILE PROJECT MANAGEMENT

The deployment of an Agile project management methodology in an existing organization faces several obstacles:

- The legacy project management processes must be displaced in some way to make room for the new process.
- The gaps that existed in the legacy process must be filled with the new process while maintaining the integrity provided by the legacy process.

Common Threads of These Methods

In an attempt to simplify the many attributes of the methods, a list of common threads can be built, using the software project attributes (table 23.2) as a framework.

Is Agile Yet Another Software Methodology Taxonomy?

Before selecting a software development method, some understanding of what type of software is to be developed is appropriate (table 23.3).[15] By partitioning software system into types, the appropriateness question can be addressed—what project management methods are appropriate for what problem domains?

FRAMEWORK FOR AGILE PROJECT MANAGEMENT METHODS

A framework for deploying Agile project management processes provides a descriptive guideline rather than a proscriptive set of rules. This framework approach provides the user a broader set of recommendations than is

TABLE 23-2. Common aspects of all methods

Thread	Compliance
Requirements Gathering	Some method of gathering requirements is needed.
Software Development or Procurement	Software must be developed (or procured) that meets the requirements.
Testing	Component and system testing are performed in some structured manner.
Personnel Management	The management of personnel is provided in some methods, but not all.
Project Management	Some means of defining tasks, measuring progress, providing feedback, and changing the course of the participants.

found in any particular named methodology. This framework is based on two foundations:

- The Software Program Managers Network Nine Best Practices[16]—which provides guidelines for project managers using practical suggestions for daily application.
- Scott Ambler's Agile Modeling framework—which provides a broad framework for creating Agile processes applied to software projects.[17]

TABLE 23-3. Software systems taxonomy

Software Type	Attributes
Management Information Systems	Software that an enterprise uses to support business and administrative operations.
Outsourced Systems	Software projects built for client organizations.
Systems Software	Software that controls a physical device such as a computer or a telephone switch.
Commercial Software	Software applications that are marketed to hundreds or even millions of clients.
Military Software	Software produced for the uniformed services.
End-User Software	Small applications written for personal use.
Web Application and e–Projects	Small-, medium-, and large-scale projects with legacy system integration, transaction processing, multimedia delivery, and Web browser-based user interfaces

AGILE PROJECT MANAGEMENT GUIDELINES

Building on the Software Program Managers Nine Best Practices, the well-established project management methods of the past, the fundamentals of any project management method, and finally common sense, a framework for Agile Project Management can be built.

Values of Agile Project Management

Before the principles of Agile Project Management can be defined, a set of underlying values is useful.

- Communication—of information within and outside an Agile project is constant. It is the responsibility of the project manager to ensure that the communication occurs effectively, clearly, and in a timely manner between the management, the contributors, and the stakeholders. Since change is constant in an Agile project, constant communication is the only means of maintaining the connections between all the participants. Going dark for any significant amount of time is simply not allowed.
- Simplicity—defines the approach to identifying the critical success factors of the project in terms of the simplest possible solution. All activities must contribute a measurable value to the project management process. Measuring the value of a project management artifact is the role of the stakeholders and the project manager. This is done by asking what is the value of this specific task, artifact, or project deliverable?
- Feedback—"optimism is an occupational hazard of software development, feedback is the cure."[18] Continuous feedback is a primary tool for defining and sustaining Agility.
- Courage—all important decisions and changes in the direction of the project need to be made with the courage. Change is part of any realistic information technology project. Dealing with the consequences of change or discarding the outcome when the decision is proven inadequate requires courage.
- Humility—the best project managers acknowledge they do not know everything. The stakeholders, project participants, and customers all have their own areas of expertise and add value to the project. An effective approach is to assume that everyone involved with the project has equal value and therefore should be treated with respect.

APPLYING AGILE PRINCIPLES IN PRACTICE

Applying these principles in practice creates the foundation for managing information technology projects in an Agile manner.

- Assume Simplicity—as the project evolves it should be assumed that the simplest solution is the best solution.[19] Overbuilding the system or any artifact of the project must be avoided. The project manager should have the courage to not perform a task or produce an artifact that is not clearly stated in the requirements as needed for the immediate benefit of the stakeholders.

- Embrace Change—since requirements evolve over time. The stakeholder understanding of the requirements will change over time. Project stakeholders themselves may change as the project makes progress. Project stakeholders may change their point of view, which in turn will change the goals and success criteria of the project management effort.
- Enabling the Next Effort is Also a Goal—the project can still be considered a failure even when the team delivers a working system to the users. Part of fulfilling the needs of the project stakeholders is to ensure that the system is robust enough to be extended over time. Using Alistair Cockburn concept, "when you are playing the software development game your secondary goal is to setup to play the next game."[20] The next phase may be the development of a major release of the system or it may simply be the operation and support of the current version of the system.
- Incremental Change—the pressure to get it right the first time can overwhelm the best project manager. Instead of futilely trying to develop an all encompassing project plan from the start, put a stake in the ground by developing a small portion of the system, or even a high-level model of a larger portion of the system, and evolve this portion over time. Or simply discard it when you no longer need it in an incremental manner.
- Maximize Stakeholder Value—the project stakeholders are investing resources— time, money, facilities, and so forth—to have a system deployed that meets their needs. Stakeholders expect their investment to be applied in the best way. By continually asking "how does this process or feature improve stakeholder value?" an Agile process can develop its own value generating processes.
- Manage with a Purpose—create artifacts of the project management process that have stakeholder value. Identify why and for whom the artifact is created. Identify a valid purpose for creating the artifact and the audience for that artifact. This principle also applies to the change to an existing artifact.
- Multiple Project Views—provide different views of the same process for different audiences. Considering the complexity of any modern information technology system construction or acquisition process, there is a need for a wide range of presentation formats in order to effectively communicate with the stakeholders, participants, and providers.
- Rapid Feedback—the time between an action and the feedback on that action must be minimized. Work closely with the stakeholders, to understand the requirements, to analyze those requirements, and develop an actionable plan, which provides numerous opportunities for feedback.
- Working Software Is the Primary Goal of the Project—the goal of any software project is to produce software that meets the needs of the project stakeholders. The goal is not to produce extraneous documentation, management artifacts, or even models of these artifacts. Any activity that does not directly contribute to the goal of producing a working system should be examined.
- Travel Light—every artifact that is created, and kept, will need to be maintained over its life cycle. The effort needed to maintain these artifacts must be balanced with their value. Not only must the effort be considered, but the risk that the artifact will create confusion over time if it is not properly maintained must be considered.

RECOMMENDATIONS TO PRACTITIONERS

Make incremental change to the requirements, project plan system, and the resulting artifacts to enable agility.

- Strive for rapid feedback to ensure the project meets the needs of all the participants and stakeholder.
- Manage with a purpose, performing only those tasks that add value to business processes supported by the system.
- Travel light, discarding processes and artifacts that do not add enduring value to the product—a working software system.

CONCLUSION

The field of Agile methods is evolving rapidly, probably too rapidly for a book-length discussion. The reader is referred to materials found in profession journals such as those published by the IEEE and ACM. Business publications as well as practice journals such as STSC's *Crosstalk* have taken up this topic as well. Numerous newsgroups and Web forums also provide information on Agile method. In the end, the applicability of an Agile method needs to be carefully considered. Choosing the proper domain is as important as choosing the proper method.

NOTES

1. Projects IN Controlled Environments (PRINCE) is a structured project management method used in the United Kingdom.

2. Project Management Body of Knowledge (PMBOK) is an ANSI Standard PMI-99-001-2000 describing the various attributes of a project management method.

3. Capability Maturity Model is a collection of model frameworks for assessing the maturity of a specific practice. Key Practice Areas are used to define the various levels of maturity. CMM now consists of: Software, People, Software Acquisition, Systems Engineering, and Integrated Product Development. The models are supported by a software process assessment standard ISO/IEC 15504.

4. SCRUM, DSDM, Crystal, Adaptive Software Development, and Extreme Programming.

5. Some proponents of these lightweight methods contend delivery of software is the only goal. Although this is an obvious outcome of the programming and integration process, there are many other deliverable artifacts associated with large-scale software projects.

6. Capers Jones's *Software Assessments, Benchmarks, and Best Practices* provides a taxonomy that is useful for defining the various domains. Management Information Systems, Outsourced systems, Systems software, Commercial software, Military software, End-User software, and Web applications, and e–project.

7. Software Development Taxonomy, www.sei.cmu.edu/legacy/kit/taxonomy.html.

8. www.swebok.org.

9. A Methodology per Project, Alistair Cockburn, Humans and Technology Technical Report, TR 99.04, October 1999. http://www.crystalmethodologies.org/articles/mpp/methodologyperproject.html

10. One source of process patterns is http://i44pc48.info.uni-karlsruhe.de/cgi-bin/OrgPatterns.

11. Aoyama, Mikio, New Age of Software Development: How Component Based Software Engineering Changes the Way of Software Development, *1998 International Workshop on Competent-Based Software Engineering,* 1998. Aoyama, Mikio, "Agile Software Process and Its Experience," *International Conference on Software Engineering,* 1998.

12. In 1992, the DOD Software Technology Strategy set the objective to reduce software problem rates by a factor of ten by the year 2000. The National Software Quality Experiment is a mechanism for obtaining core samples of software product quality. This national database provides the means to benchmark and measure progress towards the national software quality objective and contains data from 1992 through 1998.The centerpiece of the experiment is the Software Inspection Lab where data collection procedures, product checklists, and participant behaviors are packaged for operational project use. The uniform application of the experiment and the collection of consistent measurements are guaranteed through rigorous training of each participant.

13. This of course is not the contention of XP, SCRUM, ASD, and other lightweight, and now *Agile* processes. But these processes have yet to enter the stage where analytical evidence has been gathered to support the contention they produce superior results when compared to their less–lightweight cousins. This continuing debate will not be resolved in this short chapter.

14. This English proverb can be traced to a Greek proverb. In the ancient world birds were associated with the household gods and their presence was looked upon as fortuitous. Any harm done to them would bode evil for the household.

15. Jones, Capers, *Software Assessments, Benchmarks, and Best Practices,* Addison Wesley, 2000. This partitioning is not unique, but it is based on an underlying assumption that there are fundamental differences between problem domains.

16. www.spmn.com.

17. Ambler, Scott, Agile Modeling, www.agilemodeling.com. *Process Patterns: Building Large–Scale Systems Using Object Technology,* Scott Ambler, Cambridge University Press, 1998. *More Process Patterns: Delivering Large–Scale Systems Using Object Technology,* Scott Ambler, Cambridge University Press, 1999.

18. Beck, Kent, *Extreme Programming Explained,* Addison Wesley, 1999.

19. This may not always be the case but it is a good starting point.

20. http://crystalmethodologies.org/.

24

Implementing Best Practice
in Hospital Project Management

RAPHAEL M. DUA

The impact of project management on a hospital's competitive capability has not normally been seen as a benefit in the Healthcare services sector. The ability to muddle through a project using "me-too" products have placed a major premium on Healthcare providers' abilities to develop the support infrastructure to enable government program initiatives to be taken rapidly from development to delivery.

The federal and state governments' push in cost reduction processes has led to a growing appreciation of the need for a project management culture as business-critical care projects have come increasingly under the spotlight—a process accentuated by legislation-driven systems demands. Thus there is now a growing demand for project management within the industry, which must be met by companies who have a good understanding of all of the issues faced in Healthcare provision. The most important aspect besides achieving delivery on time and on budget is to ensure that all the inherent risks have been properly defined and will be well managed. What is meant by project management and what does it consist of? In itself, project management means many things to many people and is a huge subject. I will outline some of what I believe to be the more important elements due to the limitations of time of this presentation.

WHAT IS PROJECT MANAGEMENT?

Project Management Elements

Project management covers a wide area of skills and consists of a number of major elements as defined by the Project Managers Body of Knowledge, generally known as the PMBOK.

What is a Project? An Overview

A project may be defined as: "an entity in which people, resources of all forms are organised, in special way, to embark on a unique scope of work, from a defined specification, within the constraints of cost and time and resources, to achieve a beneficial outcome defined by quantitative and qualitative measures." The most important features of a project are its uniqueness and the need generally for special organization to achieve an advantageous change. Projects need to be evaluated against expected gains before the project is initiated. Many projects, which are not planned properly at the outset, are doomed to failure before they even commence and so carry a great business risk.

Structured project management techniques provide a framework for project management tools to operate. They concentrate on the definition of the project objective, determining the project organization, problem solving, and life cycle structures and the correct level of information for each part of the project structure.

The project organization and the conflicts it brings to the functional structure of a hospital have been highlighted in the past. A key role of the project manager is to come to terms with the fact that they rarely have the authority to call on resources as required, and they must negotiate with departmental managers for their cooperation. As there is little political kudos to be gained by the departmental manager, this proves to be a major hurdle to effective project management.

Projects do go wrong. However, project problems are normally due to a lack of clear objectives, poor organizational design, informal communication methods, and inadequate structured planning and risk control processes. A project could be considered to be similar to a badly behaved infant. It may well behave itself when your full attention is being given but misbehave the moment your back is turned, leaving you to wonder where you went wrong.

Risk Management Element

One of the most important areas of project management, which is not executed as often as it should be, is the risk management process and techniques, which also includes risk analysis for which the project manager needs to be practiced. There are a number of risk analysis techniques, but few, if any properly documented risk management techniques. Risk analysis techniques included sensitivity tools such as sensitivity models, Monte Carlo analysis, PERT analysis, decision trees and risk models.

As stated before, projects invariably will go wrong. The role of a project manager is to predict the potential risks to the success of the project and manage their effects before they become overwhelming. However, good decision making and management does not guarantee a good outcome—it only improves the chances. The management of risk in a project begins with its identification and analysis. The project manager can minimize the management risks in the project by ensuring that the right level of project scope and objectives, organization, planning, coordination, and control have been defined in a project charter. A major section of the project charter will provide a definition of the project brief and is a core element of effective risk, management.

It does not take a genius to know that a project has a great risk of failure if the scope and objectives are not right and not developed properly. If its objectives, standards, technical base, and general strategic planning are inadequately considered or poorly developed, the project is almost certainly destined to fail. It is critical that the design and construction are firmly managed in line with the strategic plans. The project charter clearly annunciates both effects and affects of risk in the project in its external environment (such as politics, community views, economic and site conditions, availability of financing and project phasing, and duration). It contains all the necessary definitions, interaction with those external financial, and other matters. If it is not implemented, it indicates that the project will be much harder to manage.

The importance of good project management practice in the management of risk cannot be overemphasized. However, as we know, some of the risks in Healthcare projects are unique to that activity. For example, ensuring infection control programs produce the desired results quickly. However similar projects may appear there will always be differences in the environment and the effect it has.

Best practice project management suggests that the project manager must separate the role of risk analysis from that of management. However, it is not intended to suggest that one process follow the other and when complete should not be addressed again. Project planning, risk analysis and management are an ongoing process that is best addressed as near to the event in time. This does not mean that risks should be ignored until the risk event occurs; rather that it should consider the problems of tomorrow with more effort than that spent on the problems that might occur further down the track.

Risk management must consider the importance of contingency planning for both financial and time reasons. Such planning includes the assignment of responsibilities, multilevel responses, and risk trigger setting. The importance of regular reviews and tracking is a must along with a reporting mechanism, which will ensure that all the interested project parties are fully appraise of the projects status.

The project manager must keep the right balance on the amount of effort applied in the risk management of the project. Like planning and scheduling, we run into the law of diminishing returns with project risk management. Doubling the time spent on risk analysis does not mean that the overall risk will be minimized by a further 50 percent. You are all familiar with the old 80/20 adage (80 percent of the benefit for 20 percent of the effort). The process of examining risk will provide great benefits for the minimum of effort.

Many people try to manage a project without risk analysis or project management, but empirical evidence as detailed by both KPMG and the Standish Group clearly shows that they have no control over the project and they fail. The project manager will increase their chances of successful delivery by using both project and risk management techniques, but by failing to do so hope to perform by leaving things to chance!

Negotiation Element

Many types of negotiation take place throughout the life cycle of a project, in which the project manager will take a prominent role. Negotiation is one of the many skills that a successful project manager must possess. A great deal of a project manager's time is taken up in making deals with various vendors, subcontractors, and clients in order to keep the project on track. Negotiation is about bargaining to reach a mutually acceptable outcome often known as a Win/Win situation. A good negotiator has to learn and practice the skill of negotiation; the bargaining objectives are often lost by a single careless act.

WHAT IS EARNED VALUE PERFORMANCE MANAGEMENT?

Earned Value Performance Management (EVPM) provides senior management with an accurate overview of corporate performance. It builds on the information provided by traditional scheduling techniques to plan and measure the overall productivity of a project. EVPM, through the Performance Measurement Baseline, provides focus on the bottom line assessment as to whether the plan is being implemented effectively or not and highlights problems at an early stage allowing effective management intervention. It is an objective measurement of how much work has been accomplished on a project. Earned Value Performance Measurement, Management by Objectives, and Cost Schedule Control Systems are synonymous terms. These terms have been defined in US DODI 5000.2R, BS6079 and Australian Def (AUST) 5655. Earned Value improves on the "normally used" spend plan concept (budget versus actual incurred cost) by requiring the work in process to be quantified. A major element in the definition of work to be measured is the work breakdown structure (WBS).

A WBS is developed to segregate the work scope requirements of the program into definable product elements and related services and data. The WBS is a direct representation of the work scope defined in the program statement of work and breaks that work scope into appropriate elements for cost accounting and work authorization. It is a multilevel hierarchical breakdown that shows how program costs are summarized from the lower elements to the total program level. The extent of decomposition and levels in the WBS will be determined by program management needs and contractual arrangements.

By implementing the earned value process, management can simply compare how much work has actually been completed against the amount of work planned to be accomplished. Earned value requires the project manager to plan, budget, and schedule the authorized work scope in a time-phased plan. The time phased plan in the form of a critical path network is the incremental "planned value," culminating into a performance measurement baseline. As work is accomplished, it is "earned," using the same selected budget term. Earned value compared with planned value provides a work accomplished against plan. A variance to the plan is noted as a schedule or cost deviation.

Planned Value, Earned Value, and Actual Cost data provides an objective measurement of performance, enabling trend analysis and evaluation of cost estimate at completion within multiple levels of the project. Earned Value Performance Management should be applied to every project where the owners of the final product wish to ensure that the expended resources were used efficiently. On major projects, the application of good project management tools will aid in the selection of the right course when managers need to make financial and time allocation decisions.

The key elements of performance measurement are:

- The measurement of absolute figures or just variance does not give an indication of the current status of the project.
- The value of the work obtained for the effort and resource consumed is the only true measure of project progress.
- The use of the WBS allows the project manager to focus on the parts of the project that are showing the greatest deviation. Care should be taken when considering the project as a whole. Often large negative deviations in one area are smothered by cumulative small positive deviations in other areas.
- Performance measures can be used to predict the final success, or otherwise, of the project at completion. Trend analysis is a vital component of the project manager's toolbox.
- Performance analysis is dependent on the accuracy of the tracking measures used. The only effective progress monitoring system is one in which physical deliverables are accepted against agreed quality criteria.
- Before implementing EVPM it is important that all members of the project team understand the principles and interpretation of results.
- Beware of the calculation of the Estimate to Complete (ETC) of a project or task using the reduced formula.

For cost/performance measurement to work certain systems must exist. They are:

- A time based plan
- A work breakdown structure
- A costs collection system
- An objective method of assessing progress
- A responsibility/authority matrix

THE NEED FOR CONTROL AND COORDINATION

For a project manager to be in effective control of a project then control and coordination, methods need to be implemented and there are some critical criteria that it should meet. The following list illustrates some primary areas that must be addressed by the project planning and control methodology.

- Control begins at the start of the project not just before implementation. A clear, and authorized project charter is the foundation of any good control system. Without it, the whole project is destined to fail.
- When work is planned it will need to be controlled. The effective project manager considers, for each work package, what elements are critical to completion and applies controls accordingly.
- The control system should be targeted at the agreed critical success factors not on the assumptions of the project manager.
- Control systems are a combination of ongoing monitoring and control point acceptance and review (go/no go) through the vehicle of a project steering group.
- The milestone plan allows the project manager to define the go/no go control points in the project and the start and finish criteria for each work package.
- The responsibility matrix allows the project manager to communicate clearly the needs of the project and accountabilities for completion of tasks.
- The control system needs to be balanced with the objectives of a project. These will have been defined in the Project Scope and Objectives document.
- Who will control and coordinate and how and on what contractual terms must be defined at inception not implementation.
- A coordination system is generally defined in the project charter.

CASE STUDY—THE NEW LATROBE REGIONAL HOSPITAL

The original Latrobe Regional Hospital (LRH) was a registered public hospital under the Victorian Health Services Act 1988 and functioned as part of the Victorian Department of Human Services in Australia. The diseconomies in the structure of the old LRH resulted in the Victorian State Government (through its Infrastructure Investment Policy for Victoria) to create new health service facilities in the Latrobe Valley to be provided via a Build, Own & Operate model of private-sector service delivery. This new facility was constructed at a greenfield site at Morwell East Victoria, and was being built by Multiplex Constructions Pty Ltd under the direction of Stuart Rowley, the executive director, and was operated by Australian Hospital Care Ltd. (AHCL)

In January 1997, the Victorian government signed contracts with AHCL to build the new privately owned hospital to provide hospital services to public patients. An integral part of AHCL's bid was to assume immediate management of the existing public facilities during the construction phase of the new facility. A Transitional Management Agreement (TMA) was developed to enable AHCL to introduce itself to the staff and the local community and to ease the transition into the new facility. It was thought that this period would allow the new management to commence not only the structural changes that were inevitable but also commence work on the cultural changes that would be necessary.

You would agree that it would be a difficult enough task to manage a large and complex organization over multiple sites. To do this and to undertake the complex and difficult task of bringing about cultural and structural change and at the same time become actively involved in the construction of a new hospital was always going to be a big ask. It was the acknowledgment of these unreasonable demands on the executive that led to the decision to seek the support of external consultants with expertise in project management. MPI Pty Ltd (now MPI Asia Pacific) was appointed to assist with the project and its first decisions were to establish a Project Office.

The Project Office's function was to carry out the planning, scheduling, and project management of the move from the three campuses to the new location so that it became operational from September 1, 1998. There were significant contractual imperatives for this to occur. During the initial phase of the project, the role of the Project Office was expanded to provide support services to the builder and the introduction of an issues management system as well as milestone reports.

During this transitional period it was imperative that the contracted levels of health care services to the community are maintained by the existing LRH. Through the Project Office the project schedule was managed to ensure that this was the case.

Standards from the Start

AHCL understood that acceptance of quality project management was a critical factor for new facility. According to senior management, the use of project management disciplines aided by effective project management software played a significant part in the successful opening of the new LRH five weeks ahead of schedule and on budget.

The go ahead to start building the new LRH was given in 1996, and, from the beginning; all efforts were directed contractually toward an opening date of September 1, 1998. A major complication was that at the same time the old LRH had to continue operations and convert from a public hospital management to a private hospital management model. All this occurred across three campuses up to twenty-five km. apart, with the new site located within the same area. A relationship was established with many department heads of old LRH, who then delegated unit managers to form "working parties" to cover all the aspects of the relocation of the old hospital and all its services from three campuses to the new campus. All this work had to be carried out in addition to regular duties.

Considerable executive management energy was focused on the contract date target by establishing a project steering group at AHCL's corporate office. Every part of the project was evaluated according to its criticality to the readiness and ability to open on time. The steering group consisted of representatives of the architect, the builder, the Victorian Department of Human Services, the Quantity Surveyor, an Independent Certifier; the Establishment Project Office, the Corporate Risk Manager, and the Executive Director of LRH. Regular "go/no-go" reviews were conducted; this ensured that all of the staff involved knew what was occurring with the project as well as what was expected of them. Extensive training sessions in the new practices and protocols was also given and formed an important part of the project plan.

Success

"A major factor in the successful opening of the new hospital," Stuart Rowley explains, "was the early implementation of quality project management processes and standards." The chosen project planning software was Micro Planning International's X-Pert for Window (XPW). It uses a variety of "views" of project data, including Gantt charts and Critical Path Networks and is particularly strong in resource modelling, tracking, and scheduling, as well as EVPM.

Regarding the old LRH, the initial priorities were to make the company's first high-level plans more robust and, crucially, to validate plan dates. The software was selected because of its ease of use and because its reporting and plan consolidation capability allowed the rapid pin-pointing of "hot-spots" (e.g., resource deficiencies) that required attention if the contract launch date was to be met.

Consequences

"At start-up we were not well equipped technologically and by establishing the EPO we were able to develop a positive project based culture. The emphasis on good project management undoubtedly contributed to the team working and a "can-do" attitude amongst staff," says Stuart Rowley.

Establishment Project Office

The Establishment Project Office (EPO) supports project management throughout LRH. This performs the function that in many organizations would be handled by a program manager. Typically, this type of function will take high-level project plans from operating departments and help to anticipate and resolve potential resource conflicts, using the company's overall business objectives as the benchmark to determine priorities. However, at LRH, the EPO also works closely with the various stakeholders, although project sponsors were ultimately responsible for delivering the project's business benefits; the corporate project managers are expected to drive their projects forward proactively. The EPO sought to ensure consistency in the way elements of the project management process were handled throughout the organization, all of which helps to build an effective project management culture.

Benefits

According to Stuart Rowley, the development of a project management culture via the EPO has brought significant benefits to LRH. The primary one being the defined involvement of all parties (users and developers alike) in the planning process—they are actively encouraged to challenge the assumptions on which the plans are based. Additionally, the EPO is generally advised well in advance of a project's inception, so that plans can be aggregated early and resource profiling and forecasting carried out with far greater sophistication. "Above all," says Stuart Rowley, "we have a continuous feedback loop whereby Micro Planner plans are produced in great detail for the first phase of a project, with plans for subsequent phases being refined according to experience. This process is continued beyond project completion into subsequent planning, to establish an on-going cycle of project improvement."

Typical Reports Produced by the Project Office

The following reports illustrate the typical information provided to corporate management.

The Critical Path Network for the Commissioning and Relocation Subproject Project Steering Group Report

This report was specifically designed (it became colloquially known as the "Arthurgram" so named after the chairman of the Project Steering Group) to provide a high level summary of the most critical as well as the most important milestones within the project.

As can be seen it spans the total project from the commencement of the Transition Management Agreement in 1997 to the AHCS EQuIP certification requirement date at the end of 1999. As the project progressed the "Arthurgram" was updated each fortnight to highlight the current project status.

Milestone Gantt Charts

Figures 24.1a and 24.1b are examples of the Milestone charts.

This report was designed for the human resources manager and provided the department with their specific milestones, which had to be met in order to ensure that sufficient staff would come through from the old system to the new system. It was produced in Gantt form, which provides a rapid visual picture of the major milestones and their relationship in time. However some managers preferred the data in the form of a table, which is shown below.

Task Reports

Many of the various unit managers utilized the standard task report format, which shows the name of the task, its duration, when it is scheduled to commence and finish, as well as cost analysis information. As progress occurred, the actual progress date was also entered, which enabled the project office to monitor actuals against planned dates.

Title : **Milestones for Catering**

Project : **LRH Relocation**

Commercial - In - Confidence

Date : 09-May-99   Time Now : 27-Jul-98   Sheet : 1 of 1

Task Id	Description	Baseline Date	Achieved Date	Schedule Date	Variance
Catering					
LRH23001	Catering Department - Relocation Plan Commenced	06-Apr-98	06-Apr-98	06-Apr-98	0:0
LRH23002	Menu Commenced	06-Apr-98	06-Apr-98	06-Apr-98	0:0
LRH23017	Equipment Commenced	06-Apr-98	06-Apr-98	06-Apr-98	0:0
LRH23027	Staff Commenced	06-Apr-98	06-Apr-98	06-Apr-98	0:0
LRH23036	Staff Commenced	06-Apr-98	06-Apr-98	06-Apr-98	0:0
LRH23057	Plant Assessment Commenced	06-Apr-98	06-Apr-98	06-Apr-98	0:0
LRH23090	HACCAP Commenced	06-Apr-98	06-Apr-98	06-Apr-98	0:0
LRH23082	Rosters / Protocols Commenced	14-Apr-98	14-Apr-98	14-Apr-98	0:0
LRH23077	Computers Commenced	04-May-98	04-May-98	04-May-98	0:0
LRH23089	Operating New and Existing Kitchens Commenced	11-May-98	04-May-98	04-May-98	+5:0
LRH23099	Standards For Measure	11-May-98	04-May-98	04-May-98	+5:0

FIGURE 24-1. (a) Milestone tables.

Date 18-Jul-95   Commercial - In - Confidence
Time Now 27-Jul-98
Project LRH Relocation
Output Pathology Certificates Task List
Sheet 1 of 1
Task Identity   Task Description

LRH98012 Certificate - Fire Hydrants & Hose Reels - Installation/Flow Rates

OccupancyPermit

ColinABrown

Scheduled dates: 17-Jun-98   17-Jun-98   Dur: 1:0

Actual Progress   17-Jun-98

Budgetted Cost:
Actual Cost to date:
Est. Rem. Cost
Balance from previous report.

LRH98013 Certificate - Mechanical Systems Comply Drawings,BCA & Codes

Scheduled dates: 17-Jun-98   17-Jun-98   Dur: 1:0

Actual Progress   17-Jun-98

Budgetted Cost:
Actual Cost to date:
Est. Rem. Cost
Balance from previous report.

LRH98014 Certificate - Glass installed to AS 1288 (1994)

Scheduled dates: 17-Jun-98   17-Jun-98   Dur: 1:0

Actual Progress   17-Jun-98

Budgetted Cost:
Actual Cost to date:
Est. Rem. Cost
Balance from previous report:

FIGURE 24-1. (b) Task reports.

_____ 25 _____

Conclusions and the Road Ahead

I n the *Story of Managing Projects*, we have compiled a number of chapters that deal with the process as well as the content, context, and impact of project management (PM) from a number of disciplines and industries. Thematically, the book follows a "multilegged T" (MLT) structure with the introductory chapters providing an overview/overlay of key PM concepts and subsequent chapters delving into specific PM context and practice areas (such as PM in health care, PM in construction, PM in S/W, PM in telecom, etc.).

In distilling the essence of the insights and lessons learned from the chapters presented in this book, we believe that a number of (unique or recurring) themes are emerging and are worth taking note of for future reference:

- The role of learning as a key project management competence and foundation for a number of best practices.
- The power of and necessity for knowledge management and sharing best practices.
- A better understanding of the convergence of product and service attributes in conceiving, designing, and managing projects, and in particular their dual nature in terms of possessing both tangible and intangible, static and dynamic, as well as discrete and continuous attributes.
- The complex and even nonlinear nature of most projects and their affinity if not outright dependence on knowledge assets and competences.
- The need for an integrative, systematic approach in mapping the project stake-holders.

- Understanding that many concepts and principles have been around for quite some time (such as the power and centrality of storytelling) and that they are simply being reinvented in an emerging sociotechnical context (involving for instance next generation multimedia technologies) that enhances their classical properties and value.
- The significance of and necessity for a cross-disciplinary, cross-regional perspective when reviewing key challenges and opportunities as well best (and worst) practices in PM—it seems that there are always some knowledge niches and nuggets that may be discipline-specific and geography-bound.

We believe that these key observations could facilitate achieving the objective that this manuscript serve as a platform for project management practitioners to team up with PM academics in order to provide cross-disciplinary threads of insights, lessons learned, and best practices from a variety of professions and settings as well as regions of the world where project management is enacted and shaped in the process.

INDEX

ABB (train manufacturer), 248
accounting, whole cost approach to, 297
Acela Express service, 247, 248
Activity Based Costing (ABC), 294
activity change, 134; coding of, 144, 145; feedback and, 145–48, 149; time-based perspective on, 135; timing of, 147–48
Adams, J., 201
ADePT. *See* Analytical Design Planning Technique
Advanced Research Projects Agency (ARPA), 5
aerospace industry, 10, 11, 119, 160
After Desert Storm (McDonald), 205
age groups, and technology, 59
Aggarwal, K. K., 157
Agile project management methods, 324, 327; application of, 331–32; attributes of, 327; change and, 332; communication and, 331; courage and, 331; evolving nature of, 333; feedback in, 331, 332, 333; framework for, 329–30; guidelines, 331; humility and, 331; obstacles to, 329; problems of, 325; radicality of, 327; risks with, 327; simplicity in, 331

agility, defined, 325
Aha, D. W., 127
airline companies, 160
alignment tests, 27
Allan, R. N., 158
Allen, Paul, 3
Allest, Frédéric d', 79, 81
Alstom, 248
Ambler, Scott, 330
American Society of Civil Engineers (ASCE), 198
Amtrak: Metroliner trains, 247; and NECIP, 246; project management organization of, 246; projects carried out by, 245. *See also* railway projects; railways
Analytical Design Planning Technique (ADePT), 271; applications of, 289–90; benefits of, 290–91; and building projects, 278; overview of, 272; and rescheduling of design process, 285–87; stages of, 272–74
Andrews, J. D., 157
ANOVA (one-factor analysis of variance), 319
Apollo project, 3, 4
Application Program Interfaces (APIs), 56
architects, 235

ABOUT THE CONTRIBUTORS

Glen B. Alleman has more than twenty-five years progressive responsibility in the design, development, and management of mission critical software systems provides a solid foundation for directing the development of state of the art software based systems. He is a researcher and author in the fields of project management and software process improvement, system architecture, development methodologies, fault tolerant systems design, and business process improvement. He has an M.B.A. in Systems Management from the University of Southern California and a B.S. in Physics from the University of California, Irvine.

Frank T. Anbari, (Ph.D., Project Management and Quality Enhancement, M.B.A., M.S. Engineering, PMP, PE, and ASQ Certified Six Sigma Black Belt) is a faculty member of the Project Management Program at the George Washington University. He gained extensive industrial experience serving in project leadership positions at the National Railroad Passenger Corporation (Amtrak), Day and Zimmermann, and American Water Works Service Company. He served as examiner (1993–1995) and alumni examiner (1999–2000) for the Malcolm Baldrige National Quality Award.

Simon Austin (B.Sc., Ph.D., C.Eng., MICE, FCS) is the founder director of Adept Management with specific responsibility for research, development and training. He is also Professor of Structural Engineering in the Department of Civil and Building Engineering at Loughborough University. He has been undertaking industry-focused research into design processes, modeling, integrated working and management techniques for fourteen years and is the author of numerous papers, reports, and books.

Andrew Baldwin (B.Sc., Ph.D., C.Eng., MICE) is Professor of Construction Management Systems in the Department of Civil and Building Engineering at Loughborough University. His research interests focus on the introduction of collaborative working and concurrent engineering in construction. Current research interests are focused on the of use of information and communications technology and electronic commerce to support the construction process, design management, and the legal issues of trading electronically.

Elias G. Carayannis, Ph.D., is full professor of management science, director of research on science, technology, innovation and entrepreneurship for the European Union Research Center, and co-founder and co-director of the Global and Entrepreneurial Finance Research Institute (GEFRI) at the School of Business, The George Washington University. Dr. Carayannis received his Ph.D. in technology management and MBA in finance from Rensselaer Polytechnic Institute in Troy, NY, and his BS in electrical engineering from the National Technical University of Athens, Greece. He has published more than 40 refereed journal articles and several other papers in technology management journals, as well as *The Strategic Management of Technological Learning* (CRC Press, 2000), and *Idea Makers and Idea Brokers: Intellectual Venture Capitalists* (Greenwood Press, 2003).

Raphael M. Dua is general manager of Micro Planning International maintaining involvement in the development of Micro Planner software. He has worked in the project management arena for past forty-five years developing software, planning, and scheduling projects as a consultant and as a project manager. He is working on EVPM projects in the healthcare industry in Australia and Canada. He is a member of Standards Australia International EVPM committee.

Frédéric Fontane serves as Assistant Professor in Operations Management at Ecole des Mines de Paris, France. He was educated at ESSEC Business School and University of Aix Marseille, France. He received graduate degrees in economics with a Doctorate in Operations Management. He received his Control, Electronics and Computer Engineer degree from the National Institute of Applied Sciences, Toulouse (INSA-Toulouse). His work experience includes operations management, teaching, research and consultancy. He has, in particular, studied technology management in multinational corporations of telecommunications sector. Its work is now dedicated at various issues related to supply chain management in cooperation with many manufacturing organizations (Renault, ArjoWiggins, Arcelor).

Francis Hartman, Ph.D., is a professor and past director of project management specialization (1999–2000) at the University of Calgary. He has had over 20 years of international experience in industry on capital projects and is a renowned authority on project management. He served as the NSERC/SSHRC chair (1994) in project management (Management of Technological Change), also at the University of Calgary. Prior to that, he was an adjunct professor at the University of Toronto (1986–1991) and University of British Columbia (1983–1985). Dr. Hartman is also currently the president of Quality Enhanced Decisions, Inc., and Smart Management, Inc., a local firm providing consulting services. Previously, he held various executive and leadership positions, including president of Synergy Constructors, vice president and general manager of Vanbots Construction, director and general manager of PM3-Inducon, Inc., vice president of project management for Tectonic Control, Inc., manager for Fluor Daniel-Wright Engineers Limited, and project manager of various large projects (over $500 million) for Sir William Halcrow and Partners.

Phillip Harvard has an M.B.A. in International Management form Thunderbird, a French D.E.A. in Linguistics from the University of Bordeaux and a French D.E.S.S. in Media Engineering for Education from the University of Poitiers. He lives in La Rochelle, France, with his wife and three children where he coordinates the Management Program at the general engineering school at the university.

Trevor Hine, Ph.D. has a B.A. (Hons) from the Australian National University, and a Ph.D. from the School of Brain and Cognitive Sciences at the Massachusetts Institute of Technology. He has worked at MIT, ANU, University of New South Wales, and is currently Senior Lecturer in Psychology at Griffith University.

Patrice Houdayer is Assistant Professor in Strategy at AUDENCIA-Nantes.Ecole de Management, France. He has been appointed as Deputy Director of the International Affiliated Faculty and Program Head for the New Technologies Management Program. He was educated at ESSEC Business School and University of Paris 10, France. His research interests are in the area of international strategy and innovation management. He has, in particular, studied International Strategy in R&D in multinational corporations.

Abdul Samad (Sami) Kazi is a senior research scientist at VTT, the Technical Research Centre of Finland. His research interests and experiences involve: information integration, product and process modeling, process reengineering, knowledge management, Internet-based tools and technologies, and liaisons with the industry. He is actively engaged in several European-level projects on ICT in construction.

Harold Kerzner, Ph.D., is a Professor of Systems Management at Baldwin-Wallace College. He has published or presented more than 250 papers, and has twenty-one textbooks. The Northeast Ohio PMI Chapter has initiated the Kerzner Award for excellence in Project Management. He has received a Distinguished Alumni Award from the University of Illinois and the 1998 Distinguished Service Award from and Utah State University.

Micheal D. Kull is a speaker, writer, and instructor of management and technology. He is known for his expertise in knowledge management, communities of practice, and digital storytelling. He teaches at The George Washington University and is Executive Producer of AMPLIFI, an advisory services firm for communicating knowledge through digital video.

John A. Kuprenas is a Research Assistant Professor in Civil Engineering at the University of Southern California and a Project Director with Vanir Construction Management. He is a registered Professional Civil Engineer in California. His research areas include computer applications in construction and construction processes, productivity, and quality.

Young Hoon Kwak, Ph.D., is a faculty member of the Project Management Program at Management Science Department at The George Washington University. He received his M.S. and Ph.D. in engineering and project management from the University of California, Berkeley. Dr. Kwak was the co-principal investigator of Project Management Institute's "Benefits of Project Management" study. His research interests include project management and control, project risk management and construction management. For more information, visit his homepage at http://home.gwu.edu/~kwak.

Ralph V. Locurcio, P.E., is a Senior Vice President and Director of Federal Programs at STV. Locurcio retired from the U.S. Army Corps of Engineers as a Brigadier General in 1996. A notable highlight of Locurcio's military career was his command of the Kuwait Emergency Reconstruction Office (KERO) where he led the $650M reconstruction of Kuwait's civil infrastructure following the Gulf War. Locurcio is a 1965 graduate of the U.S. Military Academy at West Point and holds a master's degree in Urban Engineering from Purdue University. He has attended executive programs at the University of Pennsylvania, Harvard University, and the U.S. Army War College. Locurcio is a Professional Civil Engineer registered in Virginia, Pennsylvania, New Jersey, and Georgia.

Hervé Mathe is Professor in Logistics Production and Service Department and Department Chairperson at ESSEC Business School, France. He holds a Doctorate from Institut Etudes Politiques Paris, a Ph.D. from Cranfield Institute of Technology, a Doctorate from Université Paris IX-Dauphine and was Bower fellow at Harvard University. He has had visiting appointments at Wharton School, SDA Bocconi, Cranfield University, and Harvard University. His work experience includes numerous consulting projects and executive courses. His research areas are service operations, global manufacturing and corporate architecture.

Maged Sedky Morcos (Ph.D., University of Leeds, 1995) worked in the industry for over than fifteen years. His industrial interests include research and training in areas of project and organization management, systems, risk, reliability and performance engineering and management. Dr. Morcos teaches different engineering and management courses. He is an associate professor of engineering management at the faculty of management sciences at University for Modern Sciences and Arts (M.S.A.), Dokki, Cairo, Egypt.

Andrew Newton (B.Eng., Ph.D., C.Eng., MICE) is Managing Director of Adept Management. Andrew is a Chartered Engineer and has previously worked within a large multidisciplinary engineering practice, undertaking a number of roles and heading numerous design studies. Andrew's industrial experience has been augmented by a Ph.D. project, the output from the research was a prototype technique called ADePT, that was awarded the 1999 Quality in Construction awards for Innovation.

Mark E. Nissen is Associate Professor of Information Systems and Management at the Naval Postgraduate School and Young Investigator for the Office of Naval Research. Mark's research focuses on using knowledge and systems for process innovation, and his publications span the information systems, project management, and related fields.

Dan P. Ono, PMP, has directed project managers within Pacific Telephone, AT&T, Lucent Technologies, and Cisco Systems for the past thirty years. His project management organizations have been responsible for projects valued at over USD $3 billion dollars. During the past several years, he has been spending his time, training, coaching, mentoring, and consulting with project managers from Lucent Technologies, Cisco Systems, and Excite@home as well as commercial training companies in Mexico, the United Kingdom, Australia, Singapore, Canada, and across the United States. Currently, Dan is the Principal Consultant of Ono & Associates.

John-Paris Pantouvakis, M.Eng., M.Sc., Ph.D., has worked as a Consultant (Greek Ministries, railway construction management company, etc.) and for Hellenic Petroleum S.A following his academic studies. In 1999, he was a temporary Lecturer (University of Thessaly, Greece). Since 2000 he has been an Assistant Professor at National National Technical University of Athens (NTUA). He has authored or coauthored several journal and conference articles and books. He is a reviewer for *Construction Management & Economics*.

Theodore H. Rosen, Ph.D., has over thirty years experience in organizational consulting, research, management facilitation, and executive coaching/leadership development. Dr. Rosen is currently on the faculty of the George Washington University School of Business and Public Management. Dr. Rosen earned his Doctorate Degree in Industrial and Organizational Psychology and has been recognized for his work by being named to "Who's Who in the East," and "Who's Who in Executives and Businesses."

Keith F. Snider is Associate Professor of Public Administration and Management at the Naval Postgraduate School. His research and teaching focuses on defense acquisition, and his recent journal publications appear in *American Review of*

Public Administration, Administration & Society, Acquisition Review Quarterly, Administrative Theory & Praxis, and *Journal of Public Procurement.*

Victor S. Sohmen is a recipient of the 1995 Canadian Governor-General's Gold Medal for academic excellence and the 2002 PMI Educational Foundation merit scholarship. His research interests include cross-cultural leadership and communication, trans-national projects, and international management. Since 1990, Victor has been a frequent contributor at regional and international conferences on project management, international business, and cost engineering.

Carolyn R. Spencer has qualifications in Psychology and Management (Queensland University) and is a Ph.D. candidate at Griffith University. Extensively experienced in change-related projects for industry and organizational contexts, current projects include strategic capability enhancements for project managers. Carolyn is a Member of the Australian Institute of Project Management, and Chair of its Industry Liaison Task Force.

Wilco Tijhuis, Ph.D., is a part-time Ass.-Professor in Construction Processes at the University of Twente, in Enschede, The Netherlands, School of Business, Public Administration and Technology, Department of Construction Process Management (http://www.sms.utwente.nl). He is also managing partner in the company WT/Consult BV—International Construction Process & Development, based in Rijssen, The Netherlands, with international activities in the field of concepts, processes and projects (http://www.wtprojects.com).

Robert James Voetsch, PMP, has twenty years project management experience with the World Health Organization, the United Nations Volunteers, and the United States Peace Corps. Currently, he is a management trainer at The University of Management and Technology and a doctoral candidate at George Washington University. His academic background includes: M.S. Project Management, George Washington University; M.A. Public Administration, American University; and, B.A. Political Science, American University. Mr. Voetsch is a certified Project Management Professional (PMP).

Cheryl J. Walker, PMP, is a managing consultant who designs and implements service both nationally and internationally. She has designed and led project management courses, authored a paper on utilizing project management for organizational change and transition, developed a project management support center, written a guidebook for a project management sales cycle, and created an e-learning course for pm practitioners. She is president of the PMI Washington DC Chapter and District Regional Advocate for Region 5, as well as a Ph.D. candidate in Organizational Behavior and Development from George Washington University.

Ian Wilson is a research fellow at the Information Systems Institute, University of Salford, UK. Ian graduated from the Information Systems Institute (then the ITI) with a BSc(Hons) in information technology in 1999. His research interests lie in the human and organizational issues involved in the development and implementation of ICT, especially with respect to virtual organizations.

Allen Woods, M.B.C.S., MIAP is the CEO of JIT Software a small software development company in Tidworth, United Kingdom. Allen has developed several management information systems for a number of organizations in both the public and private sector. His particular interest in the sphere of management science is organization modeling.